CREDO SERIES

Son of God and Son of Mary

Based on the Curriculum Framework
Course II: Who is Jesus Christ?

WRITERS
Amalee Meehan, PhD
Daniel O'Connell, PhD

GENERAL EDITOR
Thomas H. Groome, EdD

Professor Theology and Religious Education
Boston College

VERITAS
USA Office: Frisco, Texas

www.veritasreligion.com

The Subcommittee on the Catechism, United States Conference of Catholic Bishops, has found that this catechetical high school text, copyright 2013, is in conformity with the *Catechism of the Catholic Church* and that it fulfills the requirements of Core Course II of the *Doctrinal Elements of a Curriculum Framework for the Development of Catechetical Materials for Young People of High School Age.*

CREDO SERIES CONSULTANT: Maura Hyland
PUBLISHER, USA AND THEOLOGICAL EDITOR:
Ed DeStefano
TEXT CONSULTANTS:
Annette Honan
Ailís Travers
Hosffman Ospino
COPY EDITOR: Elaine Campion
DESIGN: Lir Mac Cárthaigh

INTERNET RESOURCES
There are internet resources available to support this text. Log on to www.credoseries.com

NIHIL OBSTAT
Rev. Msgr. Robert M. Coerver, S.T.L.
Censor Librorum

IMPRIMATUR
† Most Reverend Kevin J. Farrell
Bishop of Dallas
May 30, 2013

The *Nihil Obstat* and *Imprimatur* are official declarations that the work contains nothing contrary to Faith and Morals. It is not implied thereby that those granting the *Nihil Obstat* and *Imprimatur* agree with the contents, statements or opinions expressed.

SEND ALL INQUIRIES TO:
Veritas, Customer Service
P.O. Box 789
Westerville, OH 43086
Tel. 866-844-0582
info@veritasreligion.com
www.veritasreligion.com

ISBN 978 1 84730 492 6 (Student Edition)
ISBN 978 1 84730 292 2 (Teacher Resource Edition)
ISBN 978 1 84730 503 9 (E-book: Student Edition)

Printed in the United States of America
1 2 3 4 5 6 7 / 16 15 14 13

CONTENTS

CHAPTER 1

God Comes to Us

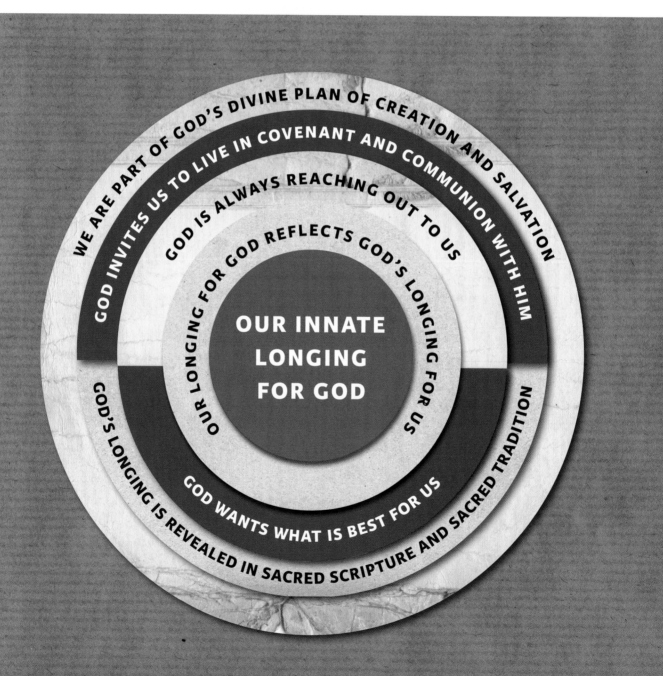

THE TEACHINGS OF THE CATHOLIC CHURCH REMIND US that 'by love God has revealed himself and given himself to man. He has thus provided the definitive, superabundant answer to the questions that man asks himself about the meaning and purpose of his life' (*Catechism of the Catholic Church* [CCC], no. 68). In this chapter we explore that God has gradually revealed his loving plan of goodness—the divine plan of Creation and Salvation—for all humanity. Sacred Scripture and Sacred Tradition pass on Divine Revelation. The fullness of Revelation is reflected in the life and teaching of the Catholic Church.

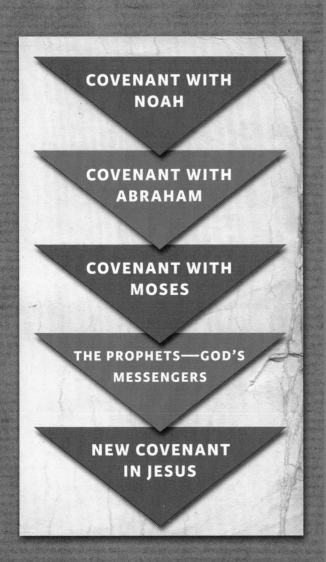

COVENANT WITH NOAH

COVENANT WITH ABRAHAM

COVENANT WITH MOSES

THE PROPHETS—GOD'S MESSENGERS

NEW COVENANT IN JESUS

Faith Focus: These teachings of the Catholic Church are the primary focus of the doctrinal content presented in this chapter:

- ◉ God has provided the definitive, superabundant answer to the questions that man asks himself about the meaning and purpose of his life;
- ◉ God has freely revealed himself and his plan of loving goodness for humanity and for all creation;
- ◉ God has fully revealed this plan by sending us his beloved Son, our Lord Jesus Christ, and the Holy Spirit;
- ◉ Through Divine Revelation we can come to know, love and serve God far beyond our natural capacity;
- ◉ Even though there will be no further Revelation after Jesus, the Holy Spirit guides the Church to gradually grasp over the course of the centuries the full meaning and significance of what God has revealed.

Discipleship Formation: As a result of studying this chapter and discovering the meaning of the faith of the Catholic Church for your life, you should be better able to:

- ◉ grow in your faith in Sacred Scripture and Sacred Tradition as the living Word of God;
- ◉ respond with the Church and personally to God, who reveals himself through his Word in Sacred Scripture and Sacred Tradition;
- ◉ more clearly encounter Jesus in Scripture, the Church, and the people and events of your life;
- ◉ respond to Christ's loving presence and his invitation to you to follow him and live in communion and intimacy with him, the Father and the Holy Spirit.

Scripture References: These Scripture references are quoted or referred to in this chapter:
OLD TESTAMENT: Genesis 3:15, 9, 12:1–4, 15:1–6 and 17; **Exodus** 34:6; **Leviticus** 26:11–13; **Deuteronomy** 4:44—6:25; **Psalms** 42:2a, 114:15, 119:89, 103, 105, 160–61; **Proverbs** 16:20 **NEW TESTAMENT: Matthew** 5:1–12, 16:24–26, 19:21, 22:1–14, 25:31–46, 28:20; **Luke** 9:3, 10:4–6, 8–10, 14:15–24; **John** 1:14–16, 3:16, 4:6–15, 14:6, 15:11, 16:13, 18:33–38a; **Hebrews** 1:1–3; **1 John** 3:1

Faith Glossary: Familiarize yourself with the meaning of these key faith terms. Definitions are found in the Glossary: **analogy of faith, apocrypha, Apostolic Tradition, Baptism, Bible, canon of Scripture, Covenant, Deposit of Faith, Divine Inspiration, Divine Providence, Divine Revelation, Ecumenical Council, evil, Fall (the), free will, Hebrews, infallibility, Magisterium, natural law, Original Sin, Paschal Mystery, redemption, Sacred Scripture, Sacred Tradition, salvation, salvation history, sanctifying grace, senses of Scripture, solidarity, traditions of the Church, Word of God**

Faith Words: Divine Providence; Divine Revelation
Learn by Heart: Hebrews 1:1–2
Learn by Example: Blessed Pope John XXIII

Who lies behind our search for happiness?

Human beings are relentless in their striving for happiness. There is always something nagging at us; something we continue to long for even at times when we are feeling 'happy'. Our culture tries to influence us in many ways, suggesting where and how we might find the answer to our search for happiness. Our culture's message is often contrary to the message and values of the Gospel. Music idols, fashion gurus, diet experts and other 'voices' fill our minds and hearts with images of whom we should work at becoming and also of the happiness we should strive to live for. These voices do their best to give us a 'makeover' that includes our buying into products and plans that are profitable to them but profit us little.

OPENING CONVERSATION
- What are some ways in which you see people seeking happiness?
- Why do we always seem to want more—even in moments when we are 'happy'?

REFLECT AND DISCUSS
- Think about the lyrics of a song or hymn or psalm with which you are familiar, where the writer is reflecting on the human search for happiness.
- Work in small groups and explore together the meaning of the songs, hymns or psalms the people in your group have chosen. What were the different writers looking for?
- Make a list of themes that are common to the group.

- Do you find any echoes of your own search for happiness?

THE SEARCH FOR HAPPINESS
When asked who they want to be and what they most desire out of life, people often respond by saying, 'I want to be happy.' The inspired human authors of Sacred Scripture often address the human heart's search for the meaning and purpose of life, and they often summarize this sense of meaning and purpose in the word 'happiness'. For example, the writer of Psalm 144 wrote: '[H]appy are the people whose God is the Lord' (Psalm 144:15). The author of the Book of Proverbs describes true wealth, '[H]appy are those who trust in the Lord' (Proverbs 16:20). These inspired human authors of the Book of Psalms and the Book of Proverbs, under the inspiration of the Holy Spirit, who is the primary author of Sacred Scripture, came to understand

and teach that their own restlessness and longing as well as the restlessness and longings of the heart of every human being are embedded in the human heart by God the Creator. Through these and other inspired writings of Sacred Scripture the Holy Spirit reveals the truth that when we truly listen to God drawing us to himself through the deepest restlessness of our heart, we find 'peace' and 'happiness'. Jesus fully revealed this truth about our desire and striving for happiness and our response to that desire in the Beatitudes.

Jesus' whole life and his teachings reveal that God desires our happiness and that we share in his joy (see John 15:11). Jesus spoke very pointedly about happiness and he revealed the nature of true happiness in the Sermon on the Mount. In the past, English translations of the Beatitudes often began: 'Happy are. . . .' Biblical scholars now teach that 'Blessed' is the more precise term. The Beatitudes are the blueprint of a true disciple of Jesus; and living the Beatitudes is the source of true joy and happiness. Christ has given us his Church to guide us in finding this inner happiness and joy.

OVER TO YOU

- Read the Sermon on the Mount in Matthew 5:1–12. What do you find strange about what Jesus said would bring people happiness?
- How will this color your own search for happiness?

In addition to his teachings in the Beatitudes, Jesus also taught on many other occasions that true human happiness is rooted in our relationship with God. (Recall Jesus' teachings in the Beatitudes and the Great Commandment.) True human happiness is accepting and responding to God's invitation to live in communion and friendship with him. God's Word, Sacred Scripture, reveals this truth about ourselves, over and over again. God is love, and he has created us to share in that love, both here on earth and in life everlasting. God alone is the source of our happiness. He has embedded this truth about ourselves in our minds and heart—at the core of our very being—and has revealed it over and over again.

God's love for us, his children (see 1 John 3:1), is beyond our understanding. The loving care and concern of God for all he has made did not end at the moment of Creation. God did not leave us alone to find our own way through life. The Catholic Church reminds us of this truth when she teaches: 'By love, God has revealed himself and given himself to man. He has thus provided the definitive, superabundant answer to the questions that man asks himself about the meaning and purpose of his life' (CCC, no. 68).

God invites each of us to live in deeper and deeper friendship with him, both now on earth in our own particular place and time, situation and circumstances and in eternal life. God's loving concern for all he has made continues to sustain its existence and preside over its development and destiny. This truth of our faith is called **Divine Providence.**

FAITH WORD

Divine Providence

Divine Providence is 'God's loving care and concern for all he has made; he continues to watch over creation, sustaining its existence and presiding over its development and destiny'.
—*United States Catholic Catechism for Adults* (USCCA), 510

GOD CREATING THE BIRDS AND THE FISHES | MARTIN DE VOS

- What does God's Revelation say about happiness? About the meaning and purpose of life?
- What does God's Word to us tell us about his role in our search for happiness?
- Have you ever felt God reaching out to you? Tell the story.
- How do you now think you can better pursue your own search for happiness?

THE MYSTERY OF EVIL AND SUFFERING

We might ask, 'If God desires our happiness, why then is there **evil** and suffering?' The **Old Testament** Books of Genesis, Psalms, Proverbs and Job and the writings of the Prophets express both the inner struggle and the faith of God's people in the midst of their sufferings. The **New Testament** describes the struggle of Jesus' disciples when faced with the upcoming suffering of their Lord. For example, St. Peter, the two disciples on the road to Emmaus and the other disciples of Jesus

could not easily understand and did not want to accept that Jesus would suffer and be put to death to fulfill his work as the Savior and Messiah. Only after the **Paschal Mystery**—'Christ's work of redemption accomplished principally by his Passion, Death, Resurrection, and glorious Ascension, whereby "dying he destroyed our death, rising he restored our life"' (CCC, Glossary; see also CCC, nos. 654 and 1067)—would the Apostles and other disciples come to understand the true power of God's love over evil. The Paschal Mystery was for them and is for us both the sign and the divine pledge that evil in any form and suffering and death will not have the last word.

Some people would argue that God directly causes suffering and other forms of evil to punish us, or simply because he really doesn't care. Our Catholic faith rejects such a view of God. God is not the direct cause of harm or evil of any kind. God is all-good and all-loving. God always cares for us. He is always present with us, in good times and in bad times. He celebrates and grieves with us. In summary, the Catholic Church teaches:

- Evil is a reality. God never causes evil nor sends suffering as punishment for sin. God only brings about what is good, and God can bring good out of evil, as the Paschal Mystery of Jesus reveals. God sometimes 'permits' evil and suffering for reasons we cannot know or understand.
- Some suffering and evil are the result of our rejection of God's plan of Creation. The suffering and other forms of evil we experience often result from our own poor or sinful choices. God gave us the gift of **free will**; sin is the result of the misuse of this gift.
- Physical suffering resulting from sickness or natural disasters arises from the disorder present in the world and is a consequence of **the Fall** and of the rejection of God's plan of goodness for all creation.
- God does not send disease, cause floods, hurricanes, tornadoes or any other kind of natural disasters to punish us or teach us a lesson; physical evil may be an opportunity for growing in faith in him and his love for us.
- Our life on earth should include an effort to be good stewards of creation and to stop contributing to this disorder.

- Jesus was confronted by the Evil One, Satan or the Devil, as were the first humans. Some evil and suffering are a result of the work of the Devil or Satan.
- Jesus worked to alleviate both physical and spiritual suffering. He taught his disciples to do likewise.
- God sent his Son to redeem us from the power of evil and sin so that we can live in eternal happiness with him, the angels, and Mary and all the saints.
- In the Passion (the suffering and Death) of Jesus we see how to respond to God with faith, hope and courage, even in the midst of suffering and tough times. God reveals in the Cross of Jesus that he suffers with us and lives in **solidarity** with all who suffer.
- In the Resurrection and Ascension of Christ, God speaks the final Word. Evil does not and will not triumph over life and goodness. We can see beyond suffering to hope and eternal life. God is love! This is our faith and the source of our hope.
- The risen Lord is always present with us as he promised (see Matthew 28:20). He is especially present with us through his Church, in her Sacraments and in the proclamation of the **Word of God**.
- People of faith who suffer witness to the reality that God, his love and goodness, never fail us.

Jesus worked to alleviate both physical and spiritual suffering. He taught his disciples to do likewise

FROM THE CATECHISM

Moved by so much suffering Christ not only allows himself to be touched by the sick, but he makes their miseries his own. . . . By his passion and death on the cross Christ has given a new meaning to suffering; it can henceforth configure us to him and unite us with his redemptive Passion.

—CCC, no. 1505

THINK, PAIR AND SHARE
- Has your attitude toward evil and suffering changed because of what you have learned?
- How have you been helped to understand and face suffering and other forms of evil in your life?
- Share your responses to these questions with a partner.

JOURNAL EXERCISE
- What wisdom have you learned about God's loving presence in your life from studying this section of the chapter? How will that help you in your search for happiness?
- In light of what you have learned, how has the significance of your chosen song, hymn or psalm changed?

God's faithful and faith-filled people have always struggled with the reality of evil and suffering. God revealed himself to be 'abounding in steadfast love and faithfulness' (Exodus 34:6). Christians look to God and his Revelation in Jesus Christ when they face suffering and other forms of evil.

God makes his love and goodness known

When Pope Julius II commissioned Michelangelo (1475–1564) to paint the story of Creation on the ceiling of the Sistine Chapel at the Vatican in Rome, Michelangelo asked the Pope how he should represent God. The Pope is alleged to have said, 'You must search your own heart to know this.' Michelangelo's Creation frescoes in the Sistine Chapel express the result of his searching his heart.

REFLECT AND DISCUSS

⊙ Look carefully at Michelangelo's fresco. Is Michelangelo depicting God reaching out to Adam, or is Adam reaching out to God, or are both God and Adam reaching out to each other?

⊙ When have you felt God's hand reaching out to you?

⊙ What response did you think God was inviting you to make?

GOD'S PLAN OF GOODNESS

Human history is, in reality, **salvation history**. It is the story of God reaching out to humanity to fulfill the divine plan of **Salvation** and also of humanity's response or lack of response to God. We give the name salvation history to the inspired record of the saving words and deeds and presence of God in the world that took place gradually over time. It is the unfolding and fulfillment of the divine plan that seeks the **redemption** of all people in Jesus Christ.

The redeeming, saving work of Christ healed what was broken by **Original Sin** and reconciled humanity with God. Original Sin is the personal sin of disobedience committed by the first human beings that resulted in the loss of living in communion and harmony with God and with all creation. Original Sin also brought suffering and death for both Adam and Eve and all human beings after them. Through Jesus' sacrifice on the Cross and his Resurrection from the dead, God's saving plan was accomplished once for all, and the 'new creation' in Christ was inaugurated.

At **Baptism** we are joined to Christ the Savior and Redeemer and are made sharers in his redeeming work. We become recipients and agents of God's saving and **sanctifying grace**. We

THE CREATION OF ADAM | MICHELANGELO

Michelangelo's Creation frescoes express the result of his searching his heart

God has revealed that he invites all people to share a life of love with him, now and eternally

receive the Holy Spirit and his grace to help us be alert for and respond to God's saving presence in our lives today. Through his Word to us in Sacred Scripture, through the Church and her Sacraments, and through the people and events of our lives, God invites and helps us to come to know and believe in his love and care for us.

THINK, PAIR AND SHARE

- Share with a partner where you see God's plan of goodness unfolding in your world.
- What people and events are manifestations of God's goodness and of his love for you?

DIVINE REVELATION

God has revealed that he invites all people to share a life of love with him, now and eternally. For example, see Matthew 22:1–14 and Luke 14:15–24. Divine Revelation began through God's action at the dawn of Creation and in his relationship of love and care for our first parents. This divine love and care, which began at Creation, continued to take place gradually over time. This Revelation continued through the covenantal relationship God entered into with Noah, Abraham, Moses and the ancient Israelites, and which culminated in Jesus Christ. Jesus is God's own Son—God's Word made flesh. (Read John 1:14–16.) Jesus is the New and Everlasting Covenant, the center and fullness of all Revelation. There will be no Revelation after him. The fullness of Revelation is reflected in the life and teaching of the Catholic Church.

God also continues to manifest himself and his love through people, through our daily experiences and the created world around us. We can come to know God through reason and experience without Divine Revelation. For example, we can come to know God and his presence when we experience something beautiful, someone loving, something precious, someone forgiving, something good and someone truthful. The order and beauty of the natural world point to God, the origin and Creator of the universe. The **natural law**, which is written upon each person's heart, and the longing for God that each person has, also point to God's existence. In the depths of our own hearts we need to be listening to God's Word for our lives today.

MOSES RECEIVES THE TEN COMMANDMENTS | JEAN WEYH

FAITH WORD

Divine Revelation

God's communication of himself and his loving plan to save us. This is a gift of self-communication, which is realized by deeds and words over time and most fully by his sending us his own divine Son, Jesus Christ.

—USCCA, 526

THE REVELATION AND ESTABLISHMENT OF THE COVENANT

The inspired writings of the Old Testament pass on the story of God reaching out and entering the Covenant with Adam and Eve, with Noah, with Abraham and his descendants, and with Moses and the Israelites. These inspired writings tell the story of how God's people both responded and did not respond to the divine invitation to enter into and live in covenant with him. The **Covenant** that God and his people entered is the solemn mutual commitment God and his people made to each other. The account of the Covenant is at the heart of salvation history and Scripture.

- **The Covenant at Creation:** God the Creator in the very act of Creation entered a covenantal relationship with humanity and all of creation. When our first parents turned their backs on this Covenant, God promised he would be faithful and restore that relationship (see Genesis 3:15).

- **The Covenant with Noah:** God made an everlasting Covenant with Noah and with all living beings. When the waters of the flood had receded, God asked Noah and his people, among other things, to have special care 'for human life' (Genesis 9:5). God promised the people 'and never again shall there be a flood to destroy the earth' (Genesis 9:11). The rainbow is a sign of this Covenant. (Read the story in Genesis 9.)

- **The Covenant with Abraham:** Later (biblical scholars set the date around 1800 BC) God and Abraham entered a Covenant. God promised that Abraham and Sarah would have many descendants, who would bring a blessing for all the nations on the earth. Abraham agreed that they would live as God's people. (Read about God's Covenant with Abraham, Sarah and their descendants in Genesis 12:1–4, Genesis 15:1–6 and Genesis 17.)

- **The Covenant at Sinai:** During the Exodus (biblical scholars set the date around 1200 BC) God, through Moses, invited the Israelites into the Covenant at Mount Sinai. The great summary of God's invitation in this Covenant was, 'I will place my dwelling in your midst . . . and will be your God and you shall be my people' (Leviticus 26:11–12). The Israelites acknowledged their relationship with God. He was their Creator and Lord and the One who saved them. They committed themselves to God and to live as God's own people. They received the Ten Commandments, summarizing the Law of the Covenant. The sign of keeping the Covenant was their keeping of the Commandments. (Read Deuteronomy 4:44—6:25.)

- **The Prophets:** While God was always faithful to the Covenant, the Israelites often failed to keep and live faithfully by the commitment they made in the Covenant. God, in his faithfulness, raised up Isaiah (whose name means 'God is salvation'), Jeremiah, Ezekiel and other prophets to remind the Israelites of his fidelity to them and to invite them back to living the Covenant as they had promised.

JESUS, THE FATHER'S DEFINITIVE WORD

At God's appointed time, he entered the 'new and everlasting covenant' with humanity. Jesus is the final and definitive Covenant between God and humankind. The New Testament proclaims, loudly and clearly, this Revelation and faith of the Church in Jesus Christ. For example, the Letter to the **Hebrews** teaches:

Long ago God spoke to our ancestors in many and various ways by the prophets, but in these last days he has spoken to us by a Son, whom he appointed heir of all things, through whom he also created the worlds. He is the reflection of God's glory and the exact imprint of God's very being, and he sustains all things by his powerful word.

—Hebrews 1:1–3

In his Person, in his way of relating to his Father and to others, and in his teachings, Jesus most clearly reveals both who God is and God's love for humanity.

LET'S PROBE DEEPER

- Work in groups of three. Each person in a group looks up and reads one of the great accounts of the Covenant in the Old Testament:
  - Genesis 9: The Covenant between God and Noah.
  - Genesis 12:1–4, Genesis 15:1–6 and Genesis 17: The Covenant between God and Abraham and his descendants.
  - Deuteronomy 4:44—6:25: The Sinai Covenant between God and the Israelites.
- Take turns explaining to the others in your group what you have read.
- What do these passages have in common?
- What different images of God are found in each passage?
- What do these passages tell us about God's wish for humanity?

NOAH'S SACRIFICE | 19TH-CENTURY STEEL ENGRAVING

WHAT ABOUT YOU PERSONALLY?

- ⊙ What words stand out for you in the passage from the Letter to the Hebrews? Do you hear there anything that is new for you?
- ⊙ How does this passage help you come to know Jesus better and deepen your faith in him?

Footprints in the Sand

One night I dreamed I was walking along the
    beach with the Lord.
Many scenes from my life flashed across the
    sky.
In each scene I noticed footprints in the sand.
Sometimes there were two sets of footprints,
other times there was one set of footprints.

This bothered me because I noticed
that during the low periods of my life,
when I was suffering from anguish, sorrow, or
    defeat,
I could see only one set of footprints.

So I said to the Lord,
'You promised me Lord
that if I followed you,
you would walk with me always.
But I have noticed that during the most trying
    periods of my life

there have been only one set of footprints in
    the sand.
Why, when I needed you most,
you have not been there for me?'

The Lord replied,
'The times when you have seen only one set
    of footprints,
is when I carried you.'

TALK IT OVER

- ⊙ What does this poem say to you for your life right now?
- ⊙ What does Jesus and his Revelation mean for your life right now?
- ⊙ Why do we say that we can and must always grow in our faith in Jesus?

JOURNAL EXERCISE

- ⊙ What is the best spiritual wisdom for your life as a disciple of Jesus that you have learned from this lesson?
- ⊙ How can you make this wisdom part of your life?

All Scripture is inspired by God

St. Francis of Assisi (c. 1181–1226) is among the most admired saints of the Church. Many people see the spiritual journey of Francis mirrored in their own life. As a young man Francis Bernardone longed for and sought happiness through success, prestige and popularity. He sought prestige in the military, a pursuit that ended in illness and in his being humiliated as a prisoner of war. He sought popularity by using his wealth and musical talents to throw lavish parties, a pursuit that ended in loneliness. All these pursuits eventually left Francis' heart empty, and he abandoned the life of Francis Bernardone for the life of St. Francis of Assisi.

A turning point on Francis' spiritual journey came in 1208. Attending Mass he heard, 'Carry no purse, no bag, no sandals; and greet no one on the road. Whatever house you enter, first say, "Peace to this house!" And if anyone is there who shares in peace, your peace will rest on that person; . . . Whenever you enter a town and its people welcome you, . . . say to them, "The kingdom of God has come near to you" (Luke 10:4–6, 8–10)'. Francis responded, 'That is what I want' and he began wearing the tunic worn by the poor of his day.

Francis divested himself of his family's wealth and possessions to follow the Lord (see Matthew 19:21). He traveled empty-handed and begged for food (see Luke 9:3). He willingly sacrificed and accepted suffering for his Lord (see Matthew 16:24–26). The 'Little Poor Man' of Assisi became renowned as the 'Joyful Troubadour of God'. Both the suffering and the joy of his Lord filled and overflowed from his heart.

REFLECT AND DISCUSS

⊙ From what you know about St. Francis of Assisi, how did his response to the above words from Scripture shape his life? How did

ST. FRANCIS OF ASSISI | ROME, ITALY

they guide him in fulfilling the desires of his heart?

⊙ Do you know anyone else who has found guidance for their life in the words of Sacred Scripture?

OVER TO YOU

⊙ What Scripture passage or passages give you guidance for your life?

SACRED SCRIPTURE: THE INSPIRED WORD OF GOD

Sacred Scripture is the inspired record of God's Revelation in history. The word 'scripture' means literally 'that which is written'. The phrase 'Sacred Scriptures of the Church' refers to the writings that the Catholic Church recognizes and accepts

as inspired by God. God is the primary author of Sacred Scripture. For this reason Sacred Scripture is 'the speech of God as it is put down in writing under the breath of the Holy Spirit' (CCC, no. 81). Therefore, the Catholic Church believes and teaches that the books of Scripture teach firmly, faithfully and without error what God wished to reveal and teach.

Inspired Word of God: God is the primary author of Scripture; God inspired its human authors. Divine inspiration is the term the Church uses to describe the gift of the Holy Spirit given to the human writers of the Bible. The inspired human authors wrote under the influence of the Holy Spirit. Using their talents and abilities, the human authors wrote the truth that God wanted people to know for their salvation. They used their personalities, their strengths and weaknesses, their worldviews and cultures to communicate words of salvation and truth to all people, of all times and places.

Canon of Scripture: The canon of Scripture is the list of Old Testament and New Testament books that the Catholic Church accepts as the inspired Word of God. These various texts, or writings, have been gathered together by the Church to form the Bible. (The English word 'bible' comes from the Greek *biblia*, meaning 'books'.) The books, or writings, in the Bible are gathered in the Old Testament—God's Revelation to the people of ancient Israel—and in the New Testament—God's Revelation in Jesus Christ. The Catholic canon of Scripture contains seventy-three books—forty-six in the Old Testament and twenty-seven in the New Testament. The Protestant canon differs from the Catholic canon. The Protestant canon does not include the Books of Ezra, Tobit, Judith, Wisdom of Solomon, Ecclesiasticus, Baruch, 1 and 2 Maccabees, and sections of other Old Testament writings. These writings are called apocrypha or deuterocanonical (meaning 'second canon') books.

Unity of Sacred Scripture: There is an unbreakable unity between the Old Testament and the New Testament. This unity 'proceeds from the unity of God's plan and his Revelation. The Old Testament prepares for the New [Testament] and the New Testament fulfills the Old [Testament]; the two shed light on each other; both are true Word of God' (CCC, no. 140).

The foundation of this unity is Jesus Christ, the Incarnate Word of God. The Gospel is the heart of all the Scriptures because Christ is its center.

Authority of Sacred Scripture: God, who is Truth, is the primary author of Sacred Scripture. For this reason the sacred texts have the authority of God and teach without error those truths which are necessary for our salvation. (See *Compendium of the Catholic Church*, no. 18.)

THINK, PAIR AND SHARE

◉ Discuss with a partner what makes the Bible so unique and vital to our life.

The Bible is not just a book of stories *about* God and his 'past' work in human history. It is not simply the record of the response of people of the past to his Word and saving presence in their lives. It is not just a source of information and knowledge about God. Sacred Scripture is the inspired Word of God, spoken not only to people of the past but also spoken to us today. Sacred Scripture is 'not a written and mute word, but the Word which is incarnate and living' (St. Bernard of Clairvaux). Through Sacred Scripture we hear God's voice, which is alive and active in our midst. Through his inspired Word God makes known to us the great truths of life—the great truths about himself, about ourselves, and about our relationship with him, with others and with all of creation.

OVER TO YOU

◉ What opportunities do you have to join with others in studying or praying Scripture? Do you avail of these opportunities?
◉ Think about creating new opportunities.

READING SACRED SCRIPTURE

'John 3:16' appears on highway billboards, on bumper stickers and on banners hanging in stadiums and arenas. The display of 'John 3:16' attests to the faith of Christians in Jesus and in the centrality of Sacred Scripture in their life. Scripture is vital to the life of Catholics. We encounter Jesus, the Word of God, when we read or listen to Scripture. We need to be nourished with both Scripture, the Word of God, and the

Eucharist, the Bread of Life. The proclamation of Scripture is part of the celebration of every Sacrament. The study of and praying with Scripture has become part of the ongoing faith life of Catholics, from early childhood through adult life.

The Church is our sure guide for what the Bible means for our lives. Every Catholic should read the Bible regularly. Every Catholic needs to take God's Word to heart and learn how to put into practice in their life its wisdom and lasting truths. Here are five 'guidelines' for reading Sacred Scripture (see CCC, nos. 112–119):

1. Pay careful attention to see how the different pieces of Scripture fit together to understand its overall meaning. It is important that we do not just lift a passage from its overall context in order to suit our purpose.
2. Read Scripture 'within the living Tradition of the whole Church'—within the context of her teachings and doctrines, worship, practices and customs, through which the Church passes on what she believes to be revealed to all generations.
3. Be attentive to the inner harmony that exists between all the truths of faith revealed by God. This inner harmony is known as the **analogy of faith**.

4. Keep in mind that interpretation of the inspired Scripture must be attentive to what God wants to reveal through the sacred authors for our salvation.
5. Distinguish between the literal and the three spiritual **senses of Scripture** (see below). The inner connection between the four senses of Scripture brings forth the full richness of Scripture for our life.

Read the Bible with expectancy; be open and ready to 'hear' the Word of God for your life. Be open to hear something new, something fresh. Jesus promised the Samaritan woman at the well that his word would always be 'fresh water', constantly springing up toward eternal life. (Read John 4:7–15.)

TALK IT OVER
- Choose one of your favorite passages from the Bible. Share it with a partner and talk about what you learn from it for your life today.
- When has the Word of God been 'fresh water' for your life?
- Share the wisdom you learned for your life as a disciple of Jesus.

JOURNAL EXERCISE
- Devise and write out a plan for reading the Bible daily.

Senses of Sacred Scripture

Literal sense: the meaning of Scripture conveyed by the words and discovered by the rules of interpretation approved by the Church.

Spiritual sense: the recognition and deeper understanding of the meanings of realities and events that the literal sense points to.
- *Allegorical sense:* the understanding and recognition of the significance of the realities and events in Christ.
- *Moral sense:* the recognition and understanding of the meaning of the realities and events for our acting justly.
- *Analogical sense:* the recognition and understanding of the eternal significance of the realities and events.

CHRIST AND THE SAMARITAN WOMAN AT THE WELL | ANGELIKA KAUFFMANN

The living Word of God

The psalmist prayed: 'Your word is a lamp to my feet/and a light to my path' (Psalm 119:105). The Word of God is a living Word. The Tradition of the Church plays a vital role in the life of people. Tradition shapes our identity. It is a lamp lighting the way we walk and live.

REFLECT AND SHARE

- Name some of the traditions in your own life—in your family, in your school, in your parish, among your friends, and so on.
- How did these traditions come about and what keeps them going?

SACRED TRADITION—SPIRITUAL WISDOM FOR LIFE

The Holy Spirit has guided the disciples of Jesus of all ages, times and places to understand the Word of God, to live and pass on the Faith, whole and entire, to the rising generations. The Spirit guides the Church to bring the Wisdom of God revealed in Jesus to questions of life and death, of suffering and injustice, of meaning and happiness. The Church reminds us of this truth when she teaches:

ST. PETER WITH THE PAPAL KEYS | VATICAN CITY

> The tradition that comes from the apostles makes progress in the church, with the help of the holy Spirit. . . . Thus, as the centuries go by, the church is always advancing towards the [fullness] of divine truth, until eventually the words of God are fulfilled in it.
> —*Constitution on Divine Revelation*, no. 8

Sacred Tradition is the living transmission, or handing on, of the message of the Gospel in the Church from the **Apostles** to their successors, the Pope and the bishops, through the ages, in an unbroken line of succession. The Latin root of the word 'tradition' is the Latin verb *tradere*, which means 'to hand on'. Tradition includes the many ways the Church, under the guidance of the Holy Spirit, develops and 'hands on' her faith to each new generation. Pride of place among the Church's Tradition is given to the great dogmas and doctrines of faith, the Sacraments and worship, and the moral teachings that are core to Catholic faith.

FROM THE CATECHISM

[E]ven if Revelation is already complete, it has not been made completely explicit; it remains for Christian faith gradually to grasp its full significance over the course of the centuries.
—CCC, no. 66

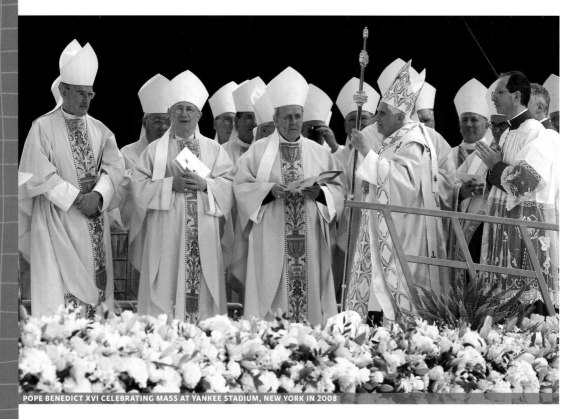

POPE BENEDICT XVI CELEBRATING MASS AT YANKEE STADIUM, NEW YORK IN 2008

The Christian life is an ongoing encounter with Jesus, the truth and Wisdom of God made flesh. This journey will find its fulfillment when we come face to face with the **Mystery** of God when our earthly journey ends. Jesus promised that the Holy Spirit, the Spirit of Truth, would guide his Church as her **Advocate** and Teacher on every step of that journey. In his final discourse to his disciples at the Last Supper, Jesus promised, 'When the Spirit of truth comes, he will guide you into all the truth' (John 16:13).

JOURNAL EXERCISE

⊙ How is your life a truthful response to your encounter with Jesus, who is 'the way, and the truth, and the life' (John 14:6)?

THE DEPOSIT OF FAITH AND THE MAGISTERIUM

Revelation is passed on under the inspiration of the Holy Spirit by God's people through Sacred Scripture and Sacred Tradition. Scripture and Tradition are the Spirit-guided ways of transmitting God's Revelation to our lives. Together Scripture and Tradition make up a single **Deposit of Faith**.

The Deposit of Faith is the 'heritage of faith contained in Sacred Scripture and Tradition, handed on in the Church from the time of the Apostles, from which the **Magisterium** draws all that it proposes for belief as divinely revealed' (USCCA, 509).

The Magisterium is the living teaching office of the Church. It is made up of the Pope, the Vicar of Christ and successor of St. Peter, and the other bishops, the successors of the other Apostles, in union with the Pope. The Magisterium guided by the Holy Spirit fulfills its task to interpret authentically the Word of God, whether in its written form (Sacred Scripture) or in the form of Tradition. Christ has blessed the Church's Magisterium with the charism of **infallibility**. This assures us that the Magisterium, in matters of faith and morals, will teach without error the truth of all that God has revealed. The Magisterium ensures that the teaching of the Apostles in matters of faith and morals is passed on without error from generation to generation until Christ returns in glory.

TRADITIONS—EXPRESSIONS OF SACRED TRADITION

The Church also has **traditions**. These traditions are the diverse ways the Church authentically celebrates and gives witness to her Tradition and faith in various times and places throughout the world. These traditions include such practices as the celebrations honoring Mary and the other saints, visits to sanctuaries and shrines, pilgrimages and processions, the Rosary and the **Stations of the Cross**, the wearing of medals and scapulars, and religious dances (see CCC, no. 1674).

The tradition of the Church is the story of a community of saints, past and present, who witness to their faith in God. Catholics and other Christians look to Abraham and Sarah, to Moses and Miriam, to David and Esther, and to many other believers whose stories are told in the Old Testament. We look to the witness of the Blessed Virgin Mary, to St. Peter and the other Apostles, to Mary Magdalene and Martha and Mary, to the martyrs and other saints. We also look to the people of faith who are part of our life today. We look to our family; to the Pope, to our bishop, parish priest and youth minister; to our teachers and other members of our parish. This 'cloud of witnesses' give us sure evidence of the existence and power of God and the presence of his saving love in our life.

As with Sacred Scripture and Tradition, the Church and her Magisterium are the guide for interpreting the authenticity of the traditions of her people. The criterion that assures the authenticity of the Church's many and diverse traditions is 'fidelity to **apostolic Tradition**, that is, the communion in the faith and the sacraments received from the apostles, a communion that is both signified and guaranteed by apostolic succession' (CCC, no. 1209).

TALK IT OVER

⊙ What is meant by the 'Tradition' of the Church? Share examples.
⊙ What is meant by the 'traditions' of the Church? Share examples.
⊙ Share the special traditions your family or parish uses to celebrate its faith.

The tradition of the Church is the story of a community of saints who witness to their faith in God

THE LAST SUPPER | MOSAIC IN BASILICA DI SAN MARCO, ITALY

JUDGE AND ACT

REVIEW WHAT YOU HAVE LEARNED

Look back over this chapter and reflect on the gift of Divine Revelation. Share what the Catholic Church teaches on these questions:

- ⊙ What is Divine Revelation?
- ⊙ What does the fact of Revelation tell us about God and his relationship with us?
- ⊙ How are Sacred Scripture and Sacred Tradition a source of encountering God?
- ⊙ What does it mean that Jesus is 'the Father's one, perfect and unsurpassable Word'?
- ⊙ What is the role of Sacred Tradition in the passing on of Divine Revelation?
- ⊙ What is the relationship and connection between Tradition and traditions?

OVER TO YOU

- ⊙ What spiritual wisdom for your life as a disciple of Jesus Christ did you discover from studying the teachings of the Catholic Church presented in this chapter?
- ⊙ Talk about how you will try to live out this spiritual wisdom in your life.

LEARN BY EXAMPLE

The story of Blessed Pope John XXIII

POPE JOHN XXIII AT THE SECOND VATICAN COUNCIL IN 1962

Blessed Pope John XXIII (1881–1963) honored both the Tradition and traditions of the Church in presenting the Gospel to the contemporary world.

John XXIII had been Pope for less than one hundred days when, to the astonishment of many, he announced that he was calling an **Ecumenical Council**. The Church throughout her history has gathered in Council to pass on her faith authentically from one generation to the next. John XXIII opened the Second Vatican Council or Vatican Council II on October 11, 1962. He gathered the bishops of the Church to read 'the signs of the times' and to address the Church's need to speak the Gospel and Tradition of the Church in a language that both clearly expressed Tradition and addressed the needs of the contemporary world. John XXIII died on June 3, 1963, and did not live to see Vatican Council II complete its work. Pope Paul VI, John XXIII's successor, closed the Council on November 21, 1965.

Pope John XXIII is much revered by both Catholics and non-Catholics. In Italy he is still affectionately known as 'Il Papa Buono' (The Good Pope). On December 3, 1963, President Lyndon Johnson posthumously awarded him the Presidential Medal of Freedom, the United States' highest civilian award. On September 3, 2000, Pope John Paul II named John XXIII a 'blessed' of the Church. In his homily at the Beatification he described John XXIII as the Pope 'who impressed the world with the friendliness of his manner which radiated the remarkable goodness of his soul'.

CREATION OF THE WORLD | BAPTISTRY OF ST. JOHN, FLORENCE, ITALY

THINK, PAIR AND SHARE

- What can Catholic teenagers learn from the example of Blessed Pope John XXIII?
- How can they give a living contemporary witness to the wisdom of the Tradition of the Church?

SHARE YOUR FAITH WITH FAMILY AND FRIENDS

- Discuss with family and friends how you can give an authentic witness to the power of the living Word of God in your lives.

JUDGE AND ACT

- Ask the Holy Spirit in prayer to guide you on your spiritual journey.
- Choose one new insight that you discovered in this chapter about your relationship with God.
- How will you make that insight part of your life as a disciple of Jesus Christ?

Pray the Sign of the Cross together.

Invitation to Prayer

LEADER

Take a moment and heighten your awareness that God, who desires to share his life with each of us, is present with us, here and now. *(Pause)*

Let us join with the psalmist and give praise and thanks to God.

The Word of God

LEADER

Happy are those . . .
 who walk in the law of the LORD.
The LORD exists forever;
 your word is firmly fixed in heaven.
(Psalm 119:89)

ALL

[My] heart stands in awe of your words.
(Psalm 119:161) *(Pause and reflect)*

LEADER

The sum of your word is truth;
 and every one of your righteous ordinances
 endures forever. (Psalm 119:160)

ALL

[My] heart stands in awe of your words.
(Psalm 119:161) *(Pause and reflect)*

LEADER

 How sweet are your words to my taste,
 sweeter than honey to my mouth!
(Psalm 119:103)

ALL

[My] heart stands in awe of your words.
(Psalm 119:161) *(Pause and reflect)*

Prayer of Intercession

LEADER

Let us lift up our hearts to God, who is always reaching out to us.

READER

Spirit of God, help us recognize and acknowledge Sacred Scripture to be your Word. May your Word help us become truer, more courageous and more generous disciples of Jesus.

ALL

We ask this in the name of Jesus.

READER

Spirit of God, help us recognize and acknowledge your wisdom in Sacred Tradition.
May we come to know you through Tradition and live ever more faithfully as disciples of Jesus.

ALL

We ask this in the name of Jesus.

Concluding Prayer

LEADER

Ever-loving God, Father of all,
you have spoken to us through your Son, your
 Word made flesh.
Send your Holy Spirit to help us
to listen to your Holy Word with care,
and to live its wisdom in our daily lives.
We ask this through Jesus Christ, your Son,
who lives and reigns with you and the Holy Spirit,
one God, for ever and ever.

ALL

Amen.

Pray the Sign of the Cross together.

CHAPTER 2

The Obedience of Faith

—Our Response to God's Invitation

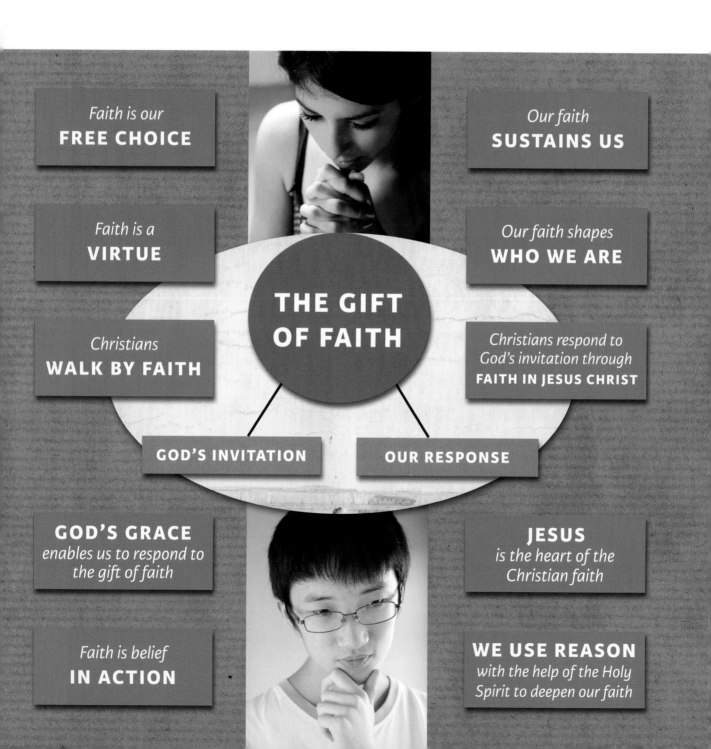

Faith is our **FREE CHOICE**

Faith is a **VIRTUE**

Christians **WALK BY FAITH**

THE GIFT OF FAITH

Our faith **SUSTAINS US**

Our faith shapes **WHO WE ARE**

Christians respond to God's invitation through **FAITH IN JESUS CHRIST**

GOD'S INVITATION

OUR RESPONSE

GOD'S GRACE enables us to respond to the gift of faith

Faith is belief **IN ACTION**

JESUS is the heart of the Christian faith

WE USE REASON with the help of the Holy Spirit to deepen our faith

FAITH IS OUR RESPONSE TO GOD'S INVITATION TO KNOW AND believe in him. In this chapter we explore the obedience of faith. We look at the teaching of the Catholic Church on faith from two perspectives: faith as a human virtue and faith as a supernatural gift and Theological Virtue. The supernatural gift and Theological Virtue of faith 'is both a gift of God and a human act by which the believer gives personal adherence to God (who invites his or her response) and freely assents to the whole truth that God has revealed' (*United States Catholic Catechism for Adults* [USCCA], 512).

FAITH IS

A SUPERNATURAL GIFT FROM GOD

A FREE RESPONSE TO GOD

NECESSARY FOR SALVATION

CHRISTIAN LIVING INVOLVES:

HANDS

HEAD

HEART

Faith Focus: These teachings of the Catholic Church are the primary focus of the doctrinal content of this chapter:
- Faith in God is both a supernatural gift from God and a free response of the person to God.
- Faith is necessary for salvation.
- Faith is a personal adherence of the whole person to God. It involves the assent of the intellect and will to the self-Revelation of God made through his deeds and words.
- Faith in God leads us to turn to him alone as our first origin and our ultimate goal. Faith leads us neither to prefer anything to him nor to substitute anything for him.
- Believing is an act of the Church. The Church's faith precedes, engenders, supports and nourishes our faith.
- Faith involves active participation in the Church community and working to spread the Faith by word and example.
- Faith in Jesus Christ leads to discipleship and has practical implications for daily life and one's relationship with Christ.

Discipleship Formation: As a result of studying this chapter and discovering the meaning of the faith of the Catholic Church for your life, you should be better able to:
- come to a deepened awareness of the presence of God in your life;
- value faith as both a gift from God and a free response to him;
- live an active faith of the 'head', 'heart' and 'hands';
- by living your faith daily, deepen your relationship with God—Father, Son and Holy Spirit.

Scripture References: These Scripture references are quoted or referred to in this chapter:
OLD TESTAMENT: **Psalms** 40:5, 119:160, 146:3–4; **Isaiah** 7:9; **Jeremiah** 17:5–6
NEW TESTAMENT: **Matthew** 5:1—7:29, 6:19–21, 7:7–11, 21, 24–29, 10:34–39, 11:25–27, 16:17, 22:37; **Mark** 1:11 and 35, 6:46, 12:30; **Luke** 4:18–19, 5:16, 10:27, 11:5–13, 18:1–8, 19:1–10, 24:13–33; **John** 14:1 and 26, 16:5–11; **Romans** 1:5, 10:17; **1 Corinthians** 12:12–26; **2 Corinthians** 5:7; **James** 2:20

Faith Glossary: Familiarize yourself with the meaning of these key faith terms. Definitions are found in the Glossary: **Body of Christ, charity (love), clergy, consecrated life, Exile (The), faith, free will, grace, Holy Trinity, hope, human person, intellect, Liturgy, Liturgy of the Hours, Liturgy of the Word, Mass, Messiah, moral passions, prayer, Sacraments, Sermon on the Mount, Theological Virtues, theology, Twelve (the), Works of Mercy, worship**

Faith Word: faith
Learn by Heart: Romans 10:17
Learn by Example: Birute, a missioner catechist

Why faith?

In June 2009 the *New York Times* asked the question 'What is faith?' Over a thousand people replied. Here are four of those responses:

- Faith is described in the Bible as 'the assurance of things hoped for, and the conviction of things not seen'.
- Faith is acting on the belief that what one does makes a difference.
- Faith is the absence of fear.
- Faith is choosing to believe that which is (for now) unproven.

REFLECT AND DISCUSS

- Is there anything missing from the above descriptions of faith? Explain.
- How do you answer the question 'What is faith?'?
- What is at the heart of Christian faith? Give reasons for your answer.

FAITH IS A HUMAN CHARACTERISTIC . . . AND MORE

In chapter 1 we explored the human desire for happiness. This desire is a touch of immortality and it reflects God's own desire for us to live in friendship with him both in the here and now and in the life everlasting after our death. What is the connection between this desire and the virtue of faith?

Faith is a universal characteristic of the **human person**. Faith impacts greatly our decisions to do what is good and our ability to trust. Faith shapes our lives, our choices, our relationships and our commitments. People of 'faith' have come to know and believe in the goodness of God, of people and of life. They live the conviction that life is meaningful; life has a good purpose.

Faith is a human virtue and a **Theological Virtue**. The human virtue of faith is the firm willingness and habit to do what is good. We acquire and grow in the human virtue of faith, as we do all human virtues, through human effort and God's grace. Faith is also one of the three Theological Virtues. The three Theological Virtues are gifts 'infused by God into the souls of the faithful to make them capable of acting as his children and of meriting eternal life' (*Catechism of the Catholic Church* [CCC], no. 1813). The Theological Virtues are **faith**, **hope** and **charity** (love).

The human virtue of faith: Have you ever heard or said, 'But I believed in you! I had faith in you!' 'Faith' plays an important role in every person's life. For example, most people acknowledge that they 'have faith in' the goodness of creation and people, and they act on that faith! They build caring and loving relationships because they have 'faith' in another person or in a group of people. Such human faith is sometimes betrayed, and when it is, that betrayal may negatively impact on our ability to grow as a person of faith. Why is that? Human faith is placed in other people and in ourselves, who are very fallible and can betray that faith. For instance, if we have been deeply hurt in the past by a parent or friend in whom we had placed our 'faith', this experience can negatively impact not only our faith in other people but also our ability to respond to God's invitation to believe in him and have faith in him.

The Theological Virtue of faith—a grace and a human act: The Theological Virtue of faith is radically different from the human virtue of faith. This Theological Virtue, which invites us to respond to God, who can neither deceive nor be deceived, is a 'supernatural' gift.

Faith is first of all a personal adherence of man to God. At the same time and inseparably, it is *a free assent to the whole truth that God has revealed. . . .* Christian faith differs from our faith in any human person. It is right and just to entrust oneself wholly to God and to believe absolutely what he says. It would be futile and false to place such faith in a creature [see Jeremiah 17:5–6; Psalms 40:5, 146:3–4].
—CCC, no. 150

Faith is a gift, or **grace**. God's grace 'precedes, prepares, and elicits our free response in faith and commitment' (USCCA, 514). Believing is possible only by the grace of the Holy Spirit. While faith is above and beyond our human power to acquire on our own, the response of faith is an authentically human act. God's grace does not take away our freedom to choose to accept or not to accept his invitation to come to know and believe in him. The Theological Virtue of faith both gives us and strengthens our ability to order our life toward God, as the First Commandment teaches. Faith in God is necessary for salvation. Faith in God leads us to turn to him alone as our first origin and our ultimate goal. The Theological Virtue of faith enables us to prefer him above anything or anyone.

- Place yourself in the presence of God, who is always inviting you to faith and giving you the grace to respond.
- How does your attitude and behavior at home, in school or in your neighborhood reflect your faith in God?

FAITH IN THE HOLY TRINITY

Faith is not only a personal act. No one can believe alone, just as no one can live alone. Christians cannot believe and live a life of faith in God without the support of the Church. Catholics acknowledge this dimension of faith at the conclusion of the **Liturgy of the Word** at **Mass**. We stand and pray the Creed; we join with the Church and profess. 'I believe. . . .'

FAITH WORD

Faith

Faith 'is both a gift of God and a human act by which the believer gives personal adherence to God (who invites his or her response) and freely assents to the whole truth that God has revealed.'
—*United States Catholic Catechism for Adults*
[USCCA], 512

In the Creed we profess faith in the **Holy Trinity**, the central mystery of the Christian faith and Christian life. We give our whole self—our mind, heart and will—to God, who revealed himself to be Father, Son and Holy Spirit. When St. Peter confessed his faith in Jesus to be the Christ, the Son of the living God, Jesus declared to him that this Revelation did not come 'from flesh and blood', but from 'my Father who is in heaven' (Matthew 16:17; see also 11:25–27). At the Last Supper Jesus promised, 'But the Advocate, the Holy Spirit, whom the Father will send in my name, will teach you everything, and remind you of all that I have said to you' (John 14:26). The Holy Spirit is the Spirit of Truth, who will help us remember and understand all that Jesus taught. The power and grace of the Holy Spirit opens our mind and heart, our intellect and will, to Divine Revelation, at whose center is Jesus Christ.

OVER TO YOU

- Search your heart. What three deep beliefs do you hold that flow from your faith in God?
- How might you allow the gift of faith to shape your attitude and behavior?

The response of faith

The Old Testament prophet Isaiah is an example of a person whose faith in God kept him going in very hard times. Isaiah lived during the **Exile**. The Exile was a time in the history of the Israelites when they were deported from their homeland and were living in a country governed by their conquerors. It was a time marked by a widespread lack of faith in God. During this time of crisis and challenge, God called Isaiah and sent him to his people to assure them of God's fidelity to them. Clinging to and giving witness to his own faith in the Lord God, Isaiah admonished and challenged the people, 'If you do not stand firm in faith, you shall not stand at all' (Isaiah 7:9).

OPENING CONVERSATION

- ◉ Who do you know or have you learned about who remained strong in their faith in God during a difficult time in their life?
- ◉ Take a moment to ask yourself, 'How firm do I stand in my faith in God?' What evidence supports your response?
- ◉ How does your faith in God affect your attitude and your behavior?

CHRISTIANS 'WALK BY FAITH'

St. Paul taught, '[W]e walk by faith' (2 Corinthians 5:7). The faith life of a Christian is neither static nor fixed. The life of faith includes the lifelong choosing to make God the center of our life. It includes our continual choosing to keep God at the center of everything that we say and do. On one occasion Jesus clearly instructed his disciples that more was demanded of them than simply their claiming by their words to be his disciples. He said, 'Not everyone who says to me, "Lord, Lord", will enter the kingdom of heaven, but only the one who does the will of my Father in heaven' (Matthew 7:21). St. James would boldly remind the early Church of this teaching of Jesus. He wrote: '[F]aith without works is dead' (James 2:20). We are not only to believe in God; our

THE PROPHET ISAIAH | RAPHAEL

whole life is to bear witness to him. We must be hearers and doers of the Word. (Read Matthew 7:24–29.)

Like St. Paul, we live in a world where it can be difficult and risky to 'walk by faith', to be a person of faith. But that should not come as a surprise. Jesus clearly taught that there would be a cost to being a person who gives their heart, mind and will totally to God. (Read Matthew 10:34–39.) Yes, living a life of faith in God as a disciple of Jesus Christ is risky. But living such a life is vital to our existence. A life of faith in God shapes who we are and who we become. Our faith shapes everything about us!

to the Word of God, Jesus Christ. We walk by faith when we match our longings for life, truth, freedom and joy—all the desires of our heart—to the way of life that Jesus Christ lived. This is another way of describing what St. Paul calls the 'obedience of faith' (Romans 1:5). To obey in faith is to submit freely to God, who is Love and Truth.

During the Rite of Baptism those who are to be baptized profess the faith of the Catholic Church into which they are about to be baptized. They renounce Satan and his works and they promise to live 'in the freedom of God's children'. After they are baptized, they are clothed in a white garment and given a candle lighted from the Easter candle, as the celebrant reminds them to 'walk always as children of the light . . . (and) keep the flame of faith alive in their hearts' so that 'when the Lord comes, may they go out to meet him with all the saints in the heavenly glory' (*Rite of Baptism for Children*, no. 127). Obeying the Word of God, revealed in Jesus Christ, is at the heart of the life of a Christian.

WHAT ABOUT YOU PERSONALLY?

⊙ How ready are you to hear, listen to and respond to the gift of faith in Christ?
⊙ How will your accepting the gift of faith affect your life?

> ### FROM THE CATECHISM
> 'Faith *seeks understanding*' [St. Anselm]: it is intrinsic to faith that a believer desires to know better the One in whom he has put his faith, and to understand better what He has revealed; a more penetrating knowledge will in turn call forth a greater faith, increasingly set afire by love.
>
> —CCC, no. 158

'FAITH SEEKS UNDERSTANDING'

At Baptism we are joined to Christ; we become adopted sons and daughters of the Father and temples of the Holy Spirit. The Holy Spirit, the divine Teacher (see John 16:5–11), abides with us and gives us the grace to see more and more clearly what faith means for our life. The Holy Spirit gives us the grace to use our intellect and rigorous thinking to come to know God better and what God has revealed. The Holy Spirit, the

TALK IT OVER

⊙ What does it mean to 'walk by faith'?
⊙ Share examples of challenges or obstacles to living your faith in God that you have encountered? How does that make walking by faith risky?

THE OBEDIENCE OF FAITH

How do Christians walk by faith? We walk by faith by our willingness to believe and trust in all that God has communicated to us. We walk by faith when we believe and give witness to what Jesus taught us about the Triune God, about others and about ourselves. St. Paul taught '[F]aith comes from what is heard, and what is heard comes through the word of Christ' (Romans 10:17). Christian faith is about obeying (from the Latin *ob-audire*, meaning 'to hear, or listen to'). It means not only listening to but also responding

Spirit of Truth, assists us to use our **intellect** and our **free will** to embrace God and all that he has revealed.

The eyes of our heart need to be informed by the sharpness of our mind—by good study of Scripture and Tradition. This is exactly what your theology class invites you to do. **Theology** is 'faith seeking understanding'. It is the study of God in which we use reason assisted by the grace of the Holy Spirit to deepen our understanding of Revelation and the faith of the Catholic Church. For those who believe, we can grow in the knowledge and experience of the reality of God through faith as well as through prayer and grace. For this reason we turn to the Church and take part in the life of the Church. The fullness of Revelation is reflected in the life and teaching of the Catholic Church. In her is found the fullness of the means of salvation.

'The sole Church of Christ, which . . . we profess to be one, holy, catholic, and apostolic, . . . subsists in the Catholic Church, which is governed by the successor of Peter and by the bishops in communion with him. Nevertheless, many elements of sanctification and of truth are found outside its visible confines' [Vatican II, *Constitution on the Church*, no. 8].
—CCC, no. 870

Reason and experience can also teach us to accept the word of other believers. Some 'doubters' claim this pursuit leads to a dead end. They claim there is a real discrepancy, almost a separation, between faith and reason. But there is no such discrepancy. All truth is from God, who is Truth. The psalmist reminds us, '[The] sum of your word is truth; / and every one of your righteous ordinances endures forever' (Psalm 119:160).

There is no contradiction between the truths of faith revealed by God and those truths, such as scientific truths, we discover by reason. Trusting in God and assenting to and living by the truths he has revealed are contrary neither to human freedom nor to human reason. The gift of faith enhances the ability of human reason to come to know the truth. God desires more for us than leaving us on our own to come to know him. He has freely revealed himself and those mysteries of faith that we could never come to know about God on our own. He has also revealed to us truths that we can come to know on our own so that we can know them with more assurance and certainty.

REFLECT AND DISCUSS

Benjamin Franklin (1706–90) once remarked, 'The way to see by Faith is to shut the Eye of Reason.'

- How does Catholic teaching on faith differ from Franklin's view?
- What arguments would you make if you were discussing the relationship between faith and reason with Franklin, or anyone who viewed faith and reason as he did?

SALVATOR MUNDI | BENEDETTO DIANA

Faith and discipleship

The risen Lord invited his disciples to faith, saying, 'Believe in God, believe also in me' (John 14:1). For a Christian, believing in God cannot be separated from believing in the One whom he sent, his beloved Son, whom the Father tells us to listen to and obey (see Mark 1:11). The risen Jesus is present with us and continues to invite people to faith. Through his Church, he invites all people to believe and trust in him and in all that he has revealed about God and about ourselves.

THE RISEN JESUS APPEARS TO THE DISCIPLES | DUCCIO DI BUONINSEGNA

REFLECT AND DISCUSS

- ⊙ What are some of the challenges the Catholic Church faces as she invites members of the Church to a deeper faith in Christ?
- ⊙ What are some of the obstacles that young people face when they seek to carry out the command to 'believe in God'?
- ⊙ How can young people come to know God through Jesus?

THE PERSON OF JESUS CHRIST: THE HEART OF CHRISTIAN FAITH AND DISCIPLESHIP

The risen Lord invites us to faith in him, who died and rose from the dead to save us from our sins and to restore us to life with God. This invitation to faith is also an invitation to discipleship. The English word 'disciple' comes from the Greek word *mathetes*, which means 'an apprentice', 'learner' or 'pupil'. Taking the meaning of 'disciple' to be that of 'an apprentice' helps us realize that becoming and being a disciple of Jesus Christ takes time—it is a lifelong process. Apprentices of Christ need time to learn, to understand and to grow in faith.

We are members of the **Body of Christ**, of which Christ is the Head. (Read 1 Corinthians 12:12–26.) We grow in faith and live as disciples of Jesus Christ with other members of the Church. To be a disciple of Christ means walking in faith as a member of the community of Jesus' apprentices—the Church on earth—in the midst of the world. We cannot make this journey alone. 'No one can believe alone, just as no one can live alone. . . . The believer has received faith from others and should hand it on to others. . . . Each believer is thus a link in the great chain of believers. I cannot believe without being carried by the faith of others, and by my faith I help support others in the faith' (CCC, no. 166).

As apprentices of Christ we join with other apprentices and learn from the Master. Receiving the Seven **Sacraments**, especially Eucharist and Penance, regularly, and active participation in the life of the Church, is essential to living a life

The prayers, good works and example of other disciples support us as we undertake our lifelong journey of faith

of faith as a disciple of Jesus. The prayers, good works and example of other disciples support us as we undertake our lifelong journey of faith and strive to base our whole lifestyle on the truths that Jesus taught by his every word and deed. We need to grow in our knowledge and understanding of those truths and in our commitment to God's Word, passed on to us through Scripture and Tradition.

THINK, PAIR AND SHARE

⊙ Page through the Sermon on the Mount in Matthew 5:1—7:29. Draw up a list of words or phrases you discover that capture Jesus' description of the life and work of his disciples.

⊙ Create a 'Values Triangle' that illustrates the words and phrases according to how you perceive their importance for the life of a disciple of Christ. On the top of your triangle place the word or phrase that captures what is, at this moment in your life of faith, *most* important to you. Then place the other words and phrases in descending order.

⊙ Share your 'Values Triangle' with a friend. Talk about how it influences the decisions you make to live your faith in Jesus Christ.

WHAT ABOUT YOU PERSONALLY?

⊙ What do you find to be the most difficult challenge or challenges to living your life as a disciple of Jesus Christ?

⊙ How does being a member of the Catholic Church support you in living your faith in Jesus Christ?

Living our faith in Christ

Zacchaeus the tax collector encountered Jesus and came to faith in him. Read Luke 19:1–10. Pay attention to how Zacchaeus' encounter with Jesus transformed his life.

REFLECT AND DISCUSS

⊙ Form into three groups. Group 1 describes how Zacchaeus is thinking at different stages in the story. Group 2 describes how Zacchaeus is feeling. Group 3 describes how Zacchaeus acts.

⊙ Each small group reports back to the class and contributes to the understanding of the encounter between Zacchaeus and Jesus.

FAITH IN CHRIST INVOLVES THE WHOLE PERSON

We give authentic witness to our faith in God when we strive to love God with all our strength, heart and mind, and our neighbor as ourselves. All the Synoptic Gospels (Matthew's, Mark's and Luke's accounts of the Gospel) add 'with all your soul'. (See Matthew 22:37, Mark 12:30 and Luke 10:27.) What is the significance of including 'soul'? In the New Testament the term used for soul is *pyschē*, which refers to one's whole being. The gift of faith invites a disciple of Christ to engage one's whole person—one's *head* (all of one's thinking, deciding and judging), one's *heart* (all of one's feelings and desires and choosing), and one's *hands* (all of one's deeds and words).

> **FROM THE CATECHISM**
> Faith is a personal adherence of the whole man to God who reveals himself. It involves an assent of the intellect and will to the self-revelation God has made through his deeds and words.
> —CCC, no. 176

Living our Catholic faith is a 'way of the head': The 'head' refers to the human gift of our intellect, our God-given ability for knowing and understanding things, for exploring the mystery of God, one's self and all of creation. The gift of faith invites and welcomes us to use our intellect. Human reason and the gift of faith, as we have already seen, are complementary partners. The faith of the Catholic Church is a most 'reasonable' faith; it is 'credible' and makes good sense. The Catholic Church encourages investigation and inquiry; she encourages people to join with her to make sense of the Faith for themselves and to share that faith with others.

JESUS AND ZACCHAEUS | NIELS LARSEN STEVNS

Read Luke 24:13–33, the account of the encounter of two of the disciples of Jesus with the risen Lord on the road to Emmaus on the morning of the Resurrection. It is a story about people's eyes being opened. The risen Lord engages the disciples, whose faith in him seems to have weakened, in conversation about their lives and their disappointment. He 'instructs' them in the whole tradition of their people, especially the writings of the Prophets that foretold the coming of the **Messiah**. Notice how the risen Christ waits and gives his two discouraged disciples time to recognize him and to renew and deepen their faith and hope. **Hope** is the third Theological Virtue. Through the virtue of hope a person 'both desires and expects the fulfilment of God's promises of things to come'

ROAD TO EMMAUS | 15TH-CENTURY FRESCO, MOMO, ITALY

(USCCA, 515). With their faith and hope renewed, the two disciples rush off back to Jerusalem, eager to share their experiences with the other disciples.

THINK, PAIR AND SHARE

- ⊙ Why do you think the faith of the disciples who were travelling on the road to Emmaus had been weakened?
- ⊙ Brainstorm with a partner a list of questions that a person today might ask about the Catholic faith.
- ⊙ Seek answers to your questions during this and future theology courses.

Living our Catholic faith is a 'way of the heart': God's invitation to faith also engages our heart. The 'heart' refers to the use of our God-given gift of free will. 'By free will one shapes one's life. Human freedom is a force for growth and maturity in truth and goodness; it attains its perfection when directed toward God, our beatitude. . . . The more one does what is good; the freer one becomes' (CCC, nos. 1731 and 1733).

This goes to what William Butler Yeats (1865–1939), the Nobel Prize winning dramatist, author and poet, described as the 'deep heart's core' of a person. Living a life of faith as a disciple of Christ includes a deep *willingness* to believe and trust in Jesus Christ and in what he has taught about the Triune God, about ourselves and about how we are to live. The Latin word *fidere*, which is the root of the English word 'faith', means 'to trust'. To have faith in God includes placing our trust in and freely giving our heart to God, who is love, goodness, faithfulness and truth. Such faith includes being aware of where our heart is. Such faith is inseparably connected with the Theological Virtue of charity, or love. Following our heart can prompt us either to chose to live out our faith in Christ or to choose not to live our faith in Christ. In the Sermon on the Mount Jesus reminded his disciples:

Do not store up for yourselves treasures on earth, where moth and rust consume and where thieves break in and steal; but store up for yourselves treasures in heaven, where neither moth nor rust consumes and where thieves do not break in and steal. For where your treasure is, there your heart will be also.

—Matthew 6:19–21

God has created every person with a free will, with the power to choose what we know is good and to love God and others and ourselves. Our God-given **moral passions** (emotions and feelings) can incline our heart to choose to do what we know is good or to choose to do what we know is evil. For example, we can respond to our feelings of anger by seeking revenge when we are bullied or treated unjustly, or we can respond by working alone or with others to correct the harm caused by such behavior. The Holy Spirit gives us the grace to learn from Jesus and to use our anger, compassion and other passions as Jesus did. The Holy Spirit gives us the

JESUS IN THE SYNAGOGUE | ENGRAVING AFTER ALEXANDRE BIDA

grace to respond with our heart and live our faith by both our words and our deeds.

THINK, PAIR AND SHARE

⊙ Share an example of a situation that drew a response from your heart.
⊙ What did your response reveal to you about what you treasured?
⊙ How did your response give witness to your faith in Jesus?

Living our Catholic faith is a 'way of the hands': The symbol of hands points to the lived commitment of a disciple of Jesus Christ. The way of the hands is about 'walking by faith' and living out in our lives the new commandment of love (charity) that Jesus taught and commanded us to live. (Read John 13:31–35; see also Matthew 22:34–40 and 1 John 2:7–17.) Charity (love) is one of the three Theological Virtues that enables us to love as God created us to love. It is the 'theological virtue by which we love God above all things for his own sake, and our neighbor as ourselves for the love of God' (CCC, Glossary; see also CCC, no. 1822).

When Jesus began his public life and ministry, he proclaimed the 'way of the hands'. He lived a life revealing the love of God for all, especially the poor and the vulnerable, thereby fulfilling the work his Father had sent him to do. In the synagogue of Nazareth he declared:

'The Spirit of the Lord is upon me,
    because he has anointed me
        to bring good news to the poor.
He has sent me to proclaim release to the
        captives
    and recovery of sight to the blind,
        to let the oppressed go free,
to proclaim the year of the Lord's favor.'
—Luke 4:18–19

Fulfilling these 'works of the Messiah' became a defining characteristic of the public life and ministry of Jesus. He healed the sick, fed the hungry, consoled the troubled, forgave sinners and welcomed all to discipleship. The **Works of Mercy**, as enumerated in the Beatitudes and the Corporal and Spiritual Works of Mercy, are the work of our hands.

Our relationship with God requires open and honest 'communication' if it is to grow and flourish

THINK, PAIR AND SHARE

- Open your Bible and page through the four accounts of the Gospel. Identify examples of Jesus fulfilling the works he announced in Luke 4:18–19.
- Discuss with a partner how you see this work being carried out in your school or parish.

OVER TO YOU

- How are you using your 'hands' to live as a disciple of Jesus? How might you roll up your sleeves and do better?

FAITH, PRAYER AND WORSHIP

Following the example of Jesus, the life of a disciple is a life of **prayer**. Together with Christ, Christians lift up our hearts to God in prayer. Jesus prayed (see Mark 1:35, 6:46; Luke 5:16) and taught us to pray (see Matthew 7:7–11, Luke 11:5–13, 18:1–8). Our relationship with God, like all relationships, requires open and honest 'communication' if it is to grow and flourish. Through our prayer and worship we communicate with God. Through this communication, which itself is a gift that is always initiated by God, we grow in faith, hope and love.

The Eucharist is the summit of the Church's **Liturgy** and life of prayer. All **worship** and prayer flow from the Sacrament of the Eucharist. The Church also prays the **Liturgy of the Hours** every day throughout the world. The Liturgy of the Hours is the official daily public prayer of the Church. Praying the Liturgy of the Hours extends the praise given to God in the Eucharist throughout the day. The hours of the day form the structure of the Liturgy of the Hours, hence its name. These 'hours' include the Office of Readings, Morning Prayer, Midmorning Prayer, Midday Prayer, Midafternoon Prayer, Evening Prayer and Night Prayer. The **clergy** (bishops, priests and deacons) and members of the **consecrated life** (members of religious communities) have traditionally had the responsibility to pray the Liturgy of the Hours. Today, an increasing number of laypeople pray the Liturgy of the Hours every day. (We will explore Christian prayer in more detail in chapter 12, 'New Life in Christ', of this text.)

OVER TO YOU

- When do you pray?
- What helps you to pray?
- Share your experience of a time when you felt God's presence with you during your prayer.

JOURNAL EXERCISE

- What wisdom for your life of faith as a disciple of Christ did you learn from your study of this section of the chapter?
- How will you make this wisdom part of your life?

REVIEW WHAT YOU HAVE LEARNED

Look back over this chapter and reflect on what it means to be a person of faith. Discuss the teaching of the Catholic Church on these statements:

- ⊙ Faith is one of the three Theological Virtues.
- ⊙ Faith is a response to God's self-Revelation and is necessary for salvation.
- ⊙ Faith is a personal act; it is the adherence of the whole person to God.
- ⊙ We come to faith in the community of the Church and not by ourselves alone.
- ⊙ Faith in Christ leads to discipleship and has practical implications for daily life and for one's relationship with Christ.

WHAT ABOUT YOU PERSONALLY?

- ⊙ What wisdom and insight did you gain from your study of this chapter about God's invitation to you to come to know him, to believe in him and to live in communion with him?
- ⊙ What might that mean for your faith journey as a disciple of Jesus Christ?

OUR RESPONSE TO JESUS' INVITATION TO FAITH IN HIM

Throughout his life Jesus *invited* people, 'Come, follow me', and welcomed a free response. Recall for a moment the incident in John's Gospel in which many of Jesus' first disciples were leaving his company because they found what he was teaching to be too challenging. Turning to the Apostles, Jesus asked, 'Do you also wish to go away?' In other words, even **the Twelve** were free to stay or go. (Read the whole story in John 6:60–71.) An uncountable number of Christians since then have chosen, as the Apostles did, to stay and believe in Jesus and to share that faith with others.

LEARN BY EXAMPLE

A story of faith in Christ in action

A catechist shares a story about the power of faith.

Birute was one of my translators for a two-week series of presentations throughout Lithuania in June 1992. The Soviets were not long gone and Lithuanians were still in the euphoria of liberation. Birute was a graceful woman with a deep peace about her. Her long auburn hair was beginning to gray, and her sad eyes reflected much suffering.

As we traveled the country, we had time to swap stories and we became friends. Birute told about the Soviet invasion of Lithuania in 1940 and the terrible persecutions that ensued. She described the particular cruelty toward people who practiced their faith. The Communists executed thousands of Church leaders and sent almost a million Lithuanians into exile and likely death in Siberia. And yet

VILNIUS CATHEDRAL, LITHUANIA

the deep Catholic faith of the Lithuanian people not only survived but thrived, as if strengthened by suffering and resistance to state-sponsored atheism.

In one of my sessions, a participant shared her childhood memory of parents pushing her through a back bedroom window when that ominous knock on the door was heard. She told of running through the fields in the dark of a neighbor's house and returning next morning to find her homestead razed and her parents gone, never to be seen again. Years later, she learned they had died in Siberia. Lithuania is full of such stories.

I asked Birute how she and the Lithuanian people endured it all. Without hesitating she said, 'Our faith saved us.' I probed, 'But did you not feel abandoned by God?' She said, 'Never! Instead, we came to understand what the Cross really means for Christian faith— not that God sends suffering, but that God suffers alongside us when it comes.'

REFLECT AND DISCERN
- What do you think Birute meant by the phrase 'Our faith saved us'? According to this account, how were the Lithuanian people saved by their faith?
- Who do you know with this sort of faith? How did they come to have it and how does it impact their lives?

SHARE YOUR FAITH WITH FAMILY AND FRIENDS
- Discuss with family and friends how faith impacts your lives. Share examples.

- Suggest how you can support one another in living your faith, in 'walking your talk'.
- Who supports you in living your faith?
- Who can you support?

JUDGE AND ACT
- How will you live your faith at home, in school, at church or with your friends?
- How far would you be prepared to go to defend your faith?

LEARN BY EXAMPLE

[F]aith comes from what is heard, and what is heard comes through the word of Christ.

ROMANS 10:17

PRAYER REFLECTION

Pray the Sign of the Cross together.

LEADER

Take some deep breaths and begin to listen to the sounds far away in the distance. Try not to think about these sounds, just hear them. (*Pause*) Listen to the sounds in this room. (*Pause*) Listen to the sounds inside yourself . . . your breathing, in and out. (*Pause*)

Now imagine yourself in your favorite place, somewhere you really like and feel good in, a place that brings you peace. Imagine you are with Jesus, who is a friend of yours. Notice what he looks like and how you feel about being with him. (*Pause*)

Now imagine him looking at you and asking you to tell him, honestly, what is the most important conviction in your life. . . . Think for a moment and then answer him, telling him why you deeply believe this. (*Pause*)

What is Jesus' response to you? Now just be silent for a moment. (*Pause*)

Finally, think about whether there are any implications or decisions you need to make because of what passed between yourself and Jesus. (*Pause*)

Breathing slowly and deeply, come back to the room.

ALL

Gracious God,
we thank you for the gift of faith.
Send us the Holy Spirit
to help us grow in our Christian faith by living as
     disciples of Jesus,
and to be open to learning from the world around
     us and from you.
We ask this through Christ our Lord. Amen.

Pray the Sign of the Cross together.

> Imagine Jesus looking at you and asking you to tell him, honestly, what is the most important conviction in your life

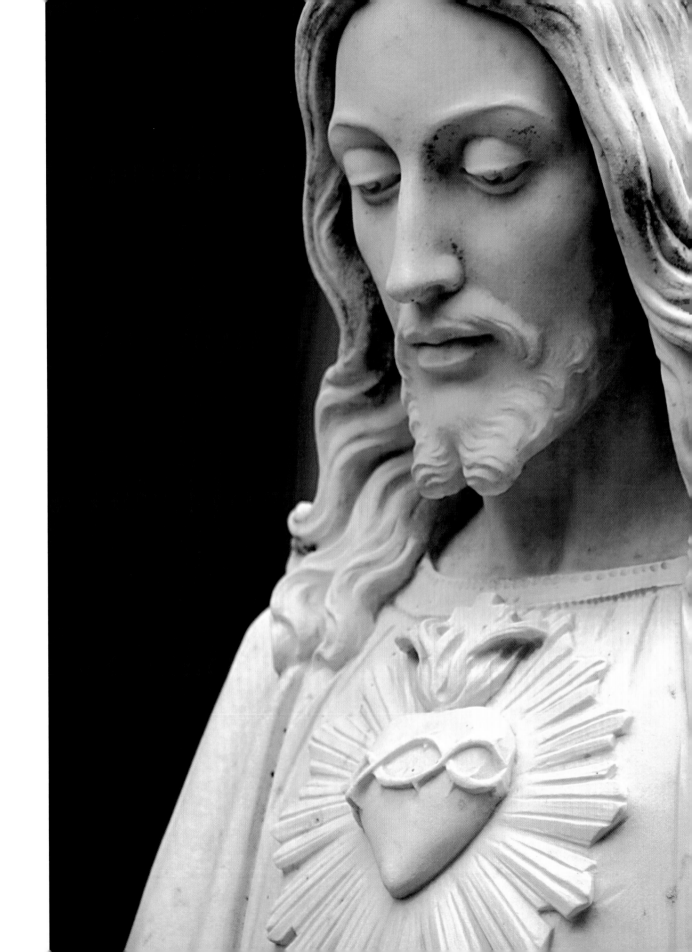

CHAPTER 3

The Catholic Church
—Our Home within God's Family

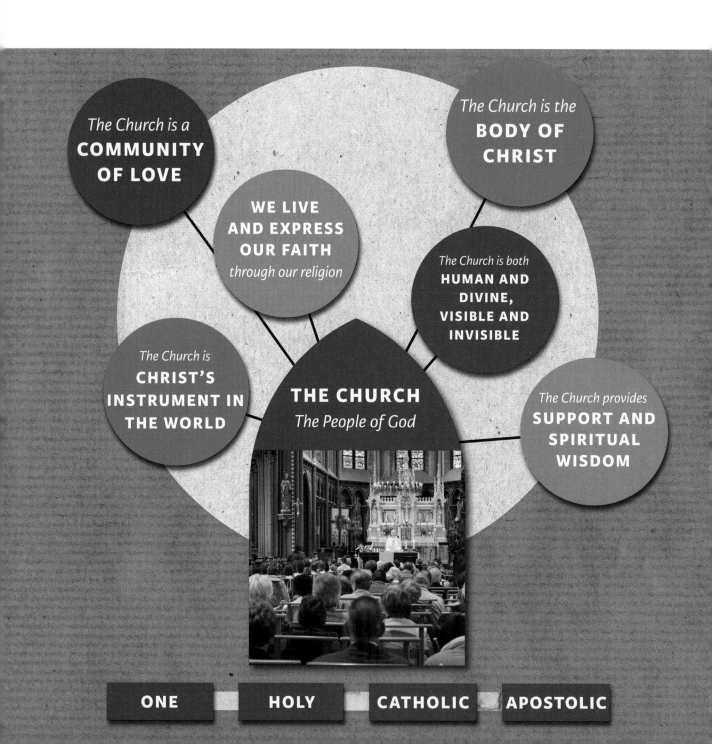

The Church is a **COMMUNITY OF LOVE**

The Church is the **BODY OF CHRIST**

WE LIVE AND EXPRESS OUR FAITH through our religion

The Church is both **HUMAN AND DIVINE, VISIBLE AND INVISIBLE**

The Church is **CHRIST'S INSTRUMENT IN THE WORLD**

THE CHURCH The People of God

The Church provides **SUPPORT AND SPIRITUAL WISDOM**

ONE   HOLY   CATHOLIC   APOSTOLIC

EVERY PERSON BY NATURE AND BY VOCATION IS RELIGIOUS.
'Coming from God, going toward God, man lives a
fully human life only if he lives by his bond with God'
(*Catechism of the Catholic Church*, no. 44). In this chapter
we explore the difference between faith and religion
and the relationship between faith and formal religious
practice. The Church, which Jesus founded, is the Body
of Christ and the new People of God in the world. The
Catholic Church, in her doctrine, life and worship, reflects
the fullness of God's Revelation in Jesus Christ. In her is
found the fullness of the means of salvation.

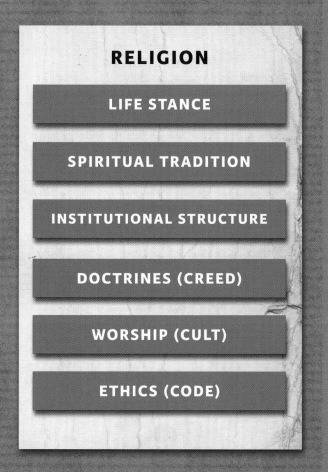

RELIGION

LIFE STANCE

SPIRITUAL TRADITION

INSTITUTIONAL STRUCTURE

DOCTRINES (CREED)

WORSHIP (CULT)

ETHICS (CODE)

Faith Focus: These teachings of the Catholic Church
are the primary focus of the doctrinal content
presented in this chapter:
- Man is by nature and vocation a religious being.
- Faith is different from religion.
- The virtue of religion is a virtue rooted in the First
  Commandment.
- The fullness of God's Revelation and the means of
  salvation are found in the Catholic Church.
- The sole Church of Christ, which in the Creed we
  profess to be one, holy, catholic and apostolic,
  subsists in the Catholic Church.
- Many elements of sanctification and of truth are
  found outside the Catholic Church.

Discipleship Formation: As a result of studying this
chapter and discovering the meaning of the faith
of the Catholic Church for your life, you should be
better able to:
- grow in your understanding and practice of the
  virtue of religion;
- articulate your faith in and understanding of the
  Church;
- come to a deeper appreciation of the significance
  of the Catholic faith for your life;
- have a clearer vision of and commitment to your
  role as an active member of the Catholic Church,
  the new People of God and the Body of Christ.

Scripture References: These Scripture references are
quoted or referred to in this chapter:
OLD TESTAMENT: **Genesis** 2:18; **Exodus** 32;
Deuteronomy 6:4
NEW TESTAMENT: **Matthew** 4:19, 23—7:29, 5:1–15
and 17, 16:13–20, 25:31–46, 26:69–75, 28:18–20; **Mark**
12:29; **John** 24:15–19; **1 Corinthians** 12:7, 12–14, 17,
20–21, 27; **Ephesians** 4:3–5; **James** 1:22; **1 Peter** 1:16,
2:9; **1 John** 1:1–3

Faith Glossary: Familiarize yourself with the
meaning of these key faith terms. Definitions are
found in the Glossary: **Beatitudes, Body of Christ,
catechumen, charisms, Church, domestic church,
Great Commandment, idolatry, Magisterium, Marks
of the Church, mystic, New Covenant, Passover,
People of God, religion, Sacrament(s), sacrament of
salvation, sanctification, virtue of religion, worship**

Faith Words: Church; Beatitudes
Learn by Heart: 1 Corinthians 12:27
Learn by Example: St. Teresa of Jesus (Ávila), Virgin
and Doctor of the Church

What is the connection between faith and religion?

OPENING CONVERSATION

⊙ Reflect on the religious profile of the local civic community to which you belong. How many churches, temples, mosques or other places of **worship** fill the landscape?

⊙ From your observation and experience, how much of a priority do **faith** and religion have in people's day-to-day lives in your community? What has led you to this conclusion?

EVERYONE IS RELIGIOUS—WHETHER THEY ACKNOWLEDGE IT OR NOT

The human person is by nature and calling a religious being. The Church reminds us of this truth when she teaches:

People look to different religions for an answer to the unsolved riddles of human existence. **Religion** refers to a set of beliefs and practices followed by those committed to the service and worship of God. The problems that weigh heavily on people's hearts today are the same as they were in ages past. What is humanity? What is the meaning and purpose of life? What is upright behavior, and what is sinful? Where does suffering originate, and what end does it serve? How can genuine happiness be found? What happens at death? What is judgment? What reward follows death? And, finally, what is the ultimate mystery which embraces our entire existence, from which we take our origin and towards which we tend?

—Vatican II, *Declaration on the Relation of the Church to Non-Christian Religions*, no. 1

Some people claim that they have no need of religion. **Atheists** claim that they do not believe in God. **Agnostics** claim that they are not sure God exists. A growing number of believers today, some of whom have been baptized, claim they are spiritual but assert that they have no need for organized religion. The events of human history, as well as the findings of social sciences, provide clear evidence, however, that the vast majority of people, either knowingly or unknowingly, have a 'faith' of some kind and join with others to express and live their faith through a particular religion. Being an active member of a community of faith and a religious tradition can motivate, guide and provide opportunities for people to join with others and 'put their faith to work', as the Gospel demands.

Sadly, some people center their life on the worship and pursuit of false gods. They live a life of idolatry. **Idolatry** 'is divinizing what is not God. Man commits idolatry whenever he honors and

reveres a creature in place of God' (CCC, no. 2113). Both Scripture and human experience clearly unmask the senselessness and tragic consequences of pursuing and centering one's life on false gods. Whether those 'gods' are the sun, the moon or the stars; whether they are emperors or entertainment or sports or business personalities; or whether they are inordinate wealth, fame or success, idolatry inevitably leads people into some form of addiction and slavery. On the other hand, a life of faith centered on God leads people to freedom and fullness of life.

FROM THE CATECHISM

It is the Church that believes first, and so bears, nourishes, and sustains my faith. Everywhere it is the Church that first confesses the Lord: 'Throughout the world the holy Church acclaims you', as we sing in the hymn *Te Deum*; with her and in her we are won over and brought to confess: 'I believe', 'We believe'. It is through the Church that we receive faith and new life in Christ by Baptism. In the *Roman Ritual*, the minister of Baptism asks the **catechumen:** 'What do you ask of God's Church?' And the answer is: 'Faith.' 'What does faith offer you?' 'Eternal life.'

—CCC, no. 168

REFLECT AND DISCUSS

⊙ Read the account of the Israelites worshiping the golden calf in Exodus 32. What led the Israelites to turn their worship away from God and to the golden calf?

⊙ What false gods in contemporary culture tempt young people? How strong is that temptation? How do you overcome it?

⊙ Where do you see people of faith and religion making a positive difference in the world today? Give concrete examples.

JOURNAL EXERCISE

⊙ Why might it be easier to put your faith to work when you are a member of a faith community?

⊙ How does being a member of the Catholic Church help you put your faith to work?

Faith finds a home in religion

The *Time Almanac* identified that there were more than 317 million adherents to twenty-five religious traditions in the United States of America in mid 2010.

REFLECT AND DISCUSS

- ⊙ Do you know anyone who is a member of another religious tradition other than Christianity?
- ⊙ Do you know people who are Christian but who are not members of the Catholic Church?
- ⊙ What words, images and actions come to mind when you hear the words 'faith' and 'religion'?
- ⊙ How would you describe the difference between faith and religion?

OVER TO YOU

- ⊙ How would you describe the relationship between faith and religion in your own life?

HOW DO RELIGIONS DEVELOP?

Faith is different from religion. Religion, as we saw in the first section of this chapter, refers to a set of beliefs and practices followed by those committed to the service and worship of God. Religion is also a virtue. The **virtue of religion** is rooted in the First Commandment. It is the habit and disposition of giving adoration to God, praying to him, and offering him the worship that belongs to him alone. The virtue of religion strengthens our ability to fulfill the promises of our Baptism. (See CCC, no. 2135.)

Most religions began with a founder, a charismatic person or group who had a powerful experience of the Divine that transformed both the way they looked at life and how they lived their lives. As they reflected upon their encounter with and placed their faith in the Divine, they tried to make sense of this experience. This eventually leads to the development of *doctrines* or *beliefs*, or *a creed*; to *worship*, or *cult*; and to *moral laws* and *ethics*, or a *'code'*. All these elements are integral features of a religion.

Judaism and Christianity are rooted in the Revelation of the one, true God and the response of the **People of God** to that Revelation. Jews profess the Shema and Christians the Creeds of the Church. Jews celebrate **Passover** and Catholics celebrate the Eucharist. Both Jews and Christians live by the **Great Commandment** and the Ten Commandments, which find their fulfillment in Jesus Christ.

FROM THE CATECHISM
Coming from God, going toward God, man lives a fully human life only if he freely lives by his bond with God.

—CCC, no. 44

THINK, PAIR AND SHARE
⊙ Taking the headings 'Creed', 'Code' and 'Cult', give other examples of each of these in the Catholic Church.

LET'S PROBE DEEPER
We'll now take a brief look at religion from three perspectives; namely, religion as a life stance, as a spiritual tradition, and as an institutional structure.

Religion as a life stance: At a very fundamental level, religion is a life stance that is centered in the relationship of its members with God. Judaism and Christianity are monotheistic religions. Both Jews and Christians believe in the one true God who first revealed himself to Abraham and of whom Moses declared, 'Hear, O Israel, the LORD our God is one LORD' (Deuteronomy 6:4; see also Mark 12:29). Jesus, the Son of God, revealed the one true God to be 'Father, Son and Holy Spirit'—the mystery of one God in three divine Persons. Faith, trust and life centered in God make life meaningful and worthwhile and give direction and a sense of ultimate purpose to the lives of believers.

Religion as a spiritual tradition: Religions are faith communities built on and expressing spiritual traditions. For Catholics, the testimony of believers who have gone before us and the testimony of faithful followers today, both Catholics and faithful non-Catholic believers, can inspire us to grow in our understanding of and practice of our faith. These traditions engage people's souls, their whole being. While the

THE HOLY TRINITY | CHURCH OF ST. MERRI, PARIS

fullness of Revelation subsists in the Catholic Church, people respond in faith to God in other religious traditions. When truth is found outside the Catholic Church, Christ's Spirit uses other Christian ecclesial communions and other religions 'as a means of salvation, whose power derives from the fullness of grace and truth that Christ has entrusted to the Catholic Church' (CCC, no. 819).

Religion as an institutional structure: Religion can also refer to the institutional structure of a particular religious tradition. Over time a

religious tradition develops a visible structure for expressing its beliefs and engaging its members in customs and practices that foster and guide their spiritual life and enable and support them to pass on its faith to the next generation. From the beginning of the Church the Apostles and other disciples of Jesus recognized that it was their duty to hand on their faith to others. In the beginning of the First Letter of John, the Apostle writes:

We declare to you what was from the beginning, what we have heard, what we have seen with our eyes, what we have looked at and touched with our hands, concerning the word of life—this life was revealed, and we have seen it and testify to it, and declare to you the eternal life that was with the Father and was revealed to us—we declare to you what we have seen and heard so that you also may have fellowship with us.

—1 John 1:1–3

Since the Creation of the first humans, the Holy Spirit has been guiding humanity to a deeper understanding of Divine Revelation and to the faithful living of that Revelation so as to bring about God's plan for the world. This same Spirit is with the Church to guide and inspire her to teach and pass on this truth in her doctrine, life and worship to every generation until Christ comes again in glory.

THE POWER OF RELIGION

The Christian life is always a life of growing in faith, in conversion toward God and becoming more Christ–like. God gave the world the Church as a unique source of grace for coming to know and believe in him. The Church, the community of Jesus' followers, supports and guides us in striving to keep God at the center of our life. A God-centered life is a life lived as Jesus lived. The Catholic Church supports and encourages her members and all people to live such a God-centered life and thereby attain a profound sense of meaning and purpose in life.

The fact of being born into the Church, however, is no guarantee of growing as a person of faith. There is the temptation to take the easy road and 'just go through the motions'. Perhaps this is what St. James the Apostle, echoing the prophets, meant when he wrote, 'But be doers of the word, and not merely hearers who deceive themselves' (James 1:22).

TALK IT OVER
- ◉ What is the importance of belonging to and participating in a religion? Give reasons for your answer.
- ◉ How does being an active member of the Catholic Church support and guide you in living your faith in Jesus Christ?

THE CHOICE TO 'GO IT ALONE'

There are many voices today that ask, 'Why belong to the Catholic Church or to any religion?' The more 'voices' that speak out in this fashion, the easier it may be to succumb to the false promises these voices make. Such voices contradict not only the evidence of human history and speak out against the collective wisdom that has guided people since the beginning of time, they also reject Jesus' invitation, 'Follow me' (Matthew 4:19). People who 'go it alone' isolate themselves from the support of a community of believers, and, in truth, deny the reality of who they have been created to be. Each one of us needs others in order to grow to be fully human and fully alive. Each one of us needs other people of faith if we are to grow as people of faith.

Should we be tempted to think this way, we need to remember that, beginning with the Book of Genesis, God revealed that he created us to live together in community. We read that God said, 'It is not good that the man should be alone; I will make him a helper as his partner' (Genesis 2:18). From the beginning God has desired that all people belong to the family of God. God gave us the Church, which was prefigured in creation, prepared for in the Old Covenant, and founded by the words and actions of Jesus Christ, to gather all humanity into that one family.

THINK, PAIR AND SHARE
- ◉ Why do you think some people try to 'go it alone' in terms of their spiritual journey?
- ◉ Do you think there are any 'real' advantages in taking such a course?
- ◉ What are the dangers of taking such a course?

The Church: The new People of God

'Outside the Church there is no salvation.' How are we to understand this affirmation of our faith? The Catholic Church teaches that those who through no fault of their own do not know Christ or the Catholic Church are not excluded from salvation; in a way known to God, all people are offered the possibility of salvation through the Church. God can offer people, including non-Christians, the grace to live out their lives as religious beings and to seek him as the origin and goal of their lives. The Catholic Church reminds us of this truth when she teaches: 'Those who, through no fault of their own, do not know the Gospel of Christ or his Church, but who nevertheless seek God with a sincere heart, and, moved by grace, try in their actions to do his will as they know it through the dictates of their conscience—those too may receive eternal salvation' (*Constitution on the Church*, no. 16).

OVER TO YOU

⊙ Imagine you are asked to explain to a non-Christian what it means to belong to the Catholic Church. Use words or symbols or images, or verse or lyrics of a song to respond.

⊙ When you are ready, share your response to the following question: Who or what has shaped your image of the Church?

FROM THE CATECHISM

The Church is both the means and the goal of God's plan: prefigured in creation, prepared for in the Old Covenant, founded by the words and actions of Jesus Christ, fulfilled by his redeeming cross and Resurrection, the Church has been manifested in the mystery of salvation by the outpouring of the Holy Spirit. She will be perfected in the glory of heaven as the assembly of all the redeemed of the earth [see Revelation 14:4].

—CCC, no. 778

JESUS FOUNDED THE CHURCH

Jesus Christ founded his **Church** and entrusted to her the fullness of the means of salvation. Christians use the word 'Church' in several inseparable ways: the Church is, first, the People that God gathers in the whole world; second, the particular or local church (diocese); and third, the liturgical (above all Eucharistic) assembly.

One of the earliest images for the Church is the 'People of God'. The word 'church' (in Latin *ecclesia* and in Greek *ekklesia*) means 'convocation' or 'assembly'. The Old Testament often used the Greek term *ekklesia* to describe the Israelites as 'the assembly of the people whom God has called together' to be his People. When the first followers of Christ identified themselves as 'Church', they were acknowledging that their roots were in God's people of the Old Testament.

The community of disciples whom Jesus gathered emerged from the community of the chosen people of Israel. At Mass, in Eucharistic Prayer I, the Catholic Church acknowledges this truth about her identity when she proclaims Abraham to be 'our father in faith'. At the Second Vatican Council the Church also reminded us of our roots when speaking of the events of the Old Testament; she taught: 'All these, however, happened as a preparation for and figure of that new and perfect covenant which was to be ratified in Christ . . . the **New Covenant** in his blood; he called a people together made up of Jews and Gentiles, which would be one, not according to the flesh, but in the Spirit' (*Constitution on the Church,* no. 9). Blessed Pope John Paul II taught this truth of our faith when he referred to Jews as 'our older brothers and sisters in faith'. The Church is deeply rooted in Judaism.

PRAYING AT THE WESTERN WALL IN JERUSALEM

THE MARKS OF THE CHURCH

In the Apostles' Creed we profess our faith in 'one, holy, catholic and apostolic' Church. 'One', 'holy', 'catholic' and 'apostolic' are the four essential characteristics, or Marks, of the Church, founded by Jesus Christ. These four **Marks of the Church** are found most fully in the Catholic Church. We introduce and take a brief look now at the Marks of the Church, and we will study them in more detail in Course IV, *The Body of Christ: The Church.*

The Church is *One*: St. Paul wrote to the Church in Ephesus: '[M]aintain the unity of the Spirit in the bond of peace. There is one body and one Spirit, just as you were called to the one hope of your calling, one Lord, one faith, one baptism, one God and Father of all, who is above all and through all and in all' (Ephesians 4:3–5). The Church is both human and divine; she is visible and invisible. She is a *sign and instrument of unity* through the presence of a visible world-wide community of the faithful sharing one Lord, one faith and one Baptism. The Church is both the sign and the means through which such unity comes about. We can see the members and the structures of the Church easily enough, but we need 'eyes of faith' to see the invisible presence of God the Holy Spirit acting in and through the Church. It is the Holy Spirit who constantly draws people into unity with God and with one another. The Church helps to build unity in a fractured world and lends great spiritual wisdom for life—a wisdom learned over many generations and centuries under the inspiration and guidance of the Holy Spirit.

FAITH WORD

Church

This term refers to the whole Catholic community of believers throughout the world. The term can also be used in the sense of a diocese or a particular parish.
—*United States Catholic Catechism for Adults* [USCCA], 507

The risen Lord commissioned the Apostles to 'make disciples of all nations. . . . And remember, I am with you always, to the end of the age'

The Church is *Holy:* The First Letter of Peter, one of the seven 'Catholic' letters in the New Testament, teaches that God called the Church to be holy, as he, the Lord God, is holy (see 1 Peter 1:16). Peter wrote: 'You are a chosen race, a royal priesthood, a holy nation, God's own people' (1 Peter 2:9). The Church is holy because God, the Holy Trinity, always lives in communion with the Church. Through the Church we receive the grace to live together, the one holy People of God, the community of disciples of Jesus Christ. Through Baptism we are once again made sharers in the very inner life of the Trinity and become members of the Church. We receive sanctifying

grace and the other graces of this Sacrament to live in right and loving relationship with God in Jesus Christ. The Holy Spirit builds up, animates and sanctifies the Church and her members, transforming us more and more into the holy People of God—despite our faults and failings.

The Church is *Catholic:* The risen Lord commissioned the Apostles to 'make disciples of all nations. . . . And remember, I am with you always, to the end of the age' (Matthew 28:19). The word 'catholic' comes from the Greek *katholikos*, which means 'universal'. The Church founded by Jesus Christ is 'catholic'. First of all, the Church is 'catholic' because Christ is always present in the Church. Second, the Church is also 'catholic' because she is sent out to make disciples of the whole human race. The Church explains:

All men are to belong to the new People of God. This People, therefore, while remaining one and only one, is to be spread throughout the whole world and to all ages in order that the design of God's will may be fulfilled.
—*Constitution on the Church*, no. 13, quoted in CCC, no. 831

From the beginning the Church has been part of God's plan to unite all people into the one family of God. 'The Church is Christ's instrument and the visible plan of God's love for humanity, because God desires that the whole human race may become one People of God' (Pope Paul VI). The Church's nature and mission is to be the sign and instrument of God's salvation in the world. The Church is the universal **sacrament of salvation** to all humankind.

The Church is *Apostolic*: Christ founded his Church on the Apostles, and under the leadership of St. Peter he gave them and their successors the responsibility to feed his sheep and tend to his lambs. (Read John 24:15–19.) The Church is always one in communion with the Pope, the successor of St. Peter—the rock on which Christ built the Church. (Read Matthew 16:13–20 and 26:69–75.) With the help of the Holy Spirit dwelling in the Church, Christ's work among us moves forward from the days of the Apostles.

REFLECT AND DISCUSS

⊙ Where do you see the Catholic Church today giving witness to the four Marks of the Church? Give specific examples.

⊙ How can the life of a Catholic today give witness to the four Marks of the Church?

JESUS TEACHES US HOW TO BE HIS CHURCH

In his words and in his actions, in every aspect of his life, Death and Resurrection, Jesus revealed to his disciples the way of being his Church

World Youth Day

The celebration of World Youth Day is a wonderful example of the many ways in which Catholics celebrate the universality of the Church. The first World Youth Day was in 1985, when young people from all over the world gathered in Rome at the invitation of Pope John Paul II. World Youth Day takes place every two to three years in different countries around the world. It is an occasion for young people to come together to share, explore and give witness to their faith. World Youth Day has been held in cities such as Buenos Aires, Czestochowa, Denver, Manila, Paris, Rome, Toronto, Cologne, Sydney and Madrid. Belonging to the Catholic Church means being a part of a worldwide Church that is united in 'one Lord, one faith, one baptism' (Ephesians 4:5).

PILGRIMS AT WORLD YOUTH DAY, SYDNEY, 2008

in the world. The Sermon on the Mount in Matthew 4:23—7:29 is Matthew's summary of Jesus' teachings on discipleship. It is a blueprint on how to live as his Church, the new People of God. The **Beatitudes** (see Matthew 5:3–11), which begin the Sermon on the Mount, are central to the Christian way of life. (We will explore the meaning of the Beatitudes at length in *Living and Loving as Disciples of Christ*, the sixth text in this *Credo* series.) The Beatitudes challenge and turn upside-down many commonly accepted values of the world. Contrary to what much of our contemporary culture teaches, the people who are considered 'blessed' are not necessarily the wealthy and privileged and powerful, but the poor, those who mourn, the meek, those who hunger and work for justice and peace, and those who suffer to do the will of God. The Beatitudes and the whole of the Sermon on the Mount teach us to live a God-centered life, as Jesus did, and not a self-centered life.

LET'S PROBE DEEPER
- ⊙ Read the Sermon on the Mount in Matthew 4:23—7:29.
- ⊙ Choose one of the teachings of Jesus in the Sermon on the Mount.
- ⊙ How does this teaching of Jesus challenge the way things are in the world?
- ⊙ Discuss the difference you think it would make if people took this teaching seriously and boldly lived by it.

WHAT ABOUT YOU PERSONALLY?
- ⊙ Talk about a time when you took this teaching seriously, or when you saw the effects of someone acting according to it.

JOURNAL EXERCISE
- ⊙ How might you respond to Jesus if he asked you about how you taking part in this work of the Church?

FAITH WORD

Beatitudes

The eight Beatitudes form part of the teaching given by Jesus during the Sermon on the Mount, which set forth fundamental attitudes and virtues for living as a faithful disciple.

—USCCA, 505

SERMON ON THE MOUNT | FRANZ XAVER KIRCHEBNER

The Church is the Body of Christ in the world

There is an ever-growing body of writing that focuses on the mystery and dignity of the human person. Some of this writing contributes to a deeper understanding, from a scientific perspective, of the power and meaning of St. Paul's teaching on the Church as the **Body of Christ**. One researcher has written:

> Everyone is some-body; we meet people through their bodies. Our bodies are great communicators— a smile or a scowl can convey so much. They also give us messages, telling us we are sad or happy, tired or thirsty, stressed or at peace. Our bodies help us to make sense of the world around us, not just the physical world, but also how we feel about things.

The human person is a unity of a body and a spiritual soul, a union of the visible and invisible. The Church likewise is both visible and invisible. She is one, yet composed of two elements, the human and the divine. When the members of the early Church began to describe who they were, they used several communal images—images pointing to a unity marked by diversity, a unity marked by the interdependence of the members of the Church.

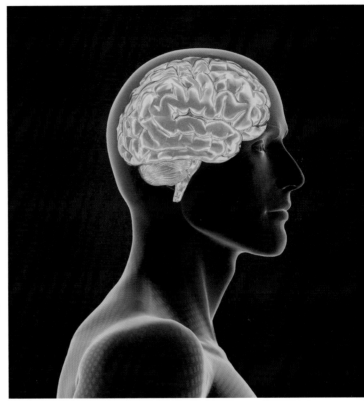

OPENING CONVERSATION
- Imagine yourself as 'the brain'. You are dependent on other parts of the body, for example, the heart and lungs, as they are on you.
- What is the unique contribution you can make to the whole body?

- How well do you think you would function without the other parts of the body?

OVER TO YOU
- When have you heard the Church described as the Body of Christ?
- How does thinking of the Church as the Body of Christ help you come to a deeper understanding of the Church and your role in the life of the Church?

THE CHURCH IS ONE BODY—THE BODY OF CHRIST
St. Paul's teaching on the Church as the 'Body of Christ' is among the most engaging and

CHRIST THE REDEEMER | RIO DE JANEIRO, BRAZIL

The image of the 'Body of Christ' teaches that every member of the Church is interrelated and is vital to the functioning of the whole Church

revealing of the images for the Church. This image of the 'Body of Christ' teaches that every member of the Church is interrelated and is vital to the functioning of the whole Church—just as every part of the human body contributes to the functioning of the whole body. St. Paul taught, 'To each is given the manifestation of the Spirit for the common good' (1 Corinthians 12:7). He went on to say:

For just as the body is one and has many members, and all the members of the body, though many, are one body, so it is with Christ. For in the one Spirit we were all baptized into one body—Jews or Greeks, slaves or free—and we were all made to drink of one Spirit. Indeed, the body does not consist of one member but of many. . . . If the whole body were an eye, where would the hearing be? If the whole body were hearing, where would the sense of smell be?. . . . There are many members, yet one body. The eye cannot say to the hand, 'I have no need of you', nor again the head to the feet, 'I have no need of you.' Now you are the body of Christ.
—1 Corinthians 12:12–14, 17, 20–21, 27

There is a wide diversity of members who make up the Body of Christ. There are laypeople, members of religious communities who vow to live the Gospel, bishops, priests and deacons, infants, children, youth, young adults, adults, wealthy and those living below the poverty line in all parts of the world. Just as with our own body, when one part is not well, our whole body is affected. Just as when one member in a family is not well, that illness, in some way, affects everyone. So, too, when one member of the Body of Christ suffers, the whole Body suffers.

Joined to Christ, at Baptism all members of the Church are to work together *in union with Christ*, the Head of the Church, according to their function in the Church. Everyone has been blessed with gifts to share and given responsibilities to fulfill. Just as the human body is one body with a diversity of interrelated parts, each of which have their own unique function, so all the members of the Church have gifts, or **charisms,** from the Holy Spirit to build up the Body of Christ in the world.

FROM THE CATECHISM

The Church is this Body of which Christ is the head: she lives from him and for him; he lives with her and in her.

—CCC, no. 807

LET'S PROBE DEEPER

◉ Look up and read Matthew 25:31–46.
◉ Discuss how this passage helps you understand the Church to be the Body of Christ in the world.
◉ Name some of the unique contributions you have seen or learned about that the Catholic Church brings to her work of being the Body of Christ in the world.

WHAT ABOUT YOU PERSONALLY?

◉ How might you respond more wholeheartedly to Jesus' words? As a member of the Body of Christ, how do you contribute to the well-being of the whole Church?
◉ How do you live out that responsibility in your family, in your school, in your parish or diocese?

JUDGE AND ACT

REVIEW WHAT YOU HAVE LEARNED

Look back over this chapter. Discuss the teaching of the Catholic Church on these statements:

⊙ Faith is different from religion.

⊙ Religion is both a virtue and a set of beliefs and practices followed by people committed to the worship and service of God.

⊙ Jesus is the fullness of God's Revelation.

⊙ The Church founded by Christ subsists in the Catholic Church.

⊙ The fullness of Revelation and the means of salvation are found in the Catholic Church.

⊙ The Church is the People of God.

⊙ The Church is the Body of Christ in the world.

⊙ The Church is the sign and instrument of salvation.

WHAT ABOUT YOU PERSONALLY?

⊙ What wisdom and insight did you learn from your study of this chapter about how you can be the Body of Christ in the world?

THE CHURCH IS OUR MOTHER AND TEACHER

The Catholic Church is our home in the family of God. She is our mother and teacher, teaching her members just as parents teach their children the language, practices and traditions of their family in the home. The **Magisterium** of the Church, guided by the Holy Spirit, faithfully and authentically teaches all that God has revealed, as well as the language and practices of our faith.

The Church fulfills her teaching responsibilities in many ways. For example, the Pope and bishops gather in Council or in Synod. The Pope may write encyclicals and many other types of official teaching documents. Bishops in the United States work together and teach through the United States Conference of Catholic Bishops. Bishops teach the people of their diocese through pastoral letters and other official documents. In this way the Church helps us to understand and live our faith.

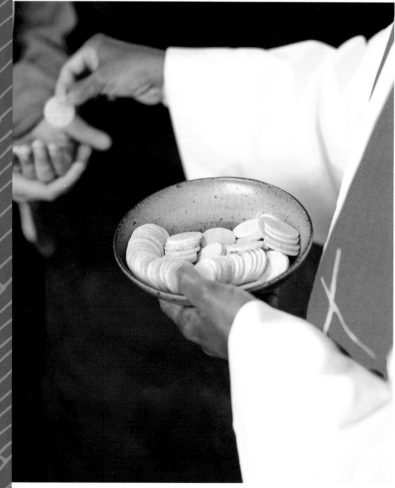

The Church nourishes us through her work of **sanctification**. Through the Eucharist and the other **Sacraments** we are made sharers in the life of God and receive the grace to live our life in Christ. We are nourished at the table of the Word and the table of the Eucharist. Through the Church we receive the Word of God and the Bread of Life. We pray with the Church and support one another as we strive to live a life of holiness. The Church nourishes our life of faith with her many traditions and devotions.

What a marvelous and blessed home we have within God's family in the Catholic Church!

The story of St. Teresa of Jesus (Ávila), virgin and Doctor of the Church

Teresa Sanchez de Cepeda y Ahumada was born in Spain in the province of Ávila in 1515. At the age of twenty Teresa entered the Carmelite Convent of the Incarnation outside Ávila, where she began reading the writings of the **mystics** of the Church. During these years Teresa experienced periods of religious ecstasy, as many mystics of the Church had before her. The memory of these mystical experiences inspired and motivated Teresa to found a Carmelite convent whose members vowed to live the Gospel in absolute poverty. In 1562 Teresa established St. Joseph's convent in Ávila. At first, the strictness of the life of the sisters became a source of scandal for many people, to the point that some citizens and the authorities of Ávila attempted to close down the convent. But the bishop and other supporters of Teresa and the sisters came to the rescue and turned the people's animosity into praise and respect for the sisters.

In March 1563 Pope Pius IV approved Teresa's way of living the Gospel, and four years later the head of the Carmelite Order gave her permission to establish other Carmelite convents. Between 1567 and 1571 she established convents in seven different parts of Spain. In total, Teresa founded seventeen convents for women, as well as many cloisters for men who wished to live the Gospel as Teresa and her sisters lived it. Teresa's followers became known as the 'Discalced', or barefoot, Carmelites.

Teresa of Jesus died in 1582; and, just forty years later, Pope Gregory XV named her a saint of the Church. In 1969 Pope Paul VI honored her with the title Doctor of the Church. This honor acknowledges the influence that her holiness of life and the wisdom in her writings contributed and

TERESA OF ÁVILA | PETER PAUL RUBENS

In 1969 Pope Paul VI honored Teresa with the title Doctor of the Church

continues to contribute to the life of the Church. The Catholic Church remembers and celebrates the life of St. Teresa of Jesus (Ávila) on October 15. At Mass on that day we pray:

O God, who through your Spirit
  raised up Saint Teresa of Jesus
  to show the Church the way to seek
  perfection,
grant that we may always be nourished
by the food of her heavenly teaching
and fired with longing for true holiness. . . .
  —'Memorial of St. Teresa of Jesus',
    Collect, *The Roman Missal*

REFLECT AND DISCUSS

⊙ What does the commitment of St. Teresa of Jesus and the Discalced Carmelites to living the Gospel say about their faith?

⊙ What power does the witness of a life of absolute poverty and renunciation of property have for Christians today? For non-believers?

SHARE YOUR FAITH WITH FAMILY AND FRIENDS

The Christian family is a **domestic church**, or Church of the home. It is a community of grace and prayer, a school of human virtues and of Christian charity.

⊙ Discuss with family and friends how family members can support one another to grow in faith.

⊙ Share ideas also on how family members can witness to others outside the home to their faith in Christ.

JOURNAL EXERCISE

⊙ Prayerfully read and reflect on these words of St. Teresa of Jesus:

Christ has no body now on earth but yours,
no hands but yours, no feet but yours.
Yours are the eyes through which is to look
    out
Christ's compassion to the world.
Yours are the feet with which he is to go about
    doing good,
and yours are the hands with which he is to
    bless us now.

⊙ Name several ways in which you strive to be what St. Teresa of Jesus described a disciple of Christ to be.

JUDGE AND ACT

⊙ What wisdom for your life have you learned from studying this chapter?

⊙ How can this wisdom help you live your life as a disciple of Jesus Christ and a member of the Catholic Church?

LEARN BY HEART

Now you are the body of Christ.

1 CORINTHIANS 12:27

Pray the Sign of the Cross together.

Invitation to Prayer

LEADER
We gather today as members of the Body of Christ.

ALL
Glory to you, Lord Jesus Christ.

Proclamation of the Word of God

READER
A reading from the First Letter of St. Paul to the Corinthians.
Read 1 Corinthians 12:12–14 and 27.
The Word of the Lord.

ALL
Thanks be to God.
Reflect silently on St. Teresa of Jesus' words:
Christ has no body now on earth but yours,
no hands but yours, no feet but yours.
Yours are the eyes through which is to look out
Christ's compassion to the world.
Yours are the feet with which he is to go about
   doing good,
and yours are the hands with which he is to bless
   us now.

Prayer of Intercession

LEADER
Jesus did not leave us orphaned. He sent us his Spirit, the Holy Spirit, to teach us to pray. Let us lift up our hearts in prayer to the Lord, who is always with us.

READER
Lord Jesus, you are the way, the truth, and the life. Help us remember that each one of us is but one part of the Body of Christ. Yet, as one part, we each have a vital role to play in caring for the entire Body of Christ in the world.

ALL
Lord, in your mercy hear our prayer.

READER
Lord Jesus, you are the way, the truth, and the life. Strengthen us to participate as fully active members of the Body of Christ, the Church.

ALL
Lord, in your mercy hear our prayer.

READER
Lord Jesus, you are the way, the truth, and the life. Guide our school community so that we will see one another as a community of equals, nurturing and wishing the best for all.

ALL
Lord, in your mercy hear our prayer.

READER
Lord Jesus, you are the way, the truth, and the life. Inspire the leaders of our Church so that they may continue to guide and support the whole Church in following Jesus, the Way, and so foster the Church's unity with God.

ALL
Lord, in your mercy hear our prayer.

LEADER
Lord God, Father of our Lord Jesus Christ,
you send us into the world
to share the Good News of Salvation with everyone.
Send your Holy Spirit
to encourage, enliven and guide us
in fulfilling this privileged responsibility.
We ask this in the name of Christ our Lord.

ALL
Amen.

All exchange a sign of peace, giving witness that you are members of the one Body of Christ, the Church.

Sending Forth

LEADER
Let us live the rest of this day and every day of our life by giving glory to God, as Jesus did, in everything we do and say.

ALL
Thanks be to God.

Pray the Sign of the Cross together.

CHAPTER 4

The Greatest Story Ever Told

—The Incarnation of the Son of God

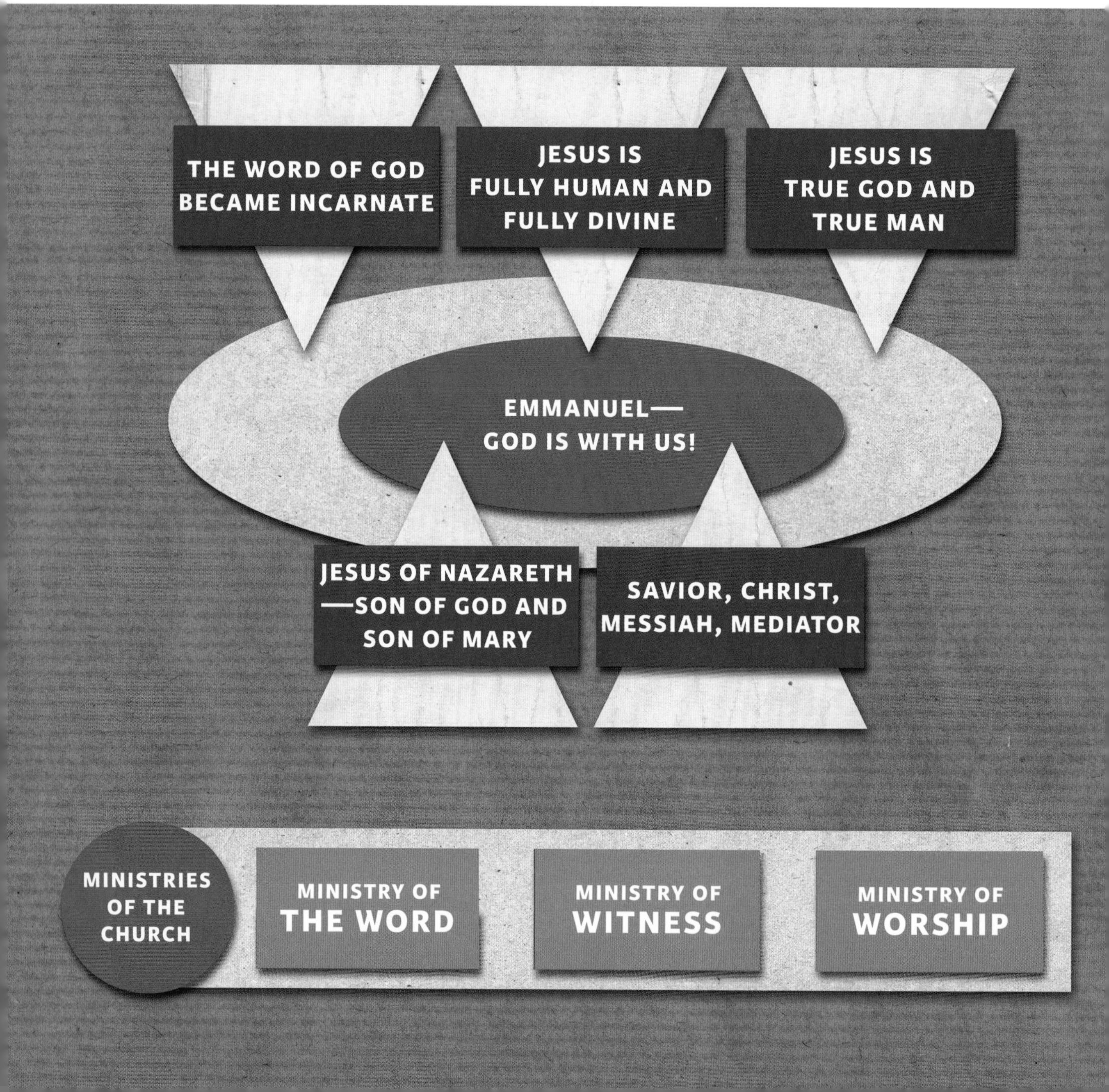

THE WORD OF GOD BECAME INCARNATE

JESUS IS FULLY HUMAN AND FULLY DIVINE

JESUS IS TRUE GOD AND TRUE MAN

EMMANUEL— GOD IS WITH US!

JESUS OF NAZARETH —SON OF GOD AND SON OF MARY

SAVIOR, CHRIST, MESSIAH, MEDIATOR

MINISTRIES OF THE CHURCH

MINISTRY OF THE WORD

MINISTRY OF WITNESS

MINISTRY OF WORSHIP

THE SON OF GOD, THE ETERNAL WORD OF GOD, became incarnate for our salvation in the Blessed Virgin Mary by the power of the Holy Spirit. In this chapter we explore the teachings of the Catholic Church on the mystery of the Incarnation: the Son of God assumed human nature without losing his divine nature. Jesus, the Son of God and the Son of Mary, is fully divine and fully human; he is true God and true man.

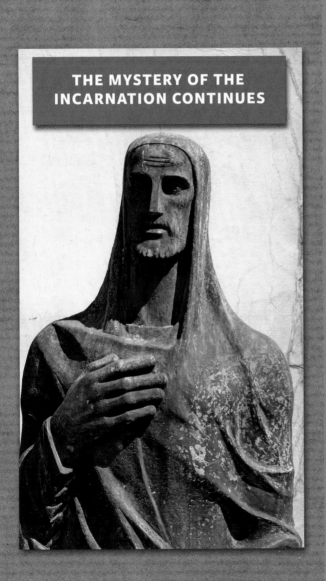

THE MYSTERY OF THE INCARNATION CONTINUES

Faith Focus: These teachings of the Catholic Church are the primary focus of the doctrinal content presented in this chapter:

⊙ Jesus Christ is the Son of God from all eternity and he is the Son of Mary from the moment of his conception in the womb of the Blessed Virgin Mary.

⊙ There is one Person in Jesus, and that is the divine Person of the Son of God.

⊙ Jesus has two natures, a human one and a divine one. The term 'Hypostatic Union' refers to this unity of God and man in one divine Person, Jesus Christ. Jesus Christ is true God and true man.

⊙ Jesus is the Logos, the Word of God, and the fulfillment of God's promise to Adam and to the people of ancient Israel.

⊙ Mary is truly the 'Mother of God' since she is the Mother of the eternal Son of God made man, who is God himself.

Discipleship Formation: As a result of studying this chapter and discovering the meaning of the faith of the Catholic Church for your life, you should be better able to:

⊙ become more aware of God's presence in your life and of how encountering that Presence impacts your life;

⊙ embrace the challenges of the meaning and message of the Incarnation in your day-to-day life;

⊙ deepen your encounter with Jesus, both in the Church and in the other events and people of your life;

⊙ come to know the risen Christ, who is present in his Church, and, consequently, be able to decide better how you can imitate Jesus as you take part in the life and mission of the Church.

Scripture References: These Scripture references are quoted or referred to in this chapter:
OLD TESTAMENT: Genesis 3:15; **Isaiah** 2:4, 11:1–3, 53:3 and 7, 61:1–2
NEW TESTAMENT: Matthew 1:18–21, 23 and 24, 28:19, 20; **Luke** 1:26–38, 4:16–21, 28–29; **John** 1:14, 17:3; **Acts of the Apostles** 2:43–47, 4:32–37; **Colossians** 2:9

Faith Glossary: Familiarize yourself with the meaning of these key faith terms. Definitions are found in the Glossary: **angel, Annunciation, consubstantial, eternal life, hypostatic union, Incarnation, Jesus (name), Kingdom of God,** *lectio divina,* **martyr, Mediator, Messiah,** *Parousia, Protoevangelium,* **salvation, Second Coming**

Faith Words: Incarnation; Christ
Learn by Heart: John 1:14
Learn by Example: Cesar Chávez, Catholic Mexican American worker for social justice

Why did God become man?

The 1965 film rendering of *The Greatest Story Ever Told*, written by the American novelist Fulton Oursler (1893–1952), was a very popular retelling of the life of Jesus. Storytelling continues to contribute to the literacy of people in all cultures. Storytellers not only pass on the stories of their communities, but they also contribute to the development of the language people use to communicate these stories. Storytellers come in a variety of forms, just as good stories do. Writers, artists and poets, screenwriters and filmmakers, composers and lyricists are all, in their own way, storytellers. Every family also has its own stories, reminiscences and anecdotes that are told and retold. Through listening to these stories children learn what is important in and to their family. They learn what it means to belong to 'their' family.

The great storytellers provide insights into the meaning and purpose of life. They speak to the universal themes that are part of human life, such as, 'Who are we?', 'Why are we here?', 'Why is there suffering and evil?' They speak to the gifts of life and death, love and friendship, forgiveness and healing, injustice and liberation, and to the reality of suffering and other forms of evil.

God, the author of Sacred Scripture, and the inspired human writers of Sacred Scripture are the most widely read storytellers. The complete Bible, which is the anthology, or collection, of seventy-six books and other inspired writings, is available today in more than 450 languages, and parts of the Bible are available in over two thousand languages.

OPENING CONVERSATION
⊙ What role does sharing stories have in your life?
⊙ What is your favorite form of storytelling? Why is that?
⊙ What stories have helped you understand the meaning of human life?

THE STORYTELLER AESOP WAS ACTIVE IN THE 6TH CENTURY BC

OVER TO YOU
⊙ What do you think is the most significant story that is told and retold in your family?
⊙ What makes it significant?

A CONTEMPORARY 'CHRISTMAS' STORY
The 'Parable of the Birds' is one storyteller's imaginative attempt to share the meaning of Christmas. Before reading the 'Parable of the Birds', let us review briefly the Catholic Church's teaching on the **Incarnation** and Nativity of Jesus. Echoing the teaching of St. John the Apostle and Evangelist, '[T]he Word became flesh and lived among us, and we have seen his glory, the glory as of a father's only son, full of grace and truth' (John 1:14), the *United States Catholic Catechism*

for *Adults* (USCCA) teaches: 'By the Incarnation, the Second Person of the Holy Trinity assumed our human nature, taking flesh in the womb of the Virgin Mary. There is one Person in Jesus and that is the divine Person of the Son of God. Jesus has two natures, a human one and a divine one' (USCCA, 515).

The Church gathers to celebrate the wondrous event and this great mystery of faith of the Incarnation each year during the liturgical season of Christmas. We celebrate that the Son of God, the Second Divine Person of the Holy Trinity, became a man while remaining God. We celebrate that Jesus Christ is true God and true man; he is fully divine and fully human. The Church uses the term **hypostatic union** to teach about and help us understand this great mystery of faith. The hypostatic union is the 'union of the divine and human natures in the one divine Person (Greek: *hypostasis*) of the Son of God, Jesus Christ' (CCC, Glossary).

O God, who wonderfully created the dignity of
    human nature
and still more wonderfully restored it,
grant, we pray,
that we may share in the divinity of Christ,
who humbled himself to share in our humanity.
           — Collect, Mass during the Day,
              The Roman Missal

Let us now read and reflect on the 'Parable of the Birds'.

Parable of the Birds

Once upon a time there was a man who looked upon Christmas as a lot of humbug. He wasn't a Scrooge. He was a kind and decent person, generous to his family, upright in all his dealings with other people. But he didn't believe all that stuff about Incarnation which churches proclaim at Christmas. And he was too honest to pretend that he did. 'I am truly sorry to distress you,' he told his wife, who was a faithful churchgoer, 'but I simply cannot understand this claim that God becomes human. It doesn't make any sense to me.'

On Christmas Eve his wife and children went to church for the midnight service. He declined to accompany them. 'I'd feel like a hypocrite,' he explained. 'I'd rather stay at home. But I'll wait up for you.'

Shortly after his family drove away in the car, snow began to fall. He went to the window and watched the flurries getting heavier and heavier. 'If we must have Christmas,' he thought, 'it's nice to have a white one.' He went back to his chair by the fireside and began to read his newspaper. A few minutes later he was startled by a thudding sound. It was quickly followed by another, then another.

He thought that someone must be throwing snowballs at his living room window. When he went to the front door to investigate, he found a flock of birds huddled miserably on the ground. They had been caught in the storm and in a desperate search for shelter had tried to fly through his window. 'I can't let these poor creatures lie there and freeze,' he thought. 'But how can I help them?' Then he remembered the barn where the children's pony was stabled. It would provide a warm shelter.

He put on his coat and galoshes and tramped through the deepening snow to the barn. He opened the door wide and turned on a light. But the birds didn't come in. 'Food will lure them in,' he thought. So he hurried back to the house for breadcrumbs, which he sprinkled on the snow to make a trail into the barn. To his dismay, the birds ignored the breadcrumbs and continued to flop around helplessly in the snow. He tried shooing them into the barn by walking around and waving his arms. They scattered in every direction— except into the warm lighted barn.

'They find me a strange and terrifying creature,' he said to himself, 'and I can't seem to think of any way to let them know they can trust me. If only I could be a bird myself for a few minutes, perhaps I could lead them to safety. . . .'

Just at that moment the church bells began to ring. He stood silent for a while, listening to the bells pealing the glad tidings of Christmas. Then he sank to his knees in the snow. 'Now I do understand,' he whispered. 'Now I see why You had to do it.'

REFLECT AND DISCUSS

⊙ What do you think the man meant when he said, 'Now I see why You had to do it'?

⊙ Does this story add to your understanding of the Christmas message? Explain.

FROM THE CATECHISM
Even when God reveals himself, God remains a mystery beyond words.

—CCC, no. 230

CUR DEUS HOMO? WHY DID GOD BECOME MAN?

The teachers and theologians of the Church have often asked and given answers to the question 'Why did God become man?' St. Bernard of Clairvaux (c. 1090–1153), the great Cistercian spiritual writer and Doctor of the Church, includes this insight in his teaching on the Incarnation: God became man in Jesus in order to know us 'from the inside' and thus be all the more likely to be merciful toward us.

At the Last Supper Jesus prayed to his Father for his disciples: '[T]his is **eternal life**, that they may know you, the only true God, and Jesus Christ whom you have sent' (John 17:3). Jesus was praying about much more than our 'knowing about' God. Jesus was revealing that he wants us to 'know' God' so intimately that it leads to a life of communion and intimacy with God that begins now and lasts forever after our death.

TALK IT OVER

⊙ Does the 'Parable of the Birds' help you in any way to understand St. Bernard's answer to the question *Cur Deus homo?* Explain.

⊙ What insights into the meaning of the Incarnation does St. Bernard's explanation give you?

ST. BERNARD OF CLAIRVAUX | 15TH-CENTURY STAINED GLASS

Incarnation

By the Incarnation, the Second Person of the Holy Trinity assumed our human nature, taking flesh in the womb of the Virgin Mary. There is one Person in Jesus and that is the divine Person of the Son of God. Jesus has two natures, a human one and a divine one.

—USCCA, 515

GOD'S FIRST PROMISE FULFILLED

The Bible opens with the accounts of Creation, the Fall, and the promise of salvation in Genesis 3:15. This initial promise of salvation is known as the *Protoevangelium*. In Genesis we read that God, speaking to the serpent, promises:

'I will put enmity between you and the woman,
    and between your offspring and hers;
he will strike your head,
    and you will strike his heel.'

—Genesis 3:15

Only Matthew's and Luke's accounts of the Gospel begin with the announcing of the fulfillment of that First Good News. We move now to explore the incredible event and mystery of the Incarnation, which you profess with the Church in the Nicene Creed:

I believe in one Lord Jesus Christ,
the Only Begotten Son of God,
born of the Father before all ages.
God from God, Light from Light,
true God from true God,
begotten, not made, **consubstantial** with the
    Father;
through him all things were made.
For us men and for our **salvation**,
he came down from heaven.

GRABOW ALTARPIECE, HAMBURG | MEISTER BERTRAM VON MINDEN

'I will put enmity between
you and the woman,
and between your offspring
and hers;
he will strike your head,
and you will strike his heel.'

GENESIS 3:15

Mary's only child is the Son of God

Christmas is the fondest feast on the Christian calendar, but we must remember that the story of Jesus' life on earth began before his birth; it began at his conception by the power of the Holy Spirit in Mary's womb. You have read and listened to the biblical telling of this story many times. No doubt you have been filled with wonder and awe pondering its many artistic renderings in portrayals in painting and music, poetry and prose. Yet its meaning is inexhaustible and your coming to grasp its meaning will be a lifelong task.

Let's begin our exploration. Read this summary of the **Annunciation**; read it slowly, dwelling on every word, imagining the scene, and be open to be surprised.

The Annunciation

The conception of Jesus in the womb of Mary by the power of the Holy Spirit was the beginning of God's fulfillment of his promise and plan to send the **Messiah.** Now, isn't it amazing that God freely chose to announce the beginning of the fulfillment of all his promises, without fanfare or celebration, to a young teenage girl? (Read Luke 1:26–38.)

God invites the Virgin Mary, through his messenger, the **angel** Gabriel, to conceive the Son of God by the power of the Holy Spirit and to give birth to and nurture him 'in whom the "whole fullness of deity" would dwell "bodily"' (CCC, no. 484, quoting from Colossians 2:9). Luke tells us that while the angel's words of invitation certainly surprised and amazed Mary, she responded, 'Here am I, the servant of the Lord; let it be with me according to your word' (Luke 1:38). Mary's response was a sign of her deep love for God and trust in him. They were the words of a strong and faith-filled young woman, who knew the implications of being pregnant before she was married.

Through Mary's 'Yes', 'the Word became flesh and lived among us, and we have seen his glory, the glory as of a father's only son,

THE ANNUNCIATION | FRA ANGELICO

full of grace and truth' (John 1:14). When Mary gave her assent, her 'Yes', to become the Mother of the Son of God, she accepted the unique and singular role God had chosen her to have in the divine plan for humanity. The Gospel of Matthew tells us that all this took place to fulfill what had been foretold in the writings of Isaiah the Prophet:

'Look, the virgin shall conceive and bear a son,
    and they shall name him Emmanuel',
which means, 'God is with us.'

—Matthew 1:23

LET'S PROBE DEEPER

The word 'Annunciation' means 'announcement'. In Luke's Annunciation account (Luke 1:26–38), the angel Gabriel announces to Mary that God has chosen her to be the Mother of the Son of God and she is to name him Jesus. The name Jesus in Hebrew means 'God saves'. Mary was a virgin, betrothed (engaged) to Joseph, a descendant of King David, the son of Jesse, through whom God's plan, as described by the prophet Isaiah, would come about. Isaiah taught:

A shoot shall come out from the stump of Jesse,
   and a branch shall grow out of his roots.
The spirit of the LORD shall rest on him,
   the spirit of wisdom and understanding,
   the spirit of counsel and might,
   the spirit of knowledge and the fear of the
      LORD.
His delight shall be in the fear of the LORD.
                —Isaiah 11:1–3

Jesus Christ the Logos, the Word of God, is the fulfillment of God's promise to Adam and Eve and to the people of ancient Israel. From all the descendants of Eve, God chose the Blessed Virgin to be the Mother of his Son. Mary is truly the Mother of God because she is the Mother of Jesus, the Incarnate Son of God. Jesus is true God and true man. He is the eternal Son of God who became man at the time God appointed, without giving up his divinity. Jesus is God himself.

REFLECT AND DISCUSS
- Share any words or phrases in the account of the Annunciation that stood out for you. Why do they stand out and what do they mean?
- What do you imagine was going on in Mary's mind and heart as she listened to the angel? Support your reflections using Luke's text.

WHAT ABOUT YOU PERSONALLY?
- What does Mary's 'Yes' mean for your own faith?

THE ANGEL'S ANNOUNCEMENT TO JOSEPH
While Luke's account of the Annunciation focuses on Mary, Matthew's account tells Joseph's side of the story. Read it slowly and carefully.

Now the birth of Jesus the Messiah took place in this way. When his mother Mary had been engaged to Joseph, but before they lived together, she was found to be with child from the Holy Spirit. Her husband Joseph, being a righteous man and unwilling to expose her to public disgrace, planned to dismiss her quietly. But just when he had resolved to do this, an angel of the Lord appeared to him in a dream and said, 'Joseph, son of David, do not be afraid to take Mary as your wife, for the child conceived in her is from the Holy Spirit. She will bear a son and you are to name him Jesus, for he will save his people from their sins'. . . . When Joseph awoke from sleep, he did as the angel of the Lord commanded him; he took her as his wife.

                —Matthew 1:18–21, 24

REFLECT AND DISCUSS
- Share any words or phrases that stood out for you in Matthew's account of the angel's announcement to Joseph. Share why they stand out and what they mean.
- From reading the angel's announcement to Joseph in Matthew's Gospel, what did you learn about the faith of Joseph? How did his faith impact his decisions in this situation?

OVER TO YOU
- What can you learn from St. Joseph about the challenges of living your own faith?

THE HOLY FAMILY | JANET MCKENZIE

The Word became flesh

At Mass on Christmas Day, Catholics pray:

Grant, we pray, almighty God,
that, as we are bathed in the new radiance of
    your incarnate Word,
the light of faith, which illumines our minds,
may also shine in our deeds.
                    —Collect, 'At the Mass at Dawn',
                                    The Roman Missal

What does your parish church look like on Christmas Eve and on Christmas Day? Is there standing room only, as there is in most Catholic parish churches? The overflowing assembly gives witness to the faith of Catholics that taking part in the celebration of the Nativity transforms the way we live our life.

READ AND REFLECT

We not only join with our parish community to celebrate the meaning of the Nativity for our life; we also reflect and pray personally, in our own words. Read these reflections of Sharon, a five-year-old child.

Sharon's Christmas Prayer

She was five,
sure of the facts,
and recited them
with slow solemnity,
convinced every word
was revelation.
She said
'They were so poor
they had only peanut butter and jelly
sandwiches to eat
and they went a long way from home
without getting lost. The lady rode
a donkey, the man walked, and the baby
was inside the lady.
They had to stay in a stable
with an ox and an ass (hee-hee)
but the Three Rich Men found them
because a star lited the roof.
Shepherds came and you could
pet the sheep but not feed them.
Then the baby was borned.

And do you know who he was?'
Her quarter eyes inflated
to silver dollars.
'The baby was God.'
And she jumped in the air,
whirled round, dove into the sofa
and buried her head under the cushion,
which is the only proper response
to the Good News of the Incarnation.

- ⊙ What do you think the poet means by saying that Sharon's response 'is the only proper response' to the news that the baby was God?
- ⊙ What is your own best response to the Incarnation?

JESUS CHRIST—GOD IS WITH US: MEDIATOR AND MESSIAH

The man who did not believe in Christmas in the 'Parable of the Birds' in section one of this chapter was willing to do almost anything to save a flock of birds that seemed destined for destruction. But, as a human being, there was a limit to what he could do. The man could not *become* a bird in order to lead them to safety. However, God became 'man' in Jesus. Jesus is 'God-with-us'. He is the only Son of the Father. He is the eternal Word of God who took on flesh (the word 'incarnation' comes from the Latin, 'to take on flesh'). In Jesus, divinity and humanity are brought into perfect union in the one divine Person. God became one of us and lived among us for our salvation. Recall these words from Matthew:

> 'Look, the virgin shall conceive and bear a son,
> and they shall name him Emmanuel,'
> which means, 'God is with us.'
> —Matthew 1:23

The name Jesus means 'God saves'. Jesus is Emmanuel; he is God with us. Jesus Christ is the bridge, or **Mediator**, between humanity and God. He is the Messiah who freed us from our sins by his suffering and Death on the Cross and brought about our reconciliation with God the Father. Jesus is the way that God most fully comes into our lives, draws us close and reconciles us with himself. By the suffering and Death on the Cross of the Incarnate Son of God, our potential for living life fully is made possible in abundance, both here on earth and in life everlasting.

The Old Testament portrayals of the Messiah, a word meaning 'Anointed One', are many and diverse. The Messiah is the Anointed One whom God would send to inaugurate his Kingdom definitively and save his people and 'atone' for their sins. For example, within the writings of the prophet Isaiah we read of a mighty ruler for justice and peace, who 'shall judge between the nations, and shall arbitrate for many peoples' (Isaiah 2:4). This same Isaiah describes the Messiah as 'a man of suffering' (Isaiah 53:3), who is 'oppressed . . . afflicted . . . like a lamb that is led to the slaughter' (Isaiah 53:7).

At the beginning of his public life and ministry, Jesus not only declared that he was indeed the Messiah, but he also described the kind of Messiah he would be. Read Luke 4:16–21. Luke goes on to tell us that Jesus' claim was not received well. '[A]ll in the synagogue were filled with rage. They got up, drove him out of the town, and led him to the brow of the hill on which their town was built, so that they might hurl him off the cliff' (Luke 4:28–29). Throughout his public life and ministry, Jesus would fulfill the description of the Messiah prefigured in the writings of the prophet Isaiah.

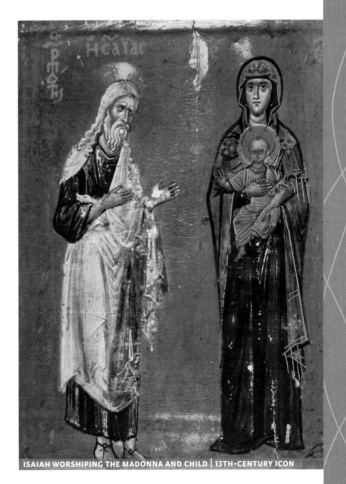

ISAIAH WORSHIPING THE MADONNA AND CHILD | 13TH-CENTURY ICON

THE RISEN CHRIST APPEARING TO HIS DISCIPLES | 19TH-CENTURY ENGRAVING

Christ

The title given to Jesus, meaning 'The Anointed One'; it comes from the Latin word *Christus*, which in its Greek root is the word for *Messiah*.

—USCCA, 507.

REFLECT AND DISCUSS

⦿ From what you have learned about the Israelites' expectations of the Messiah, why might the people in the synagogue have reacted to Jesus as Luke's account of the Gospel describes?

⦿ Do you hear Christians today reacting to Jesus in the same way as the people in the synagogue reacted to him? Explain.

THE MYSTERY OF THE INCARNATION CONTINUES—WE ARE NOT ALONE!

The risen Jesus promised, '[R]emember, I am with you always, to the end of the age' (Matthew 28:20). While the Incarnation occurred two thousand years ago, the presence of the Incarnate Son of God, God-with-us, did not end with the saving Death, Resurrection and Ascension of Jesus. The risen and glorified Christ continues to be 'God-with-us'. His presence and saving work will continue until he comes again in glory at the end of time. Christ's coming again in glory at the end of time is called his **Second Coming**, or *Parousia*. Only then will the work of the Messiah be complete. Only then will the hope expressed in the Our Father, 'Thy kingdom come', be fulfilled.

OVER TO YOU

⦿ Jesus lived and died as a Jewish man in Palestine some two thousand years ago. His ways were the ways of the Jews of that time and place. His stories and images reflect the landscape, people and teaching of that era. How, then, can young people 'imitate' Jesus in their lives today?

JOURNAL EXERCISE

⦿ Describe one thing you can begin to do in your life to imitate Jesus.

The presence and work of Christ in the world

In chapter 3 we reflected on these oft-quoted words of St. Teresa of Jesus (Ávila):

> Christ has no body now on earth but yours,
> no hands but yours, no feet but yours.
> Yours are the eyes through which is to look
> out
> Christ's **compassion** to the world.
> Yours are the feet with which he is to go about
> doing good,
> and yours are the hands with which he is to
> bless us now.

OPENING CONVERSATION

⊙ How do the words of St. Teresa of Jesus help you understand the final words of the risen Christ to his disciples, 'And remember, I am with you always, to the end of the age' (Matthew 28:20).

⊙ Who do you know to be the 'hands' and 'feet' and 'eyes' of Jesus in the world? Give reasons for your choices.

WHAT ABOUT YOU PERSONALLY?

⊙ How aware are you of the final words of Jesus to his disciples as you go about each day?

⊙ How well do the words of St. Teresa of Jesus describe you?

THE CHURCH IS THE SEED OF THE KINGDOM OF GOD

The risen Anointed One of God is with us forever. Christ is present in and with the Church and every member of the Church. The risen Christ sends us out to continue his work. This might seem like an enormous responsibility. The world is so big and has so many problems. But Jesus lives on in the Church and in the world, and his Spirit sustains us. We are not alone. We are never alone! With the help of God and the grace of the Holy Spirit, we can be the 'head', 'heart' and 'hands' of Jesus Christ in the world now.

How is the risen Lord with us? Jesus is uniquely with us in and through the Church, the Body of Christ in the world. But how is this possible? How is it possible that 'we'—the Church—are now to make Christ present to the world? The Church is a sign and sacrament of the presence of Christ at work in the world. She is, in Christ, 'a sacrament—a sign and instrument, that is, of communion with God and of the unity of the entire human race' (*Constitution on the Church*, no. 1).

The Church connects people to God and to one another. She does this through the celebration of the Sacraments and in the life of the Church in countless other ways; for example, through her living the Spiritual and Corporal Works of Mercy (see page 283 of this text). The Church works with people in education, pastoral ministry, social justice, healthcare, faith formation and in building and rebuilding communities. In all she does, the Church on earth is the seed and the beginning of that **Kingdom of God** inaugurated by Jesus. The mission of the Church, the Body of Christ in the world, is the very mission of Christ, the Head of his Body. The Church is 'the universal sacrament of salvation' *for all people*. The Church does not simply care for her own members; she, like Christ, the Head of the Church, is the visible sign of the saving presence of God in the world.

OVER TO YOU

- ⊙ In what ways do you recognize yourself as 'being' the Church to other people?
- ⊙ In what ways might your family and friends and other people recognize you as 'being' the Church to them and to those around you?

THE MINISTRIES OF THE CHURCH—ENCOUNTERING AND MAKING CHRIST PRESENT

We learn best to be Church in the world by reflecting on, learning from and imitating the events in Christ's life. Every Christian, by his or her Baptism, is joined to Christ and receives the grace of the Holy Spirit to take part in the work of the Church. As the Body of Christ, we have the vocation, mission and responsibility to make the saving presence of Christ a reality in the world today. We do this by making the light of our faith shine forth in our words and deeds. Each of the baptized fulfills this work according to their role and responsibilities within the Church. Let us take a brief look at the work of the Church from three perspectives: the Ministry of the Word, the Ministry of Witness and the Ministry of Worship.

Ministry of the Word: The baptized are called to proclaim Christ, the Word of God, to the ends of the earth. (Read Matthew 28:19.) We encounter Christ through the proclamation of God's Word, through Scripture and Tradition, in the Church. The Word of God comes as gift and gives form and direction to our lives, as it has done for

THE ANNUAL TAIZÉ GATHERING HELD IN ROTTERDAM, 2010

As the Body of Christ in the world, we must make the light of our faith shine forth in our words and deeds

literally millions of people before us—and will continue to do after us. But this does not happen automatically. We must open our hearts and minds to the grace of the Holy Spirit. We must welcome God's Word to make its home in us and give form to our life and bring that Word to others.

Ministry of Witness: The members of the early Church knew well that they must practice what they preached. They knew that they must bear witness to Jesus by living lives of faith, hope and love. (Read Acts of the Apostles 2:43–47; 4:32–37.) As members of the Catholic Church we are called to proclaim Christ not only in words but also in works, or deeds. The experience of meeting people who live their Christian faith can be truly inspiring. Why? Because in such an experience we are encountering Christ, the risen Lord and Savior in whom we profess to believe. Some Christians bear witness in a very dramatic way, as St. Peter and St. Paul did; they risk and give their life to follow Jesus, as the **martyrs** of the Church did. Every Christian is called to give such witness in the small yet important ways in which we make

sacrifices daily because of our love for God and others.

Ministry of Worship: We encounter and join with Jesus most directly through our celebration of the Seven Sacraments. The Sacraments are life-giving actions of the Holy Spirit at work in the Church. In each of the Seven Sacraments we join with Christ to give praise to the Father through the power of the Holy Spirit. We receive specific graces to live and celebrate our life in Christ and share it with others. St. Augustine of Hippo loved to tell his people at the end of Mass, 'Go and be what you have received; the Body of Christ.' This is how we are 'to be' the Church.

WHAT ABOUT YOU PERSONALLY?

- In what small but important ways can you bear witness to Jesus?
- In what ways can you 'live the Sacraments' in your everyday life?
- How might you be able to contribute to the ministries of word, witness and worship in your school? In your parish? In your home? In your local community?

JUDGE AND ACT

REVIEW WHAT YOU HAVE LEARNED

Look back over this chapter and reflect on what it means to say that the Catholic Church is our home in the family of God. Discuss the teachings of the Catholic Church on these statements:

- ◉ Jesus Christ the Logos, the Word of God, is the fulfillment of God's promise to Adam and Eve and to the people of ancient Israel.
- ◉ Jesus is true God and true man. He is fully divine and fully human.
- ◉ Jesus possesses two natures, one divine and one human, united in one divine Person.
- ◉ Mary is truly the Mother of God.
- ◉ Christ continues his presence in the world through the Church.

- ◉ The Church is the seed of the Kingdom of God.
- ◉ The Church is a sign and instrument of communion with God and of the unity of the entire human race.

WHAT ABOUT YOU PERSONALLY?

- ◉ What wisdom and insight did you learn from your study of this chapter? What might that mean for your faith journey?
- ◉ How do you think you can best contribute to the Church's work of enabling people to encounter Christ in today's world?

LEARN BY EXAMPLE

The story of Cesar Chávez

The work of Cesar Chávez gives us an example of one way in which 'the light of faith, which illumines our minds, may also shine in our deeds' (from Collect, 'At the Mass at Dawn', The Roman Missal).

Cesar Chávez (1927–93) was a Mexican American farm worker, civil rights activist and labor leader. Chávez once wrote of how he wanted the Church to be 'as Christ among us'. He said:

> What do we want the Church to do? We don't ask for more cathedrals. We don't ask for bigger churches of fine gifts. We ask for its presence with us, beside us, as Christ among us. We ask the Church to **sacrifice** with the people for social change, for justice, and for love of brother and sister. We don't ask for words. We ask for deeds. We don't ask for paternalism. We ask for servanthood.

When Chávez was ten years old the Chávez family were migrant farm workers. Chávez experienced firsthand the appalling conditions and hardships of migrant workers as he traveled all over the Southwest United States and worked on farms with them. In 1944 he joined the United States Navy and served in the Pacific in the aftermath of World War II. When he returned, Chávez joined a prominent Latino civil rights group called Community Service Organization (CSO). He championed economic and social issues, including opposing racial discrimination, and, eventually, became the national director of CSO.

Chávez soon set out to fulfill his dream of establishing an organization to protect and serve farm workers, and he founded the National Farm Workers Association, which later became the United Farm Workers (UFW) of America. For over thirty years Chávez dedicated his life to improving the dignity, respect, wages, medical benefits and conditions of farm workers throughout the United States.

Chávez had an extraordinary ability to bond with people from all walks of life— students, middle-class consumers, trade unionists, religious groups and minorities—in the search for justice. When he died in 1993, more than fifty thousand people attended his funeral in Delano, California. In 1994 President Clinton posthumously awarded Chávez the Presidential Medal of Freedom.

Chávez was a devout Catholic who often said that his struggle for justice was inspired and sustained by his deep Catholic faith. He had a strong belief in God, prayed often and attended Mass regularly. For Chávez, Catholic faith was a source of strength, connecting the Gospel mandate for justice with his struggle on behalf of the farm workers. His belief that God was with him in his work for justice gave him strength in the face of enormous opposition. The Chávez motto was '*Sí, se puede*' ('It can be done').

PAUSE AND REFLECT

Cesar Chávez was a man of prayer. Here is a prayer he wrote about his work and the people he was trying to serve:

Oración del campesino en la lucha
Prayer of the Farm Workers' Struggle

Enséñame el sufrimiento de los más desafortunados;
Así Conoceré el dolor de mi pueblo.
Show me the suffering of the most miserable;
So I will know my people's plight.

Líbrame a orar por los demás;
Porque estás presente en cada persona.
Free me to pray for others;
For you are present in every person.

Ayúdame a tomar responsabilidad de mi propia vida;
Sólo así sere libre al fin.
Help me take responsibility for my own life;
So that I can be free at last.

Concédeme valentía para servir al prójimo;
Porque en la entrega hay vida verdadera.
Grant me courage to serve others;
For in service there is true life.

Concédeme honradez y paciencia;
Para que yo pueda trabajar junto con otros trabajadores.
Give me honesty and patience;
So that I can work with other workers.

Alúmbranos con el canto y la celebración;
Para que levanten el Espíritu entre nosotros.
Bring forth song and celebration;
So that the Spirit will be alive among us.

Que el Espíritu florezca y crezca;
Para que no nos cansemos entre la lucha.
Let the Spirit flourish and grow;
So that we will never tire of the struggle.

Nos acordamos de los que han caído por la justicia;
Porque a nosotros han entregado la vida.
Let us remember those who have died for justice;
For they have given us life.

Ayúdanos a amar aún a los que nos odian;
Así podremos cambiar el mundo.
Help us love even those who hate us;
So we can change the world.
Amén.
Amen.

REFLECT AND DISCERN

- Chávez asked for the presence of the Church 'with us, beside us, as Christ among us'. What do you think he meant by this? How did he put 'flesh and blood' on this conviction?
- What does the prayer of Chávez tell you about Chávez and his faith in God-with-us?
- Share ways you can make his wisdom part of your life.

SHARE YOUR FAITH WITH FAMILY AND FRIENDS

- Talk with family and friends about how you can work together to put into practice your faith in the Incarnation.
- Discuss how this will help to bring about the Kingdom of God inaugurated by Jesus.

JUDGE AND ACT

- What are you coming to see for yourself about your living of your faith in the 'Incarnation'?
- Think of a struggle for justice that you would like to be part of so as to give witness to the saving presence of God at work in the world. How might you get involved?

LEARN BY HEART

[T]he Word became flesh and lived among us.

JOHN 1:14

Gathering and Invitation to prayer

LEADER

Recall that Jesus told us he is always with us when we gather to pray. (*Pause*) Today, we shall listen and respond to God's Word by praying according to the ancient way of praying known as *lectio divina*.

Prayer of Lectio Divina

LEADER

Open your Bible to the first chapter in Luke's Gospel. Read verses 28–31, 35 and 38 slowly, expecting that there might be a word of God's wisdom here for your life. Notice what word or image stands out for you; what resonates for you in what the angel says, and how Mary responds.

ALL

Read the passage and pause for reflection (and perhaps some sharing of thoughts on what was read).

LEADER

Reread the passage. This time as you read, pause and imagine the scene; place yourself within it as an observer. Talk to God about what you are seeing, hearing, noticing in this encounter between Mary and the angel Gabriel. (*Pause*)

ALL

Read the passage, pause and meditate on the passage. Then share your reflections, if you wish, with a partner.

LEADER

Read the passage once again. Now listen in silence for what God may be saying to you. It may help to focus on the particular word or image that seems most significant. Rest in the loving presence of God. (*Pause*)

ALL

Read the passage, pause and contemplate, or place yourself in God's presence.

LEADER

Slowly come out of contemplation. Now look into your own heart for the personal prayer you might say. (*Pause*)

ALL

Raise your prayer up to God, aloud or in the quiet of your heart.

LEADER

Now ask yourself, 'What decision is God inviting me to make?', 'What is God calling me to do?' (*Pause*)

ALL

Share decisions or overall responses to the experience. Then silently pray the words 'Thy kingdom come; thy will be done' from the Our Father as a mantra prayer.

Sending Forth

LEADER

Let us glorify the Lord by our lives.

ALL

Thanks be to God.

Pray the Sign of the Cross together.

CHAPTER 5

The Most Holy Trinity
—The Central Mystery of Christian Faith and the Christian Life

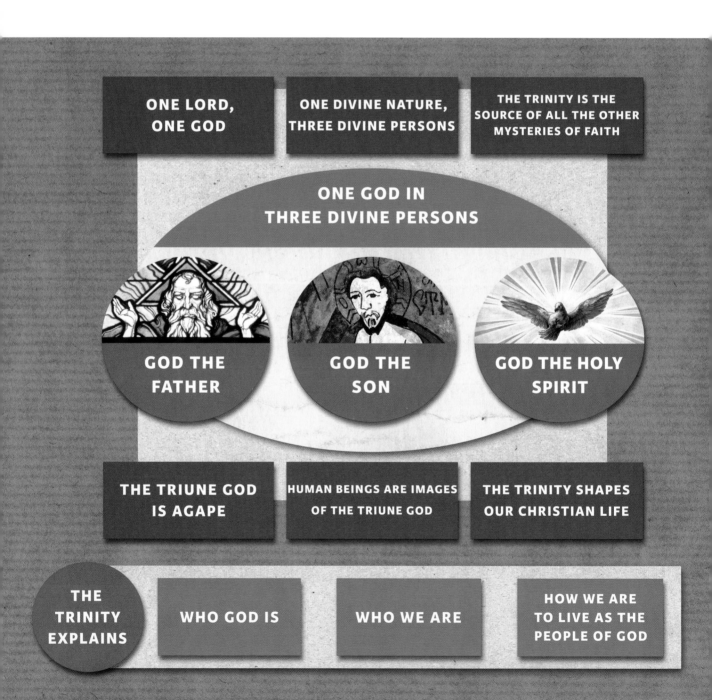

ONE LORD, ONE GOD

ONE DIVINE NATURE, THREE DIVINE PERSONS

THE TRINITY IS THE SOURCE OF ALL THE OTHER MYSTERIES OF FAITH

ONE GOD IN THREE DIVINE PERSONS

GOD THE FATHER

GOD THE SON

GOD THE HOLY SPIRIT

THE TRIUNE GOD IS AGAPE

HUMAN BEINGS ARE IMAGES OF THE TRIUNE GOD

THE TRINITY SHAPES OUR CHRISTIAN LIFE

THE TRINITY EXPLAINS

WHO GOD IS

WHO WE ARE

HOW WE ARE TO LIVE AS THE PEOPLE OF GOD

BELIEF IN THE HOLY, OR BLESSED, TRINITY IS THE central mystery of the Christian faith and life. In this chapter we explore the Catholic Church's teaching on God's self-Revelation to be a Triune God—one God in three divine Persons, Father, Son and Holy Spirit—whose very being is Truth and Love. We also explore the implications of the Revelation of the Trinity for both our understanding of who we are—persons created by the Triune God in the image and likeness of God—and what this means for how we are to live.

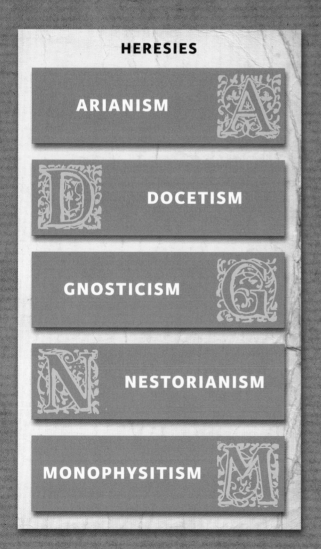

HERESIES

- **ARIANISM**
- **DOCETISM**
- **GNOSTICISM**
- **NESTORIANISM**
- **MONOPHYSITISM**

Faith Focus: These teachings of the Catholic Church are the primary focus of the doctrinal content presented in this chapter:

- ⊙ God is a Trinity: one God in three divine Persons—Father, Son and Holy Spirit. Each divine Person is God, whole and entire.
- ⊙ The three divine Persons are distinct but inseparable from one another in what they are and in what they do.
- ⊙ All three divine Persons share in the work of God in their own way.
- ⊙ All three divine Persons share the same attributes—all are all-loving, all-knowing, faithful, true, eternal and so on.
- ⊙ The three divine Persons are always in loving relationship with one another.

Discipleship Formation: As a result of studying this chapter and discovering the meaning of the faith of the Catholic Church for your life, you should be better able to:

- ⊙ discover that in your encounter with Jesus you also encounter God the Father and God the Holy Spirit;
- ⊙ appreciate more deeply that God created you in the image and likeness of the Triune God;
- ⊙ deepen your commitment to grow as a person created in the image of the Holy Trinity;
- ⊙ strive more intentionally to live in loving relationship with God and with others.

Scripture References: These Scripture references are quoted or referred to in this chapter:
OLD TESTAMENT: **Genesis** 1:2, 26; **Exodus** 3:3–15; **Leviticus** 19:18; **Deuteronomy** 6:5; **Psalm** 89:26; **Job** 1:21, 33:4; **Hosea** 11:8–9
NEW TESTAMENT: **Matthew** 1:22–23, 22:34–40, 28:19; **Mark** 12:13–17, 14:36; **Luke** 4:18, 10:25–28, 13:34; **John** 10:30, 13:34–35, 14:23, 15:9–15, 26; **1 Corinthians** 3:16, 13:1–13; **2 Corinthians** 6:16; **Galatians** 4:6; **Philippians** 2:4–11; **1 John** 4:4–16

Faith Glossary: Familiarize yourself with the meaning of these key faith terms. Definitions are found in the Glossary: **Abba, agape, analogy, consubstantial, dogma, doxology, Ecumenical Council, heresy, Holy Trinity, human person, icon, immortality**

Faith Word: Holy Trinity
Learn by Heart: 1 John 4:7
Learn by Example: Andrei Rublev, Russian icon painter

How do our relationships influence who we grow to be?

Connections Web'. Illustrate all the other ways the members of your theology class are connected beyond theology class—use present and past connections.

⊙ What do these connections say about the 'relatedness' of the members of your class?

OVER TO YOU
God has created us to live in loving relationship with him and with one another. By God's creative plan and desire, we are 'relational beings'. God has created us to live in community.

⊙ How do you think this affects how you live in relation to the other people in your family, school and wider community?

At any one time we are connected with a diversity of people in a diversity of relationships. We interact regularly with people who are part of our everyday lives, such as our families and friends, members of our parish and local community, with classmates, teammates, choir, student council members, and other students and staff in our school. We also have relationships with people who are not part of our everyday lives. We are members of a global community, or, as some would say, 'a global village'. All of our relationships influence and shape, in some way, how we grow, or do not grow, to be the person God created us to be—a **human person** endowed with the special gifts that reflect God: **immortality**, intellect, free will and the ability to love.

OPENING CONVERSATION
⊙ Members of your school community are connected in a variety of ways. Create a 'Class

THE INFLUENCE OF RELATIONSHIPS
The ways people relate have an impact, both good and bad, on the way we understand ourselves. When our family and friends accept us, when they show that they trust us and treat us with respect, these experiences tend to support how we grow to value and respect ourselves. Good and positive relationships can contribute to our developing a positive self-image. These experiences, in turn, can influence the way we view and treat other people. For example, true friends can call us to question our prejudices, selfishness and blind spots in a supportive rather than a threatening way.

The more we come to know ourselves honestly, the better we can come to relate to others in a healthy manner. We discover the world, even with its shortcomings, to be a friendly place filled with many opportunities. When this does not happen, we are more likely to develop a negative self-image. As a consequence, this may weaken our confidence to build positive and healthy relationships with other people because the self that we are offering to others is not our true self. All our experiences can influence, both positively and negatively, how we choose to relate to God.

REFLECT AND DISCUSS

- Think about the different relationships in your life. Which of these relationships are most life-giving for you? Why?
- Which of these relationships are not life-giving? Why? What can you do about this?

CREATED IN THE IMAGE OF GOD, THE MOST HOLY TRINITY

Who are we? Who is God? Answers to those questions are vital to every person. God, out of love, has responded to these questions, which he knows we are always seeking answers to. He has revealed who he is and who he created us to be. He has revealed himself to be the **Holy Trinity**—a Triune God, one God in three divine Persons. The Holy Trinity is the Revelation of God himself. In revealing his divine identity, God has also revealed who we are because he has created us in the divine image and likeness, in the image of the Trinity. Faith in the Trinity shapes and influences everything we Christians believe and how we live. The Trinity is the central mystery of Christian faith and life. The Preface at Mass on the Solemnity of the Most Holy Trinity is a statement of the Catholic Church's faith in the Trinity. In part we pray:

For with your Only Begotten Son and the Holy Spirit
you are one God, one Lord:
not in the unity of a single person,
but in a Trinity of one substance.

For what you have revealed to us of your glory
we believe equally of your Son
and of the Holy Spirit,
so that, in the confessing of the true and eternal Godhead,

> **If we develop a negative self-image, the self that we are offering to others is not our true self**

you might be adored in what is proper to each
  Person,
their unity in substance,
and their equality in majesty.
  —Preface, Solemnity of the Most Holy Trinity,
  The Roman Missal

JOURNAL EXERCISE

◉ In light of what you have learned so far
  about the Holy Trinity, what implications are
  emerging for your own life?

Under the guidance of the Holy Spirit the Church
in her doctrine, life and worship continues to
profess her faith in the Trinity. For example,
every year we profess our belief in this central
mystery of the Church when the Catholic Church
celebrates the Solemnity of the Most Holy Trinity.
We also begin every celebration of Mass by
praying, 'In the name of the Father, and of the
Son, and of the Holy Spirit'. We conclude every
Eucharistic Prayer by singing or praying aloud the
great **doxology**. We give praise and glory to the
three divine Persons of the Trinity. We pray:

Through him, and with him, and in him,
O God, almighty Father,
in the unity of the Holy Spirit,
all glory and honor is yours,
for ever and ever.

The people acclaim, 'Amen'. The word 'Amen' is
a Hebrew word found in both the Old Testament
and the New Testament that is a declaration of
assent. We will now explore the Revelation of
this mystery of who God is and its implications
for our life as disciples of Jesus Christ.

FAITH WORD

THE TRINITY | BOULBON ALTARPIECE (DETAIL)

Holy Trinity (Triune God)

The one true God, eternal, infinite, unchangeable, incomprehensible and almighty, in three divine Persons: the Father, the Son and the Holy Sprit.
—CCC, no. 202

The Revelation of the Trinity

In the Bible, a person's name often reveals their role in God's plan. For example, the name Jesus in Hebrew means 'God saves'. Think of your own first name—the history behind it, the dreams your parents had for you when they gave you that name. Are you named after a saint, a family member, or another person whom your parents admired? What about your 'family name'? What does it reveal about your family's heritage? At Baptism we are named a 'Christian'. We are baptized in the name of God, 'in the name of the Father, and of the Son, and of the Holy Spirit'.

REFLECT AND DISCUSS

- Reflect a moment on your own first name and on your family name, or surname, and what they mean to you. Share the stories behind your names.
- How does the name 'Christian' identify who you are and your role in God's plan of salvation?

FROM THE CATECHISM
The mystery of the Holy Trinity is the central mystery of the Christian faith and of Christian life. God alone can make it known to us by revealing himself as Father, Son and Holy Spirit.
—CCC, no. 261

GOD HAS GRADUALLY REVEALED HIS IDENTITY OVER TIME
We only know that God is a Triune God because God, out of love, has revealed it. We could never have come to know God to be Father, Son and Holy Spirit—one God in three divine Persons—on our own. Sacred Scripture and Sacred Tradition pass on this Revelation. For example, God revealed himself to Moses to be 'YHWH', 'I AM WHO I AM' (Exodus 3:13–15). The psalmist prays, 'You are my Father, / my God, and the Rock of my salvation' (Psalm 89:26). In his suffering Job encountered God and proclaimed, '[B]lessed be the name of the Lord' (Job 1:21), and he declared his faith in God, saying, 'The spirit of God has made me, and the breath of the Almighty gives me life' (Job 33:4).

God has revealed himself most fully by sending his Son, Jesus. Throughout his whole life Jesus revealed that he and the Father and the Holy Spirit are distinct but inseparable. Jesus said of himself, 'The Father and I are one' (John 10:30). He began his public life and ministry by declaring, 'The Spirit of the Lord is upon me' (Luke 4:18). At the Last Supper he revealed the Spirit's relationship to God the Father and God the Son. He promised his disciples, 'I will send to you the Spirit of truth who comes from the Father' (John 15:26). Just before his Ascension the risen Lord commissioned his disciples to

THE HOLY TRINITY | 19TH-CENTURY GLASS PAINTING

in Jesus to be One God, who is 'Father', 'Son' and 'Holy Spirit'.

OVER TO YOU

⦿ How might you explain the Church's faith in the Triune God? Use words, symbols, images or a combination of the three in your explanation.

THE DEVELOPMENT OF THE DOGMA OF THE TRINITY

No one has ever completely understood the mystery of the Trinity—and no one ever will. The mystery of the Triune God is far beyond the reach of human reason to understand fully and human language to express fully. The attempts at explanation have varied throughout the history of the Church. St. Augustine of Hippo spoke elegantly of 'The Lover, the Beloved, and the Love Between'. St. Patrick used his well-known analogy of the shamrock—three leaves, one stem, yet all one shamrock.

It is the responsibility of the Magisterium of the Church to interpret authentically the meaning of this Revelation. The early Church, under the guidance of the Holy Spirit, worked to find the language to express her faith in the Trinity. The language and clarity expressing the Church's faith in the Trinity emerged over time, sometimes through intense debate and not without controversy. Let us take a brief review of some of the earlier **Ecumenical Councils** of the Church that addressed this responsibility.

Council of Nicaea I (325): Pope Sylvester I, encouraged by the Roman Emperor Constantine I, gathered the bishops of the Church together to resolve the division in the Church caused by Arius (c. 250–336), a priest of the Church in Alexandria, Egypt. Arius proposed an erroneous teaching (Arianism) on the relationship between Jesus and the Father. He denied that Jesus was fully divine. The First Council of Nicaea (present-day Izink in northwestern Turkey) in 325 affirmed the apostolic teaching of the Church in the full divinity of Jesus. This Ecumenical Council of the Church taught that Jesus is truly God; he is '**consubstantial** with the Father' (meaning 'of the same substance as the Father'). The Church

baptize in the name of God the Holy Trinity, saying, 'Go therefore and make disciples of all nations, baptizing them in the name of the Father and of the Son and of the Holy Spirit' (Matthew 28:19). The work the risen Lord commissioned his disciples to do and the work the Church continues to do is the work of the Holy Trinity.

The New Testament Letters teach and pass on the faith of the Apostolic Church in the Holy Trinity. For example, St. Paul taught, 'God has sent the Spirit of his Son into our hearts, crying "**Abba**! Father!"' (Galatians 4:6). 'Abba' expresses the great intimacy between Jesus, the Son of God, and God the Father. It is an Aramaic term of endearment that Jesus used during his agony in the garden to address God the Father (see Mark 14:36). The use of the divine names—Father, Son and Holy Spirit—in the Gospel and other New Testament writings clearly expresses the faith of the Apostolic Church that God revealed himself continues to use this same language when we pray the Nicene Creed.

Council of Constantinople I (381): Nicaea I did not fully resolve the language of the Church in stating her teaching on the Trinity. Arius was sent into exile and the controversy continued, especially between Arius and St. Athanasius the Great (c. 297–373). In 381, following the death of Arius, Pope St. Damascus I, Bishop of Alexandria and Doctor of the Church, gathered the bishops in Council at Constantinople (modern-day Istanbul in Turkey). It was at this First Council of Constantinople that the teaching of Arius was officially declared a **heresy**. A heresy is a 'religious teaching that denies or contradicts truths revealed by God' (*United States Catholic Catechism for Adults* [USCCA], 514).

Council of Chalcedon (451): The Church continued to refine her language and reaffirm the apostolic faith in Jesus Christ and in the Trinity at various councils after Nicaea I and Constantinople I. In 451 Pope St. Leo I, who is also known as Pope St. Leo the Great, gathered the bishops in Council at Chalcedon, which is not far from Constantinople (Istanbul). There the

Church affirmed and accepted the Creed of the Council of Constantinople I. The Council taught that Jesus is 'consubstantial with the Father as to his divinity and consubstantial with us as to his humanity'. This teaching clarified and reaffirmed that within the one divine Person, Jesus, there are two natures, one divine nature and one human nature.

Councils of Toledo (675), of Lyons (1274) and of Florence (1442): Having affirmed the divinity of Jesus and the oneness of God, the Pope and bishops continued to turn their attention to the language to be used to express the **dogma** of the Holy Trinity. In 675 at the Council of Toledo in Spain the Church reaffirmed the apostolic faith in the Holy Spirit and the Holy Spirit's relationship to the Father and the Son. The Council reaffirmed and taught the Church's faith in the divinity of the Holy Spirit: 'The Holy Spirit, the Third Person of the Holy Trinity, is God, one and equal with the Father and the Son.' In 1274 at the Council of Lyons in France and in 1442 at the Council of Florence in Italy, the Church confessed and reaffirmed her faith in the Trinity: there is one God in three divine Persons. This is the same faith we profess with the Church today.

THE FIRST COUNCIL OF NICAEA | WALL PAINTING IN BUCHAREST, ROMANIA

- What does the Church's efforts to state clearly the meaning of the Revelation of the Trinity say to you about the work and mission of the Church?
- What can you do to grow in your understanding of the teachings of the Catholic Church on the Trinity? Why is prayer so vital to your efforts?

THE SEARCH FOR LANGUAGE TO DESCRIBE THE TRINITY

St. Augustine of Hippo, St. Thomas Aquinas and other great theologians of the Church have all highlighted the limitations of our human language for God. St. Augustine wrote: 'If you understood him, it would not be God.' St. Thomas expressed the same truth when he taught that we can only speak of God by way of **analogy**. Analogy expresses truths that cannot be fully expressed in human language. St. Thomas used 'analogy' to answer the question: How is it possible to use words drawn from finite and composite creatures to make positive statements of truth about an infinite, simple, transcendent God? Understanding the meaning of the human terms the Catholic Church uses to teach the faith of the Church is important to our understanding of the doctrine of the Trinity and other mysteries of Revelation.

Let's take a look at three words the Catholic Church uses to profess her faith in the Trinity, namely, 'substance', 'person' and 'relationship'.

Substance: In the Creed we profess Jesus, the Son of God, to be 'consubstantial', or of one substance, with the Father. All three Persons of the Trinity are of the same divine 'substance'. The Father, Son and Holy Spirit share one divine nature. The word 'substance' is a key term the Church uses to express her understanding of the Revelation of the Mystery of the Trinity. Today, we tend to have more of a scientific or physical understanding of 'substance'. This is not how the Catholic uses the word 'substance'. At the Councils of Nicaea I and Constantinople I the Church used and understood the term substance in a 'philosophical' and not a 'scientific' way.

ALLEGORY OF THE HOLY TRINITY | 17TH-CENTURY POLISH

Heresies

These early heresies of the Church continue to reappear today.

Docetism: Erroneously teaches that Jesus only appeared to be man.

Gnosticism: Erroneously teaches that Jesus only appeared to be man since the human body is corrupt.

Arianism: Erroneously teaches that Jesus is not truly God and is not of the same substance as the Father.

Nestorianism: Erroneously teaches that Jesus is only a human person joined to the divine Person of the Son of God.

Monophysitism: Erroneously teaches that the human nature had ceased to exist as such in Christ when the divine Person of God's Son assumed it.

'Substance' refers to the 'essence' of something. It names what a reality is. The Father, Son and Holy Spirit share one and the same divine nature, or the one and the same substance and essence. They are one God.

Person: The Mystery of the Trinity is the mystery of one God in three divine 'Persons'. In the time of the early Church, the Greek term for 'person' signified something different from the meaning the word has today. When we use the word 'person' today, we are usually speaking of individuals, each having their own separate identity. When we profess faith in the Trinity, one God in three 'Persons', we are not using the word 'person' to mean that there are three separate and individual Gods. The three divine Persons are distinct but not separate from one another. The distinction between the three divine Persons is revealed in the works attributed to each Person; that is, the work of Creation to the Father, the work of Salvation to the Son, and the work of Sanctification to the Holy Spirit. The reality is that the works of Creation, Salvation and Sanctification are the works of the One God. All three divine Persons are inseparable. God is both One and Three.

Relationship: The Church also speaks analogously of the 'relationship' uniting the three divine Persons. The substance, the nature or the essence, of our Triune God is such that the three distinct Persons of the Trinity live in loving relationship as One God. They are inseparable. 'The Father cannot be the Father without the Son, nor can the Son be the Son without the Father. The Holy Spirit is related to the Father and the Son who both send him forth' (USCCA, 53). All three divine Persons share the same attributes, or characteristics, that we have come to know about God from his self-Revelation. The Father, Son and Holy Spirit are infinite and eternal, almighty and all-knowing, faithful and true. Each divine Person is God whole and entire.

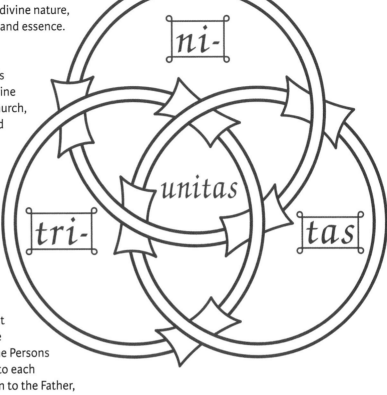

Because our correct understanding of how the Catholic Church uses these three terms is so important, let us summarize our discussion by using the words of the *Catechism*:

The Church uses (I) the term 'substance' (rendered also at times by the terms 'essence' or 'nature') to designate the divine being in its unity, (II) the term 'person' or 'hypostasis' to designate the Father, Son and Holy Spirit in the real distinction among them, and (III) the term 'relation' to designate the fact that their distinction lies in their relationship of each to the others.

—CCC, no. 252

JOURNAL EXERCISE

⊙ What new insights into the life of the Holy Trinity have you learned from your study of this chapter so far?

⊙ How can these insights help you be faithful to your name 'Christian'?

The Trinity shapes the Christian life

Praying the Sign of the Cross is a profession of faith in the Most Holy Trinity. Catholics pray the Sign of the Cross to begin our prayers in church, at home and at school. Some Catholics pray the Sign of the Cross spontaneously during the day. For example, a batter steps up to the plate and, before millions of viewers, blesses himself and awaits the opening pitch of the World Series. A graduating senior, feeling intense pressure, steps up to the free throw line in the final seconds of double overtime and blesses herself before attempting the shot that will clinch the state title.

REFLECT AND DISCUSS

◉ What are these athletes saying when they bless themselves?

◉ When do you bless yourself, or pray the Sign of the Cross? What are you saying when you do so?

OVER TO YOU

◉ Reflect for a moment on your understanding of the Church's teaching on the Trinity. What are you clear about? Not clear about?

One God in the Trinity

Now this is the Catholic faith: We worship one God in the Trinity and the Trinity in unity, without either confusing the persons or dividing the substance; for the person of the Father is one, the Son's is another, the Holy Spirit's another; but the Godhead of the Father, Son, and Holy Spirit is one, their glory equal, their majesty coeternal.
—From the Athanasian Creed

THE CREEDS OF THE CHURCH

The creeds of the Church profess the faith of the Church in the Blessed Trinity. The creeds of the Church are summary statements of the principle beliefs of the Church. Among the creeds of the Church, the Apostles' Creed, the Nicene (or Niceno-Constantinopolitan) Creed, the Athanasian Creed and the Creed of Pope Pius IV (or Creed of the Council of Trent) have a prominent place.

Turn to the Nicene Creed on page 276 of this text. Let's take a moment now to read, pray and reflect upon this powerful statement of the faith of the Church and consider its implications for living our life in Christ. Take notice that the Creed has three main parts, each stating a summary of the Church's teaching about each Person of the Trinity.

I believe in one God, the Father almighty. God is the Creator of 'all things visible and invisible', the source of all creation. God the Father is in relationship to the Son and the Holy Spirit from all eternity.

I believe in one Lord Jesus Christ. The Lord Jesus Christ is 'God from God, Light from Light, true God from true God . . . consubstantial [of one Being] with the Father'. By addressing Jesus as 'Lord', we profess our faith in the divinity of Jesus. Jesus is consubstantial with, of the same substance as, the Father. At the same time, he is distinct but not inseparable from the Father. Through the Son 'all things were made' and he shares in the creative work of the Father. The Lord Jesus Christ, the Incarnate Son of God, was incarnate of the Virgin Mary by the power of the Holy Spirit. He became man, was crucified, died, rose again and returned to the Father. With the Father and the Holy Spirit he is 'adored and glorified'. With the Father and the Holy Spirit the Son is truly God, and we worship him for he is God.

I believe in the Holy Spirit. We adore and give glory to the Holy Spirit because the Holy Spirit is Lord and Sanctifier, God 'the giver of life' who 'has spoken through the prophets'. In this third and concluding part of the Nicene Creed we also confess our belief in the Church that Christ founded to be 'one, holy, catholic and apostolic'; in one Baptism; in the forgiveness of sins; and in the final resurrection of the dead. All these works of God are the work of the Trinity.

THE TRIUNE GOD IS ONE

We are baptized in the *name* of the Father and of the Son and of the Holy Spirit and we bless ourselves as we pray 'In the name of the Father, and of the Son, and of the Holy Spirit'. We are not baptized and we do not bless ourselves in the *names* of the Father and of the Son and of the Holy Spirit. There is only *one* God who is Father and Son and Holy Spirit. We must not fall into thinking of the Trinity erroneously as being 'three Gods'. '[E]ach of [the divine Persons] is God whole and entire' [CCC, no. 253]. While the Creed we pray at Mass attributes individual works (Creation,

Salvation and Sanctification) and characteristics (almighty) to one of the divine Persons of the Trinity, those works and characteristics belong to each Person of the Trinity because God is One. The divine Persons are inseparable in what they are and in what they do. For example, what we attribute to the Father is also the work of the Son and the Holy Spirit. What we attribute to the Son is also the work of the Father and the Holy Spirit. What we attribute to the Holy Spirit is also the work of the Father and the Son. Each divine Person is also almighty, all-knowing, all-loving and eternal.

REFLECT AND DISCUSS

⊙ Reflect for a moment on your own emerging understanding of the Church's teaching on the Blessed Trinity.
⊙ What are you clear about? Not clear about?

THE HOLY TRINITY | CHURCH OF ST. CATHERINE, KARWEILER, GERMANY

GOD IS LOVE: THE IMPLICATIONS OF THE TRINITY FOR OUR LIVES

The First Letter of John teaches: 'God is love' (1 John 4:8) and 'God is love, and those who abide in love abide in God, and God abides in them' (1 John 4:16). Love was the center of Jesus' life on earth, as it is at the center of the inner life of the Holy Trinity. The deeper our insight into the inner life of the Trinity, the more we can grow in our understanding of who we are and what our faith in the Trinity calls us to be.

In 1 John 4:8 and 4:16 the inspired writer uses the Greek word *agapē* for love. The word *agapē* describes God's total 'self-gift' of unconditional and infinite love. It is out of divine love that the Holy Spirit proceeds from the Father and the Son; and it is out of divine love that God has created us in the divine image and likeness. There are other Greek words for love, such as *eros* (the word for romantic love), and *philia* (the word for the love between parents and children, among

siblings and friends). But the Love who is God is *agapē*, totally self-giving love who seeks nothing in return. It is this divine self-giving love that Jesus fully reveals on the Cross. (Read Philippians 2:4–11.) It is this same divine love that is at the heart of the Christian life. (Read 1 John 4:9–12.)

God is Triune, one God living in a divine relationship of self-giving love. The Triune God has created us in the image and likeness of God, who is Love. We are most fully human when we imitate that love by the way we live. We are most fully human when we respond to God's love and help others come to know and love God through our selfless sharing of our love for them. Agape is our constant ideal and the foundational virtue of the Christian life. (Read 1 Corinthians 13:1–13.)

THINK, PAIR AND SHARE

- ⊙ Share with a partner how this teaching helps you understand who you are called to be, and the way you are called to live.
- ⊙ Does it give you a deeper understanding of the Great Commandment? Of the new commandment Jesus gave his disciples?
- ⊙ Share how it impacts your encounter with Jesus.
- ⊙ What do you find most challenging in this teaching?

JESUS, 'THE VISIBLE IMAGE OF THE INVISIBLE GOD', MODELS THE LIFE OF GOD FOR US

In his response to the inquiry, 'What is the greatest commandment?', Jesus combined Deuteronomy 6:5 and Leviticus 19:18. He taught that the commandments given in these passages—love of God and love of neighbor—are inseparable. (Read Matthew 22:34–40; see also Mark 12:13–17; Luke

God is love, and those who abide in love abide in God

THE WASHING OF THE FEET | ST. PETER'S BASILICA, ROME

10:25–28). As he approached his death, Jesus gave his disciples the 'new commandment' that they were to follow in living the Great Commandment. He said, 'I give you a new commandment', that you love one another. Just as I have loved you, you also should love one another. By this everyone will know that you are my disciples, if you have love for one another' (John 13:34–35).

The love at the center of Jesus' life reveals the depth of the love that is at the heart of the inner life of the Triune God. This love is to be the defining characteristic of our being his disciples. We are to love one another with the love with which he loves his Father and with which he loves each one of us now. (Read John 14:23; 15:9–15.) The liturgical ritual of 'The Washing of the Feet' at the Evening Mass on Thursday of the Lord's Supper (Holy Thursday) celebrates and passes this great truth from generation to generation. During this ritual, Catholics sing the hymn 'Ubi caritas et amor, Deus ibi est' ('Wherever there is charity and

love, there is God'). Christians are to be faithful to their name by loving as Jesus, as God, loves.

REFLECT AND DISCUSS
- Where do you see Christians giving witness to their faith in the Trinity?
- What difference can Christians living their faith in the Trinity make in their families? In their local communities? In the world?

WHAT ABOUT YOU PERSONALLY?
- What difference is your faith in the Trinity making to your life? How does that faith impact your own relationship with God and with other people?
- In what ways can your life reflect the example Jesus gave in washing the feet of his disciples at the Last Supper?
- In light of what you have learned so far about the Blessed Trinity, what implications or decisions are emerging for your life?

Image-ing the Trinity in our life

WRITING THE DECLARATION OF INDEPENDENCE | JEAN LEON GEROME FERRIS

You will recall that Matthew proclaims that the birth of Jesus 'took place to fulfill what had been spoken by the Lord through the prophet: "Look, the virgin shall conceive and bear a son, and they shall name him Em·man´ū·el"' (Matthew 1:22–23, quoting Isaiah 7:14). This is a far cry from the belief of many of the founders of the United States who were Deists. Deists believe in a God who is way-out-there, somewhere in Heaven, keeping his distance from us and leaving us to our own efforts to work our way through life.

REFLECT AND DISCUSS

⊙ Do you know of any other people who proclaim a God way out there in the distance; for example, in the lyrics of a song?

⊙ For you, where is God? What consequences might your response have for your faith? For your relationship with God, with your family and friends, and with other people?

GOD IS ALWAYS PRESENT: GOD ABIDES IN US AND WE IN GOD

God has revealed that one of his attributes is that he is 'omnipresent', or he is always present and he is present everywhere. Unfortunately, many people emphasize the distance between God and the world. To such people God may be infinite and eternal, almighty and all-knowing and even all-loving, but the God of love is 'out there' and does not touch our lives. How we think of the Trinity impacts the way we encounter and respond to God, how we invite God to be part of our day-to-day life.

In chapter 4 we saw that God has revealed quite clearly that he is not 'out there' somewhere off in the distance. In and through Jesus Christ, God has revealed himself to be 'Emmanuel', 'God-with-us'. God has revealed himself as one who abides in us and invites us to abide in him. God dwells within us. St. Anselm, whom you will recall wrote *Cur Deus Homo* (Why God Became Man), professed this faith when he wrote: 'God is as close as our own heartbeat.' In fact, our heart beats with the very life of God. We are temples of the Spirit of God (1 Corinthians 3:16) and temples of the living God (2 Corinthians 6:16). God is not 'out there'. He is present and active 'in here'—in the midst of our very being and life.

God the Father, God the Son and God the Holy Spirit are intimately involved in every single aspect of our lives. God is always wishing, hoping and aching for the very best for each of us. (Read Hosea 11:8–9; Luke 13:34.) We should be filled with wonder and awe. Whenever we encounter 'charity and love' (agape) we encounter the living God. Again, we leave the final word to the Word of God, who says through the writer of the First Letter of John, whom he inspired: '[L]et us love one another, because love is from God; everyone who loves is born of God and knows God. Whoever does not love does not know God, for God is love' (1 John 4:7–8).

REFLECT AND DISCUSS

- If your image of God is of a God who is 'out there', how might that image influence your faith in God and the way you live out your faith in God? How might that image of God influence your relationship with your family, friends and other people?
- If your image of God is of a God who 'is with us', how might that change things?

THE TRINITY AND THE DEMAND FOR PEACE AND JUSTICE

Christian life is called to be an image of the Trinity—as is all human life. Since God, who is one God in three distinct divine Persons, always living in loving relationship, created us in his image and likeness, we are our best selves when we are in loving, self-giving relationships. A Trinitarian spirituality, or way of living life guided by the Holy Spirit, invites us to broaden our awareness of the presence and action of God dwelling within us and in the world around us. God is the connection, the shared relationship, who binds us together.

This faith, this reality, invites us to recognize that God calls us to work to bring about the Kingdom of God. We are to strive to cooperate with the Spirit of God and build communities founded on dignity and respect, friendship and love. It is in and through such work—such holy relationships— that we will grow in our relationship with God and others and all of God's creation.

OVER TO YOU

- What does it mean to you that God has created you and every person in the image of God, who is Father, Son and Holy Spirit?
- Where do you see people living in a way that shows they believe they are images of the Triune God? What are some of the signs and results of their doing so?
- Where do you see people not living in a way that shows they are images of the Triune God? What are some of the signs and results of their not doing so?

JOURNAL EXERCISE

- What can you do to be a clearer image of the Triune God, in whose image and likeness God has created you?

JUDGE AND ACT

REVIEW WHAT YOU HAVE LEARNED

Look back over this chapter and reflect on the Catholic Church's teachings on the Revelation of the Holy Trinity. Discuss the teaching of the Catholic Church on these statements:

⊙ The mystery of the Most Holy Trinity is the central mystery of the Christian faith.

⊙ God has gradually revealed himself over time to be a Triune God.

⊙ The three divine Persons of the Trinity are distinct from each other.

⊙ The three divine Persons of the Trinity are inseparable from each other.

⊙ The three divine Persons are always in loving relationship with each other.

⊙ The works we attribute to one divine Person of the Trinity are the work of all three divine Persons.

⊙ God has created the human person in the image and likeness of God the Holy Trinity.

WHAT ABOUT YOU PERSONALLY?

⊙ What wisdom and insight did you learn about the Trinity from your study of this chapter? What might that mean for your faith journey?

⊙ What difference will these insights make to your life—to how you try to live your faith?

⊙ Pray to the Holy Spirit to help you discern what you can 'do' with these insights.

LEARN BY EXAMPLE

The story of Andrei Rublev, Russian icon painter

The work of Andrei Rublev gives us insight into how faith in the Trinity can impact our life, no matter what our work or profession in life is.

Andrei Rublev (c. 1360–c. 1430) is regarded as one of the greatest medieval Russian icon painters. The icon painter prays and fasts throughout the process of creating the work of art. An icon is not a regular painting in the way we think of paintings today. Icon painters use a combination of figures, colors and symbols, and unite the Church's traditions of asceticism and art to create prayer-portals into the realm of God.

Rublev was a monk who lived in Russia at a time when hordes from Mongolia were invading that country and terrorizing and massacring the people. Rublev's superior asked him to paint an icon that would help the people pray to the Trinity in their suffering and afflictions. In 1410 Rublev painted his famous icon of the Trinity for the monastery of St. Sergius near Moscow. Rublev, it is thought, based his icon on 'The Hospitality

THE SAVIOR | ANDREI RUBLEV

of Abraham', a previously painted icon based on Genesis 18. Removing Abraham and Sarah from the setting, Rublev changed the focus of his icon to express his faith in the Trinity and invite others to a deeper faith in the Trinity.

Take a few moments and reflect on Rublev's icon. Look closely at the details—the figures, faces, colors, the setting and the background. Think about what the icon communicates about the substance and nature and essence of our Triune God.

First, look at Rublev's depiction of the Holy Spirit.

⊙ The Holy Spirit wears two **colors**, blue and green. What does the color green usually represent? In view of what you have learned about the Holy Spirit, what do you think the iconographer was trying to communicate by his choice of colors for the Holy Spirit?

⊙ Rublev depicts the Holy Spirit touching a table. What could this detail mean? Reflect on these words used at Mass: 'You are indeed Holy, O Lord, / the fount of all **holiness**. / Make holy, therefore, these gifts, we pray, / by sending down your Spirit upon them like the dewfall. . . .' (from Eucharistic Prayer II). What does the 'touch of the Spirit' mean for us today? For you personally?

⊙ Behind the figure of the Holy Spirit is a mountain. Where do you remember mountains featured in any of the accounts or stories from the Bible? Have you ever had a mountain experience, where God's Spirit touched your life? If so, perhaps you would like to share it.

Second, look closely at Rublev's depiction of Christ. Notice the way the figure of the Holy Spirit is leaning, drawing our eyes to the Person of Jesus Christ in the center.

⊙ What colors did Rublev use for the robe of Christ? Why do you think Rublev chose this combination of colors for Christ?

THE HOLY TRINITY | ANDREI RUBLEV

⊙ Now, look more closely at the setting. The Christ figure rests his two fingers on the table, pointing toward the cup filled with wine. What might this indicate? Behind the Christ figure there is a tree. What does this detail depict for you?

Third, look carefully at Rublev's depiction of the Father. The Christ figure is facing to our left, and once again our eyes are drawn there, to the figure of the Father.

⊙ What colors does Rublev include in his depiction of the Father? Why do you think he uses that combination? What might his use of color seek to communicate about God the Father?

⊙ Now look at the details of the setting. In one hand the Father is holding a staff, and with the other he is conferring a blessing. What might these details mean? Behind the figure of the Father, there is a house with a door and open window. What might these details signify?

Finally, take a look at one more detail.
- ⊙ In what direction are the three figures turned? What might that mean? What does it mean to you?

WHAT ABOUT YOU PERSONALLY?
- ⊙ What is the best wisdom you have learned for your understanding of the Trinity from reflecting on this icon?
- ⊙ How do you see God reflected in Rublev's icon?
- ⊙ Did your prayerful reflection on Rublev's icon help you encounter God? Explain.

SHARE YOUR FAITH WITH FAMILY AND FRIENDS
- ⊙ Discuss with family members and friends how we can show in our relationships that we believe in the Trinity.
- ⊙ In our relationships with the members of our parish, school and other communities of which we are a member, how can we be an image of the Triune God?

JUDGE AND ACT
- ⊙ Think of a struggle for peace and justice that you would like to be involved in. How could your involvement give witness to your belief in the Trinity? In the presence of the Holy Trinity at work in the world?
- ⊙ How might you get involved?

LEARN BY HEART

[L]et us love one another, because love is from God; everyone who loves is born of God and knows God.

1 JOHN 4:7

Invitation to Prayer

LEADER
Every time we gather to pray as the People of God, we pray, 'In the name of the Father, and of the Son, and of the Holy Spirit'. I now invite you to remember that God the Holy Trinity is always present with us as we pray:

ALL
In the name of the Father, and of the Son, and of the Holy Spirit. Amen.

Profession of Faith

READER
We believe in one God, the Father almighty, maker of heaven and earth.

All reflect quietly on these words.

READER
We believe in one Lord Jesus Christ, the Only Begotten Son of God, consubstantial with the Father.

All reflect quietly on these words.

READER
We believe in the Holy Spirit, the Lord, the giver of life, who proceeds from the Father and the Son.

All reflect quietly on these words.

LEADER
The Trinity is the central mystery of the Christian faith and Christian life. The First Letter of John teaches that 'love is from God; and everyone who loves is born of God' (1 John 4:7). Together let us reflect on the ancient Church chant 'Ubi caritas et amor, Deus ibi est' and how it invites us to live our faith in the Trinity. We will pause briefly after each verse.

Where charity and love are, there God is

Where charity and love are, there God is.
The love of Christ has gathered us into one flock.
Let us exult, and in Him be joyful.
Let us fear and let us love the living God.
And from a sincere heart let us love each other
(and Him).

All reflect quietly.

Where charity and love are, there God is.
Therefore, whensoever we are gathered as one:
Lest we in mind be divided, let us beware.
Let cease malicious quarrels, let strife give way.
And in the midst of us be Christ our God.

All reflect quietly.

Where charity and love are, there God is.
Together also with the blessed may we see,
Gloriously, Thy countenance, O Christ our God:
A joy which is immense, and also approved:
Through infinite ages of ages.
Amen.

All reflect quietly.

LEADER
Let us conclude our prayer reflection by recommitting ourselves to give glory to God by the way we live our lives.

ALL
Glory be to the Father,
and to the Son,
and to the Holy Spirit;
as it was in the beginning
is now, and ever shall be,
world without end. Amen.

CHAPTER 6

God the Father

—Loving Creator and Sustainer

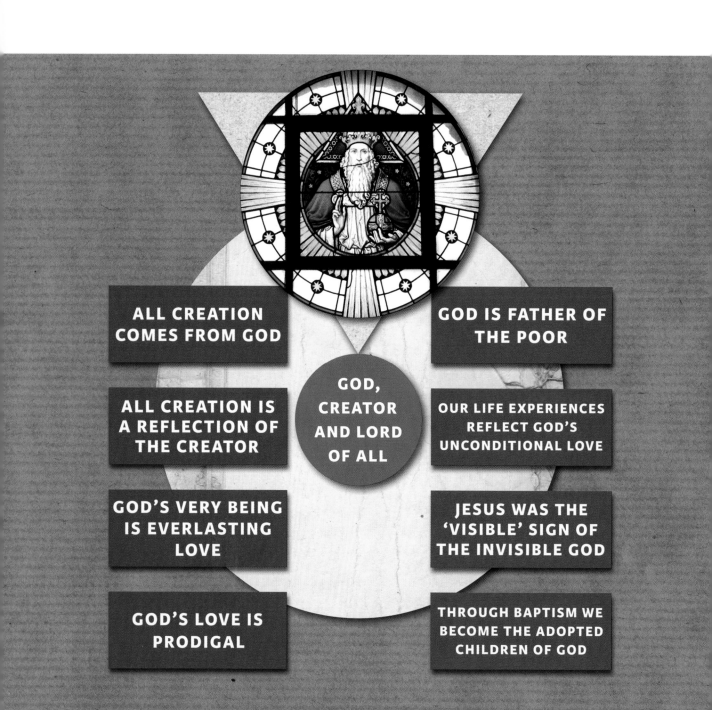

GOD, CREATOR AND LORD OF ALL

ALL CREATION COMES FROM GOD

GOD IS FATHER OF THE POOR

ALL CREATION IS A REFLECTION OF THE CREATOR

OUR LIFE EXPERIENCES REFLECT GOD'S UNCONDITIONAL LOVE

GOD'S VERY BEING IS EVERLASTING LOVE

JESUS WAS THE 'VISIBLE' SIGN OF THE INVISIBLE GOD

GOD'S LOVE IS PRODIGAL

THROUGH BAPTISM WE BECOME THE ADOPTED CHILDREN OF GOD

IN THE APOSTLES' CREED WE PROFESS OUR FAITH IN 'God, the Father almighty, Creator of heaven and earth'. God the Father is the source of all that is, visible and invisible. In this chapter we will study in more detail the teaching of the Catholic Church on God the Father, the First Divine Person of the Holy Trinity. As we deepen our understanding of this Revelation, we need to remember that the three divine Persons are inseparable in what they are and in what they do. What we say about God the Father applies equally to God the Son and God the Holy Spirit.

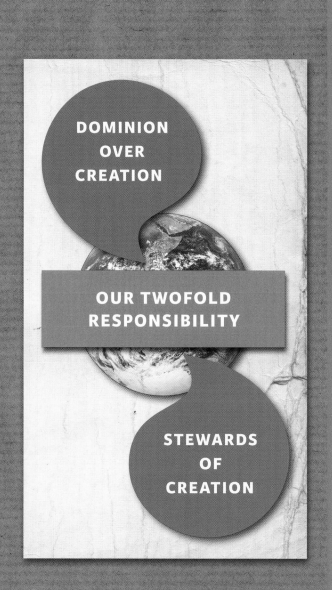

DOMINION OVER CREATION

OUR TWOFOLD RESPONSIBILITY

STEWARDS OF CREATION

Faith Focus: These teachings of the Catholic Church are the primary focus of the doctrinal content presented in this chapter:

- ⊙ God the Father is the First Divine Person of the Holy Trinity: Jesus Christ's Father and our Father.
- ⊙ God the Father is the source of all that is, visible and invisible.
- ⊙ God is Father in relation to the Son from all eternity.
- ⊙ God the Father's love is faithful, caring, healing, forgiving, just and eternal.
- ⊙ God is Father to all the baptized, to all his adopted sons and daughters, through and in the Son.
- ⊙ God the Father of mercy also cares for the unbaptized.

Discipleship Formation: As a result of studying this chapter and discovering the meaning of the faith of the Catholic Church for your life, you should be better able to:

- ⊙ discover that in your encounter with Jesus Christ you encounter God the Father;
- ⊙ value and respect yourself as an adopted child of God;
- ⊙ imagine ways to live faithfully as a child of God;
- ⊙ live out the implications for your life of your faith in God the Father, who loves you unconditionally.

Scripture References: These Scripture references are quoted or referred to in this chapter:
OLD TESTAMENT: Genesis 1:28, 2:15, 3:27; **Psalms** 8:3–6, 18:2, 38:9, 148:1–4, 7–12, 14
NEW TESTAMENT: Matthew 6:9, 13:11, 25:31–46, 26:36–46; **Mark** 14:36; **Luke** 11:2 and 9, 15:11–32, 23:46; **John** 3:16, 14:9; **Acts of the Apostles** 2:45; **Romans** 8:15; **Galatians** 4:4–6; **Colossians** 1:15–20

Faith Glossary: Familiarize yourself with the meaning of these key faith terms. Definitions are found in the Glossary: **Baptism of Desire, Creation, Creator, hermit, parable, Social Teachings (Doctrine) of the Catholic Church, stewardship, Yнwн**

Faith Words: stewardship; Social Teachings of the Catholic Church
Learn by Heart: John 3:16
Learn by Example: Julian of Norwich, hermit and spiritual writer

What does it mean to be children of God the Father?

VIEW OF THE EARTH AS SEEN BY THE APOLLO 17 CREW, 1972

On May 21, 2011 Pope Benedict XVI talked via satellite with American astronauts Mark Kelly, Ron Garin and Mike Fincke, and Italian astronaut Roberto Vitorri, who were on board the International Space Station. In the first of four questions, the Pope asked, 'From the space station you have a very different view of Earth. . . . When you are contemplating the Earth from up there, do you ever wonder about the way nations and people live together down here, or about how science and people can contribute to the cause of peace?'

OPENING CONVERSATION

◉ When you see images of planet Earth from space, what strikes you?

◉ What do these images say to you about Earth? About human beings? About God?

THE POPES AND THE EARTH

God the Father is the source of all that is, visible and invisible. All creation belongs to God—not to humanity. On numerous occasions Pope Benedict XVI, as his predecessor Blessed Pope John Paul II had done, spoke of humanity's God-given relationship with creation. Here are some examples:

The Earth is indeed a precious gift of the Creator who, in designing its intrinsic order, has given us bearings that guide us as stewards of his creation. . . . [T]he Church considers matters concerning the environment and its protection intimately linked to the theme of integral human development.
—General Audience, August 26, 2009

I would advocate the adoption of a model of development based on the centrality of the human person, on the promotion and sharing of the common good, on responsibility, on a realization of our need for a changed lifestyle, and on prudence, the virtue which tells us what needs to be done today in light of what happen tomorrow.
—Message for the Celebration of the World Day of Peace, January 1, 2010

In his homily at his inaugural Mass on March 19, 2013, Pope Francis advocated the same concern for the earth and all of God's creation. He said:

The vocation of being a 'protector' . . . means protecting all creation, the beauty of the created world, as the Book of Genesis tells us and as Saint Francis of Assisi showed us. It means respecting each of God's creatures and respecting the environment in which we live. It means protecting people . . . especially children, the elderly, those in need, who are often the last we think about. In the end, everything has been entrusted to our protection, and all of us are responsible for it. Be protectors of God's gifts!

REFLECT AND DISCUSS

- ◉ How do you think about creation? Do you consider the resources of the natural world to be our property, which we consume for ourselves alone?
- ◉ How do the teachings of Pope Benedict XVI and Pope Francis on creation help you to deepen your understanding of creation as God's gift to all people of every generation?

ST. FRANCIS OF ASSISI: PATRON OF THOSE WHO PROMOTE ECOLOGY

Blessed Pope John Paul II concluded his 1990 World Peace Day message: 'In 1979 I proclaimed Saint Francis of Assisi as the heavenly patron of those who promote ecology. . . . It is my hope that the inspiration of Saint Francis will help us ever keep alive a sense of "fraternity" with all those good and beautiful things which Almighty God has created.' St. Francis, whose name Pope Francis chose, encountered God in all creation. In 'The Canticle of the Sun' St. Francis gives glory to God for the gift of creation:

The Canticle of the Sun

Most high, all-powerful, all good, Lord!
    All praise is yours, all glory, all honor,
    and all blessing.
To you, alone, Most High, do they belong,
    No mortal lips are worthy
    to pronounce your name.
Be praised, my Lord, through all your creatures,
    especially through my lord Brother Sun,
    who brings the day; and you give light through
      him.
    And his is beautiful and radiant in all his splendor!
Of you, Most High, he bears the likeness.

ST. FRANCIS' SERMON TO THE BIRDS | GIOTTO

PRAISE THE LORD ALL THE EARTH

The work of **Creation** belongs to God alone. God alone is the **Creator**. '[O]ut of love for us' God 'made the world out of nothing, wanting to share divine life and love with us' (*United States Catholic Catechism for Adults* [USCCA], 508). While we attribute the divine work of Creation to God the Father, the work of Creation is the work of the Trinity. All three divine Persons are inseparable from one another in what they do and what they are.

The ancient people of Israel clearly believed that Yнwн, the Lord God, revealed himself to be the Creator, and that the human person is the crown of God's creation (see Psalm 8:3–6). The psalmist proclaims that the human person exists to join with all creation, even inanimate things, to give glory to God. And so, the Israelites drew creation into their chorus of praise to God.

Praise the Lord!
Praise the Lord from the heavens;
    praise him in the heights!
Praise him, all his angels;
    praise him, all his host!

Praise him, sun and moon;
    praise him all you shining stars!
Praise him, you highest heavens,
    and you waters above the heavens!

Praise the LORD from the earth,
    you sea monsters and all deeps,
fire and hail, snow and frost,
    stormy wind fulfilling his command!

Mountains and all hills,
    fruit trees and all cedars!
Wild animals and all cattle,
    creeping things and flying birds!

Kings of the earth and all peoples,
    princes and all rulers of the earth!
Young men and women alike,
    old and young together! . . .

Praise the LORD!

            —Psalms 148:1–4, 7–12, 14

The Catholic Church reminds us of this truth when she teaches: 'God created the world to show forth and communicate his glory. That his creatures should share in his truth, goodness, and beauty—this is the glory for which God created them' (*Catechism of the Catholic Church* [CCC], no. 319).

REFLECT AND DISCUSS

◉ Describe the attitude to creation that you observe in people today. How are they expressing their attitude?

◉ How does it match up with the attitude of the ancient Israelites? And why do you think this is so?

◉ How does it match up with Pope Benedict XVI's and Pope Francis' teaching on creation?

OVER TO YOU

◉ How would you describe your own attitude toward creation?

◉ How well does it match up with the teachings of the psalmist, St. Francis, Pope Benedict XVI and Pope Francis? Rate your attitude 1 to 10, with 10 indicating a very close match.

◉ What will you do to improve your attitude so as to align it with the teachings of Scripture and the Catholic Church?

FROM THE CATECHISM

God alone created the universe freely, directly and without any help. No creature has the infinite power necessary to 'create' in the proper sense of the word, that is, to produce and give being to that which had in no way possessed it (to call into existence 'out of nothing').

        —CCC, nos. 317 and 318

CREATION—A REFLECTION OF THE CREATOR

Creation is truly a reflection of the Creator. The one true God, Creator and Lord of all that is visible and invisible, can also be known with certainty from his works. The order and beauty of the natural world point to God as origin and Creator of the universe. (See CCC, nos. 46–47.) Let's listen to the words of the English poet and conservationist William Wordsworth (1770–1850).

WILLIAM WORDSWORTH | BENJAMIN ROBERT HAYDON

Tintern Abbey

. . . I have learned
To look on nature, not as in the hour
Of thoughtless youth; but hearing oftentimes
The still, sad music of humanity,
Nor harsh nor grating, though of ample power
To chasten and subdue. And I have felt
A presence that disturbs me with the joy
Of elevated thoughts; a sense sublime
Of something far more deeply interfused,
Whose dwelling is the light of setting suns,
And the round ocean and the living air,
And the blue sky, and in the mind of man.

THINK, PAIR AND SHARE

⊙ Share examples of people, verse, songs or film that give expression to encountering God in creation.
⊙ Describe how your examples give glory to God the Creator.

OVER TO YOU

⊙ Where do you see God manifesting himself to you in creation? Has this experience also been an encounter with God?
⊙ How might you give glory to God the Creator by your striving to become a better steward of creation?

STEWARDSHIP—A GOD-GIVEN RESPONSIBILITY

After God created man and woman, God blessed them and said to them, "'Be fruitful and multiply, and fill the earth and subdue it; and have dominion over . . . every living thing that moves upon the earth"' (Genesis 1:28). When God gave humanity 'dominion' over creation, he gave us the responsibility 'to till it and keep it' (Genesis 2:15). He gave us the responsibility of **stewardship**. God did not give up ownership of creation. While we may enjoy and benefit from all that God has created, creation is God's, not ours. We are to give glory and praise to God by the way we use creation. The Seventh Commandment teaches that we are to respect the integrity of creation. We are to be good and responsible stewards of creation. The **Social Teachings, or Social Doctrine, of the Catholic Church** flow from and apply this truth to daily living of the Gospel:

We show our respect for the Creator by our stewardship of creation. Care for the earth is a requirement of our faith. We are called to protect people and the planet, living our faith in relationship with all of God's creation. This environmental challenge has fundamental moral and ethical dimensions that cannot be ignored.

—USCCA, 424

FROM THE CATECHISM

Man's dominion over inanimate and other living beings is not absolute; it is limited by concern for the quality of life of his neighbor, including generations to come; it requires a religious respect for the integrity of creation.

—CCC, no. 2415;
see also Pope John Paul II, Encyclical Letter, *On the One Hundredth Anniversary of Rerum Novarum* [*Centesimus Annus*], May 1, 1991, nos. 37–38

THINK, PAIR AND SHARE

⊙ Discuss with a partner how you see the connection between 'people' and 'planet'.

⊙ Do you see a connection between fulfilling our responsibility to be good stewards of creation and the Catholic Church's teaching on respect for life?

OVER TO YOU

⊙ How do you think you are living up to your responsibility to be a good and responsible steward of all creation? How might you do better?

FAITH WORDS

Steward/Stewardship

A steward is someone who has the responsibility of caring for what belongs to another person or group of people. In the biblical accounts of Creation, God designates humanity the responsibility to have dominion over, or serve as the stewards of, creation. The root word for 'dominion' is *domus*, which means household. God has entrusted creation, his household, to humanity.

Social Teachings (Doctrine) of the Catholic Church

The official social doctrine developed by the Catholic Church in response to the industrial and technological revolutions. This social doctrine is built on the Church's reaching out and responding to orphans, widows, aliens and others from the days of the early Church.

—Based on USCCA, 528

Our faith in God the Father

OPENING CONVERSATION

The Our Father is the prayer of all Christians.

- ⊙ Quietly pray the Our Father.
- ⊙ Where and when do you pray the Our Father with others?
- ⊙ Do you pray the Our Father alone? When? Why?

THE ISRAELITES' BELIEF IN GOD THE FATHER

God, gradually over time, revealed himself to be Father, and he most fully revealed this truth about himself in his Incarnate Son, Jesus Christ. The ancient Israelites believed that God had revealed himself to be Father. Throughout the Scriptures of the Old Testament we find God named 'Father'. The name 'Father' is not a metaphor or image for God. The name 'Father' expresses an essential dimension of who God revealed himself to be. God the Father is the Creator and the giver of life. Human life is a sharing in the very breath of God. Put another way, the Israelites believed that the blood coursing through their veins pulsed with the very life of God. They had a deep faith that all of what they saw, heard, felt, touched, tasted and smelled was created and sustained by God.

And though they recognized God to be the All-powerful One, the Almighty One, they also believed and trusted the divine power to be the caring power of a Father. God was personally and intimately involved in their lives. The ancient Israelites firmly believed and placed great trust in God the Father to care for them. In the great events of the Passover, Exodus and Exile, the ancient Israelites came to believe that God alone was the One who faithfully cared for them, provided for and sustained them.

THE THIRD DAY OF CREATION | JULIUS SCHNORR VON CAROLSFELD

TALK IT OVER

- ⊙ What dimensions of creation are manifestations of God for you?
- ⊙ Share what each one says to you about God.

GOD AS 'MOTHER'—A BIBLICAL METAPHOR

While God has revealed himself to be 'Father', Sacred Scripture also speaks of God using the metaphor 'mother'. A metaphor is a figure of speech whereby a thing is spoken of as *being like* that which it only resembles. For example, 'My father is a night owl, but my mother is an early bird.' While these statements are obviously not meant to be taken literally, they speak of a truth. There is always a tension between the 'is' and 'is not' in any metaphor. To say that someone who stays up late is a 'night owl' has some truth in it. But, obviously, it is also true that the person is not an 'owl'. Metaphors reflect truth without being literally true.

Sacred Scripture and Sacred Tradition use other metaphors and other descriptive phrases to speak the truth about God and his Revelation. Scripture describes God as a king, judge, rock, gardener, lover, friend, bread-maker, washerwoman, lion, shepherd, fresh water, midwife and more. The Church helps us understand the use and power of the metaphor 'mother' for God when she teaches:

God's parental tenderness can also be expressed by the image of motherhood, which emphasizes God's immanence, the intimacy between Creator and creature. . . . God transcends the human distinction between the sexes. He is neither man nor woman: he is God.

—CCC, no. 239

Recall St. Thomas Aquinas's use of analogy. No matter how creative or powerful or precise human language may be, we need always to remember that human language can never fully define God or communicate the totality of who God is. There is always more to *understand*. Our faith seeks and desires understanding.

READ, REFLECT AND DISCUSS

⊙ Read and reflect on these words of the psalmist:

The Lord is my rock, my
    fortress, and my deliverer,
my God, my rock in whom I take refuge,
    my shield, and the horn of my **salvation**, my
    stronghold.

—Psalm 18:2

⊙ Name and share the different metaphors for God that the psalmist uses.
⊙ What attribute, or quality, of God is the psalmist communicating through each of these metaphors?
  ⊙ Which one best helps you express your faith in God?

OVER TO YOU
  ⊙ What new insights have you gained that are helping you to grow in your understanding of God the Father?

'Our Father . . . thy will be done'

OPENING CONVERSATION

- How often each day do you use the word 'will'?
- What are some meanings of the word 'will'?
- What do you mean when you pray in the Our Father, 'Thy will be done'?

Henri Nouwen (1932–96), a Dutch-born priest and psychotherapist, wrote over forty books on spirituality. In this prayer, Nouwen reflects on God's will for him:

Henri Nouwen's Prayer

Dear God
I am so afraid to open my clenched fists!
Who will I be when I have nothing left
    to hold on to?
Who will I be when I stand before you
    with empty hands?
Please help me to gradually open my hands and
    to discover that I am not what I own,
    but what you want to give me.
And what you want to give me is love,
    unconditional, everlasting love.

REFLECT AND DISCUSS

- Why do you think Nouwen was afraid to open his clenched fists? What does the phrase 'clenched fists' conjure up for you?
- Nouwen says that what God wills for us is love—unconditional, everlasting love. Is that what you also believe, and, if so, how do you respond?

JESUS REVEALS THE FATHER: 'HE WHO SEES ME SEES THE FATHER'

Jesus invites us to address God 'Father'. Who is this 'Father' whom Jesus reveals and invites us to reach out to in prayer? In John's Gospel, when the disciple Philip asks Jesus to 'show us the Father', Jesus responds, 'Whoever has seen me has seen the Father' (John 14:9). St. Paul wrote to the Church in Colossae:

He [Jesus] is the image of the invisible God, the firstborn of all creation; for in him all things in heaven and on earth were created, things visible and invisible, whether thrones or dominions or rulers or powers—all things have been created through him and for him. He himself is before all things, and in him all things hold together. He is the head of the body, the [C]hurch; he is the beginning, the firstborn from the dead,

THE CRUCIFIXION | 11TH–12TH-CENTURY IVORY

For God so loved the world that he gave his only Son, so that everyone who believes in him may not perish but may have eternal life.

JOHN 3:16

and intimacy of his relationship with the Father is perhaps most dramatically revealed at the time of his betrayal and arrest in the Garden of Gethsemane and in his suffering and Death.

Jesus, realizing full well what was in store for him, reaches out in prayer to his Father in the Garden of Gethsemane, 'My Father, if this cannot pass unless I drink it, your will be done' (Matthew 26:42). Several hours later after his scourging and crowning with thorns, his carrying the Cross and being nailed to it, and as he was slowly suffocating and experiencing the excruciating death of crucifixion, Jesus prays aloud, 'Father, into your hands I commend my spirit', and '[h]aving said this, he breathed his last' (Luke 23:46). This is the same Father to whom Jesus taught his disciples to reach out in prayer. (See Matthew 6:9, Luke 11:9.)

Through his Death and Resurrection Jesus fulfilled the divine plan of Salvation. In John 3:16 we read, 'For God so loved the world that he gave his only Son, so that everyone who believes in him may not perish but may have **eternal life**.' Through his Incarnate Son, Jesus, God the Father has revealed and accomplished his 'will' and 'desire' 'to reconcile to himself all things, whether on earth or in heaven, through the blood of his cross' (Colossians 1:20).

so that he might come to have first place in everything. For in him all the fullness of God was pleased to dwell, and through him God was pleased to reconcile to himself all things, whether on earth or in heaven, by making peace through the blood of his cross.

—Colossians 1:15–20

The more we come to know Jesus, the more we come to know the Father. The Church today reminds us of this truth of faith when she teaches: 'Jesus revealed that God is Father in an unheard-of sense: he is Father not only in being Creator; he is eternally Father in relation to his only Son who is eternally Son only in relation to his Father' (CCC, no. 240). Jesus' Revelation of the Father and the depth

The Four Evangelists, St. Paul and the other writers of the New Testament teach that the Resurrection also reveals the Father's will. '[Jesus] is . . . the firstborn from the dead' (Colossians 1:18). His sacrificial Death on the Cross was not the end. God the Father raised Jesus from the dead. The Ascension of Jesus reveals that in and through Jesus and his Death and Resurrection the fulfillment of the Father's will for humanity was accomplished and the reign of God in the world was revealed. The new creation, the Kingdom of God, was inaugurated.

WHAT ABOUT YOU PERSONALLY?

- Open your Bible and prayerfully read Matthew 26:36–46, the account of Jesus praying in the Garden of Gethsemane.
- What are your thoughts when you turn to God and pray, 'Our Father . . . thy will be done'?

FROM THE CATECHISM

Jesus' invitation to enter his kingdom comes in the form of *parables* . . . . Through his parables he invites people to the feast of his kingdom, but he also asks for a radical choice: to gain the kingdom, one must give everything. Words are not enough; deeds are required. . . . Jesus and the presence of the kingdom in this world are secretly at the heart of the parables. One must enter the kingdom, that is, become a disciple of Christ, in order to 'know the secrets of the kingdom of heaven' (Matthew 13:11). For those who stay 'outside', everything is enigmatic.
—CCC, no. 546

What are your thoughts when you turn to God and pray, 'Our Father . . . thy will be done'?

THE PARABLE OF THE PRODIGAL SON: THE WILL AND LOVE OF THE FATHER REVEALED

Jesus often used **parables** to teach. Parables are simple images or comparisons. Jesus often used parables to confront his listeners with making a radical choice about his invitation to them to enter the Kingdom of God. In the parable of the Prodigal Son, which has also been called 'The Parable of the Forgiving Father' and 'The Parable of the Prodigal and His Brother', Jesus revealed a God whose love and mercy are boundless. We will now take a fresh look at this very familiar parable from a variety of perspectives. Read Luke 15:11–32. Pause after every few verses to take notes on what stands out for you. Then bring your insights and wisdom to the whole class group. Now, let's look at this parable.

Jesus begins, 'There was a man who had two sons. The younger of them said to his father, "Father, give me the share of the property that will belong to me"' (Luke 15:11). In other words, 'Why should I wait until you die before I get my share of your 'will', of my inheritance? Give it to me now.'

JESUS IN THE GARDEN OF GETHSEMENE | BASILICA OF ST. PETER, ROME

The younger son gathered all he had and traveled to a distant country

He squandered his property in dissolute living

Reflect: *This was a shocking request for any son to make of his father in a culture that placed great emphasis on respect for parents and the rights of birth order. The younger son would have been seen to have forfeited whatever 'birthright' he might have had by making such a rude and selfish demand. So, what would Jesus' listeners have expected the father to have done? Certainly, not to give in to the younger son's demands! What are your thoughts at this point in the story?*

The younger son took his share of the property and 'traveled to a distant country, and there he squandered his property in dissolute living' (Luke 15:13). A famine comes and devastates that country, and the young man is brought so low he 'hires himself out' and is sent off 'to feed the pigs' (Luke 15:15).

Reflect: *What are your thoughts about the younger son now? Are you beginning to feel sorry for him? Does he deserve what he gets?*

The younger son soon begins to envy even the pigs. He decides to return home. He reasons, 'How many of my father's hired hands have bread enough and to spare, but here I am dying of hunger! I will get up and go to my father, and I will say to him, "Father, I have sinned against heaven and before you; I am no longer worthy to be called your son; treat me like one of your hired hands"' (Luke 15:17–19). (The son knows Jewish law. In demanding and taking the property, he forfeited the legal rewards of his birthright.)

Reflect: *What do you think of the younger son's motives for returning home? What do his thoughts reveal about the father?*

The father has been yearning for his younger son's return and is on the lookout for him. Upon seeing his son 'while he was still far off', the father's heart is 'filled with compassion' and he 'ran out and put his arms around him and kissed him' (Luke 15:20). What a welcome! Focusing totally on his son and without demanding any answers to

He would gladly have filled himself with the pods that the pigs were eating

THE STORY OF THE PRODIGAL SON | HANS SEBALD BEHAM

'I am no longer worthy to be called your son.'

LUKE 15:11—19

any questions about where he has been or what has happened to the money, and even before the son can speak the apology he has prepared, the father 'put his arms around him and kissed him'.

Reflect: *Were you surprised that the father was on the lookout for his son? Were you surprised by the father's actions upon seeing his son off in the distance? What do the father's actions reveal about the father? All that matters to the father is that his son has come home. What do you think about that?*

Spontaneously the father turns to his servants and commands them 'bring out a robe—the best one' (Luke 15:22), and a ring and sandals. (Jesus' listeners would have recognized these items as marks of honor, signs of the depth of the father's love and joy.) The father then invites everyone to join in and share his joy over the younger son's return. He orders the servants to 'get the fatted calf and kill it' (Luke 15:23) and to prepare a grand celebration. Truly, the father's love was more 'prodigal' than the son's selfishness.

Reflect: *There is no more mention of the younger son in the story. Why do you think that is so?*

Jesus does not end his parable here. He switches the parable's focus to the elder son—or to another dimension of the father's prodigal love. The 'Welcome Home' celebration is in full swing when the elder son nears home, after working in the fields all day. The son's anger rises. He refuses to share in the father's joy and join the celebration. The father comes out 'to plead' (Luke 15:28) with the elder son. The elder son stands firm, reminding his father, 'Listen! For all these years I have been working like a slave for you, and I have never disobeyed your command; yet you have never given me even a young goat so that I might celebrate with my friends' (Luke 15:29). The elder son then reminds the father of his brother's betrayal and sins. After affirming his love for his older son, the father responds, '[W]e had to celebrate and rejoice, because this brother of yours was dead and has come to life; he was lost and has been found' (Luke 15:32).

Reflect: *Does the elder son have a good point? What does the interaction between the father and the elder son reveal about the father's deepest desires, or will, for both his sons?*

REFLECT AND SHARE

- This parable has been named 'The Parable of the Prodigal Son' (the traditional title), 'The Parable of the Forgiving Father' and 'The Parable of the Prodigal and His Brother'.
- How does each of the three parable titles help you understand the meaning of Jesus' teaching? Which title captures Jesus' teaching best for you? Why?
- What does Jesus reveal in this parable about God the Father? About your relationship with God?

OVER TO YOU

- Have you ever acted like the younger son? Like the elder son? Like the father?
- What does this parable say to you about your relationship with God? With family, friends and other people?

GOD'S LOVE IS PRODIGAL

No one is outside the love and mercy of God. In this parable Jesus revealed the mystery of the abundant love of God. God's love is not to be measured in the way we normally measure human love. The word 'prodigal' means 'excessive' and has its roots in the word 'profuse', which means 'exhibiting great abundance'. God's ways are not human ways. In this parable Jesus challenges us to look beyond 'human love', which is often 'calculated', to a deeper understanding of God's compassionate and 'prodigal love'.

JOURNAL EXERCISE

- Describe your understanding of what Jesus is saying to you in this parable about what God desires for people?
- Describe a time when someone has been prodigal in their 'love' for you.
- When have you been prodigal in your outreach to others? Was there a cost to you for such abundant sharing? Explain.

In this parable Jesus revealed the mystery of the abundant love of God

THE PRODIGAL SON | AUGUSTE RODIN

We are the 'prodigal' children of God

In Baptism we are united to Jesus, the only begotten Son of the Father, and we become 'adopted' sons and daughters of God the Father. St. Paul, writing to the early Church in Galatia, reminded us of this truth of our faith. He wrote:

[W]hen the fullness of time had come, God sent his Son, born of a woman, born under the law, in order to redeem those who were under the law, so that we might receive adoption as children. And because you are children, God has sent the Spirit of his Son into our hearts, crying 'Abba! Father!'
—Galatians 4:4–6

REFLECT AND DISCUSS

- ⊙ Read Genesis 3:27. What insight do Paul's words to the Church in Galatia give you into the meaning of the creation of the human person?
- ⊙ Do you consider yourself to be a child of God?

GOD, THE FATHER OF ALL

The Arabic term **'Abba'**, which is found in Mark 14:36, Romans 8:15 and Galatians 4:6, has been translated in a variety of ways. Biblical scholars, today, agree that its use primarily expresses the personal relationship of 'child to father'. Through Baptism Christians are so united with Christ Jesus that we enter into a unique relationship with God—that of 'adopted children' of the Father.

We might ask, as the African American spiritual does, 'What of the rest of the human family?' Aren't they all 'chillun of God' called to 'fly all over God's heaven' one day? The answer, of course, is a resounding 'Yes'. We cannot impose limits on God's love, as the elder son in the parable of the Forgiving Father tried to impose on his father. Jesus revealed that God desires and wills that all people return 'home'. Jesus has given us his Church as the sign and instrument of that 'way home'. '[A]ll salvation comes from Christ the Head through the Church which is his Body' (CCC, no. 846).

Baptism, rebirth in water and the Spirit, is the ordinary entrance way to the place of salvation. This is why the Church teaches: 'Baptism is necessary for salvation for those to whom the Gospel has been proclaimed and who have had the possibility of asking for this sacrament' (CCC, no. 1257). We know that not all people come to faith in Christ, nor are all people incorporated into Christ and his Church through Baptism.

The Catholic Church has long taught that people who are not Christian can yet be saved. In the *Catechism* she teaches: '*God has bound salvation to the sacrament of baptism*', yet '*he himself is not bound by his sacraments*' (CCC, no. 1257). In other words, God can and does act apart from the Sacraments as well. One traditional explanation for how non-Christian people can be saved is that they can have '**Baptism of desire**';

that is, all who seek 'the truth and [do] the will of God in accordance with [their] understanding of it, can be saved. It may be supposed that such persons would have *desired Baptism explicitly* if they had known its necessity' (CCC, no. 1260). The Church reminds us that '[w]ithout a creator, there can be no creature' (Vatican II, *Constitution on the Church in the Modern World*, no. 36). This is the reason why believers know that the love of Christ urges them to bring the light of the Gospel to those who do not know him or who reject him.

FROM THE CATECHISM
[A]lthough in ways known to himself God can lead those who, through no fault of their own are ignorant of the Gospel, to that faith without which it is impossible to please him, nevertheless the Church still has the obligation and also the sacred right to evangelize all men.

—Vatican II, *Decree on the Missionary Activity of the Church*, no. 7

PROCLAIMING GOD'S LOVE FOR ALL PEOPLE
Sacred Scripture often reveals that God the Father has a special love for the 'poor', for orphans and for all people neglected and treated unjustly by society. Scripture also reveals that God calls us to treat all people with the dignity and respect they deserve. When this does not happen, God's people are to show, as he does, a special love for those whom others cast aside or neglect.

The Church from her beginning has always accepted her God-given responsibility to the poor and for the poor, as Jesus did and taught his disciples to do (see Matthew 25:31–46 and Acts of the Apostles 2:45). This teaching of Jesus, which calls all Christians to treat their brothers and sisters who are poor and vulnerable with 'a preferential love', is one of the foundational principles of the Catholic Church's **Social Teaching, or Social Doctrine**. The Church describes her teaching on the 'preferential option for the poor and vulnerable' in this way:

In the homily at his inaugural Mass, Pope Francis stated that the Pope must 'embrace with tender affection the whole of humanity, especially the poorest, the weakest, the least important. . . .'

POPE FRANCIS AFTER PALM SUNDAY MASS, 24 MARCH 2013

A basic moral test is how our most vulnerable members are faring

A basic moral test is how our most vulnerable members are faring. In a society marred by deepening divisions between rich and poor, our tradition recalls the story of the Last Judgment (Matthew 25:31–46) and instructs us to put the needs of the poor and vulnerable first.

The central interest of the Church's social teaching is justice for all, but especially for the helpless and the poor. It involves the removal of the symptoms and causes of poverty and injustice.

—USCCA, 423, 427

THINK, PAIR AND SHARE
⊙ What images come to mind when you hear the word 'poverty'?
⊙ Can a person be healthy and wealthy and also be 'poor'? What does it mean that God has revealed himself to be the 'Father of the poor'?

CAMPAIGN FOR HUMAN DEVELOPMENT: CATHOLIC SOCIAL DOCTRINE IN ACTION
The bishops lead the Church in the United States to put this social teaching into action in their local churches and in the Church throughout the United States and the world. The Catholic Campaign for Human Development (CCHD) is but one example of how this is happening. The CCHD works to transform lives by breaking the cycle of poverty in communities across the United States. CCHD programs are funded through annual collections in parishes. The organization funds empowerment projects for people who are living below the poverty line or on low incomes, and strives to educate the public about the root causes of poverty. CCHD conducts poverty surveys to determine the true extent of poverty in the United States and advocates to raise awareness of the numbers estimated to be living in poverty in the United States.

Here is a sample of CCHD programs:

Scenic Central dairy farmers' cooperative in Wisconsin	Enabling farmers to obtain a fair price for milk; supplying local cheese producers.
Café Reconcile in New Orleans	The café is also a school: at-risk young people receive restaurant training and learn job skills.
Safe Passage campaign, Los Angeles	Helping children's education by making their walk to school safe and secure.
Urban Oasis, Washington DC	Growing nutritious food, improving diets and contributing to soup kitchens for the destitute.
***Las Mujeres en Progreso*, New Mexico**	Day-care center at which children are taught and fed while their parents work.
Pathways Learning Center, San Francisco	Enabling Latino immigrants to learn computer skills, English and job-interview skills.

REFLECT AND DISCUSS

⊙ How do the works of the Catholic Campaign for Human Development give witness to God the Father of the poor? To God's love for all people?

⊙ What is the connection between the Catholic Church's social teaching 'the preferential option for the poor' and her teaching on respect for life?

JOURNAL EXERCISE

⊙ Review the Corporal and Spiritual Works of Mercy on page 283 of this text.

⊙ Using words or images or both, depict yourself giving witness to God the Father of the poor.

⊙ Pray to the Holy Spirit, asking for his guidance and courage to live up to God the Father's image.

JUDGE AND ACT

REVIEW WHAT YOU HAVE LEARNED

Look back over this chapter and discuss the teaching of the Catholic Church expressed in these statements:

- God the Father is the First Divine Person of the Holy Trinity. He is Jesus Christ's Father and our Father.
- God is Father in relation to the Son from all eternity.
- God the Father is the source of all that is, visible and invisible.
- The one true God can be known with certainty from his creation, by the natural light of human reason.
- All creation belongs to God. We are to be faithful stewards of God's creation.
- God the Father's love is faithful, caring, healing, forgiving, just and eternal.
- God is the Father of the poor, who calls his people to have a preferential love for the poor and the vulnerable.
- God is Father to all the baptized, to all his adopted sons and daughters through and in the Son.
- God the Father of mercy cares for the unbaptized.

RETURN OF THE PRODIGAL SON | REMBRANDT

RECALL, REFLECT AND DISCUSS

The Dutch painter and etcher Rembrandt (1606–69), in his *Return of the Prodigal Son*, portrays the younger son kneeling before the father. Rembrandt also expresses other complex emotions through the figures of the bent old man and his repentant son.

- Look carefully at how Rembrandt depicts the father. Notice the details that portray the father's emotions and character.
- How does the depiction of the father in this painting reflect the love of God the Father for every person?
- In which of the characters in Rembrandt's painting do you see yourself?

The story of Julian of Norwich (1342–c. 1416), hermit and spiritual writer

LADY JULIAN OF NORWICH | STEPHEN REID

Julian, who is also known as Julianna and Lady Julian, lived most of her life as an 'anchorite', or **hermit,** on the grounds of the Church of St. Julian in the city of Norwich, England. When she was thirty years old, Julian had a deeply mystical experience occasioned by a vision of Jesus' Passion and Death on the Cross. After praying and reflecting on this experience for many years, Julian wrote *Showings of Divine Love.* This was the first book in English to be written by a woman.

Julian championed 'God's great love for us' when the Black Death was sweeping across England and Europe. The Black Death was a bubonic plague pandemic that originated in Europe in 1347 and spread to England in 1348, where it killed almost half of the population. During this time of unprecedented panic, suffering and death, Julian wrote, 'Love is our God's meaning. Before God made us, he loved us, which love has never abated and never will.'

Julian's words of assurance to her people that they are 'endlessly loved with an endless love' and that 'God is all goodness and loves you tenderly' were a light during this time of darkness. Her deep faith in and love for Christ and her assurance that Christ's victory over death and sin was a victory once and for all, helped people to trust and hope that 'in the end, all will be well. God's love will always prevail'. In one of his catechesis on the saints, Pope Benedict XVI said of Julian of Norwich:

Julian of Norwich understood the central message for spiritual life: God is love, and it is only if one opens oneself to this love, totally and with total trust, and lets it become one's sole guide in life, that all things are transfigured, that true peace and true joy are found, and that one is able to radiate it. . . . God's promises are never greater than our expectations. If we present to God, to his immense love, the purest and deepest desires of our heart, we shall never be disappointed. 'And all will be well', 'all manner of things will be well'.

—Pope Benedict XVI, December 1, 2010

REFLECT AND DISCUSS

⊙ How does Julian's expression of her faith in God, 'God's love will always prevail', give witness to Jesus' Revelation of the Father in the parable of the Forgiving Father?

⊙ How might that same faith help you and other people as you face suffering and other forms of evil in your life?

⊙ Who do you know or have you learned about who gave witness to Jesus' Revelation that God is all goodness and loves every person tenderly?

WHAT ABOUT YOU PERSONALLY?

⊙ What spiritual wisdom can you learn from the life and teachings, courage and faith of Julian of Norwich for your own life?

SHARE YOUR FAITH WITH FAMILY AND FRIENDS

- ⊙ Explore with family members and friends the meaning of the parable of the Prodigal Son.
- ⊙ Discuss how your encounter with Jesus in listening to or reading the parable of the Prodigal Son can make a difference in your life.

JUDGE AND ACT

- ⊙ Using what you have learned in this chapter, think about how you would respond to people who ask, 'If God is all-good and all-loving and all-caring, why is there so much suffering and other forms of evil at work in the world?'
- ⊙ How is your own life a response to this question?

Gathering and Call to Prayer

LEADER

Let us give thanks to God the Father by repeating in the silence of our heart: Loving God, we give you thanks for the gift of life and for your bountiful love.

All reflect on the image of God the Father that comes to their mind and silently repeat the prayer.

LEADER

We begin our prayer in the name of God, in whose image he has created us.

All pray the Sign of the Cross together.

Proclamation of the Word of God

READER

A reading from the Gospel according to Luke.

ALL

Glory to you, O Lord.

READER

Read Luke 15:20–24.

The Gospel of the Lord.

ALL

Praise to you, Lord Jesus Christ.

All reflect prayerfully on the Word of God.

Profession of Faith

LEADER

Let us profess our faith in God the Father.

ALL

I believe in one God,
the Father almighty,
maker of heaven and earth,
of all things, visible and invisible.

Prayer of Intercession

LEADER

God our loving Father,
Jesus, your Son, taught us to pray,
'Our Father, . . . give us this day our daily bread'.
We lift up our voices and hearts with trust to you
as we pray:

READER

God our Father,
we are your adopted sons and daughters.
Strengthen us to live according to this calling.
'O Lord, all [our] longing is known to you' (*Psalm 38:9*).

ALL

Lord, hear our prayer.

READER

Help us to give you glory by our care for your creation
and to live in accordance with our responsibility to 'till it and keep it'.
'O Lord, all [our] longing is known to you' (*Psalm 38:9*).

ALL

Lord, hear our prayer.

READER

You sent your Son to be one of us and to live among us
to reveal the depth of your love for us.
Strengthen us to seek and to follow your will as he did.
'O Lord, all [our] longing is known to you' (*Psalm 38:9*).

ALL

Lord, hear our prayer.

LEADER

Ever-loving God,
help us listen to and respond to your invitation to know, love and serve you.
Send your Holy Spirit to strengthen our minds and hearts

to care for the world around us, especially for the poor, as your Son did.
We ask this through Jesus Christ, your Son, who lives and reigns with you and the Holy Spirit, one God, for ever and ever.

ALL
Amen.

Pray the Sign of the Cross together.

Help us to give you glory by our care for your creation and to live in accordance with our responsibility to 'till it and keep it'

CHAPTER 7

The Only Begotten Son of God

—Jesus Christ, God-with-Us

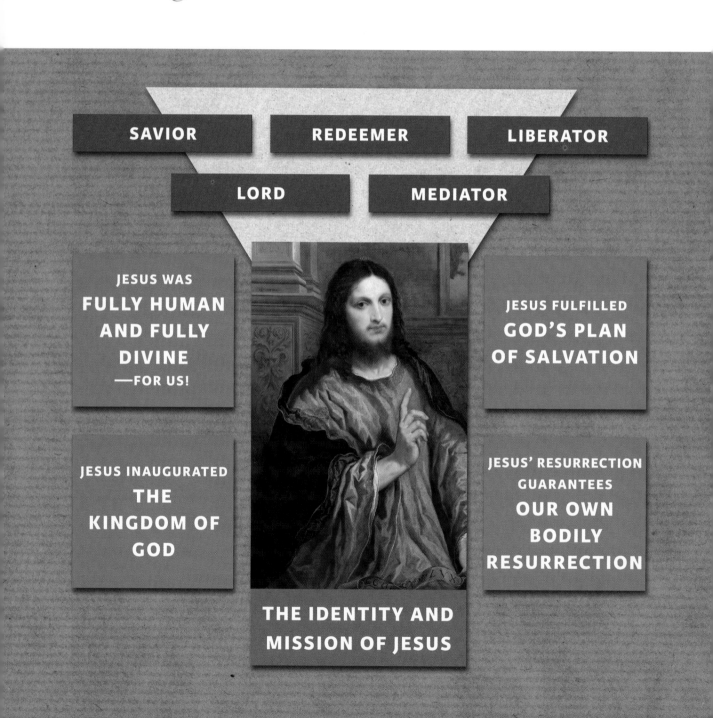

SAVIOR

REDEEMER

LIBERATOR

LORD

MEDIATOR

JESUS WAS **FULLY HUMAN AND FULLY DIVINE** —FOR US!

JESUS FULFILLED **GOD'S PLAN OF SALVATION**

JESUS INAUGURATED **THE KINGDOM OF GOD**

JESUS' RESURRECTION GUARANTEES **OUR OWN BODILY RESURRECTION**

THE IDENTITY AND MISSION OF JESUS

THE INCARNATION IS THE 'DISTINCTIVE SIGN OF THE Christian faith'. In this chapter we study in more detail the teaching of the Catholic Church on the Incarnation—'the mystery of the wonderful union of the divine and human natures in the one person of the Word' (*Catechism of the Catholic Church* [CCC], no. 483). Jesus Christ is true God and true man. He is fully human and fully divine. We explore the connection between the Incarnation and the Paschal Mystery of Jesus' Death, Resurrection and Ascension, the high point of God's divine plan of Redemption and Salvation. Jesus Christ is the Savior, the Redeemer and the one and only Mediator between God and man.

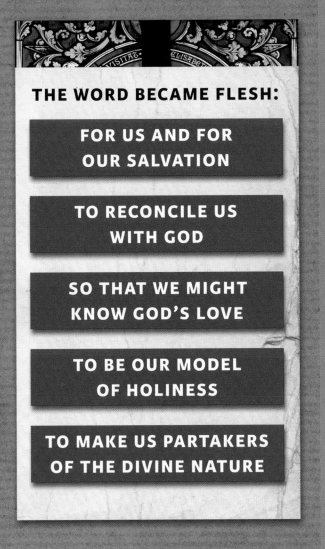

THE WORD BECAME FLESH:

FOR US AND FOR OUR SALVATION

TO RECONCILE US WITH GOD

SO THAT WE MIGHT KNOW GOD'S LOVE

TO BE OUR MODEL OF HOLINESS

TO MAKE US PARTAKERS OF THE DIVINE NATURE

Faith Focus: These teachings of the Catholic Church are the primary focus of the doctrinal content presented in this chapter:

- ◉ Jesus Christ is eternally begotten and incarnate in time.
- ◉ The Son of God is true God and consubstantial with the Father.
- ◉ Jesus Christ, the Son of Mary, is true man.
- ◉ Jesus Christ is the Savior, Redeemer and Liberator.
- ◉ Jesus Christ is the only Mediator between God and man.
- ◉ Jesus Christ is Lord.
- ◉ Jesus Christ is 'our model of holiness'.

Discipleship Formation: As a result of studying this chapter and discovering the meaning of the faith of the Catholic Church for your life, you should be better able to:

- ◉ deepen your understanding of the teachings of the Catholic Church on the mystery of the Incarnation;
- ◉ discover the difference that your faith in Jesus makes for your life;
- ◉ articulate more clearly your faith in Jesus, the Savior, Redeemer, Liberator, Lord and Mediator;
- ◉ share your faith in Jesus with more conviction;
- ◉ respond to your encounter with the risen Jesus and to the power of the Resurrection to transform the way you live your life.

Scripture References: These Scripture references are quoted or referred to in this chapter:
OLD TESTAMENT: Genesis 2:7; **Leviticus** 11:44
NEW TESTAMENT: Matthew 1:20–21, 5:11–12, 16:13–20, 25:31–46, 28:9–10, 16–20; **Mark** 1:1 and 15, 15:39, 16:9–13; **Luke** 1:67–79, 11:1, 24:13–53; **John** 1:1–3, 8:31–32, 13:15, 14:6, 15:12, 20:11–29, 21:1–19; **Acts of the Apostles** 4:12; **Romans** 14:17, 15:5; **1 Corinthians** 15:14, 20–49 and 55; **Galatians** 5:1; **Philippians** 2:5–8, 9–11; **2 Peter** 1:4; **1 John** 4:2, 9–10

Faith Glossary: Familiarize yourself with the meaning of these key faith terms. Definitions are found in the Glossary: **consubstantial, Eleven (the), expiation, hypostatic union, Incarnation, Kingdom of God, Lord, Mediator, original holiness, original justice, Original Sin, Passion (of Jesus), redemption, Resurrection, sacrifice, salvation, salvation history, sin, Son of God, Son of Man**

Faith Words: salvation; Son of God; Passion; Lord
Learn by Heart: Mark 15:39
Learn by Example: The two disciples from Emmaus

Who do you say that I am?

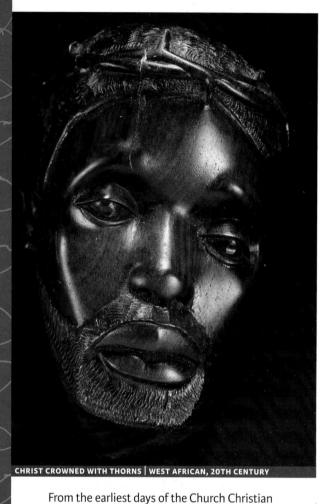

CHRIST CROWNED WITH THORNS | WEST AFRICAN, 20TH CENTURY

The Holy Spirit invites all disciples of Jesus to seek to answer the question 'Who do you say that I am?'

From the earliest days of the Church Christian artists have portrayed their image of Jesus. In some ways their art is an expression of their faith in who they have come to believe Jesus to be. Their art, you might say, is a faith-driven response to the very question that Jesus asked his first disciples, '[W]ho do you say that I am?' (Matthew 16:15).

OPENING CONVERSATION
- Recall and describe your favorite images of Jesus. Some of these images may be in this or other *Credo* texts. What does each of these images say to you about Jesus?

- Share your own response to Jesus' question, 'Who do you say that I am?'

'WHO DO YOU SAY THAT I AM?'
Jesus was travelling with his disciples on the road to Caesarea Philippi, a Roman town in the Diaspora about twenty-five miles north of the Sea of Galilee. The Diaspora was an area of settlement outside Palestine in which Jews lived. The disciples must have been muttering among themselves about who people were claiming Jesus to be and speculating on the rumors and controversies that were circulating about him. When they arrived in Caesarea Philippi Jesus asked them, 'Who do people say that the **Son of Man** is?' (Matthew 16:13). The disciples recounted to him the latest speculations they had heard. Then Jesus confronted the disciples, asking them directly, 'But who do you say that I am?' (Matthew 16:15). This is a question that the Holy Spirit invites all disciples of Jesus to seek to answer.

LET'S PROBE DEEPER
- Read Matthew 16:13–20.
- Discuss Peter's response to Jesus, 'You are the Messiah, the Son of the living God' (Matthew 16:16).

- What encounters between Jesus and the Pharisees and scribes recorded in the four accounts of the Gospel can you remember? What do those encounters reveal about what people thought of Jesus?

WHAT ABOUT YOU PERSONALLY?

- Who is the Jesus you have come to know?
- Who and what has contributed to your understanding of Jesus?
- Brainstorm and list everything that you have come to know about Jesus. Next to each item you list, name where you learned that truth about Jesus and who taught it to you.

JOURNAL EXERCISE

- Using words or an illustration, create an image of the Jesus you have come to know and in whom you believe.
- Does your image of Jesus make it easy or difficult to be his disciple? Explain.

Does your image of Jesus make it easy or difficult to be his disciple?

JESUS AND DISCIPLES ON THE ROAD TO EMMAUS | MILAN, ITALY

Jesus is the Good News

Catholics continue to share their faith in Jesus, the Incarnate Son of God, in many ways. Carlo Carretto, a renowned Italian youth leader and spiritual writer who lived for a time in the Sahara desert as a member of the Little Brothers of Blessed Charles de Foucauld (1858–1916), is but one example.

Carretto and the Stork

The Little Brothers had a fraternity among the poor families who lived by cultivating a bit of grain and a few vegetables along the Oued [a river in northern Algeria]. . . . Rabbits used to come in from round about and make short work of the little bit of green that had been acquired as the result of so much effort. By way of self-defense, one was compelled to set traps, and these became the source of a bit of meat which was generally not too bad—as long it was not fox or jackal.

One evening a flight of storks appeared in the sky above Tazrouk, bound for the north: it was spring at the time. . . . In her efforts to find somewhere to alight, a beautiful female stork put her foot right into one of the traps. All that night she lost blood, and when the dawn came it was too late. All attempts to save the poor bird were useless: she died that same day and we buried her. . . .

The flight of the storks set out once more for the north, but the partner of the dead stork stayed behind. That evening we saw the wretched bird come down near the garden, in the same place that his partner had been trapped, and fly round and round, crying. . . . This went on until sunset. The same scene was repeated next day. The flight of storks had probably reached the Mediterranean by now, and yet this lone bird was still there, searching for his companion. He stayed the entire year. . . .

The brothers became accustomed to the stork, as he did to them. He would fly into the garden and come over to take whatever morsel of meat or moistened bread the brothers offered him. . . . I remember the look in his eyes, his habit of cocking his head on one side, the regular movement of his beak, and the way he had of staring at me, as if he was trying to catch hold of me and escape his solitude. I, for my part, tried to understand him, but I remained myself, and he remained a stork. I remained imprisoned within my limitations as he did in his—limitations fixed for us by nature.

- ⊙ Why was there such a strong connection between Carretto and the stork?
- ⊙ How might Carretto's story give us insight into understanding the meaning of the Incarnation?

FROM THE CATECHISM

At the time appointed by God, the only begotten Son of the Father, the eternal Word, that is, the Word and substantial Image of the Father, became incarnate; without losing his divine nature he has assumed human nature.

—CCC, no. 479

THE WORD OF GOD BECAME FLESH IN JESUS

Every year at the Eucharistic Liturgy on Christmas Day the Church proclaims:

In the beginning was the Word, and the Word was with God, and the Word was God. He was in the beginning with God. All things came into being through him, and without him not one thing came into being.

—John 1:1–3

John the Evangelist's teaching reveals that Jesus Christ is **consubstantial** with the Father. The Word shared the same divine nature as God—'the Word was God'. Through the mystery of the **Incarnation**, God bridged the gap between humanity and divinity. For our **salvation** the **Son of God** took on flesh (took on human nature) without giving up his divinity. In the one divine Person, Jesus, the divine and human natures are united.

'Jesus Christ is true God and true man, in the unity of his divine person' (CCC, no. 480). The Son of God took on a human nature without giving up being God. Jesus Christ, the eternal Son of God, became incarnate in time. He thought with a human mind. He acted with a human will, and with a human heart he loved. He worked with human hands. He was like us in all things except sin. The Son of God, the Second Person of the Holy Trinity, embraced a human nature in order to reconcile us closer with God and with one another. He came to save, redeem and free us from the bondage of sin.

FAITH WORDS

Salvation

Salvation is the forgiveness of sins and restoration of friendship with God, which can be done by God alone.

—CCC, Glossary

Son of God

The Second Divine Person of the Holy Trinity. 'The title "Son of God" signifies the unique and eternal relationship of Jesus Christ to God his Father; he is the only Son of the Father; he is God himself. To be a Christian, one must believe that Jesus Christ is the Son of God.'

—CCC, no. 454

THE TEMPTATION OF JESUS | 19TH-CENTURY ENGRAVING

Jesus showed his humanity in every event of his human life. We see him experience hunger and thirst and temptation

'HE HUMBLED HIMSELF'

The early Church proclaimed in song the heart of the Good News: God the Father sent his Son to be one of us, to be 'like us in all things but sin'. The Letter to the Philippians, which was written some twenty years after the Death, Resurrection and Ascension of Jesus, includes a hymn that is a brief summary of the apostolic faith in Jesus. Biblical scholars think this hymn of the early Church was sung during worship and would have been widely known and prayed.

Let the same mind be in you that was in Christ Jesus,
    who, though he was in the form of God,
        did not regard equality with God
        as something to be exploited,
    but emptied himself,
        taking the form of a slave,
        being born in human likeness.
    And being found in human form,
        he humbled himself
        and became obedient to the point of
            death—
        even death on a cross.
                —Philippians 2:5–8

Jesus showed his humanity in every event of his human life—in his family life, his friendships and his socialization with others. In the four accounts of the Gospel we see Jesus experience human joy and happiness; we see him demonstrate such human virtues as fortitude, justice, temperance, prudence and compassion. We see him experience hunger and thirst and temptation. We see him grieve over the death of his friend Lazarus. 'Born in human likeness, he humbled himself' for our redemption and salvation. He became incarnate and was, indeed, like us in all things but sin.

FROM THE CATECHISM

In all of his life Jesus presents himself as *our model*. He is the 'perfect man' [*Constitution on the Church in the Modern World*, no. 38; see also Romans 15:5, Philippians 2:5], who invites us to become his disciples and follow him. In humbling himself, he has given us an example to imitate, through his prayer he draws us to pray, and by his poverty he calls us to accept freely the privation and persecutions that may come our way [see also John 13:15; Luke 11:1; Matthew 5:11—12].
                —CCC, no. 520

THE IDENTITY AND MISSION OF JESUS

The Gospel according to Mark, the earliest written account of the Gospel, begins, 'The beginning of the good news of Jesus Christ, the Son of God' (Mark 1:1). Then, near the close of Mark's Gospel, one of the soldiers who was among those who were ordered to crucify Jesus, says with awe and reverence, 'Truly this man was God's Son' (Mark 15:39). What takes place after Mark 15:39, namely, the proclamation of Jesus' **Resurrection** from the dead, is the best 'Good News' of all. It is the culminating act of God in **salvation history**. The Letter to the Philippians continues:

> Therefore God also highly exalted him
>   and gave him the name
>   that is above every name,
> so that at the name of Jesus
>   every knee should bend,
>   in heaven and on earth and under the
>   earth,
> and every tongue should confess
>   that Jesus Christ is Lord,
>   to the glory of God the Father.
> —Philippians 2:9–11

Jesus of Nazareth, who was both a historical figure and a divine Person, transcends history. In him alone the divine work of Salvation centers and is accomplished. Jesus 'the Son of God from all eternity' was not some lesser God, or just a very good and holy man who was close to God. Jesus is the eternal Son of God. Jesus is God himself, who became truly man while remaining truly God. He is the only Son of the Father. This is the Jesus in whom the Church believes. Jesus is the 'Messiah and Son of the living God'. He is the one and only **Mediator** between God and man. In the Nicene Creed we confess:

> I believe in one Lord Jesus Christ,
> the Only Begotten Son of God,
> born of the Father before all ages,
> God from God, Light from Light,
> true God from true God,
> begotten, not made, consubstantial with the
>   Father;
> through him all things were made.
> For us men and for our salvation,
> he came down from heaven,
> and by the Holy Spirit was incarnate of the
>   Virgin Mary
> and became man.

Jesus' Resurrection from the dead is the best 'Good News' of all

PAINTED WOODEN CROSSES IN A ROMANIAN VILLAGE

JESUS, 'GOD SAVES'

Near the beginning of his Gospel, Matthew gives the account of the angel Gabriel's announcement to Joseph, '[D]o not be afraid to take Mary as your wife, for the child conceived in her is from the Holy Spirit. She will bear a son, and you are to name him Jesus, for he will save his people from their sins' (Matthew 1:20–21). Matthew's first readers, who were primarily Jews who had become followers of Jesus, would clearly get the meaning of the message.

The name 'Jesus' is a succinct statement of apostolic faith and hope in Jesus. The Hebrew name Jesus means 'God saves'. The title Christ means 'Anointed One', or Messiah. In Jesus Christ, God fulfilled his promise to save his people. God fulfilled his promise in an extraordinary and unsuspected way: God himself became flesh in Jesus Christ and redeemed us and saved us from the power of sin. The Son of Mary is truly God. The child whom Mary conceived is from the Holy Spirit. 'There is salvation in no one else, for there is no other name under heaven given among mortals by which we must be saved' (Acts of the Apostles 4:12).

TALK IT OVER
◉ Why is the Incarnation the best news of the Christian faith?
◉ What is the 'best news' that you hear in the Gospel accounts of the Incarnation for your own life now? For your friends? For the life of the world?

JOURNAL EXERCISE
◉ Where do you encounter Jesus?
◉ Do the things you say and do help people encounter Jesus? Why or why not?
◉ Think of and describe one way in which you can help people encounter Jesus today.

Jesus, fully divine and fully human, for us and for all people!

ANSELM BEING MADE ARCHBISHOP OF CANTERBURY | JAMES W.E. DOYLE

The Church since the days of the Apostles has always been answering the question 'Who do you say that I am?' both for herself and for unbelievers. In the eleventh century the British theologian and Doctor of the Church St. Anselm of Canterbury (1033–1109) posed the question in this way: *'Cur Deus homo?'*—'Why did God become a man?' or 'Why God-man?'

OPENING CONVERSATION

Put on your own theological 'hat' and, from what you have learned so far, discuss:

◉ Why did God take on flesh and become man in Jesus?

◉ What difference does Jesus Christ make to people's lives? To your life?

CUR DEUS HOMO?

'Belief in the true Incarnation of the Son of God is the distinctive sign of Christian faith' (CCC, no. 463). The *Catechism of the Catholic Church* sums up, in the following manner, the reasons why the Son of God took on 'flesh' in the Incarnation:

◉ 'The Word became flesh for us in order to save us by reconciling us with God' (CCC, no. 457).

◉ 'The Word became flesh so that thus we might know God's love' (CCC, no. 458).

◉ 'The Word became flesh to be our model of holiness' (CCC, no. 459).

◉ 'The Word became flesh to make us partakers of the divine nature' (CCC, no. 460, quoting 2 Peter 1:4).

'THE WORD BECAME FLESH FOR US IN ORDER TO SAVE US BY RECONCILING US WITH GOD'

At the time appointed by God, 'the Father has sent his Son as the Savior of the world' (CCC, no. 457). The word Savior comes from the Latin *salvare*, which means 'to make safe or healthy'. Jesus is the only One who makes us 'safe' from all powers of evil. St. Gregory the Great (c. 335–c. 386), Bishop of Nyssa in central Turkey and Father of the Church, put it this way: 'Sick, our human nature demanded to be healed; fallen, to be raised up; dead, to rise again. We had lost the possession of the good; it was necessary for it to be given back to us' (quoted in CCC, no. 457). As a consequence of **Original Sin** humanity has fallen from the state of **original holiness** and **original justice**. Throughout history humanity continued to **sin** over and over again and so to turn away from God's love. God's response to all sin is the constant offering of his forgiveness and reconciliation. The Son of God became man to be the expiation for our sins, to make us sharers in God's mercy and to reconcile us with God.

'THE WORD BECAME FLESH SO THAT THUS WE MIGHT KNOW GOD'S LOVE'

The First Letter of John teaches 'God's love was revealed among us in this way: God sent his only Son into the world so that we may live through him. In this is love, not that we loved God but that he loved us and sent his Son to be the atoning sacrifice for our sins' (1 John 4:9–10). Jesus, the Word become flesh, fully and clearly reveals the love of God for each and every one of us. Through the Incarnation, in Jesus' public life and ministry, and his saving Death, Resurrection and Ascension, we 'see in flesh and blood' the depth and breadth of God's love at work in the world.

ST. ATHANASIUS | SAINT MARTIN D'YGRANDE, ALLIER, FRANCE

'THE WORD BECAME FLESH TO BE OUR MODEL OF HOLINESS'

The Son of Mary is truly and fully human. He is the revelation of the holiness to which God calls us and for which he created us. We are to be holy because God, in whose image he has created us, is holy. (See Leviticus 11:44.) God created us to live a life of holiness—to share in his life and to live in communion with him. Jesus is the way of holiness; he has revealed that way to us (see John 14:6) and made it possible for us to live it. Living a life of holiness includes 'living in right and loving relationship with God, with other people, with ourselves and with God's creation'. We are to love one another as Jesus has loved us (see John 15:12). We are to listen to Jesus as the Father commanded Peter, James and John to do at the Transfiguration. To love like Jesus means giving of ourselves for others.

> FROM THE CATECHISM
>
> 'The whole of Christ's life was a continual teaching: his silences, his miracles, his gestures, his prayer, his love for people, his special affection for the little and the poor, his acceptance of the total sacrifice on the Cross for the redemption of the world, and his Resurrection are the actualization of his word and the fulfillment of Revelation' [Pope John Paul II, *Catechesi tradendae* (*On Catechesis in Our Time*), no. 9].
>
> —CCC, no. 561

'THE WORD BECAME FLESH TO MAKE US PARTAKERS OF THE DIVINE NATURE'

St. Athanasius (c. 296–373), Bishop of Alexandria, Father and Doctor of the Church, played a central role in the formulation of the teachings of the Church in Nicaea I and the other early Councils of the Church. The Fathers of the Church are 'Church teachers and writers of the early centuries whose teachings are a crucial witness to the Tradition of the Church' (*United States Catholic Catechism for Adults* [USCCA], 513). St. Athanasius summarized the purpose of the Incarnation in the divine plan of Salvation this way: 'The only-begotten Son of God, wanting to make us sharers in his divinity, assumed our nature, so that he, made man, might make men gods.' This is an amazing statement of faith; yet, if we remember the first accounts of Creation, it should not surprise us. God created us in the divine image, sharing the very life-breath of God (see Genesis 2:7). Alive by the divine breath, we are to grow in 'godliness' by following the way of Jesus and living as disciples and apprentices of Jesus, the Master. When we do our best to live the 'way' of Jesus, we are closest to what is divine. We demonstrate to ourselves and to others who we are and who we are called to be—'flesh and blood' images of the living God.

TALK IT OVER

◉ Give one example of how Jesus showed us how to become truly human and more Godlike in how we live our lives.

ERRONEOUS TEACHINGS ON THE INCARNATION

How has the Church responded to Jesus' question, 'Who do you say that I am?' The efforts of some Christians were not always in keeping with the truths about Jesus revealed in Scripture and Tradition. Their efforts resulted in false teachings, or heresies, about Jesus that denied that Jesus is fully divine *and* fully human, that he is true God *and* true man. In teaching falsely that Jesus is either not fully divine or not fully human, these heresies deny the true nature of the mystery of the Incarnation. They deny the Church's teaching that is expressed in the doctrine of the **hypostatic union**, which we explored in detail in chapter 4 of this text, namely, that there is a union of the divine and human natures in the one divine Person (*hypostasis* in Greek) of the Son of God, Jesus Christ.

Some have falsely understood and taught that Jesus is more divine than human—someone who 'appears' to be like us but not really human. Others have falsely understood and taught that Jesus is more human than divine—not really God and no different from the many other inspirational leaders who have come and gone throughout history. Let us take a brief look at some of the major heresies about Jesus that originated and were proposed during the first five centuries of the Church—and continue to be taught in some form today.

JESUS HEALS A LEPER | WOODCUT AFTER JULIUS SCHNORR VON CAROLSFELD

Gnosticism and Docetism: Gnosticism and Docetism overemphasize the divinity of Jesus and deny his full humanity. These teachings are contrary to the Scripture and Apostolic Tradition that reveals, 'Jesus Christ has come in the flesh . . . from God' (1 John 4:2). The Church affirmed and clearly declared this to be a divinely revealed truth at the first Ecumenical Council in Nicaea in 325 when she taught that Jesus is of the same substance as (consubstantial with) the Father. The Church has continually reaffirmed this teaching at numerous later Ecumenical Councils and also at the non-ecumenical council at Antioch in 341; and we profess this faith today in the Nicene Creed.

Arianism: Arianism falsely taught that Jesus was not of the 'same substance' as God. The First Council at Nicaea rejected the Arian position and taught that Jesus is truly God; that is, he

MADONNA AND CHILD | GIOVANNI BELLINI

it. The Council of Chalcedon in 451 responded to the Monophysites and taught: 'The distinction between the natures was never abolished by their union, but rather the character proper to each of the two natures was preserved as they came together in one person *(prosopon)* and one hypostasis. In summary, Jesus was as fully human as we are; like us in all things 'yet without sin'.

THINK, PAIR AND SHARE

⊙ Pair up with a partner for a discussion on the Church's teaching on the Incarnation.
⊙ Imagine you are at the Council of Nicaea I, Ephesus and Chalcedon. Take turns playing the roles of a follower of Arianism, Nestorianism, Monophysitism and of St. Athanasius or another defender of the true meaning of the Incarnation. One partner presents the teachings of Arianism on the Incarnation; the other responds by presenting the teaching of the Catholic Church on the Incarnation. Then partners switch roles.
⊙ Do the same for Nestorianism and Monophysitism.

is of the same substance *(homoousios)* as the Father (see CCC, no. 465). In 381 the Council of Constantinople declared Arianism to be heretical.

Nestorianism: Nestorianism, the false teachings of Nestorius (c. 381–c. 451), the Patriarch of Constantinople, claimed that Jesus was two separate persons, one human and one divine. The Church, at the Council of Ephesus in 431, responded to Nestorius and his followers and decreed that Jesus is one divine Person who has two natures, a divine nature and a human nature. Jesus is both fully human and fully divine. Nestorius' teachings, in proposing that Jesus is two separate persons, also denied that Mary is 'Mother of God', stating that she only deserved the title 'Mother of Christ'. The Council of Ephesus in 431 decreed that Mary 'truly became the Mother of God by the human conception of the Son of God in her womb' (CCC, no. 466).

Monophysitism: Monophysitism falsely taught that there is only one *(mono)* nature *(physis)* in Christ; the human nature of Christ ceased to exist when the divine Person of God the Son assumed

The difficulty in expressing the mystery of the Incarnation continues today. In our stories and our images some of us tend to think of Jesus as more human than divine. Others think that Jesus is more divine than he is human. Jesus was not pretending to suffer on the Cross for us while transcending pain through his divinity; he truly suffered for us. We might find ourselves asking, 'Is Jesus mostly divine or mostly human?' The answer, of course, is that the one divine Person, Jesus Christ, is fully divine and fully human. Jesus is not just *like* God; Jesus is God fully and completely. Jesus is not just *like* us; Jesus is fully human in all ways except sin. There are two natures, one divine and one human, united in the one divine Person, Jesus.

JOURNAL EXERCISE

⊙ How would you answer the question that Jesus first asked his disciples and continues to ask you today: 'Who do you say that I am?'
⊙ What is the best wisdom for living your life as a disciple of Jesus Christ that you learned from your study of this chapter thus far?

Jesus—Savior, Redeemer, Liberator and Lord

Anger is a Poison

Ruby stepped toward him. 'Edward,' she said softly. It was the first time she had called him by name. 'Learn this from me. Holding anger is a poison. It eats you from inside. We think that hating is a weapon that attacks the person who harmed us. But hatred is a curved blade. And the harm we do, we do to ourselves.

'Forgive, Edward. Forgive. Do you remember the lightness you felt when you first arrived in heaven?'

Eddie did. *Where is my pain?*

'When we die, the soul is freed of it. But now, here, in order to move on, you must understand why you felt what you did, and

why you no longer need to feel it.'

She touched his hand.

'You need to forgive your father.'

REFLECT AND DISCUSS

⊙ What do you think of Ruby's statement, 'Holding anger is a poison'?

⊙ What is it that Eddie needs to be saved from? And how might this happen for him?

JOURNAL EXERCISE

Reflect for a few moments on these questions and then record your thoughts:

⊙ Are there things you need to be saved from? For example, is there anything that could be like a poison inside you, eating you from the inside?

⊙ When you feel you need 'saving', do you turn to Jesus? Why or why not?

THE KINGDOM AND REIGN OF GOD

The experience of evil and suffering in the world is, for some people, a poison that can lead to an expression of anger that is sometimes mistakenly aimed at God and may result in a person losing their faith in God. Jesus' whole life on earth, especially the saving event of his Death, Resurrection and Ascension, is a sign of the loving and saving activity of God in a world that is scarred by sin, evil and suffering and lacking in faith.

Jesus began his public life and ministry, we have already seen, by proclaiming that the **Kingdom of God** announced in the Old Testament was near. Jesus' announcement called people to repent of their sins and live new lives according to his Gospel (Mark 1:15). The Kingdom of God means different things to many people. Here is how the Catholic Church defines the Kingdom of God: 'The actualization of God's will for human beings proclaimed by Jesus Christ as a community of justice, peace, mercy, and love, the seed of which is the Church on earth, and the fulfillment of which is in eternity' (USCCA,

517; see also Romans 14:17). Jesus Christ, the Messiah, Redeemer, Savior, Liberator and Lord, inaugurated the Kingdom by showing people a new way of life. Central to the work of the Church—Christ the Head and her members—is the mission to proclaim Jesus and work to bring about the fullness of the Kingdom, when Christ the Lord comes again in glory at the end of time.

THINK, PAIR AND SHARE

- What are some signs that the Kingdom of God is coming about? What are some signs that the Kingdom stills needs to be brought about?
- How can working to bring about the Kingdom of God help those who ask, 'How can you say that God is good if the world continues to be racked with suffering and so many other forms of evil?'

JESUS CHRIST: REDEEMER AND SAVIOR

Jesus Christ freed us from the power and bondage of sin and death. The Catholic Church teaches that Christ accomplished his work of **redemption**. Redemption is the salvation won for us by Jesus by his paying 'the price of his own sacrificial death on the Cross to ransom us, to set us free from the slavery of sin' (CCC, Glossary). Jesus accomplished our redemption 'principally by the Paschal mystery of his blessed **Passion**, Resurrection from the dead, and glorious Ascension, whereby "dying he destroyed our death, rising he restored our life"' (CCC, no. 1067). He is the one and only Mediator between God and man.

Today the saving and redeeming power of Christ's Death, Resurrection and Ascension is celebrated and made present in the Liturgy of the Church. Its saving effects, or graces, are communicated through the Sacraments, especially the Eucharist, which is the memorial of Christ's Passover made present in the liturgical action of his Church. The Death, Resurrection and Ascension of Jesus, the Christ, can help us see beyond our suffering and remind us that God is present with us in our suffering, pain and death.

> **Redemption is the salvation won for us by Jesus by his paying the price of his own sacrificial death on the Cross to ransom us, to set us free from the slavery of sin**

⊙ Where do you encounter Jesus the Redeemer and Savior?

⊙ How does the Death, Resurrection and Ascension of Jesus help you deal with your own suffering?

JESUS CHRIST: LIBERATOR

Jesus said to the Jews who had come to believe in him, 'If you continue in my word, you are truly my disciples; and you will know the truth, and the truth will make you free' (John 8:31–32). Jesus as Liberator is an ancient metaphor that has re-emerged in our time. The word 'Liberator', meaning 'one who frees', is closely aligned with the ancient title of Messiah. Reflecting on his own experience of the risen Lord and the faith of the early Church in the risen Jesus, St. Paul wrote, 'For freedom Christ has set us free. Stand firm, therefore, and do not submit again to a yoke of slavery' (Galatians 5:1).

When we say Jesus is the Liberator, we are professing our faith in the fact that Jesus *sets us free* from the power and bondage of sin and death. Jesus empowers us to live all the values and virtues of God's Kingdom—peace and justice, love and freedom, holiness and wholeness of life for all people. He alone empowers us to resist and work against all forms of sin and evil, slavery and oppression, both personal and social. The Catholic Church reminds us of this truth: '[B]y his death, Christ liberates us from sin; by his Resurrection, he opens for us the way to a new life' (CCC, no. 654).

OVER TO YOU

⊙ Where do you encounter Jesus the Liberator?

⊙ How does your encounter with Jesus the Liberator free you?

THE RISEN AND GLORIFIED LORD

The New Testament and the Church today uses the title 'Lord' to confess that Jesus is fully and truly God. The Resurrection is God's affirmation of the life, suffering and Death of Jesus, our Lord. In the Old Testament, 'LORD', or Adonai in Hebrew, is used in place of YHWH, the divine name God revealed to Moses. The title 'Lord' indicates divine sovereignty. From her earliest

FAITH WORD

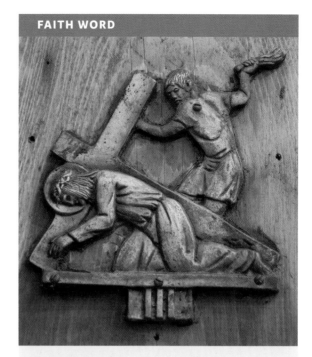

Passion

The suffering and death of Jesus. Passion or Palm Sunday begins Holy Week, during which the annual liturgical celebration of the Paschal Mystery of Christ takes place.

—CCC, Glossary

days the Church has acknowledged Jesus to be 'Lord'. The New Testament uses Lord for both God the Father and Jesus. In so doing the Church professes her faith in the full divinity of Jesus.

When the risen Lord appeared to Mary Magdalene and the other women (see Matthew 28:9–10; Mark 16:9–11; John 20:11–18) or he walked side-by-side with the two disciples who were returning to their home in Emmaus (see Luke 24:13–35) or he joined the company of St. Peter and the other disciples (see Matthew 28:16–20; Mark 16:12–13; Luke 24:36–53; John 20:19–29, 21:1–19), it was not a ghost nor Jesus in a resuscitated body who appeared to them. 'Christ's risen body is real, but glorified, not restrained by space or time' (USCCA, 525). The Resurrection confirms the 'saving', 'redeeming' and 'liberating' power of Jesus and the truth of his divinity.

CHRIST ENTHRONED | BASILICA OF ST. PAUL, ROME

Lord

The name used in Scripture for the divine name revealed to Moses. The title 'Lord' indicates divine sovereignty. To confess or invoke Jesus as Lord is to profess that he is truly and fully God.

—CCC, no. 455

OVER TO YOU

⊙ Where do you encounter the risen Lord?

⊙ Do you ever not immediately recognize the presence of the Lord with you, as happened to the two disciples on the road to Emmaus? How can you avoid this?

⊙ How do your encounters with the risen Lord strengthen you to face the challenges you will certainly meet as you strive to live as his disciple?

LET'S PROBE DEEPER: THE TRANSFORMATIVE POWER OF THE RESURRECTION

⊙ Open your Bible to the First Letter of the Corinthians and read 1 Corinthians 15:20–49.

⊙ What do the words of St. Paul reveal about the Resurrection in the divine plan of Salvation?

⊙ Give examples of situations in your local community, in the nation or in the world where you see the life-giving power of the Resurrection at work.

WHAT ABOUT YOU PERSONALLY?

⊙ What have you learned for your own life from the life-giving power of the Death, Resurrection and Ascension of Jesus?

⊙ How does your life give witness to that life-giving power? How can your life help others encounter the risen Lord?

In the Apostles' Creed we profess, 'I believe in . . . the resurrection of the body.' The Resurrection is both the promise of and our hope in our own bodily resurrection. Jesus freely accepted pain, suffering and death and transformed them into a life-giving sacrifice. Because of Jesus' Death and Resurrection on our behalf, even death has lost its sting (see 1 Corinthians 15:55). Through his Death and Resurrection, Jesus gives us his saving, healing and freeing grace to live the 'way' of Jesus. The risen Lord pours out his grace on us so we may truly become holy and grow to be our best and truest selves—the person whom God created us to be.

JUDGE AND ACT

REVIEW WHAT YOU HAVE LEARNED

Look back over this chapter and discuss the teachings of the Catholic Church expressed in these statements:

- Jesus Christ is the eternally begotten Son of God who became incarnate in time.
- Jesus is consubstantial with his Father.
- Jesus Christ, the Son of Mary, is true man and true God.
- The name 'Jesus' and the title 'Christ' reveal the mission of Jesus.
- Jesus Christ is Lord.
- Jesus Christ is Savior and Redeemer.
- Jesus Christ is Liberator.
- Jesus Christ reveals who God created us to be.

REFLECT AND DISCERN

- What is the best insight and spiritual wisdom you have learned from this chapter?
- What difference can this wisdom make to the lives of young people today?

ENCOUNTERING THE RISEN LORD TODAY

The New Testament gives the accounts of fourteen appearances of the risen and glorified Lord to many people in many places. In commenting on these accounts, one contemporary theologian remarked that something 'incomparably good' happened each time to the people who encountered the risen Lord. The same risen Lord promised, 'I am with you always, to the end of the age' (Matthew 28:20). The risen Christ has kept his promise. We encounter the risen Lord in a unique way in Sacred Scripture, in the Sacraments and in his Church, which is

THE RESURRECTION | ALBRECHT DÜRER

the sacrament of salvation in the world. We encounter him in the people and events of our lives (see Matthew 25:31–46). In our every encounter with him, the risen Lord invites us to transform our lives.

The story of the two disciples on the road to Emmaus (Luke 24:13–25)

THE ROAD TO EMMAUS | SANTO DOMINGO DE SILOS, SPAIN

Two disciples travelling home to Emmaus encounter the risen and glorified Lord and their lives are transformed.

Luke tells us that two disciples of Jesus from Emmaus, disappointed and dejected at Jesus' Death and burial, were returning home wondering about and doubting their response of discipleship. While making the seven-mile walk from Jerusalem, they encounter a 'stranger', who joins them. Walking along with the disciples, the 'stranger' engages them in dialog about what the Scripture reveals about the meaning of the events of Jesus' Death and burial—whose real meaning they did not get.

As the two disciples listen to this 'stranger', their minds and hearts become more and more open; their view of things is slowly transformed; their disappointment and dejection and doubts begin to dissipate. Overwhelmed and, no doubt, wishing to learn more, the disciples invite the 'stranger' to their home to share a meal with them. During the meal, at the breaking of bread (a New Testament phrase often used for the Eucharist), they recognize that the 'stranger' is the Lord. Their faith and hope is renewed. They rush back to Jerusalem in search of the Eleven and the other disciples to share the Good News, 'The Lord is risen'.

TALK IT OVER

- Why did the two disciples, at first, only see 'a stranger' and not 'recognize' that it was the Lord walking and talking with them?
- What does the Gospel story teach about the presence of the Lord with us today?
- Why do we not always recognize the risen and glorified Jesus in our own life?

WHAT ABOUT YOU PERSONALLY?

- How can you be more alert to the presence of the risen Jesus and more in tune to recognize and respond to him in your life?

SHARE YOUR FAITH WITH FAMILY AND FRIENDS

- Share and discuss an image of Jesus that is displayed in your family home or an image from this text. Have a good look at it and discuss what it portrays about Jesus.
- Share your faith in Jesus Christ and what this means for your life.

JUDGE AND ACT

- What difference does your faith in Jesus make to your own approach to life? Give examples.
- How will you act on that faith today and from here on out?

'Truly this man was God's Son!'

MARK 15:39

PRAYER REFLECTION

Pray the Sign of the Cross together.

LEADER

The *Benedictus*, or Canticle of Zechariah (Luke 1:67–79), is prayed daily by the Church in Morning Prayer of the Liturgy of the Hours. The *Benedictus* is a prayer of thanksgiving for God's saving action in the world. It is attributed to Zechariah, the father of John the Baptist, who was 'filled with the Holy Spirit' upon the birth of his son.

Let us pray the *Benedictus* antiphonally. One side will pray aloud a verse or verses from the *Benedictus* and the other side will respond.

ALL

Blessed be the Lord God. (*Pause and reflect.*)

SIDE 1

Blessed be the Lord God of Israel,
for he has looked favorably on his people and
redeemed them.

SIDE 2

He has raised up a mighty savior for us
in the house of his servant David,
as he spoke through the mouth of his holy
prophets from of old,
that we would be saved from our enemies and
from the hand of all who hate us.

SIDE 1

Thus he has shown the mercy promised to our
ancestors,
and has remembered his holy covenant,
the oath that he swore to our ancestor Abraham,

SIDE 2

to grant us that we, being rescued from the
hands of our enemies,
might serve him without fear, in holiness and
righteousness
before him all our days.

SIDE 1

And you, child, will be called the prophet
of the Most High;
for you will go before the Lord to prepare his
ways,

to give knowledge of salvation to his people
by the forgiveness of their sins.

SIDE 2

By the tender mercy of our God,
the dawn from on high will break upon us,
to give light to those who sit in darkness and in
the shadow of death,
to guide our feet into the way of peace.

ALL

Blessed be the Lord God. (*Pause and reflect.*)

LEADER

Let us now lift up our hearts in gratitude and praise of God the Father for sending his Son, who revealed that God is always with us, in our good times and our bad times.

One at a time, all share expressions of gratitude with the words: Lord, thank you for. . . .
After each expression of gratitude, everyone responds: Lord God, hear our prayer.
Conclude by praying the Sign of the Cross together.

THE VISITATION | MEAUX CATHEDRAL, FRANCE

CHAPTER 8

God the Holy Spirit
—The Spirit of Truth and Love

THE HOLY SPIRIT
CONTINUES JESUS' SAVING
WORK IN THE WORLD

JESUS WAS FILLED
WITH THE POWER OF
THE HOLY SPIRIT

THE HOLY SPIRIT IS
ALWAYS WITH US

GOD THE HOLY SPIRIT

THE SPIRIT OF TRUTH

THE HOLY SPIRIT TEACHES
AND EMPOWERS US TO LIVE
AS DISCIPLES OF JESUS

THE HOLY SPIRIT GIVES US
THE GRACE TO CONTINUE
JESUS' MISSION IN THE
WORLD

THE HOLY SPIRIT BUILDS,
ANIMATES AND SANCTIFIES
THE CHURCH

IN THE NICENE CREED WE PROFESS, 'I BELIEVE IN the Holy Spirit, the Lord, the giver of life, / who proceeds from the Father and the Son, / who with the Father and the Son is adored and glorified / who has spoken through the prophets'. This chapter explores the teaching of the Catholic Church on the Third Divine Person of the Holy Trinity, God the Holy Spirit. We also explore the presence and work of the Holy Spirit in the Church, in the lives of the faithful and in the world today.

SEVEN GIFTS OF THE HOLY SPIRIT

- ⊙ WISDOM
- ⊙ UNDERSTANDING
- ⊙ KNOWLEDGE
- ⊙ COUNSEL
- ⊙ FORTITUDE
- ⊙ REVERENCE
- ⊙ WONDER AND AWE IN GOD'S PRESENCE

TWELVE FRUITS OF THE HOLY SPIRIT

- ⊙ LOVE
- ⊙ JOY
- ⊙ PEACE
- ⊙ PATIENCE
- ⊙ KINDNESS
- ⊙ GOODNESS
- ⊙ GENEROSITY
- ⊙ GENTLENESS
- ⊙ FAITHFULNESS
- ⊙ MODESTY
- ⊙ SELF-CONTROL
- ⊙ CHASTITY

Faith Focus: These teachings of the Catholic Church are the primary focus of the doctrinal content presented in this chapter:
- ⊙ The Holy Spirit, the Lord and giver of life, is the Third Divine Person of the Holy Trinity.
- ⊙ The Holy Spirit eternally proceeds from the Father and the Son.
- ⊙ The Holy Spirit is only fully revealed by Jesus Christ.
- ⊙ The Holy Spirit is the Sanctifier of the Church and of her members.
- ⊙ The Seven Gifts of the Holy Spirit move us to cooperate with the graces of the Holy Spirit.
- ⊙ The Twelve Fruits of the Holy Spirit are signs of the Holy Spirit's work in the Church and in her members.

Discipleship Formation: As a result of studying this chapter and discovering the meaning of the faith of the Catholic Church for your life, you should be better able to:
- ⊙ articulate more clearly your faith in the Holy Spirit, the Lord and giver of life and the Sanctifier of the members of the Church;
- ⊙ listen and respond to the presence of the Holy Spirit in your life;
- ⊙ value and live up to your identity as a temple of the Holy Spirit;
- ⊙ share your faith in the Holy Spirit with more conviction;
- ⊙ choose ways to respond to your encounter with the Holy Spirit and to the power of Jesus' Resurrection to transform the way you live your life.

Scripture References: These Scripture references are quoted or referred to in this chapter:
OLD TESTAMENT: **Genesis** 1:1–3, 2:7; **Exodus** 40:36–38; **1 Samuel** 10:1, 16:13; **Psalms** 139:1, 3 and 7; 143:10; **Sirach** 48:1; **Isaiah** 6:1–2, 11:1–3, 61:1
NEW TESTAMENT: **Matthew** 1:20, 3:13–17, 4:1–11; **Mark** 1:9–11, 12–13; **Luke** 1:34, 3:21–22, 4:1–13 and 18, 11:13 and 20; **John** 1:29–34, 14:16, 16:13; **Acts of the Apostles** 2:1–47, 8:17–19; **Romans** 8:9 and 15, 15:19; **1 Corinthians** 3:16, 12:13; **2 Corinthians** 1:21–22, 2:2–3, 3:17, 6:10; **Galatians** 3:14, 5:16, 22–23 and 25; **1 Peter** 4:14

Faith Glossary: Familiarize yourself with the meaning of these key faith terms. Definitions are found in the Glossary: **adoration, Ascension, Fruits of the Holy Spirit, Gifts of the Holy Spirit, Holy Days of Obligation, Holy Spirit, Paraclete, Pentecost, perseverance, prayer, temptation, transubstantiation**

Faith Word: Holy Spirit
Learn by Heart: Galatians 5:25
Learn by Example: Jean Vanier and L'Arche Communities

Who and where is the Holy Spirit?

The **Holy Spirit** is the giver of life and has been at work in the world since Creation. The Holy Spirit spoke through the Old Testament prophets. Jesus promised that he and the Father would send the Holy Spirit to the disciples to be their Advocate. The Holy Spirit descended upon the disciples on Pentecost as Jesus promised. We remember and celebrate that Pentecost event and the presence of the Holy Spirit with the Church each year on Pentecost Sunday. In the Nicene Creed we pray,

'I believe in the Holy Spirit, the Lord, the giver of life, / who proceeds from the Father and the Son'. Faith in the presence and grace of the Holy Spirit is central to the life of the disciples of Jesus. Oppressed Christians, in particular, and their descendants have proclaimed their faith in the liberating presence of the Holy Spirit in their life. Here is an excerpt from a story telling of one prisoner's faith in the Spirit.

'I talked to him plain'

I went back to my cell the night before my hearing. I decided to make a prayer. It had to be on my knees. . . . I couldn't play it cheap.

So I waited until the thin kid was asleep. Then I quietly climbed down from my top bunk and bent my knees. I knelt at the foot of the bed and told God what was in my heart. I made like he was there in the flesh with me. I talked to him plain . . . no big words, no almighties. . . . I talked with him like I had wanted to talk to my old man so many years ago. I talked like a little kid and I told him of my wants and lack, of my hopes and disappointments. I asked the Big Man . . . to make a cool way for me. . . . I felt like I was someone that belonged to someone who cared. I felt like I could even cry if I wanted to, something I hadn't been able to do for years. 'God,' I concluded, 'maybe I won't be an angel but I do know I'll try not to be a blank. So in your name and in Cristo's [Christ's] name, I ask this. Amen.'

A small voice added another amen to mine. I looked up and saw the thin kid, his elbows bent, his head resting on his hand. I peered

through the semidarkness to see his face. . . . No one spoke for a long while. Then the kid whispered, 'I believe in Dios [God] also. Maybe you don't believe it, but I used to go to church and I had the hand of God upon me. I felt always like you, and I feel now warm, quiet and peaceful like there's no suffering in our hearts.'

'What is he called, Chico, this what we ask for?' I asked quietly.

'He's called Grace by the Power of the Holy Spirit,' the kid said.

The Church invites us to invoke the Holy Spirit as the interior Teacher of Christian prayer

OPENING CONVERSATION

- ◉ Why do you pray? When do you pray?
- ◉ Have you prayed like the man in prison? Explain.
- ◉ What role does praying to the Holy Spirit have in your life of prayer?

FROM THE CATECHISM

The Church invites us to invoke the Holy Spirit as the interior Teacher of Christian prayer.

—CCC, no. 2681

THE HOLY SPIRIT AND CHRISTIAN PRAYER

The Holy Spirit is ever-present with the whole Church and with each member of the Church. The Holy Spirit is the Third Divine Person of the Holy Trinity, the Lord and giver of life who proceeds from the Father and the Son, and builds up, animates and sanctifies the Church and her members. It is the Holy Spirit who moves us to respond to God's invitation to pray. **Prayer** is our response to God's invitation. Christian prayer is a personal encounter with God through Christ in the Church. The Holy Spirit, who gives life to the Church, builds up the Church and makes the Church holy, is always with us as our inspiration and guide for our prayer and for our whole lives. All we need to do is to ask.

FAITH WORD

Holy Spirit

The proper name for the Third Divine Person of the Holy Trinity; the Lord and giver of life, who proceeds from the Father and the Son, and who with the Father and the Son is adored and glorified.

DOVE OF THE HOLY SPIRIT | COIN OF THE PAPAL STATES, 1846

Hymn to the Holy Spirit

Slowly and reflectively pray this hymn to the Holy Spirit.

Father, Lord of earth and heaven,
   King to whom all gifts belong,
Give your greatest Gift, your Spirit,
   God the holy, God the strong.

Son of God, enthroned in glory,
   Send your promised Gift of grace,
Make your Church your holy Temple,
   God the Spirit's dwelling place.

Spirit, come, in peace descending
   As a Jordan, heav'nly Dove,
Seal your Church as God's anointed,
   Set our hearts on fire with love.

Stay among us, God the Father,
   Stay among us, God the Son,
Stay among us, Holy Spirit:
   Dwell within us, make us one.

—Liturgy of the Hours,
Pentecost Sunday, Morning Prayer, Hymn

JOURNAL EXERCISE

- Reflect on how the Holy Spirit might be prompting you to pray.
- What might the Holy Spirit be inviting you to change about yourself or your life?
- How can you best respond to the Spirit?

The Spirit through the ages

On the Solemnity of Pentecost Catholics pray aloud or sing the ancient sequence 'Come, Holy Spirit' (*Veni, Creator Spiritus*). This is one translation of some of the words of *Veni, Creator Spiritus*:

Come, Holy Spirit, come!
Send forth from heaven
The ray of your light.

Come, Father of the poor,
Come, giver of gifts,
Come, light of hearts. . . .

Without your grace,
There is nothing in us,
Nothing that is not harmful. . . .

Grant to thy faithful,
Those trusting in thee,
Thy sacred sevenfold gifts.

Grant the reward of virtue,
Grant the deliverance of salvation,
Grant everlasting joy. Amen. Alleluia.

REFLECT AND DISCUSS
- What do the words of 'Come, Holy Spirit!' say about the Church's faith in the Holy Spirit?
- What does this hymn suggest for your own faith?
- What other hymns to the Holy Spirit do you know?
- What other ways does the Church pray and confess her faith in the Holy Spirit?

OVER TO YOU
- What is your favorite hymn or prayer to the Holy Spirit?
- Pray these words now.

THE REVELATION OF THE HOLY SPIRIT
The Holy Spirit was first revealed in the Old Testament in the account of Creation. The

PENTECOST | FLEMISH SCHOOL, 16TH CENTURY

Revelation of the Holy Spirit at work among the People of God took place gradually over time throughout the Old Testament, and was fully revealed by, in and through Jesus Christ. St. Gregory of Nazianzus gave insight into the Church's understanding of the Revelation of the Holy Spirit when he wrote:

The Old Testament proclaimed the Father clearly, but the Son more obscurely. The New Testament revealed the Son and gave us a glimpse of the divinity of the Spirit. Now the Spirit dwells among us and grants us a clearer vision of himself.
— St. Gregory of Nazianzus, *Theological Orations*, 5, 26, quoted in CCC, no. 684

The Holy Spirit revealed in the Old Testament: *Ruach* is the Hebrew word for 'spirit', which can also be translated 'air', 'wind' or 'breath'. The Church has come to understand the use of *ruach* in the Book of Genesis as the beginning of the Revelation of the Holy Spirit. In the first account of Creation in chapter 1 of Genesis, we read:

In the beginning when God created the heavens and the earth, the earth was a formless void and darkness covered the face of the deep, while a wind [*ruach*] from God swept over the face of the waters. Then God said, 'Let there be light'; and there was light.

—Genesis 1:1–3

And, in the second account of Creation in chapter 2, we read:

[T]he Lord God formed man from the dust of the ground, and breathed into his nostrils the breath [*ruach*] of life; and the man became a living being.

—Genesis 2:7

The Revelation of the Holy Spirit continues in the Historical Books of the Old Testament. The Hebrew Scriptures tell us that it was the 'Spirit of God' who came to rest on the judges and kings, priests and prophets chosen by God, to strengthen and guide them to serve God and the People of God. For example, we read that the Lord anointed Saul to be 'ruler over his people Israel' and the 'ruler over his heritage' (1 Samuel 10:1). In the Old Testament the ritual of anointing a person was an expression that God chose and empowered the person to serve his people. It was this same Spirit of God whom the prophet Isaiah said would be with the promised Messiah (see Isaiah 61:1).

The Wisdom writings also speak of God's 'holy spirit'. For example, the psalmist prays to the spirit of the Lord God, who is always with him:

O LORD, you have searched me and known me
. . .
You search out my path and my lying down,
and are acquainted with all my ways. . . .

Where can I go from your spirit?
Or where can I flee from your presence?. . .

—Psalm 139:1, 3, 7

For the people of ancient Israel, the Spirit of God was the presence of the one true God at work in the lives of his people. '[W]hen the Church reads the Old Testament, she searches there for what the Spirit, "who has spoken through the prophets", wants to tell us about Christ' (CCC, no. 702).

A wind from God swept over the face of the waters.

GENESIS 1:2

THE ANGEL GABRIEL | SPANISH, 1300-1499

The angel Gabriel assured Joseph not to be afraid 'to take Mary as your wife, for the child conceived in her is from the Holy Spirit'

The Holy Spirit revealed in the New Testament:
The Holy Spirit who was clearly prefigured in the Old Testament is most clearly revealed in the New Testament. The Holy Spirit prepared Mary to be the Mother of Jesus, the Incarnate Son of God, and by his grace fulfilled in her the divine plan of the Father's goodness. When Mary asked the angel, 'How can this be?', he responded, 'The Holy Spirit will come upon you, and the power of the Most High will overshadow you; therefore the child to be born will be holy; he will be called the Son of God' (Luke 1:34). The angel Gabriel also assured Joseph not to be afraid 'to take Mary as your wife, for the child conceived in her is from the Holy Spirit' (Matthew 1:20). By the action of the Holy Spirit, the Father sends into the world Emmanuel, Jesus, as God with us.

At Jesus' baptism, which marked the beginning of his public life, 'the Holy Spirit descended upon him in bodily form like a dove' (Luke 3:22). Jesus is the Christ, the Messiah, the one anointed by the Father's Spirit. This presence of the Holy Spirit reveals that the Son and the Spirit are inseparable. When the Father sends the Son, he always sends the Spirit. The same Spirit continued to be with Jesus throughout his public life and ministry. In the next section of this chapter we will explore, in more detail, both the role of the Holy Spirit in the life of Jesus during his public life and ministry, and also Jesus' promise at the Last Supper to send the Spirit to dwell with his disciples.

The Revelation of the Holy Spirit continues in the Acts of the Apostles and in the New Testament letters, which state clearly that the work of the Holy Spirit continues in the Church and the world today. The Catholic Church describes the mission of the Holy Spirit this way: 'The mission of Christ and the Holy Spirit is brought to completion in the Church, which is the Body of Christ and the Temple of the Holy Spirit' (CCC, no. 737).

Titles and Images of the Holy Spirit in Scripture

Titles

Advocate (Paraclete, or Consoler): John 14:16;
1 John 2:1

Spirit of truth: John 16:13

Spirit of the Promise: Galatians 3:14

Spirit of adoption: Romans 8:15

Spirit of Christ: Romans 8:9

Spirit of the Lord: 2 Corinthians 3:17

Spirit of God: Romans 15:19

Spirit of Glory: 1 Peter 4:14

Images

Water: 1 Corinthians 12:13

Anointing: 1 Samuel 16:13; 2 Corinthians 1:21

Fire: Sirach 48:1; Acts of the Apostles 2:3–4

Cloud and light: Exodus 40:36–38; Luke
9:34–35

Seal: 2 Corinthians 1:21–22

Hand: Acts of the Apostles 8:17–19

Finger: Luke 11:20

Dove: Matthew 3:16

TALK IT OVER

◉ What do the titles and images of the Holy
Spirit reveal to you about the identity and
work of the Holy Spirit?

◉ When and how do you most recognize the
Holy Spirit at work in your school? In your
parish? In the world at large?

◉ How might the Holy Spirit work through you
to continue God's saving work?

◉ How will you invite the Holy Spirit to be
present in your life?

JOURNAL EXERCISE

◉ Choose an image of the Holy Spirit or draw
your own image of the Holy Spirit.

◉ How does that image help you encounter
Christ and live as his disciple?

The Lord, the giver of life

On most Sundays and during the celebration of **Holy Days of Obligation**, you stand with the worshiping assembly and pray the Nicene Creed. You pray in part:

- ⊙ I believe in the Holy Spirit, the Lord, the giver of life,
- ⊙ who proceeds from the Father and the Son,
- ⊙ who with the Father and the Son is adored and glorified,
- ⊙ who has spoken through the prophets.

When you pray these words, you join with the Church and profess your faith in one God in three divine Persons. The Holy Spirit, who eternally proceeds from the Father and the Son, is God. The Holy Spirit and the Father and the Son are one God in three distinct but inseparable Persons.

REFLECT AND DISCUSS

- ⊙ What have you learned so far about the Holy Spirit?
- ⊙ What does the connection between the Holy Spirit and God the Father and Jesus say to you about the work of God in your life? Does it make you think about the work of God in your life differently than you thought before?

FROM THE CATECHISM
From the beginning to the end of time whenever God sends his Son he always sends his Spirit; their mission is conjoined and inseparable.

—CCC, no. 743

JESUS IN THE POWER OF THE SPIRIT
In the previous section of this chapter we touched briefly upon the Holy Spirit's role in the life of Jesus, the Incarnate Son of God. Let us now take a more detailed look at this teaching of the Catholic Church:

When the Father sends his Word, he always sends his Breath [a traditional symbol of the Spirit]. In their joint mission, the Son and the Holy Spirit are distinct but inseparable. To be sure, it is Christ who is seen, the visible image of the invisible God, but it is the Spirit who reveals him.

—CCC, no. 689

The baptism of Jesus: All four Evangelists teach that the Holy Spirit was present at the very beginning of Jesus' public life and ministry at Jesus' baptism by John the Baptist in the River Jordan. (See Matthew 3:13–17; Mark 1:9–11; Luke 3:21–22; John 1:29–34.)

BAPTISM OF JESUS | VIBOLDONE ABBEY, MILAN, ITALY

- Look up and read John 1:29–34.
- How does this passage point to the teaching of the Catholic Church in CCC, no. 689?

OVER TO YOU
- What does this passage say to you about the Holy Spirit in your life?

The temptation of Jesus: Jesus was like us in all ways except sin. This includes the fact that he experienced **temptation**. 'Jesus himself during his life on earth was tempted, put to the test, to manifest both the opposition between himself and the devil and the triumph of his saving work over Satan' (CCC, Glossary; see also CCC, no. 538; Matthew 4:1–11; Mark 1:12–13; Luke 4:1–13). The Devil tried his best to have Jesus not only choose to turn away from his Father and the mission the Father had given him, but also to worship him and not the Father. During the times of Jesus being tempted, the Holy Spirit was there with him—the same Spirit is present with us. (See Matthew 4:1; Mark 1:12; Luke 4:1.)

- Look up and read Luke 4:1–13.
- What do each of the Devil's temptations ask Jesus to choose to do?
- What temptations do youth today face that are similar to the temptations of Jesus?
- How might the Holy Spirit help young people today to overcome temptation?

OVER TO YOU
- St. Paul told Christians, 'Your body is a temple of the Holy Spirit' (1 Corinthians 6:10). How aware are you in times of temptation that the Holy Spirit is with you? Do you call upon the Holy Spirit in times of temptation?

The public life and ministry of Jesus: After his temptation in the wilderness, Jesus returned to his hometown, Nazareth. He entered the local synagogue on the Sabbath, as was his practice, took and opened the scroll containing the writings of the prophet Isaiah, and read aloud Isaiah 61:1–2, which begins, 'The Spirit of the Lord is upon me, because he has anointed me. . . .' (Luke 4:18).

THE TEMPTATION OF JESUS | MARIENKIRCHE, ROSTOCK, GERMANY

Jesus himself during his life on earth was tempted, put to the test, to manifest both the opposition between himself and the devil and the triumph of his saving work over Satan

- Look up and read Luke 4:1–13.
- From what you have learned so far, what is the significance of being 'anointed'?
- How does Jesus choosing and reading this passage show his understanding of the connection between himself, his mission and the Holy Spirit?

OVER TO YOU
- What does this passage say to you about your Baptism and the Holy Spirit's role in helping you to live as a disciple of Jesus?

Jesus' promise to send the Holy Spirit: After he taught his disciples to pray the Lord's Prayer, Jesus continued to teach them about the need for **perseverance** in prayer. He concluded his teaching, saying, '[T]he heavenly Father [will] give the Holy Spirit to those who ask him!' (Luke 11:13). At the Last Supper Jesus repeated this promise. He assured his disciples that the Holy Spirit would come and be with them as their Teacher and Advocate (or **Paraclete**).

Jesus' promise fulfilled: After the **Ascension** Mary, the Mother of Jesus, the Eleven and other disciples returned to Jerusalem. While they were gathered in an upper room during the annual celebration of the Jewish feast of **Pentecost**, the Holy Spirit came upon them. Jesus' promise was fulfilled. Luke, the author of the Acts of the Apostles, writes, 'All of them were filled with the Holy Spirit and began to speak in other languages, as the Spirit gave them ability' (Acts of the Apostles 2:4). Jesus kept his word; the work of the Church, under the guidance of the Holy Spirit, had begun. The Holy Spirit is the 'principle agent of the whole of the Church's mission' in the world. As that work takes place throughout the ages, the mission of Christ continues.

DESCENT OF THE HOLY SPIRIT

All of them were filled with the Holy Spirit and began to speak in other languages

READ, REFLECT AND SHARE
- Look up and read Acts of the Apostles 2:1–47.
- What does this passage tell us about the faith of the Apostolic Church in the Holy Spirit?
- Where do you see Christians today giving witness to their faith in the Holy Spirit? What difference is it making?
- Name a situation in the world today where living one's faith in the Holy Spirit would make a difference. How can you play your part by the power of the Holy Spirit in making that happen?

JOURNAL EXERCISE
- Why is the Holy Spirit vital to your fulfilling your baptismal vocation to keep the flame of faith alive in your heart?

The Paraclete and Teacher

At Baptism all the newly baptized are united to the risen and glorified Christ, who gives us the Holy Spirit. We become temples of the Holy Spirit, and the Holy Spirit is at work in all the baptized. Nelson Mandela worked against the racist social system of apartheid, which Blessed Pope John Paul II condemned. Read this anecdotal summary of Mandela's work against apartheid.

The Story of Nelson Mandela

NELSON MANDELA SHORTLY AFTER HIS RELEASE FROM PRISON

Pope Benedict XVI has taught that working together to bring about the Kingdom of God inaugurated by Jesus is one way all Christians can give witness to Christ. Former president of South Africa Nelson Mandela, a person of deep Christian faith though not a Catholic, often spoke about how his faith motivated and sustained him. Many non-Catholic Christians cooperate with the Holy Spirit to continue the work Christ gave to his Church.

Here is what one person had to say about Nelson Mandela.

It would be a gross understatement to say that Mandela influenced others by his example. It is more accurate to say that he gave **inspiration** to his people. They breathed in the energy he gave them. Then they in turn exuded energy which they sent outward to him and through him. In this way he became a focus for the energy of a whole people.

Mandela was the first democratically elected president of South Africa (1994–99) and the leader of his people's struggle against the racist social system of apartheid—a social system that was strongly condemned by Blessed Pope John Paul II in his address to the United Nations Special Committee against Apartheid on July 7, 1984. Before becoming president, Mandela spent twenty-five years in prison because he had dared courageously to confront the government and its policy of apartheid.

REFLECT AND DISCUSS

⊙ How did Mandela's work mirror the words of Isaiah proclaimed by Jesus in the synagogue in Nazareth?

⊙ What unjust social policies have you seen the Catholic Church in the United States speaking out about and working against?

OVER TO YOU

⊙ When have you taken a stand against unjust social policies? Did you pay a price? Explain.

⊙ How might the Holy Spirit work through you to advocate or defend someone in need? Give examples from your experience.

THE SPIRIT OF CHRIST

St. Paul, passing on the faith of the Apostolic Church, taught that in Baptism 'we were all made to drink of one Spirit' (1 Corinthians 12:13) who is 'the Spirit of Christ' (Romans 8:9). At Baptism we are united to Christ 'the way, and the truth, and the life' (John 14:6) and the risen and glorified Lord pours out the sevenfold gift of the Holy Spirit, the Paraclete and Sanctifier, into our very being. We are made sharers in the life of God, become adopted children of the Father, brothers and sisters in Christ and temples of the Holy Spirit.

In John's account of the Gospel Jesus declares the Holy Spirit to be 'the Advocate', or Paraclete. While the exact meaning of the Greek word for *paraclete* is unclear, the origin of the Greek word actually refers to 'the one who spurs runners on in a race'. In other words, using a contemporary analogy, a 'paraclete' is similar to but not exactly like an athletic trainer or coach. The trainer and coach are teachers who prepare athletes for competition, encourage and guide athletes— even adjusting strategies—from the bench or sideline during the competition. Unlike a coach or trainer, however, the Holy Spirit never voices encouragement and strategies from the bench or sideline. The Holy Spirit is present with us and within us on the court or field, instructing and encouraging us every step of the way.

God's grace, the help and guidance of the Holy Spirit, comes to us, is offered to us and is with us through very 'ordinary' means and engages our very 'ordinary' human efforts. St. Thomas Aquinas (1225–74) summarized this truth of our faith by stating that 'grace works through nature'. When we receive God's grace in daily life, it is often through the very ordinary experiences of the people, events and things we encounter. For example, the Church uses the 'ordinary' things of water, bread, wine and oil in the celebration of the Sacraments. 'Celebrated worthily in faith, the sacraments confer the grace that they signify . . . because in them Christ himself is at work' (CCC, no. 1127).

In the Sacrament of the Eucharist the Church uses unleavened bread and wine made from grapes as Jesus did at the Last Supper. In the Eucharist, through the power of the Holy Spirit and the words and actions of the priest, who acts in *persona Christi* (the person of Christ), the bread

and wine are changed into the Body of Christ and the Blood of Christ, while the accidents (what we can touch, see, hear, taste and smell) remain unchanged. The substance of the bread becomes the Body of Christ and the substance of the wine becomes the Blood of Christ. The Catholic Church teaches this mystery of faith in her doctrine of **transubstantiation**, or 'the change in substances'. 'By the consecration the transubstantiation of the bread and wine into the Body and Blood of Christ is brought about' (CCC, no. 1413).

WHAT ABOUT YOU PERSONALLY?

⊙ Looking back, can you recognize times when God's grace, through the Holy Spirit, was at work in your life? Explain.

THE PROPHET ISAIAH | BARTHELÉMY D'EYCK

⊙ How might you give witness to the Spirit of Christ working in and through you?

THE SPIRIT OF CHRIST AT WORK IN OUR LIFE

The Church from her beginning believed that the connection between the Holy Spirit and the Church, the Body of Christ in the world, is vital to the Christian life. The Holy Spirit and the Church are inseparable. Again, St. Paul, in speaking of the Church, wrote: 'Do you not know that you are God's temple and that God's Spirit dwells in you?' (1 Corinthians 3:16). The Holy Spirit works through the life of the Church, other people and the events of our life to teach and guide us to live as faithful disciples of Jesus.

Let us now briefly explore both the work of the Spirit of Christ in our life and the signs that we are cooperating with the Holy Spirit.

THE GIFTS OF THE HOLY SPIRIT

Isaiah the Prophet foretold of the Messiah that 'the spirit of the LORD shall rest on him' (Isaiah 11:2). The prophet then lists specific gifts that the Spirit would impart to the Messiah, the Anointed One of God, the Christ. The Church names these gifts as the seven **Gifts of the Holy Spirit**. 'These gifts are permanent dispositions that move us to respond to the guidance of the Spirit. The traditional list of these gifts is derived from Isaiah 11:1–3: wisdom, understanding, knowledge, counsel [right judgment], fortitude [courage], reverence (piety), and wonder and awe in God's presence (fear of the Lord)' (*United States Catholic Catechism for Adults* [USCCA], 513). These gifts enable us to live our 'new life in the Holy Spirit'.

Wisdom. Through the Gift of Wisdom the Spirit of God teaches and guides us to see things as God sees them. The Spirit encourages us to live the spiritual wisdom taught throughout Scripture and Tradition.

The Holy Spirit helps us to show respect for the sacredness of our world and all creation

Understanding. Through the Gift of Understanding the Spirit of God teaches and guides us to an ever deeper understanding of the depth and meaning of loving God and others as Jesus did.

Knowledge. Through the Gift of Knowledge the Spirit of God teaches and guides us to grow in our knowledge and love of God. In turn, this will help us come to know what is important and of true value in life.

Counsel, or Right Judgment. Through the Gift of Counsel the Spirit of God teaches and guides us to recognize what to do in difficult situations and to be able to tell the difference between right and wrong and good and evil.

Fortitude, or Courage. Through the Gift of Fortitude the Spirit of God teaches and guides us to stand up boldly for what we believe is right and true, even when it is embarrassing or costly, and to resist temptation.

Reverence, or Piety. Through the Gift of Reverence the Spirit of God teaches and guides us to reverence God as Jesus did. The Spirit also helps us to show respect for the sacredness of our world and all creation.

Wonder and Awe in God's Presence, or Fear of the Lord. Through the Gift of Wonder and Awe before God, the Spirit of God teaches and guides us to worship and give adoration to God alone. This wonderful and awesome gift enables us to recognize and give God the glory due to him because of his holiness and greatness.

GROUP WORK: TALK IT OVER

⊙ Brainstorm and discuss examples of ways the sevenfold gift of the Holy Spirit is with us to support and teach us to live as disciples of Jesus Christ.

⊙ Share examples of times when you saw evidence of the Holy Spirit at work in the world. Use the Gifts of the Holy Spirit to explain why these were examples of the Spirit's presence and work in the world.

gentleness, and self-control. . . . If we live by the Spirit, let us also be guided by the Spirit' (Galatians 5:16, 22–23, 25).

Since the days of the Apostolic Church, Catholic Tradition has added goodness, modesty and chastity to Paul's list, bringing the list of 'the fruit of the Spirit' to twelve. The **Fruits of the Holy Spirit** are the perfections that the Holy Spirit forms in us as the 'first fruits' of eternal glory. They give witness to the presence, work and power of the Spirit of Christ at work in our life and in the world. When we live out the Gifts of the Spirit, the Fruits of the Holy Spirit pour forth in our lives.

TALK IT OVER

⊙ Who might you know or have learned about who is a witness to the Holy Spirit's active presence in the world? Give examples and support your choices by using the Gifts and/or Fruits of the Holy Spirit.

WHAT ABOUT YOU PERSONALLY?

⊙ Where do you see the Fruits of the Spirit in your own life? In the life of others?

HOLINESS OF LIFE—THE DIFFERENCE THE HOLY SPIRIT MAKES?

The Spirit is the living touch of God in our lives. Christians 'live by the Spirit'. The Holy Spirit, whom Christ pours out on his Church, builds, animates and sanctifies the whole Christian community, the Church. The Spirit of Christ prompts and supports us to live our baptismal call to holiness of life—to live in loving communion with the Trinity, with the Church and with all people and all of creation. To be holy is to be on a lifelong journey in the company of God's Spirit. The Spirit of Christ invites, teaches and guides us to live our new life in Christ by being loving, joyful, peaceful, patient, kind, good, generous, faithful, gentle, self-controlled, modest and chaste.

JOURNAL EXERCISE

⊙ Describe the life in the Spirit, the holiness of life, you desire to live.
⊙ How will you call upon the Spirit of Christ to build, animate and sanctify your life?
⊙ What can you do to work toward building such a life?

JOURNAL EXERCISE

⊙ Which gift or gifts of the Holy Spirit do you most need in your life at the moment?
⊙ How will you pray to the Holy Spirit for those gifts?

THE FRUITS OF THE HOLY SPIRIT

What are the signs that we are cooperating with the Holy Spirit to live as Jesus taught and commanded us to live? What are the signs that show we are continuing Jesus' mission of reconciling all things with God? What are the signs that we are participating effectively in bringing about the coming of the Kingdom, or reign, of God? The Church names twelve such 'signs' that are based on St. Paul's teaching in his letter to the Galatians. Paul wrote: 'Live by the Spirit . . . the fruit of the Spirit is love, joy, peace, patience, kindness, generosity, faithfulness,

JUDGE AND ACT

REVIEW WHAT YOU HAVE LEARNED

Look back over this chapter and discuss the teachings of the Catholc Church expressed in these statements:

- ◉ The Holy Spirit, the Lord and giver of life, is the Third Divine Person of the Holy Trinity.
- ◉ The Holy Spirit eternally proceeds from the Father and the Son.
- ◉ The Holy Spirit was at work before the coming of Christ.
- ◉ The Holy Spirit is only fully revealed by Jesus Christ.
- ◉ The Holy Spirit builds, animates and sanctifies the Church, the Body of Christ.

- ◉ The seven Gifts of the Holy Spirit move and support us to cooperate with God's graces to live our life as disciples of Jesus Christ.
- ◉ The twelve Fruits of the Holy Spirit are signs that the Holy Spirit is at work in the Church and in the life of her members.

WHAT ABOUT YOU PERSONALLY?

- ◉ What spiritual wisdom did you learn from your study of this chapter that deepened your awareness of the Holy Spirit's presence with you?

LEARN BY EXAMPLE

The story of Jean Vanier and L'Arche Communities

The same Paraclete who came upon the first disciples, the same Spirit who has moved many countless others throughout the history of the Church since that Pentecost, is present with us today, teaching and empowering us to go out and live as disciples of Jesus. Jean Vanier and the members of L'Arche communities is one such example.

L'Arche (Ark) is an international network of faith-based communities centered around persons with significant developmental challenges. Founded in 1964 by Jean Vanier, L'Arche began when Vanier invited three men with developmental challenges, both physical and intellectual, to live with him in a small house in France. The community that grew from this first community was characterized by profound respect and love, based in the Christian tradition of living Christ's command to 'love one another as I have loved you'. In the following piece, Jean Vanier tells the story of how L'Arche began.

In the Christmas of 1963 I was invited to be chaplain of a small institution called the Val Fleuri, which looked after men with mental disabilities. I was deeply impressed by the men there, who, it seemed to me, had a special place in God's heart. Each one seemed to have so much life, but had suffered terribly and thirsted deeply for friendship. Their desire for love touched me deeply.

Fr. Thomas (who was in charge of the institute) and I agreed that there was a great need for 'something'; indeed the French government was also ready to give financial support, but to what?

In January 1964 I went to Toronto to teach in a college there, but although I loved teaching I did not feel that Jesus wanted me to stay there. I went back to talk with Fr. Thomas. I had no big ideas about what I would do—big ideas are not my scene. I was a little naïve, but open and available for any possibilities. I wanted to follow Jesus and live the way of the Gospel.

Vanier followed what he discerned was God calling him to make a difference. He wrote,

'This was, for me, the beginning, but the L'Arche communities that were to follow were not my idea; they were God's.' Today there are over 135 L'Arche communities in thirty-six countries. In a divided world, L'Arche seeks to be a symbol of love and unity. In these communities, people with and without disabilities share their lives in homes, workshops and day programs, through which they develop their talents and work together to make the most of life. L'Arche communities are founded on mutual relationships, spirituality, expertise of care and community life. While a L'Arche community is grounded in the Christian faith, all people are welcome, regardless of religious tradition or belief.

TALK IT OVER

- ◉ How do L'Arche communities give expression to the work of the Holy Spirit in the world?
- ◉ Where else do you see the Holy Spirit at work in the Church and in her members? Give specific examples.

REFLECT AND DISCERN

- ◉ What can you learn from this story about being more open to the presence of the Spirit in your own life?

SHARE YOUR FAITH WITH FAMILY AND FRIENDS

- ◉ Talk about the Gifts of the Holy Spirit and how you can cooperate with the Holy Spirit in living as a disciple of Jesus Christ. Share practical and concrete examples.
- ◉ Pray together to the Holy Spirit to teach, animate, sanctify and support you.

JUDGE AND ACT

- ◉ Take a closer look at your life today from the perspective of the Fruits of the Holy Spirit.
- ◉ What in your life gives witness that you are truly welcoming and cooperating with the Holy Spirit?

- ◉ What in your life says that you can cooperate better with the Holy Spirit?
- ◉ Decide and put into practice what you need to do.

LEARN BY HEART

If we live by the Spirit, let us also be guided by the Spirit.

GALATIANS 5:25

THE HOLY SPIRIT | LUCA DELLA ROBBIA

Gathering

All gather in a circle, standing or seated, around a large candle. Pray the Sign of the Cross together.

Prayer of Meditation

LEADER
Come, Holy Spirit!
Fill us with your love.
Animate and sanctify us.
Move us to bring your life to the world. (*Pause*)

Close your eyes and get comfortable. (*Pause*)

Let go of any tension as you relax. (*Pause*)
Become aware of your breath (*pause*) entering
(*pause*) and leaving (*pause*) your body. (*Pause*)
Imagine yourself breathing in God's life (*pause*)
and breathing out God's love. (*Pause*)

Today we are going to imagine we were there
when Jesus was being baptized.

Picture yourself in a large crowd . . . on the banks
of the great River Jordan. . . . It is a hot, dusty day
and you are grateful to be close to the coolness
of the river. . . . You have just arrived . . . having
journeyed with some friends to see this man
called 'John the Baptizer'. . . . Moving closer, you
realize that this John the Baptist is speaking. . . .
You hear him say, 'I baptize you with water . . .
but he will baptize you with the Holy Spirit. . . .'
Through a gap in the crowds you manage to see
what is happening. . . . It is Jesus. . . . You see him
plunge down into the waters of the Jordan . . .
and then he comes up, gasping for breath. . . .
The sky above him appears to open up. . . . There
is complete silence as the crowds of people stare
in amazement. . . . Something startlingly white is
winging its way toward Jesus. . . . What looks like
a dove lands so very gently on his shoulder. . . .

You imagine you hear a voice . . . or was it
thunder? . . . saying, 'You are my Son, the Beloved;
with you I am well pleased'. . . . At those words,
Jesus lovingly reaches out and touches the
dove. . . . It swoops upward in one great, joyous
movement . . . and disappears up into the clouds
. . . leaving as mysteriously and suddenly as it
arrived. . . . Now the whole crowd is moving . . .
surging forward . . . straining to reach John and be
baptized too. . . . You feel yourself plunging into
the water. . . . Then hands grab you and haul you
up again. . . . As you stand, water streaming down
your body, you feel full of joy and energy. . . .
Something brushes your cheek . . . like the
fragile, soft brush of feathers. . . . It whispers to
you also. . . . 'You are my beloved child . . . with
you I am well pleased'. . . . What else do you
hear? . . . . Listen to what the Spirit says in your
heart now. . . . Stay with those words for a few
moments. . . . When you are ready, open your eyes
and come back to the group.

*Follow with a few moments of silence. Anyone who
wishes can now share a reflection.*

Concluding Prayer

ALL
Come, Holy Spirit,
fill the hearts of your faithful.
Enkindle in us the fire of your love.
Send forth your Spirit,
and we will be created,
and you will renew the face of the earth.
Amen.

Share a sign of peace.
Pray the Sign of the Cross together.

CHAPTER 9

Mary–Mother, Disciple and Evangelist

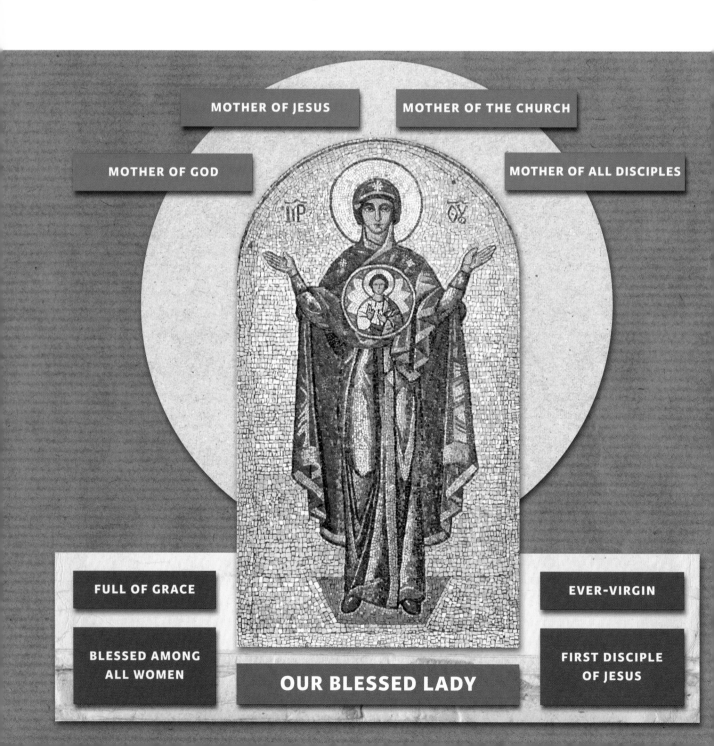

MOTHER OF JESUS

MOTHER OF THE CHURCH

MOTHER OF GOD

MOTHER OF ALL DISCIPLES

FULL OF GRACE

EVER-VIRGIN

BLESSED AMONG ALL WOMEN

OUR BLESSED LADY

FIRST DISCIPLE OF JESUS

GOD HAS GIVEN THE BLESSED VIRGIN MARY A singular role in the divine plan of Salvation. In this chapter we explore the singular graces that God has bestowed on Mary. We also look at the many titles the Church uses to honor Mary and at the liturgical feasts that remember and celebrate Mary's life and faith.

SOME MARIAN TITLES

THEOTOKOS (MOTHER OF GOD)

PANAGIA (ALL-HOLY ONE)

MEDIATRIX (MEDIATOR)

Faith Focus: These teachings of the Catholic Church are the primary focus of the doctrinal content presented in this chapter:

- ⊙ Mary is truly the Mother of God, Theotokos, since she is the Mother of the eternal Son of God.
- ⊙ Mary, from the first instant of her conception, was totally preserved from the stain of Original Sin and she remained pure from personal sin throughout her life.
- ⊙ Mary remained a virgin in conceiving her Son, in giving birth to him, and throughout her entire life.
- ⊙ Mary is the recipient of singular graces bestowed on her by virtue of the merits of her Son.
- ⊙ Mary is the first disciple of her Son.
- ⊙ Mary is the Mother of the Church.
- ⊙ Mary is the greatest saint of the Church; Catholics have a devotion to Mary that is greater than their devotion to any of the other saints of the Church.

Discipleship Formation: As a result of studying this chapter and discovering the meaning of the faith of the Catholic Church for your life, you should be better able to:

- ⊙ articulate more clearly the faith of the Catholic Church in Mary;
- ⊙ grow in your love for Mary and value her as a companion on your earthly journey;
- ⊙ share your faith in Mary with others;
- ⊙ appreciate why Mary holds a unique place in the hearts of Catholics and other Christians;
- ⊙ learn from Mary's example how to be a disciple of her Son, Jesus;
- ⊙ grow in devotion to Mary, your Mother and the Mother of the Church.

Scripture References: These Scripture references are quoted or referred to in this chapter:
OLD TESTAMENT: **Genesis** 3:14–15; **Isaiah** 7:14–17
NEW TESTAMENT: **Matthew** 2, 13:55, 5:3; **Luke** 1:26–38, 41, 46–55, 2:22–56, 4:34–35; **John** 2:1–11; 19:25–27; **Romans** 8:11; **1 Timothy** 2:5

Faith Glossary: Familiarize yourself with the meaning of these key faith terms. Definitions are found in the Glossary: **Annunciation, Assumption, Evangelist, Immaculate Conception, liturgical year,** *Magnificat,* *Mediatrix,* **New Eve,** *Panagia,* **perpetual virginity of Mary, public ministry (of Jesus),** *Theotokos,* **Visitation**

Faith Words: Immaculate Conception; Assumption
Learn by Heart: Mary's words to St. Juan Diego
Learn by Example: Nuestra Señora de Guadalupe and St. Juan Diego Cuauhtlatoatzin

Why does the Church honor Mary?

OPENING CONVERSATION

Check out what you already know about Mary. Don't worry if you are unable to answer all these questions—you will find the answers as you work through the chapter.

- What can you recall from both the Old Testament and the New Testament about Mary?
- What is the most widely prayed prayer to Mary?
- How many of the titles that the Church uses for Mary can you name?
- How many Marian feasts and devotions can you name?

A TREASURY OF MARIAN PRAYERS AND DEVOTIONS

The Catholic Church has a treasury of prayers that express her faith in Mary. Some of these prayers are in the 'Catholic Prayers, Devotions and Practices' section of this text. The Hail Mary is the most widely prayed prayer to Mary. Take a moment and silently pray the Hail Mary. Pause after each line and ask yourself, 'What do these words say about Mary?'

AVE MARIA/HAIL MARY

Dios te salve, María.
Hail Mary, full of grace,
Llena eres de gracia:
the Lord is with thee.
El Señor es contigo.
Bendita tú eres entre todas las mujeres.
Blessed art thou among women
Y bendito es el fruto de tu vientre:
Jesús.
and blessed is the fruit of thy womb, Jesus.

Santa María, Madre de Dios,
Holy Mary, Mother of God,
ruega por nosotros pecadores,
pray for us sinners,
ahora y en la hora de nuestra muerte.
Amén.
now and at the hour of our death. Amen.

REFLECT AND DISCUSS

- What truths do the words of the Hail Mary help you recall about Mary?
- When do you pray the Hail Mary? Do you sometimes pray the Hail Mary spontaneously and alone?

DEVOTION TO MARY

The Blessed Virgin Mary has always been venerated by the Church. Devotion to Mary is a deeply rooted and abiding characteristic of our Catholic faith. Catholics have a 'devotion' to Mary that is greater than their devotion to any of the other saints of the Church. Catholics do not worship Mary; we worship and give adoration only to God. Blessed John Paul II reminded us of the devotion Catholics have to Mary when he said:

Although veneration of the faithful for Mary is superior to their devotion to the other saints, it is nevertheless inferior to the cult of adoration reserved to God, from which it essentially differs. . . . While the faithful call upon Mary as 'Mother of God' and contemplate in her the highest dignity conferred upon a creature, they are still not offering her a veneration equal to that of the divine Persons. There is an infinite distance between Marian veneration and worship of the Trinity and the incarnate word.
—Blessed Pope John Paul II,
General Audience of October 22, 1997

MATER SALVATORIS | BERNHARD VOGEL, AFTER JOHANN KUPETZKY

Catholics thank and praise God for blessing Mary so profusely. We draw on her example and ask for her prayers and intercession. Mary does not have the power to answer our prayers; only God has that power. We ask Mary to intercede for us because of our trust in her and her love for us. Mary is already in Heaven and knows better than we do how to praise God and pray to him. When she and the other saints were on earth, they imitated the compassion of Jesus and cooperated with the grace of God to live the Great Commandment and the New Commandment. We believe and trust she will do the same for us and for the souls in Purgatory and that her prayers for us will be effective with her Son, Jesus. In a strict sense we do not 'pray' to Mary; rather, we pray 'in communion with her' to God. The Church reminds us of this truth when she teaches: 'Because of Mary's singular cooperation with the action of the Holy Spirit, the Church loves to pray in communion with the Virgin Mary' (*Catechism of the Catholic Church* [CCC], no. 2682).

OVER TO YOU
⊙ When and why do you pray to Mary?
⊙ What is your favorite prayer to Mary?
⊙ In what other ways do you express your devotion to Mary?

MARY'S UNIQUE ROLE IN GOD'S PLAN
The initial promise of salvation was revealed in Genesis 3:15. We read:

The LORD God said to the serpent, . . .
'I will put enmity between you and the woman,
    and between your offspring and hers;
he will strike your head,
    and you will strike his heel'.
—Genesis 3:14–15

St. Thomas Aquinas taught that Mary uttered her 'Yes' in the name of all human nature

Mary's 'Yes' overturned the course of human history. Mary's 'Yes', her free cooperation with the **grace** of the Holy Spirit, to be the Mother of the Incarnate Son of God, the One whom she would name Jesus because he would save his people from their sins, marks the beginning of the coming about of the 'new and everlasting Covenant'.

Throughout her whole life 'Mary responded with the obedience of faith' (CCC, no. 494) and in hope and out of love to everything God asked of her. 'She stands out among the poor and humble of the Lord, who confidently hope for and receive salvation from him' (Vatican II, *Constitution on the Church*, no. 55).

The Church has come to understand that the 'woman' prefigures Mary and her 'offspring' prefigures Jesus. The Devil will have no power over her and her 'offspring'. Mary's 'Yes' was the beginning of the fulfillment of the divine promise made in Genesis 3:15. Mary is the **New Eve**. Mary is honored as the Glory of Israel, the Tower of David and the Ark of the Covenant. She was the culmination of a long line of such holy women as Sarah, Rebecca, Rachel, Miriam, Deborah, Hannah, Judith and Esther.

St. Thomas Aquinas taught that Mary uttered her 'Yes' 'in the name of all human nature'. The *Catechism* adds, 'By her obedience she became the new Eve, mother of the living' (CCC, no. 511).

THINK, PAIR AND SHARE

- Look up and read Matthew 2; Luke 2:22–38, 41–52 and John 2:1–11, 19:25–27.
- Work with a partner to create a 'Profile of Mary' based on these Gospel passages.
- What does your profile reveal about the early Church's belief in Mary?

WHAT ABOUT YOU PERSONALLY?

- What most inspires you about Mary?

Hail Mary, full of grace, . . .
Blessed are you among women

What hymns to Mary do you sing with your parish at Mass? One hymnal commonly used in Catholic churches in the United States of America lists more than twenty-five Marian hymns, the earliest of which dates from the year 1080. The 'Ave Maria' is the most commonly sung hymn to Mary. You will remember that its opening words are from the angel Gabriel's greeting to Mary at the **Annunciation**: 'Greetings, favored one! The Lord is with you' (Luke 1:28). Catholics around the world repeat this salutation and greeting every time we pray or sing the Hail Mary, the Ave Maria.

Gabriel's Greeting

Hail Mary, full of grace,
The Lord is with thee.

Spanish
Dios te salve, María, llena eres de gracia,
el Señor es contigo.

Tagalog (spoken in the Philippines)
Aba Ginoong Maria, napupuno ka ng grasiya,
Ang Panginoong Diyos ay sumasaiyo.

Indonesian
Salam Maria penuh rahmat Tuhan besertamu,
Terpujilah engkau diantara wanita.

Luganda (spoken in Uganda)
Mirembe Maria,
ojjudde eneema,
Omukama ali nawe.

THE ANNUNCIATION | JEAN BELLEGAMBE

OPENING CONVERSATION
⊙ What is your favorite Marian hymn? Why is it your favorite?
⊙ Share the lyrics of that hymn and explain what they say about Mary.

MARY, FULL OF GRACE: FREE FROM ALL SIN
God chose Mary to be the Mother of his Incarnate Son, Jesus, 'from all eternity' for her extraordinary role in the divine plan of Salvation (CCC, no. 488). The Catholic Church has come to understand the angel's words, 'Greetings, favored

one! The Lord is with you' (Luke 1:28), to mean that God blessed Mary with the singular grace of being free from sin from the first moment of her conception in the womb of her mother, St. Anne. The Catholic Church names this singular grace the **Immaculate Conception.** Pope Pius IX in 1854 in his Apostolic Constitution *Ineffabilis Deus* ('God Ineffable') defined the Immaculate Conception of Mary to be a dogma of the faith. An Apostolic Constitution is a formal decree by the Pope to the whole Church declaring an official teaching of the Catholic Church. *Ineffabilis Deus* teaches:

The most Blessed Virgin Mary was, from the first moment of her conception, by a singular grace and privilege of almighty God and by virtue of the merits of Jesus Christ, Savior of the human race, preserved immune from all stain of original sin.

—*Ineffabilis Deus*, Pius IX, quoted in CCC, no. 491

God blessed Mary more than any other created person by choosing her to bear the One who 'takes away the sins of the world'. Because of her role as the Mother of God's own Son, God has given her this singular grace.

FROM THE CATECHISM
What the Catholic faith believes about Mary is based on what it believes about Christ, and what it teaches about Mary illumines in turn its faith in Christ.

—CCC, no. 487

FAITH WORD

IMMACULATE CONCEPTION | JUAN ANTONIO DE FRÍAS Y ESCALANTE

Immaculate Conception

A dogma of the Church that teaches that Mary was conceived without Original Sin due to the anticipated redemptive graces of her Son, Jesus.
—*United States Catholic Catechism for Adults (USCCA)*, 515

LET'S PROBE DEEPER
- Read Luke 1:26–38, Luke's account of the Annunciation, and reflect on the qualities that Mary displayed; for example, she believed; she heard God's will; she accepted that God had chosen her to be the Mother of the Savior; she trusted God.
- Which of Mary's qualities do you see in yourself? Would you like to develop in yourself?
- Pray to Mary to help you develop these qualities.

MARIAN DEVOTION: EXPRESSED IN MARY'S TITLES
The Catholic Church uses many titles to express her faith in and devotion to Mary. You can read many of these titles in the Litany of the Blessed Virgin Mary (or the Litany of Loreto). We will now briefly explore the faith of the Church that is

expressed in the titles **Theotokos** (Mother of God, or God-Bearer), **Panagia** (All-holy), Blessed Virgin and **Mediatrix** (Mediator).

Theotokos: *Theotokos,* meaning 'God-Bearer' or 'Mother of God', is the singular most important title for Mary. In the fifth century, Nestorius, the Patriarch of Constantinople, proposed that there were two separate persons in Christ, one divine and one human. As a consequence of his teaching, Nestorius also erroneously taught that Mary was the mother of the human Jesus but not of the divine Person, Jesus; and so she did not deserve the title *Theotokos,* Mother of God. The Church condemned Nestorius and his teaching as heresy at the Ecumenical Council held in Ephesus in 431 and she decreed that Mary is truly the Mother of God 'since she is the mother of the eternal Son of God made man, who is God himself' (CCC, no. 509).

Panagia: 'The Fathers of the Eastern tradition call the Mother of God "the All-Holy" (*Panagia*) and celebrate her as "free from any stain of sin, as though fashioned by the Holy Spirit and formed as a new creature" [*Constitution on the Church*, no. 56]' (CCC, no. 493). Mary is 'the most excellent fruit of redemption' (CCC, no. 508); she is indeed 'full of grace', the *Holy* Mother of God. By the grace of God Mary remained free from any stain of sin, from both Original Sin and from every personal sin, her whole life long (see CCC, no. 493). Mary's singular graces did not take away her free will. She still had the free will to say 'Yes' or 'No' to God throughout her life on earth.

Panagia iconography

An icon (from the Greek *eikōn* meaning 'image') is a religious work of art, most commonly a painting. *Panagia* is also the term for a particular type of icon of Mary. In a *panagia* icon Mary faces the viewer directly. She is also usually depicted full length with her hands in the *orans* (prayer) position and with the image of Christ as a child in front of her chest.

The *panagia* icon on this page is an icon of the late-seventeenth-century Russian school. You can see the influence of Byzantine art in the solemn and static posture and in the pensive look on the Virgin's face. Christ is shown in a roundel on the Virgin's chest to indicate symbolically that he is in her womb. The archangels, the halo of the Virgin, and the roundel containing the image of Christ suggest a triangle, the Trinity. The Virgin is turned outward, drawing the person looking at the icon into relationship with her and her child.

RUSSIAN SCHOOL, LATE 17TH-CENTURY PANAGIA ICON

Blessed Virgin: The Church, from her beginning, came to believe that Mary's conception of her only Son was by the power of the Holy Spirit. It was in 'the fulfillment of the divine promise given through the prophet Isaiah, "Behold, a virgin shall conceive and bear a son"' (CCC, no. 497; see also Isaiah 7:14–17). The Church grew in her understanding of the Scriptures and of the Incarnation. She also grew in her understanding that Mary was 'always a virgin'. This teaching of the Church is named the **perpetual virginity of Mary.** 'Mary "remained a virgin in conceiving her Son, a virgin in giving birth to him, a virgin in carrying him, a virgin in nursing him at her breast, always a virgin": with her whole being she is "the handmaid of the Lord"'(CCC, no. 510). Mary's perpetual virginity 'is *the sign of her faith* . . . and of her undivided gift of herself to God's will' (CCC, no. 506).

Some Christians and non-believers object to the Catholic Church's teaching on the perpetual virginity of Mary. They base their objection on the grounds that the New Testament speaks of the 'brothers and sisters' of Jesus. The use of those terms, however, needs to be understood within the context of the time and culture in which Jesus and the members of the Apostolic Church lived. In the world of that time, such terms did not necessarily mean siblings; these were common terms also used for cousins and even close friends.

Mediatrix: A *panagia* icon is often placed in the apse of the sanctuary, above the altar, in Eastern churches. Its presence there symbolically points to Mary's privilege as an intercessor and Mediatrix between people and Christ. The title Mediatrix does not in any way deny that Jesus Christ alone is the 'one *mediator* between God and the human race' (1 Timothy 2:5). Pope John Paul II reminded us that the Church's honoring Mary as Mediatrix flows from and is linked to her motherhood. He taught: 'Mary's mediation is essentially defined by her divine motherhood. Recognition of her role as Mediatrix is moreover implicit in the expression "our Mother"' (General Audience, October 1, 1997). Mary is the Mother of God and the Mother of the Church.

OVER TO YOU

⊙ What is your favorite title for Mary?
⊙ How does that title influence your relationship with Mary?
⊙ How does honoring Mary with that title deepen your relationship with Jesus Christ?

JOURNAL EXERCISE

⊙ Using the title for Mary that you selected, compose your own prayer to Mary.
⊙ Learn this prayer by heart and pray it often.

CELEBRATING THE CHURCH'S FAITH IN MARY

The Catholic Church all over the world celebrates many feast days throughout the **liturgical year** to honor Mary. During these celebrations the Church gives thanks and praise to God for his wonderful gift of Mary. Here are some of the Marian feasts the Catholic Church in the United States of America celebrates:

Solemnity of Mary, Mother of God (January 1). The Church gathers to remember and celebrate Mary's role and title—*Theotokos*, Mother of God. On this same day each year, the Catholic Church also celebrates World Peace Day. Many people pray to Mary, Queen of Peace, and ask for her

OUR LADY OF PERPETUAL HELP

help in bringing peace to the world. This Solemnity of Mary, Mother of God, is also a Holy Day of Obligation in the United States of America.

Feast of the Presentation of the Lord (February 2). On this day the faithful remember and celebrate Mary and Joseph's presenting Jesus in the Temple at Jerusalem shortly after his birth and dedicating him to God, according to Jewish custom and law.

Solemnity of the Annunciation of the Lord (March 25). The Church gathers to remember and celebrate the conception of Jesus in the womb of the Virgin Mary by the power of the Holy Spirit.

Feast of the Visitation of the Blessed Virgin Mary (May 31). The Church gathers to remember and celebrate Mary's visit to Elizabeth. The whole month of May is one of special devotion to Mary.

Solemnity of the Assumption of the Blessed Virgin Mary (August 15). The Church gathers to remember and celebrate that Mary, at the end of her life on earth, was assumed, body and soul, into Heaven. Mary's Assumption is a foreshadowing of our own 'resurrection of the body'. This feast is a Holy Day of Obligation in the United States of America.

Feast of the Nativity of the Blessed Virgin Mary (September 8). The Church gathers to remember and celebrate the beginning of Mary's life on earth and the dawning of the fulfillment of the divine plan of Salvation.

Solemnity of the Immaculate Conception of the Blessed Virgin Mary: Patronal Feast Day of the United States of America (December 8). The Church gathers to remember and celebrate that Mary was conceived in the womb of St. Anne, her mother, without Original Sin, and she remained free from sin her whole life. This feast is a Holy Day of Obligation in the United States of America.

AZULEJO TILEWORK IN PORTO, PORTUGAL

Feast of Our Lady of Guadalupe (December 12). The Church gathers to remember and celebrate Mary's appearance to St. Juan Diego and her proclamation of God's love for all people. Mary, the Virgin of Guadalupe, is Patron of the Americas.

TALK IT OVER
- How does your parish celebrate these or other Marian feasts?
- In what other ways does your parish community venerate and show its love for Mary?

OVER TO YOU
- Look up all the Marian feasts celebrated by the Church. On your calendar, mark the dates on which these feasts are celebrated.
- Join with the Church on those days. Celebrate your faith and share your love for Mary.

The motherhood of Mary

Each year on the second Sunday of May, people of all faiths celebrate Mother's Day in the United States of America. The celebration of a day set aside to honor mothers began in 1870, and President Woodrow Wilson proclaimed it a national holiday in 1914. Annual celebrations honoring mothers and celebrating motherhood take place in more than forty countries in other parts of the world, most often in March, April or May.

Catholics honor and celebrate the motherhood of Mary during the entire month of May. The custom of Christians dedicating May to Mary can be dated back to medieval times. Today, we decorate Marian shrines and make a special effort to pray the Rosary daily during May. Many schools and parishes hold a May Crowning. Some families set up and decorate a shrine to Mary in their home.

OPENING CONVERSATION

- ☉ How does your family celebrate Mother's Day? Share any unique customs your family may have.
- ☉ How does your parish honor Mary during the month of May? Share any unique customs your parish may have.
- ☉ How does your family celebrate May as the month of Mary in your home?

THE MOTHERHOOD OF MARY

We have already explored that the most important honor we give to Mary is venerating her as 'Mother'. Mary is the Mother of God, the Mother of Jesus and the Mother of the Church. The Litany of Loreto, or the Litany of the Blessed Virgin Mary, also honors Mary as 'Mother of divine grace', 'Most pure', Mother of chaste love', 'Mother and Virgin', 'Sinless Mother', 'Dearest of mothers', 'Model of motherhood', 'Mother of good counsel', 'Mother of our Creator' and 'Mother of our Savior'. All our devotion to Mary flows from her motherhood. Let us take a look at Mary's role in the life of her Son.

Infancy and early years of Jesus: The Gospels according to Matthew and Luke tell us that while she was a young virgin and probably a teenager and only betrothed (engaged) to Joseph, Mary conceived Jesus by the power of the Holy Spirit. She gave birth to her Son in the poorest of circumstances, fled from a murderous ruler and became a refugee in a strange country. We also know that when Mary and her husband, Joseph, presented Jesus

CHRIST IN THE HOUSE OF HIS PARENTS | JOHN EVERETT MILLAIS

It is safe to conclude that Jesus learned the skill of carpentry from Joseph

in the Temple, they were greeted by an elderly holy man named Simeon and an elderly holy woman, Anna, both of whom recognized Jesus to be the promised Messiah. They praised God, and Simeon proclaimed, 'My eyes have seen your salvation', and he alerted Mary that 'a sword will pierce your own soul too'. These were daunting words for a young teenage mother to hear and to keep in her heart as she loved and cared for her son in Nazareth, where he 'grew and became strong, filled with wisdom; and the favor of God was upon him'. (Read Luke 2:22–35, 39.)

There is nothing more known of the infancy and childhood years of Jesus except for the notable incident when the Holy Family traveled with their relatives to Jerusalem for the annual celebration of Passover when Jesus was twelve years old. At the conclusion of the festival, Jesus stayed behind, and Mary and Joseph left the family caravan and, with 'great anxiety', searched for their only Son. They found him in the Temple, 'sitting among the teachers, listening to them and asking them questions'. Luke continues:

He said to them, 'Why were you searching for me? Did you not know that I must be in my Father's house?' But they did not understand what he said to them. Then he went down with them and came to Nazareth, and was obedient to them. His mother treasured all these things in her heart. And Jesus increased in wisdom and in years, and in divine and human favor.

—Luke 2:49–52

The hidden years of Jesus: During those years in Nazareth (perhaps about eighteen years) Jesus 'increased in wisdom and in years, and in divine and human favor' (Luke 2:52). Since Jesus is identified as 'the carpenter's son' (Matthew 13:55), it is safe to conclude that, during those years in Nazareth (which are also named 'the hidden years' of Jesus' life), Jesus learned the skill of carpentry and other building skills from Joseph. He also took part regularly in the life of the local synagogue. Remembering the prophecy of Simeon about her own broken heart, Mary must also have had a heavy heart about Jesus' safety and his future as she pondered the words of Simeon in the Temple:

THE MARRIAGE AT CANA | GERARD DAVID

Jesus' public ministry began with his response to his mother's request at the wedding feast at Cana

'This child is destined for the falling and the rising of many in Israel, and to be a sign that will be opposed so that the inner thoughts of many will be revealed—and a sword will piece your own soul too.'

—Luke 4:34–35

It was during those hidden years in Nazareth that Joseph, according to ancient tradition, died, leaving Mary to care for her Son as a single parent. Jesus truly grew in wisdom and in years, and his mother certainly had a significant role in his life as a teenager and young adult.

The public life and last days of Jesus: Once again, the four accounts of the Gospel contain few instances of Mary taking part in Jesus' public life and ministry from the time of his baptism to his Crucifixion. In the Fourth Gospel John tells us that, at the wedding feast at Cana (read John 2:1–11) in Galilee, Mary knew that Jesus' time had come. When the newly married couple's wedding ran out of wine, she brought this dilemma to Jesus' attention, overruled his hesitation, and told the servants to obey his instructions. His **public ministry** began with his response to his mother's request.

While little is written about Mary accompanying Jesus during the three years of his public life and ministry, the Gospel tells us that she was a witness to the Paschal Mystery of Christ's suffering, Death and Resurrection. Mary was present with her Son during his final days and hours. Mary, Mother Most Sorrowful, stood at the foot of the Cross with the other women disciples of her Son and 'the disciple whom Jesus loved' (read John 19:25–27). We cannot begin to imagine the depth of her grief as she looked upon her suffering Son and listened to his final words. The sword that Simeon had spoken of had surely pierced her heart.

- How does the 'motherhood of Mary' inspire you to live your life as a disciple of her Son?
- What detail from the life of Mary do you find most inspiring and most challenging for your own life as a disciple of Jesus?
- How does it lead you to a deeper faith in her Son?

MARY'S LAST DAYS ON EARTH

The Gospels speak neither of Mary's final days on earth nor of her death. Sacred Tradition, reflecting the beliefs of the Apostolic Church, teaches that, at the end of Mary's life on earth, God brought her whole person, body and soul, to Heaven, to share in the glory of her Son. In his 1950 Apostolic Constitution *The Most Bountiful God* (*Munificentissimus Deus*), Pope Pius XII proclaimed this belief, which is called the **Assumption**, to be a dogma of faith revealed by God. Mary's Assumption is a symbol of our hope that our bodies will be raised from the dead on the last day. 'The resurrection of the body means not only that the immortal soul will live on after death, but that even our "mortal bodies" [see Romans 8:11] will come to life again' (CCC Glossary; see also CCC, no. 988).

JOURNAL EXERCISE

- Create your own artistic expression of the motherhood of Mary in words or images.
- Share your work with family and friends.

THE ASSUMPTION | LORENZO LOTTO

FAITH WORD

Assumption

The dogma that when the Blessed Virgin Mary's earthly life was finished, because she was sinless, she was kept from corruption and taken soul and body into heavenly glory.

—USCCA, 505

Mary, the first disciple and first evangelist

The *Catholic Almanac* identifies more than one hundred and five religious communities in the United States who commit to live the Gospel after the example of Mary, the first disciple of her Son. In addition, there are numerous laypeople who are members of organizations and movements approved by the Catholic Church who seek to live a life of holiness and discipleship as Mary did. One example of the latter is the 'Magnificat' movement.

Magnificat was set up by a group of Catholic women from the Archdiocese of New Orleans whose members commit to live out the spirit of Mary's visit to Elizabeth. Magnificat's first function took place on October 7, 1981. Among the many objectives of Magnificat is to sponsor the 'Magnificat Meal'. The Magnificat Meal is a two- to three-hour gathering that takes place at least four times a year. Women come together and engage in communal worship and prayer and listen to one woman's personal expression of God's action in her life.

MADONNA OF THE MAGNIFICAT | BOTTICELLI

OPENING CONVERSATION

- Do you know of any similar movement in your area where young people can share their faith by reaching out to people in need?
- How do you see people's devotion to Mary shaping their faith life?

OVER TO YOU

- If you are not already involved in such a group, might you become involved, or perhaps even suggest to your friends that you think about setting up such a group?

THE MAGNIFICAT: MARY'S CANTICLE OF FAITH AND PRAISE

The Gospel account of the Visitation in Luke 1:39–56 tells of Mary travelling 'in haste' after the Annunciation to visit Elizabeth, her elderly and pregnant relative. Luke the Evangelist writes that upon her arrival at Elizabeth's and Zechariah's home, Elizabeth's unborn son (St. John the Baptist) 'leaped in her womb' when Elizabeth heard Mary's greeting; and Elizabeth, 'filled with the Holy Spirit', exclaimed: 'Blessed are you among women, and blessed is the fruit of your womb' (Luke 1:41). In response, Mary burst into prayer, praising God, 'My soul magnifies the Lord.' Mary's prayer of praise is known as the *Magnificat*. (Read the *Magnificat* in Luke 1:46–55.) The *Magnificat* is 'the song both of the Mother of God and of the Church' (CCC, no. 2619). The Church prays the *Magnificat* and praises God every day as part of Evening Prayer of the Liturgy of the Hours. Praying the *Magnificat* regularly provides Christians with an inspiration, a vision and a model for living the Gospel.

Blessed Pope John Paul II in his 1987 encyclical letter *Mother of the Redeemer* (*Redemptoris Mater*) reminds us: 'the truth about the God who saves . . . cannot be separated from the manifestation of his love of preference for the poor and humble, that love which, celebrated in the *Magnificat*, is later expressed in the words and works of Jesus' (*Mother of the Redeemer*, no. 37). The 'humble' radiate in their life an acknowledgment that God alone is the center of their life. The humble recognize themselves to be truly poor. They acknowledge that all they are and all their blessings are gifts from the Lord. Such humility is known as 'poverty of spirit'; it the source of true wealth. 'Blessed are the poor in spirit, for theirs is the kingdom of heaven' (Matthew 5:3).

THINK, PAIR AND SHARE

⊙ What does the Canticle of Mary, or the *Magnificat*, reveal about Mary?
⊙ How does the Magnificat movement described above manifest the faith of Mary expressed in the *Magnificat*?
⊙ Why is Mary such a model for all Christians?

OVER TO YOU

⊙ How can the *Magnificat* be a source of inspiration for you as you strive to be a disciple of Jesus?

MARY, MODEL OF FAITH— FIRST DISCIPLE AND FIRST EVANGELIST

Mary is the first disciple of her Son. She is our model of faith and discipleship. The Church at the Second Vatican Council (1962–65) summarized Mary's faith and discipleship:

Committing herself whole-heartedly to God's saving will and impeded by no sin, she devoted herself totally, as a handmaid of the Lord, to the person and work of her Son, under him and with him, serving the mystery of redemption, by the grace of Almighty God. . . . [T]he holy Fathers see Mary . . . as freely cooperating in the work of human salvation through faith and obedience.

—*Constitution on the Church*, no. 56

Elizabeth exclaimed: 'Blessed are you among women, and blessed is the fruit of your womb'

THE VISITATION (DETAIL) | JACOPO PONTORMO

Mary was also the first evangelist; she was the first to announce the Good News of Salvation. Mary was 'the first messenger of the gospel', as Bishop Perrier of Lourdes has called her. With wonder and awe she shared the joy that filled her heart. The account of the Visitation reminds us that being a disciple of Jesus does not only include delivering a message in words; it also includes sharing the Good News with others in a way that fosters their encounter with Jesus, as Mary's encounter with Elizabeth did. Mary is the handmaid of the Lord; she is a model of faith, hope and love for God. At the Annunciation she committed herself totally to God and to the vocation to which God called her, saying, 'Here am I, the servant of the Lord' (Luke 1:38). Mary was ready to give her total self to the Lord, accepting while not yet knowing the cost. The depth of that commitment was fully revealed at the foot of the Cross, and the joy of that commitment was revealed at the Resurrection and her own Assumption.

TALK IT OVER

⊙ What aspects of Mary's life model discipleship for you?

⊙ How can you integrate these qualities into your own life?

⊙ Give an example of these qualities in action in your school or parish.

MARY, MOTHER OF OUR CHURCH

The Fourth Gospel passes on this encounter of Mary and 'the beloved disciple' with her dying Son. 'When Jesus saw his mother and the disciple whom he loved standing beside her, he said to his mother, "Woman, here is your son." Then he said to the disciple, "Here is your mother" (John 19:26–27).

From apostolic times the Church has interpreted these words of Jesus as his 'handing over' his mother to be the Mother of all his disciples. Mary, the Mother of Jesus, the Incarnate Son of God, is our Mother, too. She is the Mother of the Church; she is the 'Help of Christians'. Mary guides and supports us to continue the work of her Son, the work of the Church. Mary is 'the symbol and the most perfect realization of the Church' (CCC, no. 507). '[I]n a very special way she cooperated by her obedience, faith, hope, and burning charity in the work of the Savior in restoring supernatural life to souls. For this reason she is mother to us in the order of grace' (*Constitution on the Church*, no. 61). Mary is the first and best flowering of who and what we have been called to become.

JOURNAL EXERCISE

⊙ Think of your own family and friendships. How can you bring the spirit of the *Magnificat* to them?

⊙ How can family members and friends help one another to live their faith in Jesus?

JUDGE AND ACT

REVIEW WHAT YOU HAVE LEARNED

Look back over this chapter and reflect on the teachings of the Catholic Church on the Blessed Virgin Mary and her unique role in the life of the Church and in the life of each member of the Church.

- Mary is truly the Mother of God, *Theotokos*, since she is the Mother of the eternal Son of God.
- Mary, from the first instant of her conception, was totally preserved from the stain of Original Sin and she remained pure from personal sin throughout her life.
- Mary remained a virgin in conceiving her Son, in giving birth to him, and throughout her entire life.
- Mary is the recipient of singular graces bestowed on her by virtue of the merits of her Son.
- Mary is the first evangelist and the first disciple of her Son.
- Mary is the Mother of the Church.
- Mary is the greatest saint of the Church; Catholics have a devotion to Mary that is greater than their devotion to any other saint of the Church. There is a distinct difference between the Church's veneration of Mary and her worship of God.

OVER TO YOU

- What wisdom for your life did you learn from exploring Mary as the first disciple and first evangelist?

LEARN BY EXAMPLE

The story of Nuestra Señora de Guadalupe and St. Juan Diego Cuauhtlatoatzin

Our Blessed Lady appeared to Juan Diego, a Nahuatl (Aztec) Indian convert to Christianity, at dawn on December 9, 1531, on Tepeyac Hill near Mexico City as Juan made his way to Mass. After identifying herself to be 'Mary, the Mother of the True God', 'the Lady' asked Juan to go and tell the Bishop of Mexico City that she was requesting that a shrine be built on the spot where she appeared. The shrine was to be a sign and witness of her love, compassion and protection, especially for people in need. After listening to Juan, the bishop simply dismissed him.

'The Lady' appeared to Juan on two further occasions, each time instructing him to return to the bishop and deliver her request. On December 12, while Juan Diego was on his way to bring a priest to his dying uncle, 'The

Lady' appeared to him for the fourth time, assuring Juan of his uncle's recovery. She then told him to go to a frosty summit of the rocky and barren hill and gather roses—a strange request since it would be very unusual to find roses in December. Juan did what 'The Lady' asked and returned with the roses. She arranged the roses in his cloak and sent him, yet again, to the bishop.

When Juan opened up his cloak to show the roses to the bishop, they saw a beautiful image of 'The Lady'. The bishop now realized the truth of Juan's request and soon after he began the building of the shrine on the top of Mount Tepeyac. The image you see on the previous page can still be seen behind the main altar in the present Basilica of Our Lady of Guadalupe, which is near the site of the original basilica. Millions of pilgrims from all over Mexico and the world visit the basilica to venerate Nuestra Señora de Guadalupe to implore her intercession, in response to her promise to Juan, 'I am here as your mother.'

Juan Diego was canonized on July 31, 2002 by Blessed Pope John Paul II. The Pope also declared Our Lady of Guadalupe to be the Patron of the Americas. The Feast of Our Lady of Guadalupe is celebrated on December 12 and the memorial of St. Juan Diego Cuauhtlatoatzin on December 9.

REFLECT AND SHARE

⊙ Reflect on these words that Mary spoke to Juan Diego: 'I am here as your mother'.

⊙ Share how you respond to these words.

OVER TO YOU

⊙ Read and reflect on this prayer to Our Lady of Guadalupe:

God of power and mercy,
you blessed the Americas at Tepeyac
with the presence of the Virgin Mary of
    Guadalupe.
May her prayers help all men and women
to accept each other as brothers and sisters.
Through your justice present in our hearts,
may your peace reign in the world.
We ask this through our Lord Jesus Christ, your
    Son,
who lives and reigns with you and the Holy
    Spirit,
one God for ever and ever. Amen.

SHARE YOUR FAITH WITH FAMILY AND FRIENDS

⊙ In what ways is Mary the model for your life as a disciple of Jesus Christ?

⊙ Share your devotion to Mary with family and friends. Perhaps you might also share what you have learned about Mary through your study of this chapter.

⊙ Discuss how devotion to Mary might impact your relationship with one another.

JUDGE AND ACT

⊙ In Mary's honor, choose some act of justice or compassion that you can do with your friends to be a living witness of God to the downtrodden and poor.

BRONZE RELIEF OF JUAN DIEGO | GUADALUPE SHRINE, MEXICO

LEARN BY HEART

'I am here as your mother.'

MARY'S WORDS TO ST. JUAN DIEGO

Invitation to Prayer

LEADER

Our closing prayer reflection is a meditation on the icon of the Black Madonna of Częstochowa. Our Lady of Częstochowa is revered and honored as the Queen and Protector of Poland. Every year thousands of pilgrims visit Częstochowa and the National Shrine of Our Lady of Częstochowa in Doylestown, Pennsylvania to express their love and devotion to Mary.

We begin by asking the Holy Trinity to guide our meditation.

All pray the Sign of the Cross together.

Prayer of Meditation

All spend some time in silence looking at the colors, background, clothes, facial expressions and other details of the icon.

Reflect in silence on these questions:
- What do the details reveal about the faith of the artist?
- What do the details say to you about Mary?
- In what ways does your reflection on this icon deepen your faith? Motivate you to live your faith?

Volunteers may now share their reflections.

Concluding Prayer

LEADER

Together, let us lift up our hearts to Mary and pray:

ALL

Holy Mother of Częstochowa,
   you are full of grace, goodness and mercy.

THE BLACK MADONNA OF CZĘSTOCHOWA

Our Lady of Częstochowa is revered and honored as the Queen and Protector of Poland

I consecrate to you all my thoughts, words and
      actions—my soul and body.
I beseech your blessings and especially your
      prayers for my salvation.
Today I consecrate myself to you, good Mother,
      totally—
      with body and soul amid joy and sufferings,
      to obtain for myself and others your blessings
      on this earth and eternal life in heaven.
Amen.

CHAPTER 10

The Son of Mary: Our Exemplar and Model

JESUS, GOD'S LOVE INCARNATE

GOD REVEALS HIMSELF IN JESUS

JESUS SHOWS US 'THE WAY' TO RESPOND TO GOD

JESUS TEACHES US HOW TO BE FULLY ALIVE, FULLY HUMAN

JESUS REVEALS THE MERCY AND FORGIVENESS OF GOD

JESUS SHOWS US HOW TO LOVE

JESUS SHOWS US WHAT TRUE FRIENDSHIP MEANS

JESUS MAKES IT POSSIBLE FOR US TO KNOW WHOM GOD CREATED US TO BE

THE CATHOLIC CHURCH TEACHES THAT JESUS IS our exemplar and model. In the one divine Person of Jesus the divine nature and a human nature are united. Jesus Christ is truly divine and truly human. Jesus is truly human in all ways except sin. In this chapter we explore how Jesus reveals the dignity and vocation of what it means to be human. We discover the meaning of Jesus' Revelation 'I am the way, and the truth, and the life' (John 14:6) for our life.

KEY CHARACTERISTICS OF JESUS' HUMANITY

AUTHENTICITY

FORGIVENESS AND MERCY

COMPASSION

Faith Focus: These teachings of the Catholic Church are the primary focus of the doctrinal content presented in this chapter:
- ◉ God created the human person in his image and likeness. To be fully human means to accept the person God created us to be.
- ◉ We must respect the dignity of the human person.
- ◉ The Incarnation affirms that we are created good, but in need of salvation, and are meant for the glory of God.
- ◉ Jesus 'is the image of the invisible God, the firstborn of all creation' (Colossians 1:15).
- ◉ 'Man is predestined to reproduce the image of God's Son made man . . . so that Christ shall be the first-born of a multitude of brothers and sisters.' (CCC, no. 381)
- ◉ Jesus invites us to believe in him, to invite him into our hearts and to follow him and his teaching as the path that leads to fullness of life.
- ◉ The baptized are to conform themselves to Christ until he is formed in them.

Discipleship Formation: As a result of studying this chapter and discovering the meaning of the faith of the Catholic Church for your life, you should be better able to:
- ◉ work toward becoming the person whom God created you to be;
- ◉ grow in holiness of life, in your relationship with God the Father, Son and Holy Spirit;
- ◉ respond more intentionally to your encounter with Jesus in Scripture, in the Church and in the people and events of your life;
- ◉ resolve to imitate Jesus and integrate his values into the way you live your life.

Scripture References: These Scripture references are quoted or referred to in this chapter:
OLD TESTAMENT: **Genesis** 1:27, 12:1–4; **Exodus** 34:5–6; **Deuteronomy** 4:37, 7:8–9, 10:15; **2 Samuel** 7:28; **Isaiah** 43:1–7, 49:14–15, 54:8–10, 62:4–5; **Jeremiah** 31:3; **Ezekiel** 16; **Hosea** 2, 11; **Psalms** 85:11, 119:160, 138:2; **Wisdom** 13:1–9; **Malachi** 2:6
NEW TESTAMENT: **Matthew** 3:13–17, 4:1–11, 5:1—7:29, 9:36, 10:1–4, 12:1–14, 14:14, 17:1–9, 18:21–22,19:8–9, 23:37, 26:26–29, 27:55, 28:18; **Mark** 1:9–11, 12–13, 15, 21–28, 2:8–10, 13–17, 3:13–19, 4:12–13 and 40, 5:36, 6:50, 9:2–8, 12:14, 14:22–26, 16:17–20; **Luke** 2:46, 51–52, 3:21–22, 4:1–13, 16–19, 31–37, 6:12–21, 7:11–17, 9:28–36, 10:41–42, 13:10–17, 15:2, 22:14–23; **John** 1:14, 29–51, 2:1–12, 3:16, 4:1–42, 6:63, 7:46, 9:1–41, 11:1–44, 13:1–20, 31–35; 14:6, 8–10, 15:12–17, 17:20–26, 20:31, 21:15–19; **Romans** 4:18, 15:5; **1 Corinthians** 2:7–16, 11:23–26; **Ephesians** 3:9–12; **Philippians** 2:5; **Colossians** 1:15–17, 18; **1 John** 4:7–8, 16

Faith Glossary: Familiarize yourself with the meaning of these key faith terms. Definitions are found in the Glossary: **adoration, compassion, eternal life, Kingdom of God, miracle(s), preferential option for the poor, Redemption, social sin, solidarity, Theological Virtues, Transfiguration**

Faith words: miracle; solidarity
Learn by Heart: John 14:6
Learn by Example: St. Maria Goretti, virgin and martyr

What is the meaning of the Incarnation for us?

All human beings are on a quest. We all search for the meaning and purpose of our life. We ask a myriad of questions to discover the direction to take to make that quest successfully. In fact, the very word 'question' is built on the root 'quest', from the Latin verb *quaerere*, meaning, 'to search, to look for, to navigate, to ask'. Human beings make their life-quest in a variety of ways. Christians follow the way of Jesus. Jesus is the exemplar and model for our life-quest. He is 'the way, and the truth, and the life' (John 14:6). We accept Jesus' invitation, 'Follow me' (Matthew 4:19).

OPENING CONVERSATION

⊙ Consider these statements that reflect issues and questions of concern to young people:
- Things got really bad for me last year, and I nearly dropped out of school. I wondered, 'What's the point?'
- Sometimes I wonder, 'Why am I not better looking, more popular, never good enough to make first chair?'
- What am I going to do after high school? How can I become a 'success'?

⊙ What other life questions are important to ask?

OVER TO YOU

⊙ What are some of the current 'big' questions you are asking? From your many encounters with Jesus in Scripture and the Church, how do you hear Jesus responding?

'WHAT ARE YOU LOOKING FOR?'

The first disciples of Jesus lived during a time of 'expectation'. They were wondering and looking for answers to their questions about the coming Messiah, the Anointed One and Savior whom God promised to send to his people. When John the Baptist was with Andrew and another one of his disciples, John 'watched Jesus walk by' and exclaimed, 'Look, here is the Lamb of God!' (John 1:36). The two disciples began to follow Jesus. Seeing them, Jesus asked, 'What are you looking for?' (John 1:38). Andrew and the other disciple went off with Jesus and remained with him for the rest of the day, no doubt asking him many questions. Sometime later that same day Andrew left the conversation to find his brother, Simon Peter. When he did, he told Peter, 'We have found the Messiah' (John 1:41), and brought him to Jesus.

TALK IT OVER

- Read John 1:35–51.
- What role does questioning have in this Gospel passage?
- What do you think led Andrew to say, 'We have found the Messiah'?

OVER TO YOU

- Imagine Jesus turns to you and asks, 'What are you looking for? Why are you following me?' What is your response?

WHO AM I?

All of life's questions, in some way, are connected with the fundamental question, 'Who am I?' For example, the seemingly simple question 'What will I wear today?' is really asking, 'Who do I want others to know me as?' What we wear gives expression to who we think we are. But there is another underlying question, the answer to which gives direction to our quest. The question is: 'To whom do I go to seek the answers to my questions about life?' Christians answer that question with 'Jesus'. Jesus is the Word of God. His words 'are spirit and life' (John 6:63). Jesus embodies what has been revealed in and through creation. Jesus 'is the image of the invisible God, the firstborn of all creation; for in him all things in heaven and on earth were created, things visible and invisible, whether thrones or dominions or rulers or powers—all things have been created through him and for him. He himself is before all things, and in him all things hold together' (Colossians 1:15–17). The more we come to know

Jesus, the more we come to know ourselves and the person God created us to be. The **Theological Virtues** empower and guide us in this quest.

> ### FROM THE CATECHISM
> Man is predestined to reproduce the image of God's Son made man, . . . so that Christ shall be the first-born of a multitude of brothers and sisters.
>
> —CCC, no. 381

The quest for truth: St. Irenaeus (c. 125–c. 200), bishop of Lyons in modern-day France and Father of the Church, taught: 'The glory of God is the human person fully alive.' The quest for truth about ourselves is ultimately the quest for God, who is Truth (see Deuteronomy 7:9; 2 Samuel 7:28; Psalm 119:160; Wisdom 13:1–9; Malachi 2:6). To strive to be fully human means to cooperate with the grace of God to work at becoming people who are endowed with the special gifts that reflect God: immortality, intellect, free will and the ability to love (see CCC, nos. 356–358, 1702–1706). The Theological Virtue of Faith empowers us to make this quest successfully.

CHRIST EXPOUNDING THE LAW | EDWARD SMITH AFTER DA VINCI

The quest for love: The quest for love is the quest for God, who revealed himself to be love (see 1 John 4:7–8). In Jesus God has revealed his innermost secret (see 1 Corinthians 2:7–16; Ephesians 3:9–12): 'God himself is an eternal exchange of love, Father, Son, and Holy Spirit, and he has destined us to share in that exchange' (CCC, no. 221). (See also Deuteronomy 4:37, 7:8, 10:15; Isaiah 43:1–7, 49:14–15, 54:8–10, 62:4–5; Jeremiah 31:3; Ezekiel 16; Hosea 2, 11; John 3:16; 1 John 4:8, 16.) The more we come to know Jesus and respond to his command to love as he loved (see John 13:31–35), the more we come to know ourselves and the person God created us to be. In Jesus we see that our deepest desire to love and to be loved is central to our growth as children of God. The Theological Virtue of Love empowers us to make this quest successfully.

Hope—the inner, God-given energy for our quest: St. Paul in his Letter to the Romans uses the phrase 'hoping against hope' to describe the power of the virtue of hope. When speaking of Abraham's response to God's invitation (see Genesis 12:1–4), St. Paul wrote, 'Hoping against hope, [Abraham] believed that he would become "the father of many nations"' (Romans 4:18). The Theological Virtue of Hope strengthens us in both our desire and quest to become fully human—to grow to become a clear 'image of God's Son made man'. Hope is the confident expectation that God's desire will come about. Hope is rooted in the very nature of God and is revealed in his unwavering fidelity in keeping and fulfilling his promises (see Exodus 34:6; Psalm 85:11, 138:2). Hope assures us that God desires what is good and best for each and every person.

THINK, PAIR AND SHARE

We see such faith, love and hope at work in the lives of women, men and children of the Church who have lived or are living in some of the most cruel and inhuman places and conditions.

- ⊙ What is the connection between truth and love and hope for a Christian striving to become the person God created them to be?
- ⊙ Who do you know or have read or learned about that models such a life? Discuss with a partner how they 'reproduce the image of God's Son made man' (CCC, no. 381).

JOURNAL EXERCISE

- ⊙ Using words or images, describe or depict how you are striving to be a living image, or icon, of Christ.

The mysteries of Jesus' life

Every Sunday at Mass we listen to the proclamation of the Gospel. Over a three-year cycle we listen to the Gospels of Matthew (Year A), Mark (Year B) and Luke (Year C), and to the Gospel of John during all three years. During the liturgical seasons of Advent, Christmas, Lent and Easter and on various Solemnities of the Lord Jesus we listen to the Gospel accounts of the major events in the story of God's saving work in Jesus. During Ordinary Time we mostly listen to and reflect on the events of Jesus' public life and ministry. Ordinary Time takes place between the end of the Christmas season and the beginning of Lent, and from the Sunday after Pentecost to the Solemnity of Christ the King.

CHRIST IN MAJESTY AND THE FOUR EVANGELISTS | 13TH-CENTURY IVORY

OPENING CONVERSATION

- From hearing the Gospel proclaimed at Mass and from your study of the Gospels and the life of Jesus in theology class, you have already come to know many of the details of the earthly life and saving work of Jesus. List as many key events in Jesus' life as you can.
- Work with a partner. Assemble all the events under the heading 'The Mysteries of Jesus' Life'.

OVER TO YOU

- What is your favorite Gospel story about Jesus?
- How does this story help you come to know Jesus?
- How does it inspire you to live as his disciple?

JESUS: TRUE GOD AND TRUE MAN

At the heart of all Revelation and of the Catholic faith is a Person, Jesus Christ, who is both fully divine and fully human and who is worthy of our belief, **adoration** and love. Jesus is the center—the heart and the defining feature—of our Catholic faith and life. Who is this Jesus who invites us to discipleship?

The four Evangelists (Matthew, Mark, Luke and John) wrote their accounts of the Gospel to pass on the faith of the Apostolic Church in Jesus, which had been passed down by word of mouth. St. John, toward the conclusion of his account of the Gospel, states why he wrote his Gospel: 'so that you may come to believe that Jesus is the Messiah, the Son of God, and that through believing you may have life in his name' (John 20:31). When we read or listen to the Gospels being proclaimed, we are not simply reading writings *about* Jesus. We encounter the risen Lord himself, the Word of God, who invites us to believe in him and to invite him into our hearts and to follow him and his teaching. He is the 'way' that leads to *life* both here on earth and life everlasting. The quest for that *life* is what drives every person.

THINK, PAIR AND SHARE

- Think for a moment about the Jesus you have come to encounter and to know from your reading of or listening to the four accounts of the Gospel.

- Work with a partner and draw up two lists. On one list, name the things you have learned about Jesus that reveal his divinity. On the second, list some of the things that point to his humanity. Share thoughts on how each list helps you come to know Jesus and live as his disciple.
- Join up with another pair of students and assemble your combined image of Jesus, true God and true man.

In all of his life Jesus presents himself as our *model*. He is the 'perfect man' [Vatican II, *Constitution on the Church in the Modern World*, no. 38; see also Romans 15:5, Philippians 2:5], who invites us to become his disciples and follow him' (CCC, no. 520). He 'enables us *to live in him* all that he himself lived, and *he lives it in us*' (CCC, no. 521).

THE MYSTERIES OF THE EARTHLY LIFE OF JESUS

Jesus was born, raised, lived and died. His every deed and word 'is a mystery of *redemption*' (CCC, no. 517). His whole life, his Incarnation, Death, Resurrection and Ascension, is the Revelation that we are good but in need of salvation and are meant for **eternal life** with God. Jesus' whole life is the Revelation of God saving us from the power of sin and death, reconciling us to himself, and restoring fallen humanity to our original vocation of holiness of life with God.

Infancy, Early Years and Hidden Life

(See CCC, nos. 522–534, 564.)

- **Conception and birth.** The Incarnation affirms that we are created good, but in need of salvation, and are meant for eternal glory with God. After a long time of preparation among the people of God, Jesus was born of the Virgin Mary by the power of the Holy Spirit. His birthplace—a stable in Bethlehem—already signifies his solidarity with the poor and the marginalized.

- **Magi and presentation in the Temple.** The three wise men from the East, or Magi, came bearing gifts, signifying that Jesus had been born for the whole world. Jesus' circumcision and presentation in the Temple were 'the sign of his incorporation into Abraham's descendants, into the people of the **covenant**' (CCC, no. 527).

- **Flight into Egypt and return to Nazareth.** Herod ordered the massacre of all children of two years of age and under living in Bethlehem and its surroundings out of his fear that the 'newborn king of the Jews' would threaten his power. Mary and Joseph, warned of this pending massacre in a dream, fled into Egypt, and returned after the death of Herod to raise their child in Nazareth.

- **Finding in the Temple.** When Jesus was twelve years old the Holy Family made the annual pilgrimage to Jerusalem to celebrate Passover and they were ready to return home when Mary and Joseph found that Jesus was not with them. 'They found him in the Temple, sitting among the teachers, listening to them and asking them questions. . . . Then he went down with them and came to Nazareth, and was obedient to them. . . . And Jesus increased in wisdom and in years, and in divine and human favor' (Luke 2:46, 51–52).

- **Hidden life.** For the next eighteen years or so, until he was about thirty years old, Jesus lived a life quite similar to the people of Nazareth of his time. 'By his obedience to Mary and Joseph, as well as by his humble work during the long years in Nazareth, Jesus gives us the example of holiness in the daily life of family and work' (CCC, no. 564).

Public Life and Ministry

(See CCC, nos. 535–560, 565–570.)

The mysteries of Jesus' public life and ministry reveal to us the meaning of being his true disciples.

- ⊙ **Announcement of the Kingdom of God.** The Gospel according to Mark tells us that Jesus' public life began with his proclamation and inauguration of the **Kingdom of God**. 'The time is fulfilled, and the kingdom of God has come near; repent, and believe in the good news' (Mark 1:15).
- ⊙ **Baptism and Transfiguration.** All three Synoptic Gospels give an account of the baptism of Jesus (see Matthew 3:13–17; Mark 1:9–11; Luke 3:21–22; see also John 1:29–34) and of the **Transfiguration** (see Matthew 17:1–9; Mark 9:2–8; Luke 9:28–36). Both the baptism and Transfiguration of Jesus reveal his identity and mission. Matthew concludes his account of the baptism of Jesus: 'just as [Jesus] came up from the water, suddenly the heavens were opened to him and he saw the Spirit of God descending like a dove and alighting on him. And a voice from **heaven** said, "This is my Son, the Beloved, with whom I am well pleased" ' (Matthew 3:16–17). This Revelation of the divinity of Jesus by God the Father was echoed again at the Transfiguration. Luke tells us that the disciples Peter, James and John heard a voice from Heaven say, 'This is my Son, my Chosen; listen to him!' (Luke 9:35).
- ⊙ **The Messiah and his work.** After his Temptation (see Matthew 4:1–11; Mark 1:12–13; Luke 4:1–13), Jesus returned to Nazareth. He entered the synagogue and announced that he was the Messiah and proclaimed his mission (see Luke 4:16–19). Jesus had a special outreach to the poor and made 'active love toward [the poor] the condition for entering his kingdom' (CCC, no. 544). Witnessing to God's love by caring for both the spiritual and bodily needs of people was clearly a central aspect of Jesus' public life and ministry (see Luke 6:18–19).
- ⊙ **The call of the Twelve.** Jesus gathered disciples around him, both women and men. From those disciples Jesus chose the Twelve (see Matthew 10:1–4; Mark 3:13–19a; Luke 6:12–16) to be his closest disciples, the Apostles who would be the leaders among all his disciples. From among the Twelve, he appointed St. Peter to be the leader of the Apostles (see John 21:15–19).
- ⊙ **Miracles of Jesus.** Jesus worked many **miracles**. According to the Fourth Gospel, Jesus' mother, Mary, prompted Jesus to perform his first miracle at the wedding feast at Cana in Galilee. (Read John 2:1–12.) The miracles of Jesus 'strengthen faith in the One who does his Father's works; they bear witness that he is the Son of God' (CCC, no. 548). Jesus' miracles are signs of God's saving work in the world opposing 'the earthly evils of hunger, injustice, illness, and death' (CCC, no. 549).
- ⊙ **Jesus, the Teacher.** Throughout his public life Jesus was respected as a rabbi who taught with the authority of God (see Matthew 5:27–32, 7:28–29, 19:8–9, 28:18; Mark 1:21–28, 2:10, 4:12–13, 16:17–20; Luke 4:31–37; John 7:46). Jesus came to fulfill the law and the prophets (see Matthew 5:17) and he devoted much of his time to teaching. Many of those teachings are gathered in the Sermon on the Mount in Matthew's Gospel (see Matthew 5:1—7:29).
- ⊙ **Final entry into Jerusalem.** Jesus was ever journeying toward Jerusalem—and his final destiny. On his final entry into Jerusalem he entered the holy city riding on a donkey as the people hailed him and welcomed him as they would a king. Later that week, on the night before he died, Jesus gathered with

his disciples for the Passover meal. There, he washed their feet (see John 13:1–20); and, anticipating his Death, he instituted the Eucharist (see Matthew 26:26–29; Mark 14:22–25; Luke 22:14–23; 1 Corinthians 11:23–26).

- ⊙ **Passion and glorification: The Final, or Last, Days; Crucifixion and Burial and Descent into Hell.** After Jesus' betrayal and arrest, his trial and suffering, soldiers from the Roman army crucified him on the hill of Calvary, just outside the city of Jerusalem. The Fourth Gospel tells us that Mary, his mother, and the disciple whom he loved, and other faithful women disciples stood at the foot of the Cross witnessing his death. Before sundown on the day of his death, one of his disciples, Joseph of Arimathea, after requesting permission, buried the body of Jesus in an unused tomb. Jesus truly experienced 'the condition of death, the separation of his soul from his body'. And 'between the time he expired on the cross and the time he was raised from the dead', he joined the others 'in the realm of the dead' (CCC, nos. 624, 632).
- ⊙ **Resurrection and Ascension.** Christ is the 'firstborn from the dead' (Colossians 1:18). 'On the third day Jesus rose again in accordance with the Scriptures. He ascended into heaven and is seated at the right hand of the Father. He will come again in glory to judge the living and the dead, and his kingdom will have no end' (Nicene Creed). 'Jesus Christ, the head

FAITH WORD

Miracle

Miracles are signs of the presence of God at work among us. 'The miracles and other deeds of Jesus are acts of compassion and signs of the Kingdom and salvation' (*United States Catholic Catechism for Adults* [USCCA], 80).

of the Church, precedes us into the Father's glorious kingdom so that we, the members of his Body, may live in the hope of one day being with him for ever' (CCC, no. 666).

TALK IT OVER
- ⊙ What is the key message of the Death, Resurrection and Ascension of Jesus?
- ⊙ Why is the Death, Resurrection and Ascension of Jesus the heart and center of the Gospel?
- ⊙ What questions about human life does the Death, Resurrection and Ascension of Jesus answer?

JOURNAL EXERCISE
- ⊙ Reflect on this teaching of our Catholic faith: Jesus showed his humanity in every event of his human life.
- ⊙ Choose and reflect on one Gospel passage from the life and ministry of Jesus. How does that passage help you encounter Jesus and respond to his invitation to live as his disciple?

Jesus was like us in all things but sin

John's Gospel opens with this description of Jesus, 'And the Word became flesh and lived among us, and we have seen his glory, the glory as of a father's only son, full of grace and truth' (John 1:14). Jesus' deeds and words were truth and love in action. You may have heard it said of an individual that she or he 'talks the talk' but doesn't 'walk the walk'. Well, Jesus steadfastly and faithfully did both. In today's language Jesus' life was 'authentic'.

OPENING CONVERSATION

- ◉ What qualities of human beings point to their being 'authentic'?
- ◉ Who do you know either personally or have come to know in another way who is 'authentic'? Give examples and your reasons.
- ◉ List some of the characteristics of Jesus that you have come to know that witnessed that he lived what he preached. Was he always true to whom he claimed to be?

JESUS WAS ALWAYS TRUE TO HIS IDENTITY AND HIS MISSION

For Christians, Jesus reveals most clearly what it means to be 'authentic'. Jesus, first and above all, lived to do his Father's will. He was always true to being the Son of the Father and to fulfilling the mission the Father gave him. Jesus was one with his Father. He did not base what he said and did on his desire to seek the acceptance or approval of people. He was always faithful to his identity. Recall this dialogue between Jesus and Philip the Apostle:

Philip said to him, 'Lord, show us the Father, and we will be satisfied.' Jesus said to him, 'Have I been with you all this time, Philip, and you still do not know me? Whoever has seen me has seen the Father. How can you say, "Show us the Father"? Do you not believe that I am in the Father and the Father is in me? The words that I say to you I do not speak on my own; but the Father who dwells in me does his works.'

—John 14:8–10

None of his avowed enemies ever accused Jesus of hypocrisy! They accused him of many other things, such as eating with sinners and tax collectors (Mark 2:13–17), inviting tax collectors to be his disciples (Mark 2:14), and healing on the Sabbath (Luke 13:10–17). Some of his enemies also acknowledged that Jesus was a person of his word who taught with authority. For example, Mark tells us that, on one occasion, some Pharisees, when they tried to entrap him so they could bring him up on charges, addressed Jesus, saying, 'Teacher, we know that you are sincere,

CHRIST AND THE WOMAN TAKEN IN ADULTERY | LUCAS CRANACH THE YOUNGER

Jesus is the exemplar and model of mercy and forgiveness who lives in us and we in him

and show deference to no one; for you do not regard people with partiality, but teach the way of God in accordance with truth' (Mark 12:14).

TALK IT OVER
⊙ What other examples can you give of Jesus speaking and living the truth—even when others, including his disciples, were not ready to accept it?

WHAT ABOUT YOU PERSONALLY?
⊙ What helps you to be authentic—true to yourself, true to your word? What prevents you, or people in general, from being authentic?
⊙ How does the witness of Jesus' life help you overcome those obstacles?

GOD OF MERCY AND FORGIVENESS
When he revealed his name and identity to Moses, God declared, 'The LORD, the LORD, a God merciful and gracious, slow to anger, and abounding in steadfast love and faithfulness' (Exodus 34:5–6); Moses then confesses that the Lord is a forgiving God (see Exodus 7). Jesus was the mercy and forgiveness of God 'made flesh'. In his own saving Death and Resurrection he revealed the 'life-changing', 'world-changing'

power of God's mercy and forgiveness. Jesus is the exemplar and model of mercy and forgiveness who lives in us and we in him.

In the Beatitudes Jesus taught, 'Blessed are the merciful, for they will receive mercy' (Matthew 5:7). On another occasion, St. Peter asked Jesus, 'Lord, if another member of the church sins against me, how often should I forgive? As many as seven times?' Jesus responded, 'Not seven times, but, I tell you, seventy-seven times' (Matthew 18:21–22). In other words, there can be no limit to a person's forgiveness. Without God's grace, given to us through Jesus, such mercy and forgiveness would be impossible. It is only by God's grace that we *can* follow the example of Jesus, who lives in us and we in him.

TALK IT OVER
⊙ What other examples can you give of Jesus witnessing to God's mercy and forgiveness?

WHAT ABOUT YOU PERSONALLY?
⊙ What helps you to be a person of mercy and forgiveness? What prevents you, or people in general, from being merciful and forgiving?
⊙ How does the witness of Jesus' life help you overcome those obstacles?

THE COMPASSION OF JESUS

Many New Testament scholars point to compassion as being one of the defining characteristics of Jesus' life. In the Bible the English word 'compassion' is a translation of a Greek word meaning 'womb' and of a Hebrew word that is also translated as 'mercy'. Compassion is the quality of a person who so closely identifies with the suffering and condition of another person that the suffering of the other becomes their own, 'enters their womb'. The Latin roots of the English word 'compassion' are *cum* and *passio*, which mean 'suffering with'.

All through the Gospels, even when the word 'compassion' is not explicitly used, we can feel the power of compassion at the heart of Jesus' life. Recall for a moment some of the incidents in the Gospel when Jesus expressed and acted upon the depth of his feelings for others. For example:

⦿ Jesus wept at the death of his friend Lazarus (see John 11:35).

⦿ Jesus described the crowd as being 'like sheep without a shepherd' (Matthew 9:36).

⦿ Jesus saw and felt the suffering of people as his own and 'he had compassion for them and cured their sick' (Matthew 14:14).

⦿ Jesus looked out over the city of Jerusalem and lamented the refusal of God's people to respond to his love and concern for them (see Matthew 23:37).

⦿ Jesus, moved by the tears of a widowed mother upon the loss of her son, comforted and assured her, 'Do not weep'. Then he raised her son back to life again. (Read that story in Luke 7:11–17.)

⦿ Time and time again Jesus said to people, 'Don't cry', 'Don't worry', 'Don't be afraid'. (See Mark 4:40; 5:36; 6:50; Matthew 6:25–34; Luke 10:41–42.) Within these sayings we recognize Jesus' kindness, gentleness and care for people—his compassion.

RESURRECTION OF THE WIDOW'S SON | JAMES TISSOT

Jesus is our exemplar and model for our own witnessing to God's compassion for people. As Jesus was moved by the suffering of others and acted to alleviate this suffering, we, his disciples, are to do likewise. From its very foundation, the Church has carried out works of mercy and compassion; for example, by feeding the hungry, caring for orphans, defending the weak, educating the young and elderly, serving those in need of health care, providing shelter for the homeless, and so on. These works, which put the Great Commandment and Jesus' new commandment into practice, are summed up by the Church in the Corporal and Spiritual Works of Mercy, which are listed on page 283 of this text.

THINK, PAIR AND SHARE

- Share with a partner other examples of Jesus witnessing God's compassion for people.
- How did people respond to Jesus' compassion?

- What would a society look like if 'compassion' was its driving force?
- Think of a time when you showed compassion. Describe the situation and why you responded with compassion. How did your compassion make a difference for the person or people in the situation?

WHAT ABOUT YOU PERSONALLY?

- Has anyone treated you with compassion? How did you respond?
- What difference did that act of compassion make to your life?

JOURNAL EXERCISE

- What helps you to be a compassionate person? What prevents you, or people in general, from being compassionate?
- How does the witness of Jesus' life help you overcome those obstacles?

'I have called you friends. . . .'

What are the qualities of a true friend? Do you consider yourself to be a true friend?

These were among Jesus' final words to his disciples: 'This is my commandment, that you love one another as I have loved you. No one has greater love than this, to lay down one's life for one's friends. You are my friends if you do what I command you. I do not call you servants any longer, because the servant does not know what the master is doing; but I have called you friends, because I have made known to you everything that I have heard from my Father. You did not choose me, but I chose you. And I appointed you to go and bear fruit' (John 15:12–16a). As he had done so often in the parables, Jesus used a common life-experience to help his disciples come to understand the depth of the relationship that bonded them. In this case he used the metaphor 'friend'.

OPENING CONVERSATION

⊙ What are the qualities of a true friend? Do you consider yourself to be a true friend? Explain.

⊙ Now recall and draw up a list of ways in which Jesus showed his disciples that he was their 'friend'. Compare that list with your responses to the previous question.

OVER TO YOU

⊙ Do you ever take Jesus' words to his disciples to heart and think of Jesus as *your* friend? Explain.

⊙ How is Jesus a model for your own life as a true and loyal friend?

JESUS: TRUE 'FRIEND'

Jesus' whole life, from the Incarnation through his Death, Resurrection and Ascension, was a mystery of the **redemption** of humanity. Jesus revealed and gave witness to the saving and healing love of God that is offered to all people. This was evident in Jesus' teaching and treatment of 'saints' and sinners; the healthy and the sick; the spiritually, economically and socially poor;

THE RAISING OF LAZARUS | VINCENT VAN GOGH

Great sorrow and sadness in death indicates the presence of great love and affection during life

Jew, Samaritan and Gentile; men and women. He came to fulfill his Father's will to reconcile all people to a life of communion and intimacy with God. He commissioned and empowered his Church to be the sign and instrument of that saving grace. Through the Church God continues to work out our sanctification in the world.

Jesus helped his disciples come to know the meaning of his life by calling them 'friends'. Jesus' friendship with his disciples is portrayed in his friendship with Mary, Martha and Lazarus. Read John 11:1–44. In this moving and heartfelt episode, Jesus revealed his obedience, fidelity and love both for his Father and for his friends. He wept as he grieved with Martha and Mary at the death of their brother and his close friend, and then he responded by bringing Lazarus back to life. In the account we discover the Evangelist's portrayal of the identity of Jesus and his saving work among us. Great sorrow and sadness in death indicates

the presence of great love and affection during life.

At the Last Supper, speaking of his Crucifixion, Jesus declared, 'No one has greater love than this, to lay down one's life for his friends. You are my friends if you do what I command you. I do not call you servants any longer, because the servant does not know what the master is doing; but I have called you friends, because I have made known to you everything that I have heard from my Father. You did not choose me but I chose you. And I appointed you to go and bear fruit, fruit that will last, so that the Father will give you whatever you ask in my name. I am giving you these commands so that you may love one another' (John 15:13–17). Later at that same meal, Jesus further revealed the depth and nature of his friendship with his disciples; he prayed that his disciples would be one with him as he and the Father are one. (Read John 17:20–26.)

Preferential Option for the Poor and Vulnerable

The sacredness of human life and the dignity of the human person is the foundation of the Social Teaching, or Social Doctrine, of the Catholic Church. Flowing from that principle is the principle of the '**Preferential Option for the Poor and Vulnerable**' which 'instructs us to put the needs of the poor and vulnerable first' (see USCCA, 422–423).

The central interest of the Church's social teaching is justice for all, but especially for the helpless and the poor. It involves the removal of the symptoms and causes of poverty and injustice.

—USCCA, 427

THE POOR AND VULNERABLE

Jesus lived in **solidarity** with the poor and vulnerable. He brought the good news of God's love and compassion to sinners and to the sick—people to whom Jewish law of his day was far from friendly. (Read Matthew 5:17–48, 12:1–14.) Through Jesus' 'befriending' sinners and others whom Jewish law labelled to be 'unclean' and thus to be avoided, the scribes and Pharisees often denounced him for acting against the prescriptions of Jewish law. By his actions Jesus revealed the universality of God's love for all people and the true meaning and demands of the Great Commandment and the Ten Commandments. Jesus revealed that God lives in solidarity with all people.

The spiritually poor: Jesus invited 'sinners' and those searching for God into his circle of disciples, 'friends'. Recall Jesus' call of Matthew the tax collector to be one of his Apostles, and the Fourth Gospel's account of Jesus' encounter with the Samaritan woman in John 4:1–42. These and similar actions of Jesus especially infuriated the scribes and Pharisees, who denounced Jesus, saying, 'This fellow welcomes sinners and eats with them' (Luke 15:2). 'Public sinners' included people who had sinful, or 'unclean', professions, such as prostitutes, tax collectors (publicans), robbers, herdsmen, usurers (people who lent money and collected interest on the loan). Public sinners made up a

social class of their own in Jewish society in Jesus' time. Jewish law classified them as 'outcasts'; they were people to be avoided, and if someone came into contact with such a person, he or she would now also be 'unclean'. On many occasions Jesus reached out to sinners and invited them to repent and to be his disciples. In reaching out to sinners, Jesus proclaimed and revealed that God offers his saving love to all people.

The economically poor and oppressed: The teachings and deeds of Jesus proclaimed good news to the poor, to captives, and to the oppressed (see Luke 4:18). Jesus' whole life assured the poor of God's fidelity to and love for them:

JESUS HEALS THE SICK | CHURCH OF ST. BARTHÉLEMY, ALSACE, FRANCE

Blessed are you who are poor,
 for yours is the kingdom of God.
Blessed are you who are hungry now,
 for you will be filled.

—Luke 6:20–21

God expressed his love for the economically poor throughout the Scriptures of ancient Israel. Jesus did the same and fulfilled the Law and the Prophets. The Old Testament, over and over again, names widows and orphans to be among the poorest of the poor because the social structures of the ancient world made them totally dependent on others to provide for them. The Old Testament prophets, over and over again, speak of God's wrath over these **social sins** and admonish against making the economically poor the targets of unfair and unjust treatment. Social sins are sins that produce unjust social laws and oppressive institutions that are contrary to and work against the goodness and love

of God. Social sins are the consequence and the cumulative effect of the personal sins of individuals. Jesus repeated the teachings of the prophets and reassured the poor of God's special love for them by his constant concern for them.

The sick: Jesus often reached out in solidarity to and healed people suffering from disease and other forms of illness. According to Jewish teaching and law in the time of Jesus, sickness was the direct result of possession by the Devil (see Luke 13:10–17, Jesus curing the crippled woman), or punishment by God (see John 9:1–41, the questioning of the Pharisees concerning whose sin was responsible for the man being born blind.) Because of the association of sickness with the Devil or sin, a person's illness excluded them from participation in the life of Jewish society, including participating in synagogue or Temple prayer and worship. Jesus rejected this teaching and practice as false. On occasion, the Evangelists tell us he 'touched' the sick to heal them. This act, according to the purity codes of Jewish law of his time, had the effect of making Jesus himself 'unclean'—and thus to be avoided.

Women: God created the human person male and female in his image and likeness. (Read Genesis 1:27.) This is the reason we must respect the God-given dignity of every person. The social structures of Jesus' time relegated women to an 'inferior' status in Jewish society. All three Synoptic Gospels—Matthew, Mark and Luke—state that there were women among the disciples of Jesus from the beginning of his ministry in Galilee and that they were still with him at the foot of the Cross. (See Matthew 27:55.) Jesus' public relationship with women was contrary to many customs of his time. For example, when Jesus asked the woman at Jacob's Well for a drink, she responded, 'How is it that you, a Jew, ask a drink of me, a woman of Samaria?' And the Evangelist explains, 'Jews do not share things in common with Samaritans' (John 4:9). Later in the passage, the Evangelist comments that when Jesus' disciples, who had left Jesus to buy food, returned and saw Jesus in conversation with the woman, they 'were astonished that he was speaking with a woman, but no one said, "What do you want?" or "Why are you speaking with her?"' (John 4:27). In Jesus' time, Jewish men were not to speak to women in public as Jesus spoke to the Samaritan woman and freely to other women in public.

TALK IT OVER

- ◉ What people are marginalized and victimized in society today? Why and how are they marginalized? Make a list. Discuss: How would Jesus want you to reach out to those suffering from disrespect and acts of injustice?
- ◉ How do you see the Church responding to and living in solidarity with all people as Jesus did? Are you following the example of Jesus and joining in that work?

WHAT ABOUT YOU PERSONALLY?

- ◉ Compare your own attitude and actions toward people with those of Jesus.
- ◉ Do you take part in or have you suffered from acts of bullying? Why is bullying contrary to the way a disciple of Jesus is to live?

In Jesus' time, Jewish men were not to speak to women in public as Jesus spoke to the Samaritan woman and freely to other women in public

THE SAMARITAN WOMAN AT THE WELL | AGIA FOTINI CHURCH, CRETE

JUDGE AND ACT

REVIEW WHAT YOU HAVE LEARNED

Look back over this chapter and reflect on how Jesus is the Exemplar and Model for your life and the life of all human beings. Discuss the teaching of the Catholic Church on these statements:

⊙ The Incarnation affirms that the human person is meant for the glory of God.

⊙ Jesus is the 'visible image of the invisible God'.

⊙ The human person is predestined to reproduce the image of God's Son made man.

⊙ The Theological Virtues of faith, hope and charity (love) give direction to and empower the human quest for happiness.

⊙ In all of his life Jesus presents himself as our model. He 'enables us *to live in him* all that he himself lived, and *he lives it in us*'.

⊙ Jesus lived a life of mercy, forgiveness and compassion; we, his disciples, are to do likewise.

⊙ Jesus affirmed the dignity of all people. We are called to do the same.

THE HUMAN PERSON—*IMAGO DEI*

Jesus constantly opposed anything and anyone that would undermine the dignity of any person. In this way Jesus affirmed the Revelation of God in the first book of the Bible, the Book of Genesis, where we are told that we are created in the image of God. This Revelation and teaching of the Catholic Church is the fundamental source of our human dignity. We have been created in the divine image and restored to it by God's saving work in Jesus Christ.

> It is in Christ, 'the image of the invisible God', that man has been created 'in the image and likeness' of the Creator. It is in Christ, Redeemer and Savior, that the divine image, disfigured . . . by the first sin, has been restored to its original beauty and ennobled by the grace of God.
> —CCC, no. 1701

Because of this truth we are obligated and have the God-given responsibility to respect ourselves and every person—even when we are abhorred by the despicable things that they may do. Every person has a God-given dignity and worth and every person is worthy of respect. Every person is precious in the eyes of God. No one, not even ourselves, can take our dignity away. We are who we are; we are images of the living God, the beloved of God.

OVER TO YOU

⊙ Are there people or groups in the United States today who are treated in ways whereby their full dignity is not respected and valued? Explain your answer.

⊙ What undermines a person's dignity and how can this happen?

⊙ How can communities work to ensure that all people have what they need in order to live with dignity?

⊙ From what you have learned so far, how and why should our Christian faith motivate us to defend the dignity of all people?

The story of St. Maria Goretti, virgin and martyr

ST. MARIA GORETTI | FATHER WILLIAM HART MCNICHOLS

The life of St. Maria Goretti (1890–1902), patron of youth and victims of rape, exemplifies her faith in Christ and the cost she was willing to pay for living a life of fidelity to God and to the way of Jesus.

Maria's family were sharecroppers. After her father died when she was nine, Maria was raised by her mom. When Maria was twelve her mother assumed the farming tasks to provide for the family. Unable to handle these tasks alone, she shared in the work with a count and his teenage son. Maria, in turn, took on many of the responsibilities of caring for her siblings. Things did not work out very well, as the count and his son abused the family by keeping most of the profits from their joint farming efforts.

The count's son Alessandro, seeing and taking advantage of the poverty and desperation of Maria and her family, demanded that Maria work for him, and he verbally abused her for not completing the tasks he gave her. Alessandro's verbal abuse led to his attempts to sexually abuse Maria. When Alessandro attempted to rape her, Maria forcefully refused him once again. Wild with anger, Alessandro stabbed Maria fourteen times. Maria was taken to hospital and survived for twenty hours before she died.

Maria's dying hours reflected the depth of her faith and how she modeled her young life on Christ. She did something that would capture much air time on cable news today. When asked if she forgave the man who had tried to rape and murder her, Maria replied, 'Yes, for the love of Jesus I forgive him. I want him to be with me in Paradise.'

Alessandro was tried and convicted and sentenced to thirty years in prison. While there, he had a vision of Maria. He repented and turned his life around. When he was released from prison, Alessandro visited Maria's mother and asked for her forgiveness. For the remainder of his life he worked as a gardener in a Franciscan monastery.

In 1950 Pope Pius XII named Maria Goretti a saint, making her the youngest saint of the Church. Over two hundred and fifty thousand people attended her canonization. Maria's mother and Alessandro were among those who attended. Maria's mother was the first mother ever to witness the canonization of her child. The Catholic Church remembers and celebrates the life of St. Maria Goretti on July 6. In the Collect at Mass we pray,

O God, author of innocence and lover of
    chastity,
who bestowed the grace of martyrdom
on your servant handmaid, the Virgin Saint
    Maria Goretti, in her youth,
grant, we pray, through her intercession,
that, as you gave her a crown for her
    steadfastness,
so we, too, may be firm
in obeying your commandments.

JESUS SPEAKS TO HIS DISCIPLES | 11TH-CENTURY ILLUMINATED MANUSCRIPT

REFLECT AND DISCERN

- ⊙ What does Maria Goretti's life and death tell you about what it means to be truly human and a disciple of Jesus?
- ⊙ Do young people today experience abuse similar to the abuse Maria suffered? How can Maria's example help them deal with that abuse?

SHARE YOUR FAITH WITH FAMILY AND FRIENDS

- ⊙ Share practical ideas on ways you can work at living a fully human life by developing some of the characteristics Jesus exemplified in his life.

JOURNAL EXERCISE

At the conclusion of the celebration of Mass, the priest or deacon may send us forth using the words, 'Go in peace, glorifying the Lord by your life.' We respond, 'Thanks be to God.'

- ⊙ How will you glorify God with your life?

JUDGE AND ACT

- ⊙ What wisdom for your life have you learned from studying this chapter? What does this mean for your life as a disciple of Jesus Christ and a member of the Catholic Church?

LEARN BY HEART

'I am the way, and the truth, and the life.'

JOHN 14:6

Gathering

All pray the Sign of the Cross together and place yourselves in the presence of the Triune God.

Invitation to Prayer

LEADER

Our concluding prayer is a prayer of meditation. Close your eyes and become quiet and still. (*Pause*)

Think about what is going on in your life at this time. What questions or issues, worries or concerns do you have? What are your hopes and joys? (*Pause*)

Now let us listen to God's own Word to us. As we do so, let us imagine we are onlookers, seeing and hearing the event unfolding in our presence.

Proclamation and Meditation on the Word of God

READER

A reading from the holy Gospel according to Luke. *Proclaim Luke 7:36–50.*
The Gospel of the Lord.

ALL

Praise to you, Lord Jesus Christ.
All reflect quietly for a few moments.

LEADER

We will now listen to the story again. This time, as you listen to it, imagine yourself as one of the characters—perhaps as the woman, or as Simon the Pharisee, or as one of the other people in the room. In your mind, become part of the scene, joining in and talking with the other characters. Be conscious of your feelings, thoughts, imaginings and memories. Be conscious of the sounds, sights, smells and tastes that surround you in that place.

READER

Read Luke 7:36–50 slowly.

LEADER

Reflect quietly for a few moments as you silently respond to these questions:

What are you feeling now? What are you thinking? What memories or issues from your own life come to mind? (*Pause*)

What is God saying to you through this Gospel story? What spiritual wisdom are you hearing from it for your life? (*Pause*)

Is there an invitation in this story for you, a decision to be made? (*Pause*)

LEADER

Draw your prayer to a close now with a petition or prayer of thanks to God.

All spend a few moments in silent prayer praying the refrain 'O Lord, your love is steadfast' (based on Psalm 69:13, 16) as a mantra-prayer.

LEADER

Let us now join together and pray as Jesus taught us.

ALL

Our Father. . . .

LEADER

Let us glorify the Lord with our lives.

ALL

Let us glorify the Lord with our lives.

Pray the Sign of the Cross together.

CHAPTER 11

The Road to New Life in Christ

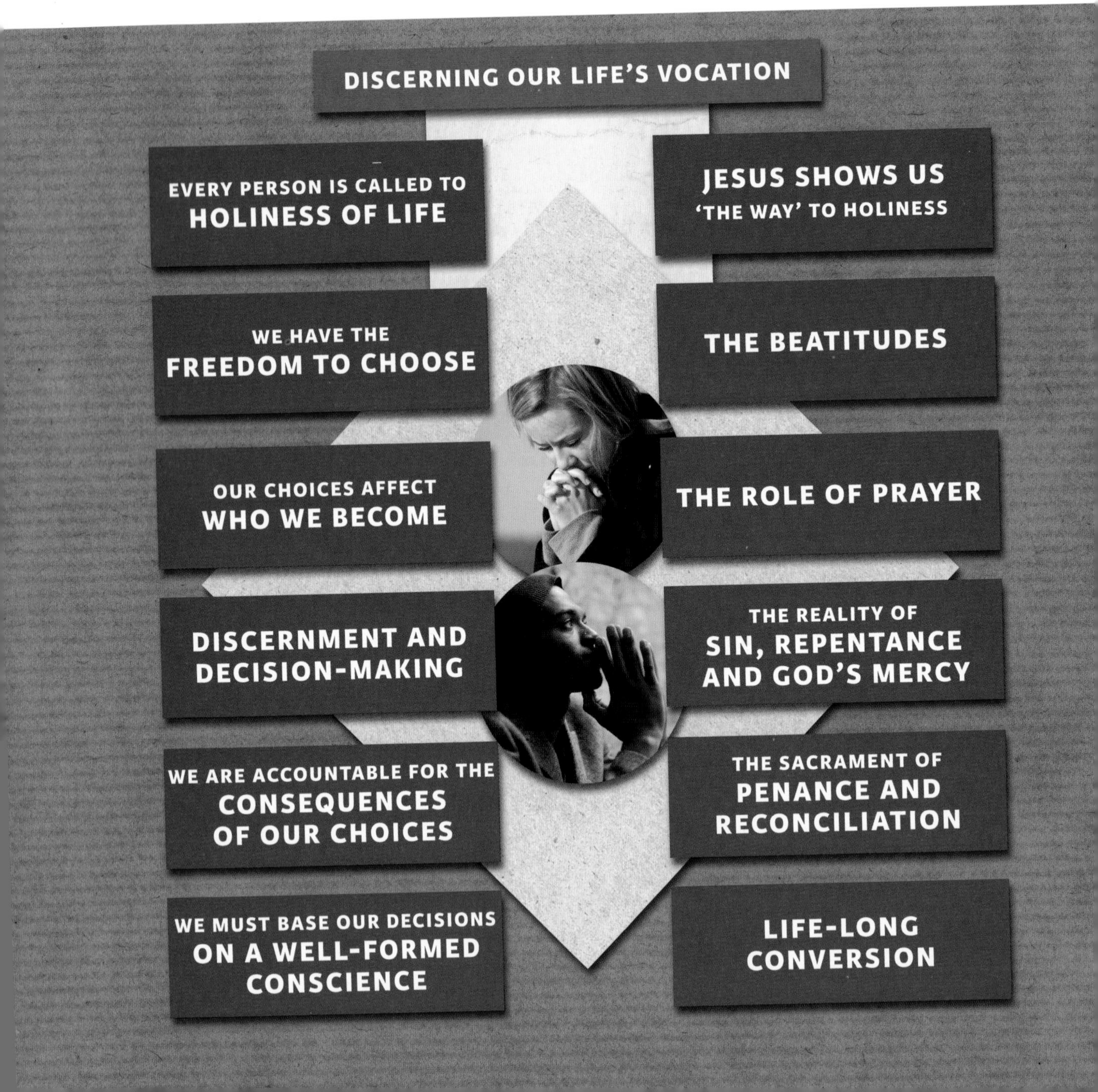

DISCERNING OUR LIFE'S VOCATION

EVERY PERSON IS CALLED TO **HOLINESS OF LIFE**

JESUS SHOWS US **'THE WAY' TO HOLINESS**

WE HAVE THE **FREEDOM TO CHOOSE**

THE BEATITUDES

OUR CHOICES AFFECT **WHO WE BECOME**

THE ROLE OF PRAYER

DISCERNMENT AND DECISION-MAKING

THE REALITY OF **SIN, REPENTANCE AND GOD'S MERCY**

WE ARE ACCOUNTABLE FOR THE **CONSEQUENCES OF OUR CHOICES**

THE SACRAMENT OF **PENANCE AND RECONCILIATION**

WE MUST BASE OUR DECISIONS **ON A WELL-FORMED CONSCIENCE**

LIFE-LONG CONVERSION

JESUS INVITES US TO BELIEVE IN HIM, TO INVITE HIM into our hearts and to follow him and his teachings. Jesus began his public life by announcing, 'The time is fulfilled, and the kingdom of God has come near; repent, and believe in the good news' (Mark 1:15). In this chapter we continue our study of the Catholic Church's teachings on what it means to be truly human and a faithful disciple of Jesus Christ. We explore the Holy Spirit's invitation, or call, to conversion and holiness of life, which seeks to keep God and doing the will of God at the center of our life.

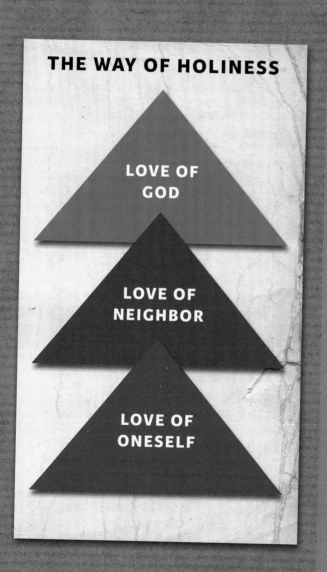

THE WAY OF HOLINESS

LOVE OF GOD

LOVE OF NEIGHBOR

LOVE OF ONESELF

Faith Focus: These teachings of the Catholic Church are the primary focus of the doctrinal content of this chapter.
- Joined to Christ in Baptism, we can grow in holiness and goodness.
- The 'common vocation of all Christ's disciples [is] a vocation to holiness of life and to the mission of evangelizing the world'. God also calls each person to a particular vocation.
- Jesus invites us to believe in him, to invite him into our hearts and to follow him and his teaching as the path that leads to fullness and holiness of life.
- Jesus teaches us how to be single-hearted in our desire for God.
- Jesus Christ redeems us and gives us his grace so that we can choose the good according to God's will and resist temptation.
- Jesus reveals the depth of God's mercy and forgiveness.
- Jesus reveals the way to repentance and conversion. His grace strengthens us to offset the disordered affections and divided hearts with which we live.

Discipleship Formation: As a result of studying this chapter and discovering the meaning of the faith of the Catholic Church for your life, you should be better able to:
- articulate the teachings of the Catholic Church on the dignity and destiny of the human person;
- include prayer and discernment in your decision-making;
- appreciate that the risen Christ is with you as your light and guide on your life's journey, especially when you endure hardships in living your life in Christ;
- grow in intimacy with God through the regular reception of the Sacraments of the Eucharist and Penance and Reconciliation.

Scripture References: These Scripture references are quoted or referred to in this chapter:
OLD TESTAMENT: Genesis 1:27–28, 3:1–19, 4:10–17; **Leviticus** 19:18; **Deuteronomy** 6:5; **1 Samuel** 3:1–21; **Psalms** 119:1–2, 10, 45, 47 and 105; **Isaiah** 49:14–17; **Jeremiah** 1:4–19; **Zechariah** 12:10
NEW TESTAMENT: Matthew 4:8–10, 5:1–11, 22:35–40; **Mark** 1:15, 12:28–31; **Luke** 1:26–38, 4:34, 6:20–22 and 35, 10:25–38, 15:11–32; **John** 3:16–17, 8:32, 13:34–35, 19:37; **Acts of the Apostles** 9:1–25, 13:1—14:28, 15:36—18:17, 18:24—20:16; **Romans** 7:19, 8:21; **1 Corinthians** 3:16–17, 12:13; **2 Corinthians** 3:17; 6:16; **Galatians** 5:1; **Ephesians** 4:12, 14–16; **1 Timothy** 6:12; **2 Timothy** 4:7; **1 John** 1:8, 9

Faith Glossary: Familiarize yourself with the meaning of these key faith terms. Definitions are found in the Glossary: **actual graces, Beatitudes, charisms, conscience, conversion, discernment, evangelization, grace, holiness, Kingdom of God, Law of Love, morality, moral life, redemption, salvation, sanctifying grace, sin, vocation**

Faith Words: vocation; holiness; conscience; morality
Learn by Heart: 2 Corinthians 3:17
Learn by Example: Dorothy Day, Servant of God

Who does God call me to become?

All parents have a natural and sincere desire to want nothing but the very best for their children. This desire is universal and so 'innate', so natural, that the Bible uses the image of a parent's love for their children to speak about God's love for his people. For example, Isaiah the Prophet speaks of the depth of love bonding a 'nursing mother' and her child to assure the Israelites living in exile of the Lord God's love for them and of God's desire for their well-being. Speaking in God's name the prophet announces the promise of the coming of a new Exodus and **salvation**. Their sorrow will be replaced with joy.

But Zion said, 'The LORD has forsaken me,
    my Lord has forgotten me.'
Can a woman forget her nursing child,
    or show no compassion for the child of her
        womb?
Even these may forget,
    yet I will not forget you.

See, I have inscribed you on the palms of my hands;
    your walls are continually before me.
Your builders outdo your destroyers,
    and those who laid you waste go away from
        you.

—Isaiah 49:14–17

Jesus also used the image of a parent's love to reveal the depth of God's love and desire for all humanity. Recall the parable of the Prodigal Son in Luke 15:11–32, whose meaning you explored in chapter 6. Compare Jesus' teaching about God in this parable with the words of Isaiah.

OPENING CONVERSATION
- What do the words of Isaiah and the parable of the Prodigal Son help you come to know about God's love for you? What do they have in common?
- What do you recognize as the very best hopes and desires that your parents have for you?
- Why do you think they have such hopes and desires?

REFLECT AND DISCUSS
- Now, fast forward and imagine yourself as a parent sharing your love with a son or daughter. What would be some of your best hopes and desires for your child? Draw up a list.
- Having imagined what your parents' 'best hopes and desires' (their best wishes) for you might be, what do you think God's 'best wishes' are for you?
- Work with a friend and pool your wisdom to create a list of what you think would be God's best wishes for all people.
- Bring your list back to the whole group. Create a class list under the heading 'God's Best Wishes for Us'.

Vocation

The term given to the call to each person from God; everyone has been called to holiness and eternal life, especially in Baptism. Each person can also be called more specifically to the priesthood or to religious life, to married life, and to single life, as well as to a particular profession or service.

—*United States Catholic Catechism for Adults* (USCCA), 531

DISCERNING OUR PARTICULAR VOCATION

All the baptized are called to **holiness** of life and to participate in the Church's mission of evangelization. **Evangelization** is the 'ministry and mission of proclaiming and witnessing Christ and his Gospel with the intention of deepening the faith of believers and inviting others to be baptized and initiated into the Church' (USCCA, 512). Together with God's grace and the advice and support of family and other members of the Church, each one of us strives to discern, know, prepare for and take the necessary steps to live out this **vocation** in a particular way. The Holy Spirit guides us in this process of **discernment** of our particular vocation. Discernment is a form of prayerful reflection; it is coming to know and choosing one's vocation. Prayerful discernment is an essential tool in answering the critical life-question that you will face and may already be thinking about: What am I to do with my God-given gifts and talents? So, it is wise to bring God into this process.

The pinnacle of the divine act of Creation was the creation of Adam and Eve. In the Book of Genesis we read: 'So God created [man] in his image, / in the image of God he created them; / male and female he created them.' Then 'God blessed them, and God said to them, "Be fruitful and multiply, . . . and have dominion over the fish of the sea and over the birds of the air and over every living thing that moves upon the earth"' (Genesis 1:27–28). God created the man and woman, humanity, to live in community. And the family is the basic human community. For

SIXTH DAY OF CREATION | CHURCH OF LA MADELEINE, TROYES, FRANCE

Christians, the family is the domestic church, or church of the home. It is in the family that children first learn to live out the vocation they share with all the baptized. Parents fulfill, in part, their vocation, as the Fourth Commandment teaches, by caring for the well-being of their children—for 'their physical, spiritual, intellectual, emotional, and moral needs' (USCCA, 378). First and foremost, Catholic and other Christian parents fulfill this responsibility by bringing up their children 'to keep God's commandment as Christ taught us, by loving God and neighbor' (from *Rite of Baptism for Children*, no. 77).

A second key dimension of parental responsibility is to work at discerning the gifts (talents, skills, personality traits and so on) of their children and to guide their children to come to know, develop and use those God-given gifts out of love and gratitude to God. In other words, parents are to support their children to discover their particular God-given vocation.

In the Catholic Church there are many vocations to holiness of life and service to the

THE ANNUNCIATION | SANDRO BOTTICELLI

God called and invited Moses, Jeremiah and the Blessed Virgin Mary to take part in the work of God

mission of the Church. These vocations are grouped into three 'states of life'. These states of life are the clergy, or hierarchy, which includes bishops, priests and deacons; the laity, which includes the married life and single life; and the consecrated life, which includes all, both clergy and laity, who profess the evangelical (gospel) counsels of poverty, chastity and obedience. The faithful live their vocation to the consecrated life in a variety of ways approved by the Church, including as members of religious orders and communities, as consecrated virgins, as monks and hermits, as members of secular institutes and societies of apostolic life.

No matter what your particular vocation might be in the future, you should be open and ready to respond to God's call, as the young Samuel was ready and responded. (Read 1 Samuel 3:1–21). Here are some guidelines to help you prepare for and discern your vocation:

- ⊙ Ask the Holy Spirit to guide your discernment. Then ask yourself:
- ⊙ What am I good at? (Know, respect and honor your God-given talents and gifts.)
- ⊙ What would I enjoy? (Remember, God desires what is good for you.)
- ⊙ What would I find worthwhile? (Fulfill your calling to be a wise steward of the skills and talents with which God has blessed you.)
- ⊙ As you weigh the different options, talk them over with God in prayer, and seek the advice of people of faith whom you trust.

LET'S PROBE DEEPER
- ⊙ Read the accounts of God calling and inviting Moses (Exodus 3:1–17, 4:10–17), Jeremiah (Jeremiah 1:4–19) and the Blessed Virgin Mary (Luke 1:26–38) to take part in the work of God.
- ⊙ In what ways are these vocation stories similar? In what ways do they differ?
- ⊙ In what one way are they all similar?

WHAT ABOUT YOU PERSONALLY?
- ⊙ To what degree have you identified your own vocation in life or even the direction your life might take?
- ⊙ What has influenced you to move in this direction?
- ⊙ What steps are you taking or what plans are you making in order to live out this vocation?

The universal call to holiness of life

The Church teaches that the 'common vocation of all Christ's disciples [is] a vocation to holiness [of life] and to the mission of evangelizing the world' (*Catechism of the Catholic Church* [CCC], no. 1533). This is your vocation right now.

OPENING CONVERSATION

Throughout this text, in particular in chapter 7, you have explored the teaching of Scripture and the Catholic Church on holiness. Recall for a moment what you have learned so far about holiness and striving for holiness of life. Then share responses to these questions:

◉ What does 'being holy' mean?
◉ What would come to mind if you heard a friend of yours described as 'holy'?

HOLINESS OF LIFE

C. S. Lewis (1898–1963) is a widely read writer who converted from atheism to Christianity. You are more than likely familiar with his fictional series *The Chronicles of Narnia*, which has sold over 100 million copies in forty-seven languages. Lewis was also a Christian apologist, or a defender and explainer of the Christian faith. In his classic apologetic work titled *Mere Christianity*, which focuses on the moral law of knowing and choosing the good, Lewis shares his understanding of 'holiness'. He says that, if we allow it, God will make the smallest and feeblest of us into dazzling people, pulsating with an energy and joy and wisdom and love that we cannot now imagine. We are like a mirror reflecting back to God something of God's own boundless power and goodness and delight. What a possibility! God desires and calls every person, Christian and non-Christian, believer and non-believer, to holiness of life. God also makes it possible for every person to live in communion with him, now and after death.

OVER TO YOU

◉ Who do you know who reflects some of the qualities of holiness described by Lewis?
◉ Do you reflect any of these qualities?

FROM THE CATECHISM

'All Christians in any state or walk of life are called to the fullness of Christian life and to the perfection of charity' [*Constitution on the Church*, no. 40 § 2]. All are called to holiness: 'Be perfect, as your heavenly Father is perfect' [Matthew 5:48].

—CCC, no. 2013

C.S. LEWIS IN THE EARLY 1960S

JESUS, 'THE WAY' TO HOLINESS OF LIFE

By the Incarnation and his saving Death, Resurrection and Ascension, Jesus unites us to God and reveals to us both who we are and our call to holiness of life. Each member of the Church strives for holiness by living as a disciple of Jesus. Within the Church, the 'Body of Christ', every member has a vital part to play. As St. Paul explains, every member brings special gifts and all gifts are given 'for building up the body of Christ' (Ephesians 4:12). The Church gives the name **charisms** to these special gifts.

At Baptism we profess faith in Jesus, we invite him into our hearts and we promise to follow him and his teachings as the path that leads to holiness of life. We receive the gift of **sanctifying grace**; all our sins, Original and personal, are forgiven. We are joined to Christ, the Holy One of God (see Luke 4:34), and we receive the gift of the Holy Spirit and become a temple of God, a temple of the Holy Spirit (see 1 Corinthians 3:16–17; 2 Corinthians 6:16). We receive the graces to respond to and live out this vocation within and through the Church, the community of Jesus' disciples.

St. Paul explained, '[I]n the one Spirit we were all baptized into one body—Jews or Greeks, slaves or free—and we were all made to drink of one Spirit' (1 Corinthians 12:13). And in the Letter to the Ephesians we read, 'We must no longer be children . . . [b]ut speaking the truth in love, we must grow up in every way into him who is the head, into Christ . . . each part . . . working properly, promotes the body's growth in building itself up in love' (Ephesians 4:14–16).

OVER TO YOU

- ⊙ What do you think it means to 'grow up in every way into Christ'?
- ⊙ Name some of the ways that you are already 'growing up' in faith.
- ⊙ Name some of the ways in which you would like to grow more.

THE WAY OF HOLINESS—THE WAY OF LOVE

Jesus taught that the true and authentic life of holiness is the way of charity, or love. In other words, we are to live as Jesus did and commanded his disciples to live: 'I give you a new commandment, that you love one another. Just as I have loved you, you also should love one another. By this everyone will know that you are my disciples, if you have love for one

ST. PAUL | MOSAIC IN VERIA, GREECE

FAITH WORD

Holiness

Holiness is a state of goodness in which a person lives in communion with God, who is Father, Son and Holy Spirit, and, with the help of God's **grace**, the action of the Holy Spirit and a life of prayer, is freed from sin and evil. (Based on USCCA, 514)

THE SERMON ON THE MOUNT | ANDREAS BRUGGER

another' (John 13:34–35). Let us briefly review Jesus' teachings on the Great Commandment (see Matthew 22:35–40, Mark 12:28–31, Luke 10:25–37) and on the **Beatitudes** (see Matthew 5:1–11; Luke 6:20–22) to help us understand the meaning of striving to live the way of holiness revealed by Jesus.

The Great Commandment: love of God, love of neighbor, love of self

In Luke's account of this Gospel episode, a lawyer asks Jesus, 'Teacher, what must I do to inherit eternal life?' In Matthew and Mark, the question posed to Jesus is, 'Which commandment in the law is the greatest?' This is a similar question to the one the lawyer asks in Luke's Gospel, for surely it is by living the 'Greatest Commandment'

that one finds eternal life. Eternal life in Heaven is inseparably united with the way we live our life on earth.

In Luke, Jesus responds by asking the lawyer a question, thereby getting the lawyer to answer his own question. In Matthew and Mark, Jesus answers the question: '"You shall love the Lord your God with all your heart, and with all your soul, and with all your mind". This is the greatest and first commandment. And a second is like it: "You shall love your neighbor as yourself"'. Now, both of these commandments, or laws, are at the root of the moral code of the Torah of the Old Testament—love of God in Deuteronomy 6:5 and love of neighbor as oneself in Leviticus 19:18. Why then the question?

In Luke's version the lawyer persists by asking, 'And who is my neighbor?' In response, Jesus tells the parable of the Good Samaritan. Here and many times throughout his life, Jesus makes it clear that the heart of living a full and authentic human life is the living of the Greatest Commandment. Our love for God expressed in our love for our neighbor is the only way to fullness of life for ourselves. It is the surest way to love ourselves. The new commandment and the Great Commandment demand true self-love.

Jesus' words about the **Law of Love** summarized his actions. Jesus continuously opened up the meaning of his words about living the Law of Love not only by his teaching but, more importantly, by his love for his Father and for all people. His life on earth clearly revealed what it means for us to live a life of goodness and holiness; that is, to live a moral life. What an amazing and challenging way of life Jesus preached by his words *and* deeds!

TALK IT OVER
- Review all three Gospel accounts of Jesus' teaching on the Greatest Commandment. Note the similarities and differences.
- What does Jesus' teaching reveal about the vocation all Christians are called to live?
- What is the message here for young people of your age?
- Share your best conclusions.

WHAT ABOUT YOU PERSONALLY?
- What is the best wisdom you have learned from this review?

'Blessed are . . . .'

If the Greatest Commandment summarizes the Law of God's reign, or Kingdom, the Beatitudes give us insight into the deeper meaning of that Law. The Beatitudes reveal the actions and attitudes characteristic of the Christian life.

Both Matthew and Luke give an account of Jesus teaching the Beatitudes. Read Matthew 5:1–11 and Luke 6:20–22. The first words of each of the Beatitudes are 'Blessed are'. Some translations of the Beatitudes begin with 'Happy are'. In Hebrew the word for 'blessed' is the noun *ašrę*, and in Greek it is the noun *makarios*. Both of these words can be translated as 'blessed' or 'happy'. What is the connection between being blessed and being happy? How can a person be 'persecuted for righteousness' sake' (Matthew 5:10) and still be blessed? How can a person be happy when people 'hate you, and when they exclude you, revile you and defame you' (Luke 6:22) for living as a disciple of Jesus? Understanding the connection between 'happy' and 'blessed' within the context of Sacred

What is the connection between being blessed and being happy?

Scripture is essential to our understanding this apparent dilemma.

Jesus' whole life on earth gives witness that the qualities named in the Beatitudes are signs of a person striving to live in communion with God, of striving to live for the **Kingdom of God**. By living the Beatitudes we can experience true joy and happiness in this life and we can confidently hope for eternal happiness with God in Heaven. 'The Beatitudes are at the heart of Jesus' preaching' (CCC, no. 1716), and they confront us to discern what we truly treasure in our hearts. The Beatitudes:

- fulfill God's promises to Abraham and his descendants about the Kingdom of God;
- teach us to love God above all things, to choose not to let anyone or anything take priority over our relationship with God;
- point us to the final end for which God created us, namely, a life centered in God and with God, now and forever;
- assure us that life with God, both here on earth and in Heaven, is a gift;
- ask that we discern and decide on how we value earthly goods and what role the pursuit of earthly goods plays in our life;
- set the standards by which we live our life on earth.

THINK, PAIR AND SHARE
- Think about and share with a partner the connection you see between the Law of Love and the Beatitudes.
- What is the connection between holiness and happiness? Between being 'blessed' and holiness?
- Who have you learned about or know that has lived or is striving to live the Law of Love and the Beatitudes? Be specific.

OVER TO YOU
- Do you consider yourself blessed when people 'exclude you, revile you, defame you' (Luke 6:22) for living as a disciple of Jesus?
- Do you intentionally try to fashion your life by the Law of Love and the Beatitudes? What challenges do you face?
- Who and what helps you overcome those challenges and obstacles?

Christ has set us free to live as disciples of Jesus

⊙ Where do you see the freedom of people fostered by those in authority? Hindered by those in society?
⊙ How might you strive to be truly free? Help others to be truly free?

TRUE HUMAN FREEDOM

St. Paul wrote, 'For freedom Christ has set us free' (Galatians 5:1). Jesus Christ is the Redeemer and Savior. He has redeemed us from slavery to sin. He has revealed that Jesus is the truth and the way of living in true freedom. St. Paul also clearly taught that we can only truly exercise this freedom with the grace of the Holy Spirit. He wrote that only when we cooperate with the grace of the Holy Spirit will we be free (see 2 Corinthians 3:17). Jesus is the Messiah, the One anointed by the Spirit, who has set us free so we can live in hope that we 'will obtain the freedom of the glory of the children of God' (Roman 8:21).

The most fundamental freedom that Jesus Christ won for us was freedom *from* the power of sin and the freedom *to* live for and with God—*the freedom to live* for the Kingdom of God. The exercise of this freedom always involves a deep inner struggle, which St. Paul himself experienced. St. Paul described this 'battle: 'I do not do the good I want, but the evil I do not want is what I do' (Romans 7:19). To Timothy, Paul's friend and missionary companion, he wrote, 'Fight the good fight of the faith' (1 Timothy 6:12). Paul knew and experienced both the costs and the rewards of living the moral life, namely, of doing what is good and avoiding what is evil. He knew well that the Kingdom of God belongs to those who seek God above all else (see Luke 6:20). Their 'reward will be great, and [they] will be children of the Most High' (Luke 6:35).

There is much talk about freedom in families, in schools, in society. Often young people seek to be free from the control of parents and other forms of authority. They want to be free to make their own decisions. Groups in society want to be free from too much regulation and oversight. They speak of free markets. But the exercise of freedom is always 'regulated'. Our gift of free will requires that we know that what we choose to say or do is truly good and that it truly is for our own good and the good of others. When authority chooses to 'regulate' the freedom of its members, those in authority also must be sure that what they are doing is 'truly good' and is truly good for society.

OPENING CONVERSATION

⊙ How would you describe freedom?
⊙ How do the gifts of our intellect and free will serve the freedom of a person?

The freedom we enjoy in Jesus Christ also comes with great responsibility. We are accountable for all the consequences of our decisions. We have the responsibility to learn how to develop or form our **conscience** correctly and to base our moral decisions on a well-formed conscience. To fulfill this responsibility we read and study Sacred Scripture and the teachings of the Catholic Church; we receive the Sacraments, especially the Eucharist and Penance, and pray regularly; we seek the advice of people of faith; we learn from the witness and example of the saints and those who faithfully live the Gospel. All these disciplines can help us, with the grace of God, to judge and know what is good and what is evil. They help us to exercise faithfully the freedom to live for the Kingdom of God and as children of God.

The grace of Christ heals and empowers our exercise of our intellect and free will. It does not curtail our freedom nor is it a revival taking away our freedom. The Spirit of Christ helps us to know and choose the truth and good that God has placed in every human heart. The Fourth Gospel teaches: 'Then Jesus said to the Jews who had believed in him, "If you continue in my word, you are truly my disciples; you will know the truth, and the truth will make you free' (John 8:31–32).

REFLECT AND DISCUSS

⊙ When you think of Jesus as 'Liberator', the One who set us free from the power of sin and death, what comes to mind in relation to your own life? Freedom from what? Freedom for what?

FROM THE CATECHISM

In man, true freedom is an 'outstanding manifestation of the divine image'.

—*Constitution on the Church in the Modern World*, no. 17, quoted in CCC, no. 1712

FAITH WORDS

Conscience

'Moral conscience, present at the heart of the person, enjoins [the person] at the appropriate moment to do good and to avoid evil. It also judges particular choices, approving those that are good and denouncing those that are evil.' When we listen to our conscience, we 'can hear God speaking'.

—CCC, no. 1777

Morality

Morality refers to the goodness or evil of particular actions. For a Catholic, it also refers to the manner of life and action formed according to the teaching laid down by Christ Jesus and authoritatively interpreted by the Church.

—USCCA, 520

Download Now

WE *CAN* MAKE MORAL DECISIONS: GOOD AND TRUE DECISIONS

God has created every person to be an image of God and has blessed us, as we have seen in chapter 10, with unique gifts that reflect God, namely, immortality, intellect, free will and the ability to love. 'Endowed with a spiritual soul, with intellect and with free will, the human person is from his very conception ordered to God and destined for eternal beatitude' (CCC, no. 1711). But, as Genesis clearly teaches, we are free to order our life to God and free to accept and seek a life of happiness with God or to choose the opposite. We are free to accept the grace of Christ to live the new commandment here on earth and enjoy eternal happiness in the glory of Heaven. We have the ability to come to know and to seek and to do what is true and good. Our intellect and will, supported by God's grace, enable us to know and to choose freely the path of goodness over the path of evil, the path that leads to God or away from God. Such wonderful gifts bring with them awesome responsibilities.

We come face to face with a wide variety of choices and decisions every day. Some of our choices are well-informed and good; others are not. Scripture, the teachings of the Catholic Church and our everyday experiences remind us that the human person 'still desires the good' but everyone's 'nature bears the wound of original sin' (CCC, no. 1707). While we do not always live as our best selves, we can be sure of one thing—God always desires what is best for us. With God's help, with God's grace, we *can and do* make good decisions. God desires and helps us to be the best person we can possibly be. Here are some simple questions to ask in every situation when you are trying to make good choices:

- ◉ What is the real issue involved here?
- ◉ What are my options?—Lay them out!
- ◉ What are the likely consequences to each option for myself? For others?
- ◉ What does my Catholic faith teach me to do?
- ◉ What would Jesus do? (WWJD)

TALK IT OVER

- ◉ Discuss the type of circumstances or influences that might lead you and other young people to make good decisions.

The effects of Original Sin draw us away from choosing to live a God-centered life and toward living a self-centered life

THE GARDEN OF EDEN | VITTSKÖVLE KYRKA, SWEDEN

⊙ Then think of and share the kind of things that might influence you and other young people to make bad decisions.

WHAT ABOUT YOU PERSONALLY?

⊙ Think of an important choice or decision you have made recently.
⊙ How did your Catholic faith influence your decision?
⊙ Is there anything about your decision that you would change now? If so, what would you do differently? Why?

JOURNAL EXERCISE

⊙ Draw a mind-map under the heading 'The People and Things That Influence Me in Making Important Decisions'. When you have completed your mind-map, rank in order of priority the most important influences for you. For example, if you consider that your parents would have the biggest influence on you, then put the number '1' beside them, and so on.
⊙ Think about how you would rank the influence of friends, peers, family, teachers and coaches, the Church, the civil law, the media, famous people and so on.
⊙ Evaluate your priorities based upon what you have learned so far about making decisions to live as Jesus taught us, his disciples, to live.

THE REALITY OF SIN AND GOD'S MERCY

Jesus teaches us to lead a life of conversion and he gives us the gift of the Holy Spirit to help us. The Spirit of Christ empowers us with the grace of God to offset our disordered affections and divided heart. The Beatitudes (see Matthew 5:1–11 and Luke 6:20–23) 'shed light on the actions and attitudes characteristic of the Christian life. . . .' and 'respond to the natural desire for happiness. . . . [They] reveal the goal of human existence, the ultimate end of human acts: God calls us to his own beatitude' (CCC, nos. 1717, 1718 and 1719). Jesus' call to repentance is a call to be single-hearted in our desire for God and to focus our life on God. Making moral decisions, choosing what is good and true, and living the new life in Christ that we receive at Baptism, takes courage.

The effects of Original Sin draw us away from choosing to live a God-centered life and toward living a self-centered life. The biblical story of the Fall teaches that what 'appears' to be good is sometimes, in reality, evil (see Genesis 3:1–19) and needs to be rejected (see Matthew 4:8–10). Recall for a moment that the Devil's greatest strategy was one of deception. We are sometimes lied to, or tempted to see evil as a good and to choose evil as good. We are tempted to **sin**. We sin when we freely and knowingly give into temptation and choose what we know is evil over what we know

is good. The First Letter of John admonishes us not to lie to ourselves but to acknowledge the truth of our human weakness. We read: 'If we say that we have no sin, we deceive ourselves, and the truth is not in us' (1 John 1:8). Such self-deception eventually contributes to our failure to recover and grow in holiness. 'To receive [God's] mercy, we must admit our faults' (CCC, no. 1847).

Earlier in this New Testament Letter, we read, 'If we confess our sins, he who is faithful and just will forgive us our sins' (1 John 1:9). Scripture, over and over again, assures us that God's mercy is always there for us when we fail or fall short. God has most fully revealed his mercy in Jesus, who has freed us from the power of evil and death and saved us from our sins. The Son of God became incarnate by the power of the Holy Spirit for our salvation. 'For us men and for our salvation, / he came down from heaven' (Nicene Creed). We receive God's mercy at Baptism when we are first made sharers in the suffering, Death and Resurrection of Christ. God sent his Son to redeem everyone from sin so that all can share an eternal life with him (see John 3:16–17). Jesus now lives and establishes a relationship with each

and every one of us, particularly through the sacramental life of the Church.

After Baptism we continue to receive this mercy in numerous ways through the Church, especially through the Sacrament of Eucharist and the Sacraments of Healing, Penance and Anointing of the Sick. The ancient spiritual practice of examining one's conscience not only prepares us for celebrating the Sacrament of Penance and Reconciliation, but it also helps us to discern, or figure out, the daily efforts we make (and do not make) to live 'the way' of Jesus. It helps us to 'face ourselves' honestly, to recognize our sins as well as our graces, and to be constantly alert for how to grow in holiness of life.

God also helps us to know and sense his love and mercy through the people and events of our lives. The kindness and forgiveness of others are reminders of the divine love and mercy.

JOURNAL EXERCISE

- ◉ Write about a time when you were particularly aware of your human weakness. Were you tempted to hide and not acknowledge it?
- ◉ What are the consequences of hiding our human weakness? Of acknowledging it?

The road to conversion

There is an old adage that goes something like, 'We learn from our mistakes'. Someone else put it this way, 'Our greatest glory is not in never falling, but in rising every time we fall'.

OPENING CONVERSATION

⊙ Do you know any similar adages? Share them with the group.
⊙ What do these adages say to you about human weakness?
⊙ What do they say to you about the Christian life?

THE CONVERSION OF SAUL

There are many stories of **conversion** in both the Old Testament and the New Testament. One of the most dramatic and well known is St. Luke's account of the conversion of Saul in Acts of the Apostles 9:1–25. Luke describes the zeal and passion with which Saul the Pharisee sought out Jesus' disciples to harm them before he became Paul, the Apostle to the Gentiles. Luke writes that Saul was 'breathing threats and murder against the disciples of the Lord' (Acts 9:1). This zeal moved Saul to request letters of introduction to the synagogues at Damascus from the high priest in Jerusalem. If Saul found any man or woman worshiping Jesus or proclaiming that Jesus was the Son of God, the letters would give Saul the authority to arrest them and bring them back to Jerusalem to be punished.

With letters in hand Saul set off for Damascus with a contingent of helpers. The story in Acts goes like this:

Now as he was going along and approaching Damascus, suddenly a light from heaven flashed around him. He fell to the ground and heard a voice saying to him, 'Saul, Saul, why do you persecute me?' He asked, 'Who are you, Lord?'

The reply came, 'I am Jesus, whom you are persecuting.'

—Acts of the Apostles 9:3–5

When the vision had cleared and the voice had finished speaking, Saul got up from the ground. Though his eyes were open, he could see nothing. His helpers had to lead him by the hand like a child into Damascus, where he stayed for three days, without sight, neither eating nor drinking.

About that time, Jesus appeared to Ananias, a disciple of Jesus in Damascus, and asked him to lay his hands on Saul so that he might regain his sight. Ananias 'laid his hands on Saul and said,

CONVERSION OF ST. PAUL | TRINITY ALTAR, WAWEL, KRAKÓW, POLAND

"Brother Saul, the Lord Jesus, who appeared to you on your way here, has sent me so that you may regain your sight and be filled with the Holy Spirit" ' (Acts of the Apostles 9:17). Immediately something like scales fell from Saul's eyes, and his sight was restored. 'Then he got up and was baptized, and after taking some food, he regained his strength' (Acts of the Apostles 9:18–19). After spending 'several days . . . with the disciples in Damascus', Saul, who now would use his Roman name, Paul, 'began to proclaim Jesus in the synagogues, saying, "He is the Son of God"' (Acts of the Apostles 9:19–20). By using his Roman name 'Paul', he was signaling the 'turning around' of his life.

Paul now spent his every waking moment zealously preaching and striving to live the Gospel. He founded many churches in lands far away from Jerusalem and Palestine. Paul the Apostle, the Apostle to the Gentiles (non-Jews), was the first great missionary to the Gentiles. The details of the missionary journeys of Paul are recorded in Acts of the Apostles 13:1—14:28; 15:36—18:17 and 18:24—20:16.

For Paul, conversion was a lifelong effort, as it is for all Christians. As we saw earlier, his journey was filled with ups and downs, with successes and failures. It was, in his own words, 'a fight'. Later, toward the end of his life, Paul wrote to Timothy, his friend and companion on many of his missionary journeys, 'I have fought the good fight, I have finished the race, I have kept the faith' (2 Timothy 4:7).

REFLECT AND DISCUSS

- ⊙ Why is Saul (St. Paul) considered to be a great convert?
- ⊙ What do you think gave Paul the courage and strength to keep going?
- ⊙ What can you learn from Paul's conversion experience?
- ⊙ How might young people today experience conversion?

FROM THE CATECHISM

Conversion means turning around one's life toward God and trying to live holier lives according to the Gospel. 'Conversion is first of all a work of the grace of God who makes our hearts return to him. . . . God gives us the strength to begin anew. It is in discovering the greatness of God's love that our heart is shaken by the horror and weight of sin

ST. PAUL CONFESSES HIS CHRISTIANITY | CHRISTOPH ANTON MAYR

Paul spent his every waking moment zealously preaching and striving to live the Gospel

Ongoing conversion requires each of us to be honest, first and foremost with ourselves, about our sins, slips and slacking off

and begins to fear offending God by sin and being separated from him. The human heart is converted by looking upon him whom our sins have pierced' [see also John 19:37; Zechariah 12:10].
—CCC, nos. 1431, 1432

LIFELONG CONVERSION

The Christian life is one of lifelong conversion; it is a lifelong dying to sin and rising to newness of life in Christ. Jesus' call to repentance and conversion is, first and foremost, a call to an interior conversion, a conversion of the heart. Such a conversion is a radical reorientation, a radical 'turning around' and facing anew toward God. Jesus desires and calls us to live our life, as he did, with a singleness of purpose—we center our life on God. This includes a life of repentance, a turning away from evil, with repugnance for the evil actions we have committed and the harm they have brought upon others and ourselves, and a firm desire and commitment to change our life and, with God's grace, to sin no more and to avoid whatever might lead us to sin. While Baptism is the moment of our first conversion, the decision to become a disciple of Jesus and turn our lives fully toward God needs to be renewed over and over again. Conversion is a lifelong process that never ends until we finally rest in God and see God face to face.

The truth is that none of us are as good as we could be or should be or appear to be. Ongoing conversion requires each of us to be honest, first and foremost with ourselves, about our sins, slips and slacking off, about the times when we do wrong, or do not do the good that we should do. Such conversion is the result of the work of both God's Spirit within us and our efforts to collaborate with the presence and graces of the Holy Spirit in our life. The journey toward holiness of life is always ahead of us.

Most conversions happen bit by bit—two steps forward, one step back—across a lifetime. As we learn about ourselves, about others and about God, as we work on our relationships, as we make better decisions, and as we participate in the life of the Church, gradually we grow closer to God and to becoming our true selves.

JOURNAL EXERCISE

- Name four or five 'high points' in your own faith journey.
- Where did you see the Holy Spirit at work in each event or experience? What evidence leads you to that conclusion?
- Discern how these past experiences might shape your future journey of ongoing conversion, your growth in holiness of life.

JUDGE AND ACT

REVIEW WHAT YOU HAVE LEARNED

Reflect on your dignity as an image of God and on your vocation to fullness and holiness of life. Discuss the teaching of the Catholic Church on these statements:

⊙ Jesus invites us to believe in him, to invite him into our hearts, and to follow him and his teaching, which leads to fullness and holiness of life.

⊙ Jesus teaches us how to be single-hearted in our desire for God.

⊙ The 'common vocation of all Christ's disciples [is] a vocation to holiness [of life] and to the mission of evangelizing the world' (CCC, no. 1533). God also calls each person to a particular vocation.

⊙ Jesus Christ redeems us and gives us his grace so that we can choose the good according to God's will and resist temptation.

⊙ Jesus reveals the depth of God's mercy and forgiveness.

⊙ Jesus reveals the way to repentance and conversion. His grace strengthens us to offset the disordered affections and divided hearts with which we live.

WHAT ABOUT YOU PERSONALLY?

⊙ How do you understand the call to Christian discipleship—what is involved, its major demands, its best hopes?

⊙ How do you understand conversion in your own life—where you are on the journey, where you have come from, the next steps along the way?

⊙ What decisions do you want to make in response to what you have learned in this chapter?

LEARN BY EXAMPLE

The story of Dorothy Day (1897–1980), Servant of God—a life of conversion to Christ

Dorothy Day, early in her life, found it very difficult to believe in God. After the trauma she suffered from consenting to have an abortion and the failure of her first marriage, Dorothy became pregnant again. This time she was determined to give birth to her baby, whom she named Tamar. This decision and the events that followed awakened Dorothy to the existence and presence of God in her life. Against the objections of the atheist father of Tamar, Dorothy came to the decision to embrace the faith of the Catholic Church. Before Dorothy's own Baptism in December 1927, Tamar was baptized a Catholic. In her 1952 biography, *The Long Loneliness*, Dorothy recalled that on the day after her own Baptism, she received Holy Communion with great joy in her heart.

DOROTHY DAY IN 1916

Dorothy lived out her newly embraced faith in Christ by serving the poor and those treated unjustly and neglected by society. On May Day 1933 Dorothy and Peter Maurin began the *Catholic Worker*, a monthly newspaper devoted to social justice and active non-violence. Dorothy converted the newspaper's office into a 'home of hospitality' for the homeless poor. This is how she described her missionary work with the poor:

> What we would like to do is change the world—make it a little simpler for people to feed, clothe and shelter themselves as God intended them to do. By fighting for better conditions, by crying out

unceasingly for the rights of the workers, of the poor, of the destitute . . . we can to a certain extent change the world; we can work for the oasis, the little cell of joy and peace in a harried world.

Dorothy Day's conversion led to her work of evangelization. Right up until her death in 1980, Dorothy was boldly speaking out against injustice and working for peace in the world. In March 2000, her cause for canonization to sainthood was introduced and she was officially declared 'a Servant of God'.

TALK IT OVER

- ⊙ What can we learn from Dorothy Day's conversion from being an 'unbeliever' to her embracing faith in Jesus Christ?
- ⊙ How was dedicating her life to helping others and working for 'the little cell of joy and peace in a harried world' a sign of her lifelong efforts of conversion and bringing the Gospel to the world?
- ⊙ What choices do we need to make to help our own ongoing 'conversion'?

OVER TO YOU

- ⊙ What wisdom for your life can you learn from the example of Dorothy Day?
- ⊙ Is this the type of wisdom that appeals to people today? Why or why not?

SHARE YOUR FAITH WITH FAMILY AND FRIENDS

- ⊙ Look back at the journal entry you made at the conclusion of section four, 'Think It Through', of this chapter.
- ⊙ Share the activity with your family and friends, and invite them to share their faith story.
- ⊙ Discuss ways you can support one another in your efforts to deepen your understanding of living your faith   in Christ.
- ⊙ Pray together, asking the Holy Spirit to teach and guide you in your efforts.

JUDGE AND ACT

- ⊙ Prayerfully reread the Beatitudes in Matthew 5:1–11.

- ⊙ Select one Beatitude that you will strive to live.
- ⊙ How will living that Beatitude help you strive for holiness of life?

LEARN BY HEART

[W]here the Spirit of the Lord is, there is freedom.

2 CORINTHIANS 3:17

A Prayer of Meditation

Pray the Sign of the Cross.

In the quiet of your heart, pray:

Happy are those whose way is blameless,
> who walk in the law of the LORD.
Happy are those who keep his decrees,
> who seek him with their whole heart, . . .
With my whole heart I seek you;
> do not let me stray from your
> commandments. . . .
I shall walk at liberty,
> for I have sought your precepts. . . .
I find my delight in your commandments,
> because I love them. . . .
Your word is a lamp to my feet
> and a light to my path. . . .
> —Psalm 119:1–2, 10, 45, 47, 105

Take a moment to breathe deeply. Allow your memory to wander back over this past week, over the things that felt good as well as those you would rather forget. (*Pause*)

Think of a moment when you made a choice that took you nearer to God. (*Pause*)

Now think of a moment of choice that took you further away from God. (*Pause*)

Remember, we are not forced to make choices based on fear of what others may or may not think of us, on keeping up appearances, or on anxiety, or because we want control. Our best choices are made out of love and truth. What motivates you in making your choices? (*Pause*)

Ask God the Holy Spirit to help you make choices that are loving and true—choices that lead you to walk the path of goodness and holiness. (*Pause*)

In the quiet of your heart, pray:

Loving God, you created us out of love.
You created the world out of love.
You created us out of such love
> that you created us in your image and
> likeness.
Help us become more and more aware of your
> Spirit,
who is always present with us,
who is our Companion and Teacher,
who guides us to make decisions—everyday
> decisions as well as ones that have a big
> impact on our lives.
Help us to discern your will and to choose what is
> most loving and true. Amen.

Conclude by praying:
Glory be to the Father,
and to the Son,
and to the Holy Spirit;
as it was in the beginning,
is now, and ever shall be,
world without end. Amen.

CHAPTER 12

New Life in Christ

THE RESURRECTION IS THE BASIS OF OUR FAITH AND HOPE

JESUS PASSED OVER THROUGH DEATH TO A NEW AND GLORIFIED LIFE

THROUGH THE SACRAMENTS AND OUR LIFE IN THE CHURCH WE ARE MADE SHARERS IN CHRIST'S NEW LIFE

JESUS TRIUMPHED OVER SIN AND DEATH AND THE POWER OF EVIL

BAPTISM IS THE DOORWAY TO NEW LIFE IN CHRIST

WE TOO CAN TRIUMPH BECAUSE OF GOD'S SAVING WORK IN JESUS CHRIST

PRAYER NURTURES OUR LIFE IN CHRIST

THE PASCHAL MYSTERY CONTINUES ON IN THE WORLD TODAY

THE LORD'S PRAYER IS A SUMMARY OF THE GOSPEL

THE 'WAY' OF JESUS IS THE ONLY ROAD TO TRUE HAPPINESS

BAPTISM UNITES US WITH CHRIST, AND WE RECEIVE new life in him. In this chapter we continue our study of the common vocation of all the baptized to grow in holiness. We explore the centrality of prayer in the Christian life. All Christians pray the Our Father, which is a summary of the Gospel and the most perfect of prayers. Praying the Our Father teaches us both how to pray and how to live our gift of new life in Christ.

FORMS OF CHRISTIAN PRAYER

BLESSING AND ADORATION

THANKSGIVING

PETITION

INTERCESSION

PRAISE

Faith Focus: These teachings of the Catholic Church are the primary focus of the doctrinal content presented in this chapter.
- Conformed to Christ, we can grow in holiness of life and goodness.
- Jesus teaches us to pray and teaches us through prayer.
- There are five basic forms of Christian prayer that are rooted in Sacred Scripture.
- Christians express their prayer in three basic ways: vocal prayer, mediation and contemplation.
- The Lord's Prayer is a summary of the Gospel and the prayer of all Christians.
- Christians address their prayer primarily to the Father.
- Christians also pray to Jesus and in the name of Jesus, who intercedes for us.
- Christians also pray to the Holy Spirit, who teaches us to pray.

Discipleship Formation: As a result of studying this chapter and discovering the meaning of the faith of the Catholic Church for your life, you should be better able to:
- articulate the teaching of Jesus on true happiness and relate your understanding of that teaching to your striving to live a life of holiness and goodness;
- understand the meaning of the Paschal Mystery for your life;
- identify moral struggles and dilemmas in your life of faith and trust in the presence of God to teach and support you in facing those struggles successfully;
- develop a sincere practice of daily prayer, using its many forms and expressions;
- build your life on the petitions of the Lord's Prayer, which is a summary of the Gospel.

Scripture References: These Scripture references are quoted or referred to in this chapter:
OLD TESTAMENT: **Exodus** 11:1—12:32; **Isaiah** 11:1–5, 6–9
NEW TESTAMENT: **Matthew** 5:10–12, 6:7–13, 21 and 33, 16:22–26, 18:21–22,26:36–46, 28:20; **Mark** 1:9–11, 35 and 4–41, 2:5, 5:28 and 36, 6:46, 7:6–7 and 29; **Luke** 3:21, 4:13, 5:16, 6:12, 22–23, 7:37–38, 9:18, 28 and 36, 11:2–13, 18:1–14, 22:32, 41–42, 23:39–43; **John** 1:29, 14:13, 15:5, 9–17, 16:24–33, 17:15; **Romans** 6:4–5, 7:19, 14:17; **1 Corinthians** 5:7, 10:13; 15:17–18; **Galatians** 5:25; **Ephesians** 4:9–10; **Philippians** 2:8; **Colossians** 1:15, 18; **1 Thessalonians** 5:17

Faith Glossary: Familiarize yourself with the meaning of these key faith terms. Definitions are found in the Glossary: **beatitude, blessings, conversion, Divine Providence, faith, Jesus Prayer, Kingdom of God, Liturgy of the Hours, Lord's Prayer, Paschal Mystery, perseverance, Redemption, temptation**

Learn by Heart: Romans 6:5
Learn by Example: The Trappists and Thomas Merton

Why do Christians live with hope?

SHERLOCK HOLMES BATTLING THE EVIL PROF. MORIARTY | SIDNEY PAGET

The struggle with good and evil is a central dynamic in every person's life. In chapter 11 you listened to St. Paul describe this very struggle in his own life; he wrote: 'I do not do the good I want, but the evil I do not want is what I do' (Romans 7:19). This human struggle is so universal that it is a central theme in Sacred Scripture, in the writings of the spiritual masters of the Church, as well as in numerous works of literature, prose and poetry, film and theater, opera, hymns and other musical classics.

OPENING CONVERSATION

⊙ What works of literature, prose or poetry, film or music have you read, listened to or watched whose central theme is the struggle between good and evil?

⊙ What Scripture accounts can you recall that focus on the struggle between good and evil?

⊙ How is Jesus' life, Death and Resurrection the ultimate battle between good and evil?

⊙ Where do you see this battle taking place in the world today?

⊙ How can young people today successfully triumph over evil? What helps us to do good when we see a wrong being perpetrated?

OVER TO YOU

⊙ What do you consider to be some of the ultimate 'struggles' between good and evil in your life?

⊙ How does your **faith** in Christ support and guide you in those struggles?

JESUS TRIUMPHED OVER SIN AND DEATH AND THE POWER OF EVIL

There are the ordinary and everyday struggles between good and evil that we all encounter, and then there are the 'big struggles' of life that carry huge burdens with them. As individuals, as local communities, as nations and as a global community, we face tremendous moral struggles between good and evil, peace and violence, justice and injustice, love and hate, hope and despair, faith and doubt, and the list goes on.

Christians face these struggles today, as we have always done, with rock-solid faith and hope. Christian hope is more than wishful thinking. Hope is one of the three Theological Virtues and is rooted in the very nature of God, who is Love and Truth and is always faithful to his Word. Hope is the assurance that all our battles with evil will ultimately be successfully won because of God's saving work in Jesus Christ. The Resurrection of Jesus Christ is the foundation of Christian faith and hope. St. Paul taught, 'If Christ has not been raised, your faith is futile and you are still in your sins' (1 Corinthians 15:17–18).

At Baptism we die to sin, are buried with Christ, and rise to new life in him. Because of Christ, St. Paul taught, 'we too might walk in newness of life' (Romans 6:4). This 'newness of life' refers to both a newness of life here on earth as well as in the life everlasting after our bodily death. Jesus Christ, our Savior and Redeemer and risen Lord, is the 'firstborn of the dead' (Colossians 1:18). United to the risen Lord, we live with the assurance that life will triumph over all forms of evil—good will triumph over evil, peace over war, love over hate, justice over injustice. God's reign *will prevail,* as Isaiah the Prophet envisioned:

The wolf shall live with the lamb,
      the leopard shall lie down with the kid,
the calf and the lion and the fatling together,
         and a little child shall lead
            them.
The cow and the bear shall gaze,
      their young shall lie down
         together;
      and the lion shall eat straw
         like the ox.
The nursing child shall play over
         the hole of the asp,
      and the weaned child shall
         put its hand on the adder's
         den.
They will not hurt or destroy
      on all my holy mountain,
for the earth will be full of the
knowledge of the LORD
      as the waters cover the sea.
                              —Isaiah 11:6–9

READ, REFLECT AND SHARE

◉ Read Isaiah 11:1–5. What is the connection between this passage and Isaiah 11:6–9?
◉ How do these passages find their fulfillment in Jesus?

◉ Where do you see Isaiah's vision becoming a reality today?

OVER TO YOU

◉ Talk about a time when you found yourself involved in a situation in which Isaiah's vision was being made a reality.

THE PATH TO HOLINESS AND GOODNESS: TRUE HAPPINESS

Isaiah's vision speaks to the deepest desire of the human heart. Many words and phrases are used to capture the meaning of that desire; 'peace', 'happiness', 'being blessed', 'life everlasting' and 'eternal life' are but a few. Jesus described the deepest desire of our heart to be 'a treasure' (see Matthew 6:21). He clearly revealed that our deepest desire is to be 'blessed'—to live life with God. The Catholic Church restates this universal truth in the *Catechism* with these words: '[T]he natural desire for happiness . . . is of divine origin. God has placed it in the human heart in order to draw [us] to the One who alone can fulfill it' (*Catechism of the Catholic Church* [CCC], no. 1718).

THE RESURRECTION | NOTRE-DAME DU ROSAIRE, LOURDES

Jesus clearly taught that happiness and belonging to the 'Kingdom of God' (the 'Kingdom of Heaven') are connected. Our true happiness and **beatitude**, which begins here on earth, will find fulfillment in our life after death. Then we will live in eternal beatitude (the eternal happiness of Heaven) in communion with God. The 'way' of Jesus is the only road to true happiness. It is the path to fullness of life, to growth in holiness and goodness. The way of Jesus is the only road to becoming fully and truly blessed. While travelling that road is enormously consoling, assuring, affirming and hope-filled, it is, at the same time, tremendously challenging and demanding and costly. Jesus taught:

If any want to become my followers, let them deny themselves and take up their cross and follow me. For those who want to save their life will lose it, and those who lose their life for my sake will find it. For what will it profit them if they gain the whole world but forfeit their life? Or what will they give in return for their life?
—Matthew 16:24–26

The way of Jesus is the only road to becoming fully and truly blessed

TALK IT OVER

Talk about some people whom you have already learned about in the *Credo* series or that you know about from other sources who have suffered because of their decision to travel the 'way' of Jesus.

JOURNAL EXERCISE

⊙ What are some moral choices that you have made that 'cost' you?
⊙ Did the accompanying cost—suffering—take away from your true happiness? Explain.
⊙ How does hope guide and sustain you in your life-quest for happiness?

Passing over from death to newness of life in Christ

Many of the events of our life manifest the natural movement of dying and rising. For example, we might experience dying and rising in our friendships; we may break up or fall out with a friend and are left feeling really upset; but then we reach out and reconcile and are filled with a renewed life. Reflecting on these events and experiences can remind us of the Christian life—of our dying to sin and rising to new life in Christ.

REFLECT AND DISCUSS
- Where have you experienced the process of dying and rising in nature?
- Think about your own life in Christ. What dying or rising have you experienced today, this week, or this past year?
- What might these experiences say to you about living as a person reborn in the waters of Baptism?

OVER TO YOU
- How have these experiences contributed to your understanding of your life as a disciple of Jesus Christ? To your growth as a disciple of Jesus Christ?

BAPTISM IS THE DOORWAY TO NEW LIFE IN CHRIST
The Christian life is, as we explored in chapter 11, a lifelong **conversion** to holiness and goodness of life. Our new life in Christ is a continual, lifelong dying to sin, of choosing what is good over what is evil. Moral choices can be difficult to make, and suffering often accompanies the making of those choices (see Matthew 5:10–12; Luke 6:22–23). Jesus passed over through death to a new and glorified life. Baptism is the first Sacrament of Christian Initiation and is the doorway to the Christian life. Through Baptism we are reborn as children of God and become members of Christ.

St. Paul taught:

Therefore we have been buried with him by baptism into death, so that, just as Christ was raised from the dead by the glory of the Father, so we too might walk in newness of life. For if we have been united with him in a death like his, we will certainly be united with him in a resurrection like his.

—Romans 6:4–5

In Baptism we are joined to the risen and glorified Christ and are made sharers in these saving events. We are incorporated into the Church, the Body of Christ in the world. We receive the gift of the Holy Spirit and are restored to holiness of life. We receive the grace(s) and power of the Holy Spirit to align our lives with

THE RESURRECTION | CHURCH OF ST. VITUS, RAVENSBURG, GERMANY

Christ as we make our earthly journey. The Church at the Second Vatican Council reaffirmed the truth of our faith: 'Thus by Baptism men and women are implanted in the paschal mystery of Christ: they die with him, are buried with him, and rise with him' (*Constitution on the Sacred Liturgy*, no. 6).

> **FROM THE CATECHISM**
>
> Holy Baptism is the basis of the whole Christian life, the gateway to life in the Spirit . . . and the door which gives access to the other sacraments. Through Baptism we are freed from sin and reborn as [children] of God; we become members of Christ, are incorporated into the Church and made sharers in her mission: 'Baptism is the sacrament of regeneration through water in the word' [Roman Catechism II, 2, 5].
>
> —CCC, no. 1213

'THE LAMB OF GOD WHO TAKES AWAY THE SIN OF THE WORLD'

John the Baptist, the day after he baptized Jesus in the waters of the Jordan River, saw Jesus approaching him and declared, 'Here is the Lamb of God who takes away the sin of the world' (John 1:29). John's proclamation, 'Here is the Lamb of God', would certainly have reminded the first disciples of Jesus, most of whom were Jewish, of how God saved his people from their slavery in Egypt. In particular, John's proclamation would have reminded them of the time when, at God's command, their ancestors sprinkled the blood of a lamb on the doorposts of their homes during the Tenth Plague, and the angel of death passed over their homes, sparing the lives of first-born males from death. (Read Exodus 11:1—12:32.) They would have seen in John's proclamation, as we believe today, that these Old Testament events prefigured the saving work of God in the **Paschal Mystery** of Jesus.

Jesus is 'our paschal lamb' (1 Corinthians 5:7). Jesus 'is acknowledged in the New Testament as the Lamb of God, who takes away the sins of the world; he is the Paschal Lamb, the symbol of Israel's **redemption** at the first Passover' (CCC Glossary; see also CCC, nos. 571, 608). The word 'paschal' comes from the Hebrew word *pesach*, meaning 'passover'. The saving work of Jesus' dying and rising 'is *paschal* because it is Christ's passing into death and passing over it into new life. It is a *mystery* because it is a visible sign of an invisible act of God' (see *United States Catholic Catechism for Adults* [USCCA], 522–523). The Paschal Mystery is the final and definitive Passover. In Jesus, our Redeemer and Savior, God's infinite saving love is most fully revealed and the divine promise and plan of Salvation and Redemption is fulfilled.

LAMB OF GOD | ALTAR MOSAIC, ALTHOFEN, AUSTRIA

'Here is the Lamb of God who takes away the sin of the world!'

JOHN 1:29

PASSOVER | 19TH-CENTURY ENGRAVING

THINK, PAIR AND SHARE

- What does the Passover event of the Exodus tell us about God?
- What does it prefigure about the work of Jesus?
- How does it help you understand the faith of the Church in Jesus, the Paschal Lamb of God?

OVER TO YOU

- What 'passovers' might you have experienced on your faith journey?
- How have these events in your life helped you come to know Jesus better? To know yourself and your vocation to a life of holiness and goodness better?
- What implications does the Paschal Mystery have for your everyday life?

The Paschal Mystery of Christ happened once and for all over two thousand years ago, but it continues and is made present in the Church today, especially through the celebration of the Seven Sacraments, and particularly the Eucharist. In and with and through Christ, humanity can pass over from bondage to sin and evil and from death itself into newness of life. Through our being made sharers in the Paschal Mystery, we take part in the day-to-day process of dying and rising to new life in Christ—in the process of conversion that we explored in chapter 11.

READ, REFLECT AND SHARE

Silently and prayerfully read the account of the baptism of Jesus in Mark 1:9–11.

- Work with a partner and read the passage out loud to each other, replacing the words 'My Son' with the name of your partner.
- Share your thoughts on these questions:
  - What difference does believing and trusting that you are God's beloved child make to how you see and respond to the struggle between good and evil in your own life? In the world around you?
  - What evil do you see in the world that arises from not seeing, valuing and respecting all people as God's beloved children?
  - Where in the world today do you see evidence of Christians treating one another as 'beloved' children of the same Father? What good results from this?

Communion with God through prayer

acknowledge it or not, people need to pray! But praying and prayer mean different things to different people. St. John Damascene (c. 676–749), Father of the Church, spiritual writer and poet, described prayer as 'raising your mind and heart to God, or requesting good things from God'. St. Thérèse of Lisieux (1873–97), the Little Flower, who was a member of the Carmelite Order and who died at the age of twenty-four, centered her life on prayer. In her autobiography she wrote: 'For me prayer is a movement of the heart; it is a simple glance toward Heaven; it is a cry of gratitude and love in times of trial as well as in times of joy; finally, it is something great, supernatural, which expands my soul and unites me to Jesus. . . . I have not the courage to look through books for beautiful prayers. . . . I do like a child who does not know how to read; I say very simply to God what I want to say, and He always understands me.' In short, prayer is conversation and communion with God.

OPENING CONVERSATION

- ⊙ Why, where and when do you pray?
- ⊙ When and where do you see your family, friends and other people praying?
- ⊙ Why do you think other people pray?
- ⊙ Work with a partner to come up with and agree on a definition of prayer.

FROM THE CATECHISM

Man may forget his Creator, or hide far from his face; he may run after idols or accuse the deity of having abandoned him; yet the living and true God tirelessly calls each person to that mysterious encounter known as prayer.

—CCC, no. 2567

PRAYER IS LOVING CONVERSATION WITH GOD

The Church invites us to pray regularly. Praying regularly is vital not only to the life of a Christian, but to the life of every person. Whether we

THINK, PAIR AND SHARE

- ⊙ Think for a moment about your relationships with your family, friends and other significant people in your life.
- ⊙ Are there similarities between the reasons friends spend time talking together and the reasons people pray? Talk about this with a partner.
- ⊙ What would the relationships you identified be like if there was no regular conversation or other form of communication between you and them?

FORMS AND EXPRESSIONS OF CHRISTIAN PRAYER

Christian prayer is 'the living relationship of the children of God with their Father who is good beyond all measure, with his Son Jesus Christ and with the Holy Spirit . . . the habit of being in the presence of the thrice-holy God and in communion with him' (CCC, no. 2565). Christians pray in many ways. Whenever, wherever and whatever way we choose to pray, our prayer is first and foremost a response to God's invitation to us to share our deepest feelings and thoughts and our joys and sorrows with him.

There are five basic forms of Christian prayer, which are found in both the Old Testament and the New Testament and have been part of the Christian practice of prayer since the time of Jesus and the Apostles. Filled with wonder and awe over God's love for us, we might pray a *prayer of blessing and adoration* and tell God that he is the center of our life. We might pray a *prayer of thanksgiving* and tell God we are grateful for the many **blessings** that fill our life. We might pray a *prayer of petition* and tell God we are sorry for our sins and acknowledge that we offended him or did harm to someone or even to ourselves. We might pray a *prayer of intercession* and share with God our concerns for a family member or a friend or for people in the world who suffer. Finally, we may simply share with God how 'awesome' he is and pray a *prayer of praise*.

We can express any of the above prayer forms in three ways. Christian Tradition names these three major expressions of prayer to be: *vocal prayer,* spoken aloud or in the quiet of our heart; prayer of *meditation;* and prayer of *contemplation*. We can sing as the psalmist did; we can dance as Miriam the sister of Moses did. We might even paint, as Christian artists have done since the earliest days of the Church.

THREE KEYS TO GOOD PRAYER

Each of the forms and expressions of Christian prayer, in its own way, provides wisdom about what makes good and true prayer. It is always possible to pray. For some people, prayer is easiest when they simply speak openly to God from their hearts, just as they would speak to a family member, close friend, or teacher or other adult in whom they trust. The key is to find a way of praying that you are comfortable with, that enables you to open your heart and that you are likely to practice regularly. The Church offers these wise counsels:

First: Ask first and foremost to do God's will, whatever it may be. '[S]trive first for the kingdom of God', and then everything 'will be given to you as well' (Matthew 6:33).

Second: Speak whatever is in your heart. Be totally honest with God. There is no need to 'heap up empty phrases' because 'your Father knows what you need before you ask' (Matthew 6:7, 8).

MIRIAM DANCING | ANSELM FEUERBACH

Third: Approach God with humility. Humility is the virtue that acknowledges that God is God and we are his beloved children. Approach God with a humble and contrite heart.

OBSTACLES TO PRAYER

St. Teresa of Jesus, St. John of the Cross, Blessed Mother Teresa of Calcutta and other people of prayer have described obstacles that they faced in their life of prayer. When we look at our own life of prayer, we discover that we, at one time or another, face these same obstacles. Here is a summary of those obstacles and some suggestions to deal with them:

Distraction. We have too many things on our mind, and our mind drifts to other things. Rather than wrestling with the distractions, we should acknowledge them, set them aside and humbly return to our prayer.

No interest. Sometimes we just do not want to pray or do not feel like praying. When that happens we need to hang in there with prayer. The experience of having a tough time with prayer, and yet hanging in there, can bring special growth to our lives in faith.

Weakness or lack of faith. Sometimes we just move along smoothly day by day, not giving much thought to God. We rely too much on our self. When this happens, remember the words of Jesus, 'Apart from me you can do nothing' (John 15:5).

Despair and disillusion. Ever feel that God has not heard your prayer? You have kept on asking and asking but have gotten no response? When this happens try to remember that God does care and always wants the best for you. So much depends on what we believe about God in times like this.

READ, REFLECT AND SHARE

- ⊙ Read and reflect on Matthew 26:36–46, the prayer of Jesus in the Garden of Gethsemane.
- ⊙ What does the fact that Jesus shared his heartfelt desires with his Father, not once but three times, say to you?
- ⊙ When you feel that your prayer seems to go unanswered, how might reflecting on Jesus' prayer in the Garden of Gethsemane help you to trust in God and persevere in your prayer?

PRAY REGULARLY AND PERSEVERE

St. Paul wrote, 'Pray without ceasing' (1 Thessalonians 5:17). Just as breathing is vital to our physical life, praying is vital to our spiritual life as disciples of Christ. We need to keep in

It is always possible to pray; we can pray any time and in any place and in any way we want

touch with God on a regular basis—even more than we 'text' our closest friend. 'Prayer requires time, attention, and effort' (USCCA, 476). Prayer requires perseverance. **Perseverance** is the moral virtue, or good habit, of staying with what is good in times when we are distracted or tempted not to do what we know is the will of God. Awareness of these three features of prayer gives us the vision and can strengthen our commitment to pray without ceasing:

First: *'It is always possible to pray'* (CCC, no. 2743). We can pray any time and in any place and in any way we want. We can turn to God even for the briefest moment, while walking, surfing the net, queuing at the arena to get our tickets and so on.

Second: *'Prayer is a vital necessity'* (CCC, no. 2744). Through prayer we can come to know God and do his will. Prayer helps us live life to the full (see John 10:10).

Third: 'Prayer and *Christian life* are *inseparable'* (CCC, no. 2745). It is not possible to be a Christian without praying. Through prayer we open our hearts and minds to the transforming grace of the Holy Spirit so as to be more conformed to Jesus Christ.

READ, REFLECT AND SHARE

◉ Read and reflect on the following quotations, pausing briefly after each one:
 – 'We must remember God more often than we draw breath.' (St. Gregory of Nazianzus)
 – 'Whether or not our prayer is heard depends not on the number of words but on the fervor of our souls.' (St. John Chrysostom)

◉ In what ways does the wisdom of these two renowned spiritual writers of the Church mirror your own understanding and practice of prayer? How are they different? Share your thoughts.

WHAT ABOUT YOU PERSONALLY?

◉ Would you say that you are a person of prayer? Is prayer as much a part of your life as breathing?

◉ What might you do to make prayer part of the rhythm of your life?

Jesus teaches us to pray

Someone once wrote, 'All true prayer somehow confesses our absolute dependence on the Lord of life and death. It is, therefore, a deep and vital contact with him whom we know not only as Lord but as Father.'

in solitude and in secret, the prayer of Jesus involves a loving adherence to the will of the Father even to the Cross and an absolute confidence in being heard.

—CCC, nos. 2600 and 2620

OPENING CONVERSATION

⊙ What does it mean to say that we are absolutely dependent on God?

⊙ What do you think the writer's description of God as 'Lord and Father' means?

⊙ What other ways would you describe God to whom you pray? Explain your choice.

FROM THE CATECHISM

Jesus' prayer [is always] a humble and trusting commitment of his human will to the loving will of the Father. . . .

Jesus' filial prayer is the perfect model of prayer in the New Testament. Often done

JESUS, OUR MODEL FOR PRAYER

Jesus often prayed. Jesus prayed in solitude. He took time out and 'went aside' to be in direct conversation with his Father. Jesus prayed before making decisions about fulfilling his mission (see Luke 3:21; 6:12; 9:18, 28; 22:32, 41–44). He often went off by himself to pray at the height of the pressing demands of his public life and ministry (see Mark 1:35, 6:46; Luke 5:16).

Jesus also took the time to teach his disciples to pray and about prayer. After the disciples witnessed Jesus praying, they asked, 'Lord, teach us to pray, as John taught his disciples' (Luke 11:1). In response Jesus taught them the **Lord's Prayer**.

God is our Father, our Abba, whom we approach in prayer with confidence and trust. (Read Matthew 6:9–13; Luke 11:2–4.) In the Sermon on the Mount Jesus taught that praying is much more than words. He instructed his disciples: 'When you are praying, do not heap up empty phrases as the Gentiles do; for they think that they will be heard because of their many words. Do not be like them' (Matthew 6:7). On another occasion Jesus taught his disciples (and at the same time admonished some Pharisees and scribes) that true prayer is not simply about filling God's 'ears' with many 'empty' words. Quoting the writings of the

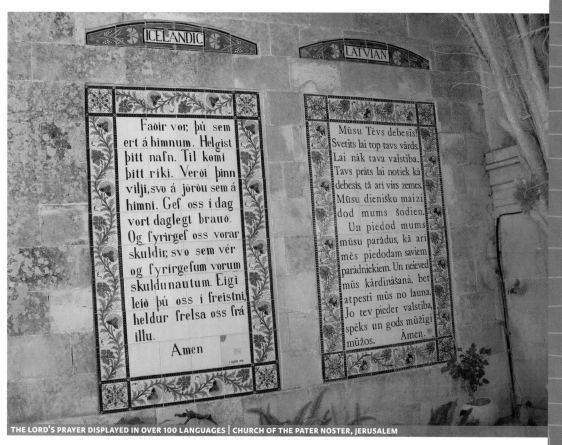

THE LORD'S PRAYER DISPLAYED IN OVER 100 LANGUAGES | CHURCH OF THE PATER NOSTER, JERUSALEM

prophet Isaiah, Jesus said to the Pharisees and scribes:

'Isaiah prophesized rightly about you hypocrites, as it is written,

"This people honors me with their lips,
    but their hearts are far from me,
in vain do they worship me,
    teaching human precepts as doctrines."'

—Mark 7:6–7

We live in a 'communion of love with the Father' (CCC, no. 2615), whom we, empowered by the Holy Spirit, approach through Christ and with Christ. Christ is our way to the Father, and he has taught us by his word and example how to pray with humility (see Luke 18:9–14) and perseverance (see Luke 11:5–13; 18:1–8). True prayer gives witness to our faith in God and our relationship to him.

LET'S PROBE DEEPER

⊙ Choose one of these three parables of Jesus about prayer from Luke's account of the Gospel:

- Luke 11:5–13: The parable of the Obstinate Friend
- Luke 18:1–8: The parable of the Widow and the Unjust Judge
- Luke 18:9–14: The parable of the Pharisee and the Tax Collector

⊙ Read the parable prayerfully and place yourself in the parable. Pause and jot down what you hear Jesus saying to you about prayer.

⊙ Design an image that represents the wisdom of the message of the parable.

⊙ Make a decision on how you can incorporate this wisdom into your own prayer life.

⊙ Write the decision in your journal. As you write your decision, ask the Holy Spirit to guide you to put it into practice.

FROM THE CATECHISM

The Lord's Prayer brings us into communion with the Father and with his Son, Jesus Christ. At the same time it reveals us to ourselves.

—CCC, no. 2799

THE LORD'S PRAYER (PATER NOSTER) | ILLUMINATED BOOK, C. 1500

prays the Lord's Prayer during the celebration of Mass and of all the other Sacraments. She prays it throughout the day from dawn to late evening in the **Liturgy of the Hours** when she gathers in prayer. Given the diversity of time zones across the world, we might say that the Catholic Church prays the Lord's Prayer 24/7, 365 days a year.

OVER TO YOU

⊙ When do you pray the Lord's Prayer?

⊙ How might pausing during the day and silently praying the Lord's Prayer impact your day? Make you more aware that God is your companion?

⊙ If you pray the Our Father in a language other than English, invite a friend to pray it with you in that language.

LET'S PROBE DEEPER: THE SUMMARY OF THE GOSPEL

We will now take a closer look at the meaning of the Lord's Prayer. In summary, the opening words, 'Our Father, who art in heaven', praise God and acknowledge that we are his children. In the remaining lines of the Lord's Prayer we petition God for the grace and help to live as his children. The first three petitions—'Hallowed be thy name', 'Thy kingdom come' and 'Thy will be done'—give praise and glory to God. We put ourselves at God's service, and pray to glorify his name and serve the Kingdom and his divine will. In the next four lines we petition God to give us and all people the graces to live as his faithful children. We pray 'Give *us*. . . .', 'Forgive *us*. . . .', 'Lead *us* not. . . .' and 'Deliver *us*. . . .' Let us explore now how praying the Lord's Prayer honors and gives glory to God and also guides us in our effort to live as Jesus taught us.

'Our Father, . . .'

We approach God the Father, as Jesus did, with the confidence and trust of children. We acknowledge humbly that he has adopted us as his children in his only Son, and, indeed, he is the Creator, the Father of all people. In praying 'Our Father' we exclude no one. We reject individualism and division; we commit ourselves to promote a love for all people and for the whole

'PRAY THEN IN THIS WAY: OUR FATHER. . . .'

The Our Father, also known as the Lord's Prayer because it 'is taught and given to us by the Lord Jesus' (CCC, no. 2765), is the common prayer of all Christians. The early Church writer Tertullian (c. 160–c. 225), summarizing the importance of the Lord's Prayer in the life of the early Church, wrote that 'the Lord's Prayer is truly the summary of the whole gospel' (*On Prayer*, quoted in CCC, no. 2774). St. Thomas Aquinas, in the thirteenth century, taught that 'the Lord's prayer is the most perfect of prayers' (*Summa Theologiae*, II–II, 83, 9). Praying the Lord's Prayer teaches us how to approach God in prayer and seek what we need to live the Gospel.

The 'Didache', or 'The Teachings of the Twelve Apostles', is a second-century three-part treatise. In the second part, which describes the prayer and worship life of the early Church, the author writes that the Church prayed the Lord's Prayer three times a day. The Catholic Church today continues to pray the Lord's Prayer daily. She

of creation. Finally, '[w]hen we say "Our" Father, we are invoking the new Covenant in Jesus Christ, communion with the Holy Trinity, and the divine love which spreads through the Church to encompass the world' (CCC, no. 2801).

'Who art in heaven'

Heaven 'does not refer to a place but to God's majesty and his presence in the hearts of the just' (CCC, no 2802).

God has given us the gift of life and existence to glorify him by our life and live in communion with him, for ever and ever. Tradition has named the eternal state of our eternal communion with God the **Beatific Vision**. Jesus descended from Heaven and, because of him, one day we can ascend there with him (see Ephesians 4:9–10).

'Hallowed be thy name'

The Third Commandment commands: 'You shall not take the name of the Lord your God in vain.' In other words, we are to give glory to the name of God—to God—in all we say and do. Our lives should speak the truth of 'who we are', sons and daughters of the thrice-holy God. When we

DANTE'S VISION OF HEAVEN | GUSTAVE DORÉ

pray this first of the seven petitions of the Lord's Prayer, we bless and adore God, the Holy One, who alone is the source of all holiness. 'To hallow' is to respect and value and reverence someone as holy. We acknowledge humbly who God is and who we are.

'Thy kingdom come'

St. Paul teaches that 'the kingdom of God [is] righteousness and peace and joy in the Holy Spirit' (Romans 14:17). The **Kingdom of God** was a central theme of Jesus' preaching. Since Pentecost, the coming of that reign is the work of the Spirit of the Lord who 'complete[s] his work on earth and brings us the fullness of grace' [*Roman Missal*, Eucharistic Prayer IV]. 'The Church looks first to Christ's return and the final coming of the Reign of God. [She] also prays for the growth of the Kingdom of God in the "today" of our own lives' (CCC, no. 2859). Every time we strive to live the Greatest Commandment and the Beatitudes, we take part in that work.

'Thy will be done on earth as it is in heaven'

Jesus obediently fulfilled the will of his Father (see Matthew 26:42 and Philippians 2:8) and he calls us to do the same. (Read John 15:9–17 and John 16:25–33.) After his Death and Resurrection the risen Lord commissioned the Apostles, saying, in part, '[teach] them to obey everything that I have commanded you' (Matthew 28:20). This is the work of every individual Christian and the work of the Church as a whole. We are also to proclaim the will of God by the way we live so that all people and all societies may know and strive to conform their wills to the will of God.

Heaven does not refer to a place but to God's majesty and his presence in the hearts of the just

'Give us this day our daily bread'

In this petition we are telling God that we trust in his loving care and concern for all he has made, in **Divine Providence**. We believe and trust in him to be the giver and the sustainer of all life, body and soul, material and spiritual. We pray for both ourselves and all people who hunger, spiritually and materially. We acknowledge our solidarity with the poor and we commit, by the power of the Holy Spirit, to feed the poor by working against all hunger. We bring the 'bread of justice' to the world so that justice is established 'in personal and social, economic and international relations, without ever forgetting that there are no just structures without people who want to be just' (CCC, no. 2832).

'And forgive us our trespasses, as we forgive those who trespass against us'

We are to forgive as Jesus forgave. Joined to Christ at Baptism and made sharers in his sacrifice on the Cross, we receive the grace to forgive as he did. We receive the grace to '[b]e merciful, just as your Father is merciful' (Luke 6:36). The ability to forgive as Jesus did is made possible by the work of the Spirit of Jesus in our life (see Galatians 5:25). In the Sermon on the Mount Jesus taught his disciples the depth of forgiveness that he demands of his disciples. To Peter's question 'Lord, if another member of the church sins against me, how often should I forgive? As many as seven times?', Jesus' response 'Not seven times, but I tell you, seventy-seven times' (Matthew 18:21–22) more than likely stunned Peter and the others listening on. In other words, 'Place no limits on your forgiveness. Strive to be as perfect in your forgiveness toward others as God is in his forgiveness of you.' Should we fail, we can encounter and turn to the forgiving Lord in the Sacrament of Penance and Reconciliation.

'And lead us not into temptation'

Our understanding of the meaning of the word 'lead' in this petition of the Lord's Prayer is important. The original Greek word used in this text that we translate as 'lead' can also be translated to give us both 'do not allow us to

CHRIST BREAKING BREAD AT EMMAUS | PIER LEONE GHEZZI

THE TEMPTATION OF JESUS | SAINT-SULPICE-DE-FAVIÈRES, ESSONNE, FRANCE

enter into' and 'do not let us yield to' **temptation**. God the Holy Spirit is with us in the thick and thin of our battle with evil, as he was with Jesus in the desert during his time of temptation. St. Paul, who experienced this battle and fought the good fight, wrote: 'No [temptation] has overtaken you that is not common to everyone. God is faithful, and he will not let you be [tempted] beyond your strength, but with the [temptation] he will also provide the way out so that you may be able to endure it' (1 Corinthians 10:13). In this petition we ask God to give us the knowledge to know temptation, and the grace to overcome it.

'But deliver us from evil'

In this petition we pray, in communion with the whole Church, 'for the deliverance of the whole human family' (CCC, no. 2850). At the Last Supper, Jesus prayed to his Father, 'I am not asking you to take them out of the world, but I ask you to protect them from the evil one' (John 17:15)—the same evil one, the Devil, who tempted him at the beginning of and throughout

his life (see Luke 4:13). The Devil is always at work in our life and in the world. We pray 'deliver us from evil', acknowledging that we cannot face temptation alone, single-handedly. We need God's many graces and the support of our brothers and sisters in faith. We pray with the hope that good will triumph over evil, love over hate, injustice over justice, peace over war.

REFLECT AND SHARE

⊙ Reflect on the Lord's Prayer as 'The Summary of the Gospel'.
⊙ Share your reflections with a partner and then create together a 'Profile of a Disciple of Jesus'. Include passages from the Gospel in your portrait.

JOURNAL EXERCISE

⊙ Reflect on the events and challenges you routinely face in living as a faithful disciple of Jesus and child of God.
⊙ How will you put the words of the Lord's Prayer into action in your own life?

JUDGE AND ACT

REVIEW WHAT YOU HAVE LEARNED

Look back over this chapter and reflect on your vocation to live the new life in Christ you received at Baptism. Discuss the teachings of the Catholic Church on these statements:

- ⊙ Conformed to Christ, we can grow in holiness of life and goodness.
- ⊙ Christians pray five basic forms of prayer that are rooted in Scripture: Prayer of Blessing and Adoration, Prayer of Petition, Prayer of Intercession, Prayer of Thanksgiving, and Prayer of Praise
- ⊙ Christians express their prayer in three basic ways: vocal prayer, meditation, and contemplation.
- ⊙ Jesus teaches us to pray and teaches us through prayer.
- ⊙ The Lord's Prayer is the prayer of all Christians; it is a summary of the Gospel and the most perfect of prayers.

WHAT ABOUT YOU PERSONALLY?

- ⊙ What are some of the best insights and spiritual wisdom that you have learned from this chapter?
- ⊙ What are the most significant obstacles and challenges you encounter when praying? How can you work to overcome them?

THE PRAYER OF CHRISTIANS

The prayer of Christians acknowledges that we are adopted children of the Father. The prayers of the Church, the Body of Christ, are addressed primarily to God the Father through the power of the Holy Spirit in the name of Jesus, the Head of his Body, the Church. Although Christians address their prayer primarily to God the Father, as Jesus did and as he taught us to do, Christians also pray to Jesus and the Holy Spirit. Jesus is the Incarnate Son of God, who intercedes for us (see John 14:13, 16:24). Christians pray to him and in his name.

Sometimes we simply pray the name 'Jesus' over and over again, either aloud or within the quiet of our heart. Indeed, 'the invocation of the holy name of Jesus is the simplest way of praying' (CCC, no. 2668). For example, the **Jesus Prayer**, 'Lord Jesus Christ, Son of the living God, have mercy on us sinners', which is based on Luke 18:10–14, dates back to the fifth century and comes to us from the Church in the East. The risen and glorified Lord continues to intercede for us as he did so often for others during his life on earth. Jesus Christ himself answers prayers addressed to him. (Read Mark 1:40–41; 2:5; 5:28, 36; 7:29; Luke 7:37–38; 23:39–43.)

JESUS PRAYS ON THE MOUNT OF OLIVES | ENGRAVING AFTER ALEXANDRE BIDA

Christians address their prayer primarily to God the Father, as Jesus did and as he taught us to do

The story of the Trappists and Thomas Merton (1915–68)

Thomas Merton was a Trappist monk, poet and widely read spiritual writer. He converted to Roman Catholicism on November 16, 1938 while a student at Columbia University. Three years later, Merton decided to enter the Abbey of Gethsemani, a community of Cistercian monks of the Strict Observance, or Trappists. The daily schedule of life of a Trappist includes communal and private prayer, contemplation, study and manual labor. Trappists spend at least four hours a day in chapel, chanting their praises of God. When they are not praying aloud in chapel, their daily life is one of silence. They vow to speak only in praise of God or when the fulfillment of their responsibilities requires it.

Merton described his life of prayer and the importance of prayer for his life. He wrote:

My Lord God, I have no idea where I am
going.
I do not see the road ahead of me.
I cannot know for certain where it will end.
Nor do I really know myself,
and the fact that I think that I am following
your will
does not mean that I am actually doing so.
But I believe that the desire to please you
does in fact please you.
And I hope I have that desire in all that I am
doing.
I hope that I will never do anything apart
from that desire.
And I know that if I do this
you will lead me by the right road
though I may know nothing about it.

Therefore I will trust you always
though I may seem to be lost
and in the shadow of death.
I will not fear, for you are ever with me,
and you will never leave me to face my
perils alone.

Merton believed that prayer must speak aloud, and in his many writings he addressed moral issues of our day that were contrary to the Gospel. These included racism and the inordinate race of nations to arm themselves for war. A strong supporter of non-violence, he described the civil rights movement in the United States as 'the greatest example of Christian faith in action in the social history of the United States'.

REFLECT AND DISCERN

⊙ Thomas Merton made an active choice as a young man to be baptized into the Catholic faith. What does his decision suggest for you? What active choices can you make regarding your own Baptism?

⊙ How do you think Merton's support for non-violence and the civil rights movement were linked to his prayer life? To his praying the Our Father?

Where can you make time during the day for prayer?

OVER TO YOU

- Take a few moments to reread and reflect prayerfully on Thomas Merton's prayer.
- How does this prayer speak to you?
- Is this a prayer you could incorporate into your own prayer life? How would you go about doing so?

SHARE YOUR FAITH WITH FAMILY AND FRIENDS

- Pray the Lord's Prayer regularly with your family and friends. Together, choose a line or phrase or a word that resonates with you in a special way.
- Discuss how together you can make that line or phrase or word come alive in your life.

JUDGE AND ACT

- How can you respond to St. Paul's advice to pray ceaselessly?
- Write down the recurring events that make up a typical day for you and arrange those events according to the time of day they regularly occur.

- Where can you make time throughout the day for prayer? Are there obstacles preventing you from including praying on a regular basis? How might you overcome them?

LEARN BY HEART

> [If] we have been united with him in a death like his, we will certainly be united with him in a resurrection like his.

ROMANS 6:5

Invitation to Prayer

LEADER
Let us place ourselves in the presence of the thrice-holy God.

All pray the Sign of the Cross together.

LEADER
O God, who founded the salvation of the human race on the Incarnation of your Word,
give your peoples the mercy they implore,
so that they all may know there is no other name
  to be invoked,
but the Name of your Only Begotten Son.
Who lives and reigns with you in the unity of the
  Holy Spirit,
one God, for ever and ever.
ALL
Amen.
> —Collect, Feast of the Holy Name of Jesus,
> *The Roman Missal*

Proclamation of the Word of God

READER
A reading from the Letter to Philemon.
Proclaim Philemon 2:10–11.
The word of the Lord.
ALL
Thanks be to God.

All quietly reflect on the name Jesus.
Say the name Jesus.
Does hearing the name Jesus heighten your
awareness of his presence with you?
Does saying the name Jesus heighten your
awareness of his presence with you?
Open your heart and mind in prayerful conversation
with your Lord.

Response to God's Word

LEADER
Lord Jesus, we ask you to guide us and give us your grace to make our living the prayer you taught us the plan for living our life as your disciple. We pray together:

READER
(All respond 'Jesus, save your people' after each
petition.)
Lord, be merciful
From every evil
From every sin
From the snares of the Devil
From your anger
From the spirit of infidelity
From everlasting death
From neglect of your Holy Spirit
By the mystery of your Incarnation
By your birth
By your childhood
By your hidden life
By your public ministry
By your agony and crucifixion
By your abandonment
By your grief and sorrow
By your death and burial
By your rising to new life
By your return in glory to your Father
By your gift of the Holy Eucharist
By your joy and glory
> —From Litany of the Holy Name of Jesus

ALL
Silently or aloud, add your own petitions.

LEADER
Let us pray:
ALL
Lord, may we who honor the holy name of Jesus
enjoy his friendship in this life
and be filled with eternal joy in the Kingdom
where he lives and reigns for ever and ever. Amen.

CHAPTER 13

From Here to Eternity

—The Last Things

DEATH DOES NOT HAVE THE FINAL WORD

IN DEATH, LIFE IS CHANGED, NOT ENDED

DEATH IS THE DOORWAY TO ETERNAL LIFE

WE ARE CALLED TO HOLINESS OF LIFE

WE WILL BE HELD ACCOUNTABLE FOR OUR EARTHLY ACTIONS

THE CHURCH'S TEACHING ON LIFE AFTER DEATH

THE LAST JUDGMENT: GOD'S POWER OVER EVIL WILL FINALLY BE REVEALED

GOD WILL BE OUR JUDGE

THE JUST WILL REIGN WITH CHRIST FOR EVER

THE SAINTS IN HEAVEN ARE OUR PARTNERS IN DISCIPLESHIP

IN HIS PRAYER TO HIS FATHER FOR HIS DISCIPLES AT THE Last Supper, Jesus acknowledged that he was sent to give eternal life to all who believe in him. He then described eternal life: 'And this is eternal life, that they may know you, the only true God, and Jesus Christ whom you have sent' (John 17:3). In this final chapter we examine the teachings of the Catholic faith about eternal life—life after death. We explore the Church's teachings on the Last Things—death and Judgment, Purgatory, Heaven and Hell. We also take a closer look at the Communion of Saints and the relationship of the faithful on earth with all the faithful who have died.

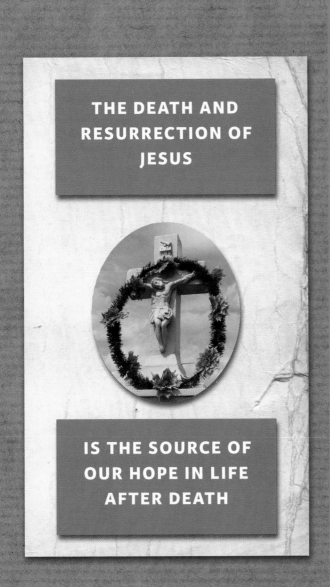

THE DEATH AND RESURRECTION OF JESUS

IS THE SOURCE OF OUR HOPE IN LIFE AFTER DEATH

Faith Focus: These teachings of the Catholic Church are the primary focus of the doctrinal content presented in this chapter.

- At the moment of death our life is changed, not ended. Death is the doorway to life everlasting.
- God will judge every person's life on earth both at the moment of his or her death and when Christ comes again in glory.
- After death we will live in a state of eternal happiness with God, or Heaven; or we will live in a state of eternal alienation from God and his love, or Hell.
- The faithful who die in a state of grace but who have not yet reached a state of love for God and holiness of life that enables them to enter a life of eternal happiness with God must undergo a process of purification, or Purgatory.
- All the faithful, both those living on earth and those who have died, are united with one another in the Communion of Saints.

Discipleship Formation: As a result of studying this chapter and discovering the meaning of the faith of the Catholic Church for your life, you should be better able to:

- articulate the teachings of the Catholic Church on the Last Things: death, Judgment, Heaven, Purgatory and Hell;
- value the importance of living as your 'best' self in light of the life of the world to come;
- take inspiration from the example of the lives of the saints of the Church, both living and dead;
- acknowledge that you belong to and are supported by the Communion of Saints;
- trust in your own prayers to the saints and for loved ones who have died;
- trust in God's mercy and forgiveness.

Scripture References: These Scripture references are quoted or referred to in this chapter:
OLD TESTAMENT: **2 Maccabees** 12:45; **Psalms** 6:5; **Wisdom** 3:1–5; **Isaiah** 38:18, 52:15, 64:3; **Jeremiah** 29:10–14; **Daniel** 12:2
NEW TESTAMENT: **Matthew** 5:22, 26 and 29, 10:28, 12:32, 13:41–42 and 50, 25:31–46; **Mark** 9:43–48; **Luke** 16:19–31, 17:1–3, 22:42, 23:43; **John** 13:31–35, 14:1–3, 17:1–26; **Romans** 5:12–14, 6:23, 8:18–25; **1 Corinthians** 2:9, 3:11–15, 15:28; **Colossians** 1:18; **2 Timothy** 2:11; **Hebrews** 9:27, 12:1; **2 Peter** 3:1–13; **1 John** 3:14–15; **Revelation** 21:1, 4

Faith Glossary: Familiarize yourself with the meaning of these key faith terms. Definitions are found in the Glossary: **Beatific Vision, Communion of Saints, death, eternal life, Heaven, Hell, immortality, Kingdom of God, Last Judgment, Particular Judgment, Purgatory, Resurrection, soul**

Faith Words: Last Judgment; Beatific Vision
Learn by Heart: 2 Timothy 2:11
Learn by Example: *Día de los Muertos*

Ever wonder about life after death?

ANGEL OF GRIEF | WILLIAM WETMORE STORY

Have you experienced the death of a family member or friend? Do you recall watching the reporting of the shooting of the twenty students and six staff and faculty at Sandy Hook Elementary School on December 14, 2012, or the reporting of other senseless killing and 'deaths'?

OPENING REFLECTION

- ◉ What would you say to someone who is suffering and grieving because of the death of a friend or family member?
- ◉ What do *you* think happens when we die?

LIFE AFTER DEATH

Father Ronald Rolheiser, a member of the Missionary Oblates of Mary Immaculate, is a Catholic theologian, speaker and spiritual writer. He has given much thought to the reality of life after **death** and how it should affect our lives in the here and now. Let's hear what he has to say.

If we say that belief in an afterlife does not (and should not) affect how we live our lives, we're simply out of touch with some of the deeper things that motivate us. It makes a huge difference, unconsciously, as to how restless or peaceful we are. When we no longer believe in a life hereafter, we will, one way or the other, put unfair, restless pressure on this life.

Belief in life after death is important, not because it can affect our present lives with fears of hellfire or with the promise of a heaven that can be a soothing narcotic when life can't deliver what we want, but because only the infinite can provide the proper horizon against which to view the finite. . . .

If, for example, we don't believe in life after death . . . how do we keep the demons of restlessness, disappointment, sadness, jealousy, self-pity and cynicism at bay?

THINK, PAIR AND SHARE

- ◉ With a partner, summarize your understanding of what Fr. Rolheiser is saying.
- ◉ Discuss why you agree or disagree with him.
- ◉ How might 'taking the long view' of eternity give everything in this life a proper perspective?

Father Rolheiser continues:

If this life alone has to carry everything, how tragic then to be poor, to lack opportunity, to not be healthy, to not have a perfect body, to lack the talent to adequately express ourselves; how tragic then to not regularly experience ecstasy in love, to not find a perfect soul mate, to have to sleep alone; how permanently tragic then to have been the victim of some accident, to have been abused, to be wounded, less than whole; . . . how tragic then to have to face death with our lives still incomplete; how tragic then to have to miss out on any of life's pleasures; how tragic then to find ourselves always in lives too small for us, small-time, small-town, unknown, our dreams reduced to ashes, nostalgia, jealousy, frustration; how tragic then to contemplate what might have been, to have made wrong choices; how tragic then simply to be alone on a Friday night; how tragic then to have to spend a holiday without someone special to share it with; how tragic then to live in a body, a family, a marriage, a home, a world and a life which can never give us the full symphony nor ever take away our deepest restlessness and longing.

Belief in a life after this one isn't meant to make us live in fear of hellfire or in the infantile hope that if we're good we'll get a reward for it after we die. Belief in life after death is meant to give us proper vision so that we can, precisely, enjoy the real joys of this life without perpetually crucifying ourselves because they, and we, aren't perfect.

OVER TO YOU

- ⊙ Do Fr. Rolheiser's words 'If this life alone has to carry everything, how tragic then to be poor, to lack opportunity, to not be healthy, to not have a perfect body. . . .' connect with your view of the relationhship between life on earth and eternal life?
- ⊙ See if you can describe or share your image of the life after death with a partner.

FROM THE CATECHISM

Because of Christ, Christian death has a positive meaning. . . . Our living now in friendship with God will continue into eternity.

—CCC, no. 1010

Belief in life after death is meant to give us proper vision so that we can, precisely, enjoy the real joys of this life without perpetually crucifying ourselves because they, and we, aren't perfect.

FR. RONALD ROLHEISER

DEATH: THE DOORWAY TO ETERNAL LIFE

God has created the human person to be a unity of a body and a **soul**. By death our soul is separated from our body. The soul is the immortal part of who we are that lives after the death of our body. 'Death is the natural and inevitable end of life on earth' (*United States Catholic Catechism for Adults* [USCCA], 153). Everyone will come face to face with death.

A defining characteristic of all the great religions of the world is their view of and teachings on death. For Christians, death is the doorway to eternal life. And the **Resurrection** is the basis of our hope that we, too, will live in a new way after our physical death. Christ is the 'firstborn from the dead' (Colossians 1:18). The risen and glorified Christ lives forever. The Resurrection offers the most consoling and influential way of facing and even celebrating the death of our body, and we wait in hope for the Second Coming, or *Parousia*, of Christ, when he will return in glory and our bodies will rise again.

Catholics celebrate this faith when they gather for the Funeral Mass. We celebrate and express this faith and hope in the white vestments the priest often wears and in the white pall that we place over the casket in which the body of our loved one lies. We express and celebrate this faith and hope in the prayers and songs. For example, in Preface I for the Dead we proclaim:

In him [Christ] the hope of blessed resurrection
    has dawned,
that those saddened by the certainty of dying
might be consoled by the promise of
    immortality to come.
Indeed for your faithful, Lord,
life is changed not ended,
and, when this earthly dwelling turns to dust,
an eternal dwelling is made ready for them in
    heaven.
    —*The Roman Missal*, Preface I for the Dead

The words of this Preface confess the Christian faith that death is not the end of our life; it is a change in the way we live. In the Nicene Creed we profess that we look forward to 'the resurrection of the dead and the life of the world to come'. We profess this same faith in 'life everlasting' in the Apostles' Creed. **Eternal life** is living for ever with God in the happiness of Heaven, entered after death by the souls of those who die in the grace and friendship of God.

TALK IT OVER

⊙ What difference can the faith of the Church make to the formation of our attitude toward our own death? Toward the way we live now?

A HINDU 'SADHU' SEEKS TO ACHIEVE REINCARNATION THROUGH RENUNCIATION

Reincarnation

Some people, such as Hindus, teach that after people die, they will come back to life on earth in some *new form*, and that they will keep coming back to a life on earth in an ongoing cycle of *new forms* until their spirits finally reach a state of perfection or oneness with the Divine. This understanding of death is called reincarnation. The Catholic Church rejects this understanding of human life and death as being contrary to what God has revealed, to the teachings of Scripture and Tradition. There is no 'reincarnation' after death. (See Hebrews 9:27.)

Death and Judgment

In the face of death, ultimate questions about the meaning of life emerge. We may ask: What is the purpose of life? Why am I here? To whom do I belong? Instead of causing us to fall into the kind of despair that Fr. Rolheiser described at the beginning of this chapter, death and life after death can give us tremendous hope. There, all wrongs will be righted, all injustice called to account, all wounds and brokenness healed. There, 'God . . . will wipe every tear. . . . Death will be no more' (Revelation 21:4). Just imagine, all the good you do in this life helps to make you who you are, and that will 'remain' with you in eternity.

When we are touched by death, we see things from a different perspective. Death exposes the superficial, selfish and shallow parts of our lives. We are forced to think about what is really important and truly valuable to us.

OPENING CONVERSATION

⊙ When have you experienced the death of a family member or friend or neighbor? Or learned about the tragic death of someone or of a group of people? What were your thoughts about death and dying at that time?

⊙ Read and evaluate these views on death from five young people:

– I don't think about it; it doesn't make any sense to me. I don't know anyone who has died. I mean, who thinks about death? It's weird. (Sasha, age 15)

– I never thought much about death until my mom became very ill, and then I couldn't avoid it. She was a great mom, full of life and fun. It was terrible when she died. I hope I'll meet her again. (Patrick, age 17)

– I do believe in life after death though I don't know what exactly it will be like. I believe that Jesus rose from the dead and that we will too. (Cindy, age 18)

– I think death is like a passageway, from this world into the next, and that there is something after it, like Heaven, but I don't know what that really means. I hope I will see people I love after I die. (Elena, age 16)

– I don't think there's anything beyond this world. When you're dead, that's it. There's nothing. No Heaven, no **Hell**, nothing. (Adam, age 17)

REFLECT AND DISCUSS

⊙ Whom do you identify with most—Sasha, Patrick, Cindy, Elena or Adam? Whom do you identify with least? Explain your responses.

'Father, if you are willing, remove this cup from me; yet, not my will but yours be done.'

LUKE 22:42

JESUS IN THE GARDEN OF GETHSEMANE | EL GRECO

⦿ Does any one of these views or a combination of views on death and life after death reflect your current understanding of the teaching of the Catholic Church on death?

DEATH IN THE SACRED SCRIPTURE

In the Old Testament the belief of God's people in life after death emerges gradually. At first, death was understood as the passage from the land of the living to *sheol,* the dark unhappy realm of the dead, where there is little to cheer about and no praise of God (see Psalm 6:5 and Isaiah 38:18). Later on, the Old Testament reveals the understanding of death as the separation of the body and soul (see Wisdom 3:1–5) and suggests that there will be a judgment after death and a possible resurrection of the body. The Book of Daniel, which was written sometime in the second century before the birth of Christ, during a time of great persecution, provides a vision of hope in the face of certain death. Daniel declares, 'Many of those who sleep in the dust of the earth shall awake, some to everlasting life, and some to shame and everlasting contempt' (Daniel 12:2).

Referring to his own imminent death, Jesus said, 'Father, if you are willing, remove this cup from me; yet, not my will but yours be done' (Luke 22:42). How Jesus faced his own death is the model for every human death. Jesus accepted death knowing that it was only through his Death that he could accomplish what his life had promised. In Jesus' Death we see the power of love and friendship overcoming the forces of evil in the world. Jesus' Death brought both the promise of new life to the whole world and the power to bring that new life to its fullness.

The New Testament builds upon these views and clearly reveals that there is life after death, with a judgment of how we have lived that has eternal consequences. St. Paul picks up the understanding of the meaning of the first sin of Adam and Eve as causing death (see Romans 5:12–14 and 6:23). However, this death has been overcome by the Death and Resurrection of Jesus. In his letter to his friend and companion Timothy, St. Paul teaches: 'The saying is sure: If we have died with [Christ], we will also live with him' (2 Timothy 2:11). At Mass we profess this mystery of faith when we pray aloud or sing, 'We proclaim your Death, O Lord, and profess your Resurrection until you come again' (*The Roman Missal*). Christ has defeated both death and sin;

and through the graces of Baptism and the other Sacraments, so can we.

REFLECT AND DISCUSS

⊙ Imagine a friend challenges the notion of life after death; how would you argue for it?

OVER TO YOU

⊙ What strikes you as true from what we have just read. Why?

⊙ What strikes you as surprising? Why?

⊙ What are the implications for our lives? Why?

FROM THE CATECHISM
Just as Christ is risen and lives for ever, so all of us will rise at the last day.

—CCC, no. 1016

JUDGMENT AFTER DEATH

Just before he died, Jesus assured the repentant good thief, whom tradition names Dismas, 'Truly I tell you, today you will be with me in Paradise' (Luke 23:43). The dying Jesus dramatically and compassionately revealed that God alone and no human tribunal is the judge of our life. Our judgment is in the hands of a merciful God. On other occasions, Jesus also taught that there is a clear connection between the way we live our life on earth and our life after death. In the parable of the Rich Man and Lazarus in Luke 16:19–31, Jesus teaches us that the way we live our life on earth has consequences for our life after death. In the parable of the Judgment of Nations in Matthew 25:31–46, he teaches that God will hold us accountable for how we have lived our life on earth.

Christian faith distinguishes between the **Particular Judgment** and the **Last Judgment**. The Particular Judgment is the individual judgment of a person that takes place at the moment of a person's death. Our whole life—our actions, our thoughts, our feelings, past and present—will be open to God and also to us. It is a moment of utter honesty in the presence of God. We will see ourselves as we really are—the person we have freely chosen to become. There will be no more masks, no more hiding, pretending and fooling ourselves. This judgment will be a time of searing

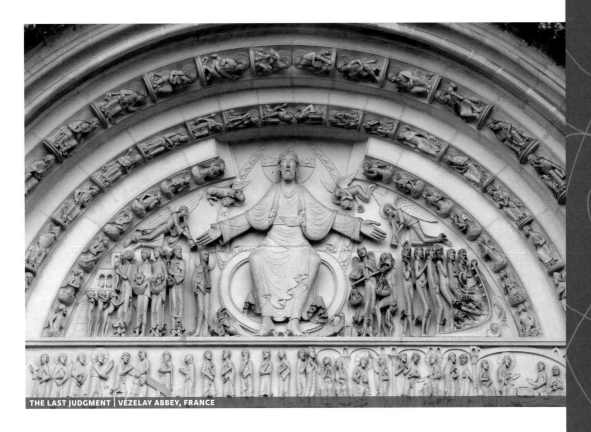
THE LAST JUDGMENT | VÉZELAY ABBEY, FRANCE

truthfulness. It will be a time when we will have to take full responsibility for our life on earth.

In the Synoptic Gospels the Last Judgment is often revealed in the condemnation of sinners who do not repent. When this judgment takes place, it is final, outside and beyond history. In the Apostles' Creed we profess that the risen Jesus will come again 'to judge the living and the dead'. In the Nicene Creed we profess that the risen Jesus 'ascended into heaven. . . . He will come again in glory to judge the living and the dead, and his kingdom will have no end'. (Read 2 Peter 3:1–13.) 'The Last Judgment will reveal that God's justice triumphs over all the injustices committed by his creatures and that God's love is stronger than death' (CCC, no. 1040).

At the Last, or Final, Judgment, all things will finally be made right. God's power over evil will finally be revealed. God's reign will conquer the efforts of the powers of evil and death for ever and ever. Christ 'will come again in glory to judge the living and the dead and his kingdom will have no end (Nicene Creed). Each of us will appear in our own 'resurrected' bodies before Christ, the Just Judge of the living and the dead, to give an account of our life. People who die in friendship with God are People of God beyond death. All creation itself will be transformed into a new heaven and a new earth. (Read Romans 8:18–25 and Revelation 21:1.) The **Kingdom of God** will come in its fullness 'so that God may be all in all' (1 Corinthians 15:28). God's original plan of goodness for all creation, visible and invisible, material and spiritual, will finally be restored as he promised. All creation will join in one voice to give glory to God forever.

FROM THE CATECHISM
Those who die in God's grace and friendship and are perfectly purified live for ever with Christ.

—CCC, no. 1023

FAITH WORD

Last Judgment
The moment at the end of time when everyone will appear before Christ and receive an eternal recompense in accord with their earthly life.

—USCCA, 517

THE LAST JUDGMENT | FRA ANGELICO

READ, REFLECT AND SHARE

⊙ Read the parable of the Judgment of Nations in Matthew 25:31–46. In this parable Jesus gives an amazing and most revealing description of this Final Judgment of all people.

⊙ What is the criterion on which God will judge people?

⊙ What other teachings of Jesus help us understand this criterion; for example, his giving his disciples the new commandment at the Last Supper in John 13:31–35. Use your Bible to help you locate and identify these teachings.

CREATE A PARABLE

⊙ Work in small groups and create a contemporary version of the parable of the Judgment of Nations.

⊙ Choose your audience; for example, world leaders gathered at the United Nations or a world summit, members of Congress, bankers, energy suppliers, and so on.

⊙ Use images from the life and culture of your audience.

⊙ Now create your parable and share it with the whole class.

'Truly I tell you, just as you did it to one of the least of these who are members of my family, you did it to me.'

MATTHEW 25:40

WHAT ABOUT YOU PERSONALLY?

⊙ Do you identify with the 'sheep' or the 'goats' in the parable? Perhaps, a little of both?

⊙ Relate your thoughts to what you learned about conversion in chapter 11.

⊙ How do you think you would feel if you knew that the Last Judgment was to happen very soon? Would you be well prepared for it? What might you reassess in your life?

Heaven, Purgatory and Hell

PARADISE | GIOVANNI DI PAOLO

Since the days of the early Church, Christians have professed their belief in Heaven, **Purgatory**, and Hell. These three states of life after death have been represented by many images and in different genres of story, painting, sculpture and music, and today in film and television.

OPENING CONVERSATION

⊙ Work in three groups to gather and pool your knowledge to provide as many examples as you can of Heaven, Purgatory and Hell depicted in film, television, art and music. Be as imaginative as you can, and remember, you do not have to agree with these depictions.

⊙ One group will deal with depictions of Heaven; a second group will deal with depictions of Purgatory; a third group will deal with depictions of Hell.

⊙ Each group shares with the whole class the results of its discussion.

REFLECT AND DISCUSS

⊙ What image is the most powerful for you? Explain.
⊙ Did any image coincide with your own ideas on Heaven, Purgatory or Hell? How?
⊙ Did any image conflict with your own ideas on Heaven, Purgatory or Hell? How?

OVER TO YOU

⊙ What did you learn from this exercise about where people find or how they develop their images of Heaven, Purgatory and Hell?

> FROM THE CATECHISM
> This perfect life with the Most Holy Trinity— this communion of life and love with the Trinity, with the Virgin Mary, the angels and all the blessed—is called 'heaven'. Heaven is the ultimate end and fulfillment of the deepest human longings, the state of supreme, definitive happiness.
> —CCC, no. 1024

HEAVEN

St. Paul, summarizing the teaching of Isaiah the Prophet, indirectly speaks of the 'wonder' and 'mystery' of life after death when he teaches: 'What no eye has seen, nor ear heard, nor the human heart conceived, what God has prepared for those who love him' (1 Corinthians 2:9; see also Isaiah 52:15; 64:3). Now recall St. Augustine of Hippo's well-known statement about the human search for happiness: 'Our hearts are restless, O Lord, until they rest in you.' St. Augustine was, in one sense, speaking of Heaven. This renowned Doctor and Father of the Church was teaching that Heaven is not so much a place as it is a state of eternal happiness. Heaven is being in the presence of God, face to face. Heaven is, first and above all, living in communion and intimacy with God, who is Love. The Church uses the term **Beatific Vision** to describe this eternal and intimate communion and happiness with God. 'This mystery of blessed communion with God . . . is beyond all understanding and description' (CCC, no. 1027).

For Christians, Heaven is also being with Christ and living in the presence of Christ forever. This hope is based, in part, on these words of Jesus at the Last Supper to his disciples, who were troubled over his death:

'Do not let your hearts be troubled. Believe in God, believe also in me. In my Father's house there are many dwelling places. If it were not so, would I have told you that I go to prepare a place for you? And if I go and prepare a place for you, I will come again and will take you to myself, so that where I am, there you may be also.'

—John 14:1–3

All the faithful departed gathered around Christ form the Church of Heaven. They have a concern for us, who are still making our earthly pilgrimage, and they intercede for us. They join with us, the angels, and Mary and all the saints in giving glory to God—Father, Son and Holy Spirit.

LET'S PROBE DEEPER: SCRIPTURE SEARCH AND REFLECTION

- Jesus often taught about and used many images for Heaven; for example, see Matthew 13:31–50 and Matthew 22:1–14.
- Look up and read those passages and search for other passages in which Jesus speaks of Heaven.
- Create a profile based on your reading.

ETERNAL HAPPINESS FOR ALL

What about all those people who do not come to faith in Jesus? Is there a place for them in Heaven? St. Peter teaches that God desires that all people live in eternal happiness. God does not want anyone to perish (see 2 Peter 3:9). The depth of this desire has been clearly revealed in and through Jesus Christ. The Church knows we cannot place limits on God's mercy and it teaches

THE BEATIFIC VISION | WILLIAM BLAKE

FAITH WORD

Beatific Vision

The seeing of God face to face; being and living in the presence of God in heavenly glory. The Beatific Vision is the foundation of the happiness (or beatitude) of Heaven.

—See CCC, Glossary; see also
CCC, nos. 1028, 1720

that many people, some knowingly and others unknowingly, choose to live as Jesus revealed. And so the Church, always and everywhere, continues to invite all people to come to know and believe in Christ so that they may hear the words of eternal life.

Christ commands us to proclaim the Gospel to all peoples until he comes again in glory. As Christians we cannot simply be concerned for our own attainment of salvation and eternal life of happiness with God. The love for God drives us to do everything we can to help our neighbor come to eternal life and to avoid saying or doing anything that may be an obstacle to their coming to faith in Christ. Christ admonished his disciples and warns us: 'Occasions for stumbling are bound to come, but woe to anyone by whom they come! It would be better for you if a millstone were hung around your neck and you were thrown into the sea than for you to cause one of these little ones to stumble' (Luke 17:1–3). We journey through life on earth together. We are companions on the path to life.

OVER TO YOU

⊙ In light of the above teaching of the Catholic Church on Heaven, create a visual or verbal image of Heaven that shares your hope for Heaven, a life of eternal beatitude with God.

The purification of Purgatory is another sign of God's 'prodigal' and unconditional merciful love

PURGATORY

At the moment of their death there may be people who, while they have, for the most part, lived a good and holy life, still bear some of the damaging effects and consequences of their personal sins. God, in the mystery of his infinite merciful love, continues to reach out to them and gives them the opportunity to undergo that purification necessary before achieving full union with him, with the angels, and with Mary and all the blessed in Heaven. The Church has named this state of purification 'Purgatory'. Purgatory is a temporary process through which we shed our residual selfishness and sin and are freed from the temporal punishment of sin 'so as to achieve the holiness necessary to enter the joy of God' (CCC, no. 1054). This purification is not a sign of God's vengeance or desire to punish. It is but another sign of his 'prodigal' and unconditional merciful love and of his desire that all live in and share in his love forever. Since Purgatory takes place after life on earth and therefore outside of time, we cannot say that Purgatory is either long or short in terms of time as we know and experience it in our life on earth.

DANTE'S VISION OF PURGATORY | GUSTAVE DORÉ

COLORFUL CANDLES ARE LIT IN CEMETERIES IN POLAND ON ALL SOULS' DAY

Catholics set aside All Souls' Day each year to pray and intercede for all the faithful departed

We see a glimpse of the Revelation of the reality of Purgatory in the Old Testament. In the Second Book of Maccabees, which was written in the late second century before the birth of Christ, we read, 'Therefore [Judas Maccabeus] made atonement for the dead, that they might be delivered from their sin' (2 Maccabees 12:45). This Revelation is the foundation of the Church's doctrine of Purgatory. People believed that the dead needed prayers to help them as they came face to face with God. The early Church's belief in Purgatory is passed on in the New Testament. (Check out Matthew 5:26 and 12:32 and 1 Corinthians 3:11–15.) While these texts do not make explicit mention of the name Purgatory, the Catholic Church, guided by the Holy Spirit, sees in Sacred Scripture the Revelation of the reality that we can make up for sins in both this world and the next.

The Church for centuries has passed on this faith of the Apostolic Church in many ways, including the celebration of All Souls' Day on November 2. Catholics set aside November 2 each year to pray and intercede for all the faithful departed. So, just as we can communicate with and pray for someone who is living, we can

communicate with and pray for someone who has died. Our Catholic faith gives us a vision of life that addresses those feelings of 'unfinished business' with someone who has died. We can not only work for and do good things that benefit people who are living on earth; we can also do acts of goodness and love that can benefit the faithful departed. Pope Paul VI, who was Pope from June 21, 1963 to August 6, 1978, reminded us of the bond that unites the Church on earth with the Church of Heaven. He taught:

DANTE'S VISION OF HELL | GUSTAVE DORÉ

Hell is a self-imposed permanent and eternal alienation and exclusion from Love, who is God

A perennial link of charity exists between the faithful who have already reached their heavenly home, those who are expiating their sins in Purgatory and those who are still pilgrims on earth. Between them there is an abundant exchange of all good things.

—*Indulgentiarum Doctrina* [On the Doctrine and the Practice of Indulgences], no. 5

One cherished Catholic practice of praying for those who have died is to have the holy **sacrifice** of the Mass offered for the repose of the soul of a departed relative or friend. During each celebration of Mass, we raise up our prayers for all the faithful departed. Catholics also have the tradition of pausing during the day to remember their loved ones who have died and to pray, 'Eternal rest grant unto them, O Lord, and let perpetual light shine upon them. May they rest in peace. Amen'.

OVER TO YOU

⊙ In light of the above explanation, create a visual or verbal image of Purgatory that makes sense to you.

HELL

Jesus' last prayer for his first disciples was that they would come to know the love that his Father has for him and for them and that they would so share in that love that they would be one with him and the Father as the Father and he are one. (Read John 17.) Jesus not only desires such happiness for us, but he offers us all the graces and opportunities to move us to freely choose to accept the divine invitation. Jesus himself warned his disciples and us that those who do not live by his commandment of love of God and neighbor will be separated from him in life everlasting

Indulgences

An indulgence is a partial or the full remission of sins before God or the temporal punishment that still remains of sins whose guilt is forgiven. Indulgences may be obtained by a properly disposed member of the Christian faithful for themselves or for the dead. Indulgences are granted through the Church, the minister of the saving work of Christ.

(read Matthew 25:31–46; see also Matthew 5:22, 29, 10:28, 13:41–42, 50; Mark 9:43–48). The First Letter of John teaches 'We know that we have passed from death to life because we love one another. Whoever does not love abides in death. All who hate a brother or sister are murderers, and you know that murderers do not have eternal life abiding in them' (1 John 3:14–15). The state of living eternally separated from God's love is named 'Hell'. As with Heaven and Purgatory, Hell is not so much a physical place as we often imagine. It is a state of being, a self-imposed permanent and eternal alienation and exclusion from Love, who is God.

Hell is the eternal state of our choosing to live a life separated from God forever. Hell is the consequence of a person freely and knowingly choosing not to have the life of happiness for which God created him or her and for which he or she longs. The paradox of the mystery of God's unconditional love is that God respects the choices we knowingly and freely make, as we must accept their consequences. The most devastating misuse of our freedom is to turn our backs on God and spurn his love, not just temporarily but eternally. Blessed Pope John Paul II described the reality of Hell in this way: 'Hell is the definitive rejection of God, a state for those who freely and definitively separate themselves from God, the source of all life and joy.' The consequence of this choice is a self-imposed, eternal alienation from God.

OVER TO YOU

⊙ In light of the above explanation of the teaching of the Catholic Church on Hell, create a visual or verbal image of Hell that makes sense to you.

REFLECT AND DISCUSS

⊙ Share your images of Heaven, Purgatory and Hell in light of what you have learned in this chapter. Discuss:
  – What wisdom have you learned from your shared images?
  – Have your own earlier images of Heaven, Purgatory and Hell changed in any way as a result of what you learned in this chapter? If so, how?
  – What are some of the practical implications of what you have learned for your life right here and right now on earth?

The First Letter of John teaches: 'We know that we have passed from death to life because we love one another.'

Communion of the living and the dead

Read this reflection by Fr. Ronald Rolheiser, whom you met at the opening of this chapter, on how death can leave much unfinished business:

> I was once counseling a man, a priest in his fifties, who was still unable to forgive himself because when he was a young, shy and frightened boy of seven, and his mother lay dying, he was too afraid to give her a hug when she asked for it. More than forty years later, he still nursed guilt and a deep regret for this unfinished business with his long-dead mother.

Death can leave much unfinished business. Some people die unexpectedly and long before their time. Others can be left behind feeling unforgiven or unforgiving. Some people are full of regret for things not said or done, or indeed for things said or done that they now regret, and alienated from the one who has died. Death can appear to take away the opportunity to put right what needs attention and it can seem like the issues will never be resolved.

REFLECT AND DISCUSS

- Have you ever had the experience of being left with unfinished business? Perhaps you wanted to tell somebody about your plans for the future, but you didn't get around to it. Maybe you felt guilty for breaking the confidence of a good friend.
- How do you respond to the belief that it is possible to resolve matters with someone who has died?

THE COMMUNION OF SAINTS

Do you think of yourself as a 'saint'? St. Paul would have called you just that. The name 'saint' is usually reserved for someone who now lives in Heaven. But, we are 'saints in progress'. We are saints in the sense that St. Paul used the term. We are called to give glory to God by living a holy life on earth and forever with God after our life on earth ends. The vast majority of the time, holiness is lived in the very ordinary things and events of our daily life. Sainthood, 'holiness of life', is not so much accomplished through heroic acts as through perseverance in the daily living of our faith in the ordinary, everyday events of life— as St. Thérèse of Lisieux modeled so well for us.

There is a real connection between the faithful who are living on earth and the faithful living in life after death. Joined to Christ in

The Communion of Saints is a communion of holy people, living and dead. It is also a communion of 'holy things'

ALTARCITO AT A TAXI STAND IN ACAPULCO, MEXICO

Baptism, there is a bond that unites the members of the Church on earth, the souls in Purgatory and the Church in Heaven. All the faithful belong to the one Body of Christ. The bond of Baptism is never broken, not even by death. We call this connection the **Communion of Saints**. The communion of saints is a communion of holy people, living and dead. It is also a communion of 'holy things' (CCC, no. 948): the faithful share in the faith of the Church; in the Sacraments, especially the Eucharist, and in the gifts each one has been given for the good of all; and they share their possessions and live in solidarity with all people.

To deepen our own appreciation for our life in the Communion of Saints, we need first to get our heads around the notion that *we are* members of such a community, a community of holy people. We live in communion with Christ and with one another both here on earth and in the life everlasting.

THINK, PAIR AND SHARE

- Who are the 'saints' on earth whom you know? What are the signs that show they are holy?
- How do you respond to the belief that being a saint is accomplished by living our faith in Christ in the ordinary, everyday events of life?
- What does the call to be a saint mean for the lives of young people today?

OVER TO YOU

- Just like we talk to the saints, we can talk to family and friends who have died. Do you talk with someone you know who has died? Do you thank them? Ask for forgiveness?

El Altarcito

When you visit a Hispanic Catholic household, you are likely to find a special place or corner where family members have built an *altarcito* (Spanish for 'little altar'). The *altarcito* is a place where people put sacred images of Jesus, Mary and the saints alongside other religious objects such as crosses, medals, rosary beads and prayer cards. Some *altarcitos* will have a Bible available for people to read when praying. Others have pictures of relatives and friends who have died or who are away for some reason (for example, migrants, soldiers, students).

The *altarcito* is a reminder that the world is a sacred space, where God becomes present in many ways and especially in our homes. For many Latinos(as), as well as for many other Catholics around the world, the *altarcito* is the place where one learns in a very visual way that 'God is with us', that Mary and the saints are part of our family, that prayer brings the family together, and that when we need to encounter God here and now we can do so at this sacred place within our home. The *altarcito* does not replace participation in the liturgical life of the Church; rather, it extends the Liturgy into the home.

SAINTS IN HEAVEN: MODELS AND PARTNERS IN DISCIPLESHIP

Mary and the other saints model for us how we might live the life of a saint. The saints are our 'great cloud of witnesses' (Hebrews 12:1) who show us the many ways by which we can live holy lives as faithful disciples of Jesus. To be a saint, a faithful disciple of Christ, the Holy One of God, can sound way out of our reach. But when we look to the life of such saints as St. Benedict of Nursia and his twin sister St. Scholastica, St. Francis and St. Clare of Assisi, St. Hedwig and St. Casimir, St. Thérèse of Lisieux and her parents, St. Frances Cabrini and St. Vincent de Paul, St. Anrê Tran An Dung and St. Andrew Kim Taegon, and St. Rose of Lima and St. Lorenzo Ruiz, we begin to get a practical sense of how to go about living holy and good lives as Jesus did and taught us to do.

We can also think of the people whom the Church has named and honors to be 'saints' or 'blessed', who lived in the Americas, such as St. Elizabeth Ann Seton, St. Martin de Porres, Blessed Juan Bautista and Blessed Jacinto de los Angeles, St. Juan Diego Cuauhtlatoatzin, St. Kateri Tekakwitha, St. Marianne Cope, St. Katharine Drexel and St. Pierre Toussaint. All of these disciples of Jesus were 'ordinary' people like ourselves— even the very famous saints who did amazing and heroic things.

Through the lives of all the saints 'God shows, vividly, to humanity his presence and his face. He speaks to us in them and offers us a sign of his kingdom, to which we are powerfully attracted, so great a cloud of witnesses are we given' (Vatican II, *Constitution on the Church*, no. 50).

Patron saints: People often have a 'patron saint' to whom they look in a special way for good example, for prayers and intercession. If you are named after a saint, or if your school or parish has a patron saint, then that saint could be your patron saint too. This tradition of the Church gives a sense of having a particular friend and model in Heaven, an 'insider' who can help you live as a friend of God.

Praying to the saints: We look to the saints both as models and as intercessors. We learn from their example and speak with them (pray to them). We talk things over with them and ask their help in living as a friend of God, in much the same way as we would speak to trusted family members and friends. We ask the saints to join our prayers to their own and bring them to God, who alone can answer our prayers. On the Solemnity of All Saints, November 1, we remember and celebrate the lives of all the saints, those whom the Church has canonized and all the other saints who now live in the eternal presence of God. You may have loved ones among them.

TALK IT OVER

⊙ Share with one another something you know about one of the saints who helps you live as a disciple of Christ.

OVER TO YOU

⊙ How do you evaluate the Catholic tradition of looking to the saints for good example and prayers of intercession? Does this tradition still have a place in our world today? Why or why not?

⊙ Who among the saints—famous or anonymous—might you choose to learn from and pray to, and why this particular saint?

ELIZABETH ANN SETON | 19TH-CENTURY ENGRAVING

JUDGE AND ACT

REVIEW WHAT YOU HAVE LEARNED

Look back over this chapter and reflect on what you have learned about the Catholic Church's teachings on the Last Things; namely, death and Judgment, Heaven, Purgatory and Hell. Share your understanding of the teaching of the Catholic Church on these statements:

- All the faithful belong to the Communion of Saints that unites all the faithful, both those living on earth and those who have died.
- At the moment of death our life is changed, not ended. Death is the doorway to life everlasting.
- Every person's life on earth is judged at the moment of his or her death and when Christ comes again in glory.
- Every person receives the eternal consequences of how he or she has cooperated with the grace of God and lived their life in this world.
- After death the faithful will live in a state of eternal happiness with God, or Heaven.
- The faithful who die in a state of holiness of life and love of God but who have not yet reached the degree of holiness of life that enables them to be invited to enjoy eternal life, must undergo a process of purification, or Purgatory.
- After death those who turn their backs on God's love and spurn him will live in a state of eternal alienation from God, or Hell.
- All the faithful living on earth and those who have died form the Communion of Saints, the holy People of God.

REFLECT AND DISCERN

- What are some implications of the teaching of the Catholic Church on life after death for your present lifestyle—your values, commitments, priorities and best hopes?

LEARN BY EXAMPLE

The story of Día de los Muertos

Catholics in Mexico, Mexican American Catholics and Catholics in other Central American countries have a special regard for the memory of *los muertos* (the dead) in their religious traditions. They usually celebrate *El día de los Muertos*, the Day of the Dead, on November 1 and 2, when the Church celebrates the Feasts of All Saints and All Souls respectively.

DAY OF THE DEAD, JANITZIO, MICHOACAN, MEXICO

On the *Día de los Muertos* a number of religious and cultural traditions come together in unique ways. Without a doubt, Catholicism has strongly shaped the celebration, but it is not the only influence. Certain indigenous traditions come alive through many of the rituals that are part of the celebration, such as dances, songs, prayers, and the preparing and sharing of food—especially the favorite dishes of the remembered dead. People also create colorful *altares* (altars) around the graves of their beloved dead. On these altars, symbols of life and death share the same space—as if there is little difference between them.

Ultimately, *Día de los Muertos* is an affirmation of life: death does not have the final word. This celebration—not a lamentation—reflects the rock-solid conviction that Jesus Christ has conquered death and that the living and the dead remain united in the one Body of Christ.

THE LAST JUDGMENT (CENTER PANELS) | ROGIER VAN DER WEYDEN

THINK, PAIR AND SHARE

⊙ Does your family celebrate your communion with the saints of God, with all the faithful who have died? Share your experiences.

⊙ Talk about how your parish celebrates any special customs that honor or celebrate the lives of the saints.

WHAT ABOUT YOU PERSONALLY?

The core message of the Catholic Church's teaching on the 'Last Things' is that at the moment of our death our life is transformed. The quality of the life everlasting we will have is a consequence of the way we have lived our life on earth.

⊙ Choose three great truths about death, judgment, life after death and the Communion of Saints that you learned during your exploration of this chapter.

⊙ What are they and why did you choose them?

⊙ What hopes and challenges do they offer you?

⊙ How can you take these truths to heart and allow them to permeate your daily life from here on?

SHARE YOUR FAITH WITH FAMILY AND FRIENDS

⊙ Think about all the people who have shared their faith with you, especially by the example of their life.

⊙ Name those people and share with family members and friends what it was in their lives that helped you come to a deeper lived faith in Jesus Christ.

OVER TO YOU

⊙ How do you think the way you are living now is impacting others?

⊙ If someone were to post your 'obituary' on line right now, what part of it would focus on the role your faith in Christ played in your life? Would you be satisfied?

JUDGE AND ACT

⊙ Choose one of the truths of our faith that you named in the 'What About You Personally?' activity.

⊙ Think about what difference this truth of the Church might make to how you live your life.

⊙ Decide now: What role do you want the Communion of Saints to have in your life of faith?

LEARN BY HEART

If we have died with [Christ], we will also live with him.

2 TIMOTHY 2:11

PRAYER REFLECTION

LEADER
Converse with God for a few moments in the quiet of your heart.
(Pause for silent reflection.)

LEADER
Let us begin our prayer very much aware that God is with us.
ALL
Pray the Sign of the Cross together.

LEADER
Together let us pray:
ALL
Something in me is stirring;
I think it's the part of me
that waits in lonely exile
and yearns for a homeland.
(Pause for silent reflection)

READER
A reading from the Book of the Prophet Jeremiah.
Proclaim Jeremiah 29:10–14.
The Word of the Lord.

ALL
Thanks be to God.

READER
Loving God, through the guidance of all the saints, living and dead, give us the courage to act with practical love in our lives. We pray to the Lord.
ALL
Lord, hear our prayer.

LEADER
I now invite other prayers from the group.

Students who wish to do so may offer their individual prayers, to which all respond: 'Lord, hear our prayer.'

LEADER
Loving God, you have heard the prayers we have spoken and you know the ones deep in our hearts. We ask you to grant them, through Christ our Lord.

ALL
Amen.

LEADER
We will now invoke the help of the saints to live our faith with joy and integrity. Respond 'Pray for us' after each petition.

READER
Holy Mary, Mother of God
St. Michael
Holy angels of God
St. John the Baptist
St. Joseph
Sts. Peter and Paul and all the Apostles
St. Mary Magdalene
St. Stephen
St. Perpetua and St. Felicity
St. Augustine and St. Athanasius
St. Francis and St. Dominic
St. Martin de Porres and St. Rose of Lima
St. Teresa of Jesus and St. Thérèse of Lisieux
St. Anrê Tran An Dung and St. Andrew Kim Taegon
St. Lorenzo Ruiz and St. Juan Diego
St. Hedwig and St. Casimir
St. Elizabeth Ann Seton and St. Katharine Drexel
St. Kateri Tekakwitha and St. Marianne Cope
All you holy people.

LEADER
We invite all who wish to invoke the names of other saints, or holy persons, perhaps from your family history or from your family's faith life, to do so.

ALL
Respond 'Pray for us' *at the conclusion of the last petition.*

LEADER
God of our ancestors who set their hearts on you,
of those who fell asleep in peace,
and of those who won the martyrs' violent
    crown:
we are surrounded by these witnesses as by
    clouds of fragrant incense.
In this age we would be counted in this
    communion of saints;
keep us always in their good and blessed
    company.
In their midst we make every prayer through
    Christ who is Lord for ever and ever.

ALL
Amen.

Conclude by praying the Sign of the Cross together.

CATHOLIC PRAYERS, DEVOTIONS AND PRACTICES

SIGN OF THE CROSS
In the name of the Father,
and of the Son,
and of the Holy Spirit. Amen.

OUR FATHER (LORD'S PRAYER)
Our Father who art in heaven,
hallowed be thy name;
thy kingdom come,
thy will be done
on earth as it is in heaven.
Give us this day our daily bread,
and forgive us our trespasses,
as we forgive those who trespass against us;
and lead us not into temptation,
but deliver us from evil. Amen.

GLORY PRAYER (DOXOLOGY)
Glory be to the Father,
and to the Son,
and to the Holy Spirit;
as it was in the beginning
is now, and ever shall be,
world without end. Amen.

PRAYER TO THE HOLY SPIRIT
Come, Holy Spirit, fill the hearts of your faithful.
And kindle in them the fire of your love.
Send forth your Spirit and they shall be created.
And you shall renew the face of the earth.

O God, by the light of the Holy Spirit you have
    taught the hearts of your faithful.
In the same Spirit, help us to know what is truly
    right and always to rejoice in your consolation.
We ask this through Christ, our Lord. Amen.

HAIL MARY
Hail Mary, full of grace,
the Lord is with thee.
Blessed art thou among women
and blessed is the fruit of thy womb, Jesus.
Holy Mary, Mother of God,

pray for us sinners,
now and at the hour of our death. Amen.

APOSTLES' CREED
I believe in God,
the Father almighty,
Creator of heaven and earth,
and in Jesus Christ, his only Son, our Lord,
who was conceived by the Holy Spirit,
born of the Virgin Mary,
suffered under Pontius Pilate,
was crucified, died, and was buried;
he descended into hell;
on the third day he rose again from the dead;
he ascended into heaven,
and is seated at the right hand of God the Father
    almighty,
from there he will come to judge the living and
    the dead.

I believe in the Holy Spirit,
the holy catholic Church,
the communion of saints,
the forgiveness of sins,
the resurrection of the body,
and life everlasting. Amen.

NICENE CREED
I believe in one God,
the Father almighty,
maker of heaven and earth,
of all things visible and invisible.

I believe in one Lord Jesus Christ,
the Only Begotten Son of God,
born of the Father before all ages.
God from God, Light from Light,
true God from true God,
begotten, not made, consubstantial with the
    Father;
through him all things were made.
For us men and for our salvation
he came down from heaven,

and by the Holy Spirit was incarnate of the Virgin
    Mary,
and became man.

For our sake he was crucified under Pontius Pilate,
he suffered death and was buried,
and rose again on the third day
in accordance with the Scriptures.
He ascended into heaven
and is seated at the right hand of the Father.
He will come again in glory
to judge the living and the dead,
and his kingdom will have no end.

I believe in the Holy Spirit, the Lord, the giver of life,
who proceeds from the Father and the Son,
who with the Father and the Son is adored and
    glorified,
who has spoken through the prophets.

I believe in one, holy, catholic and apostolic
    Church.
I confess one Baptism for the forgiveness of sins
and I look forward to the resurrection of the dead
and the life of the world to come. Amen.

JESUS PRAYER
Lord Jesus Christ, Son of God, have mercy on me,
    a sinner. Amen.

ACT OF FAITH
O my God, I firmly believe that you are one God
in three divine Persons, Father, Son, and Holy
Spirit. I believe that your divine Son became man
and died for our sins and that he will come to
judge the living and the dead. I believe these and
all the truths which the Holy Catholic Church
teaches because you have revealed them, who
are eternal truth and wisdom, who can neither
deceive nor be deceived. In this faith I intend to
live and die. Amen.

ACT OF HOPE
O Lord God, I hope by your grace for the pardon
of all my sins and after life here to gain eternal
happiness because you have promised it, who are
infinitely powerful, faithful, kind, and merciful. In
this hope I intend to live and die. Amen.

ACT OF LOVE
O Lord God, I love you above all things and I love
my neighbor for your sake because you are the
highest, infinite and perfect good, worthy of all
my love. In this love I intend to live and die. Amen.

PRAYER FOR VOCATIONS
Loving Mother, Our Lady of Guadalupe,
you asked Juan Diego to help build a Church that
    would serve a new people in a new land.
You left your image upon his cloak as a visible
    sign of your love for us,
so that we may come to believe in your Son, Jesus
    the Christ.
Our Lady of Guadalupe and St. Juan Diego,
help us respond to God's call to build your Son's
    Church today.
Help us recognize our personal vocation to serve
    God as married or single persons or priests,
    brothers or sisters as our way to help extend
    the Reign of God here on earth.
Help us pay attention to the promptings of the
    Holy Spirit.
May all of us have the courage of Juan Diego to
    say 'Yes' to our personal call!
May we encourage one another to follow Jesus,
    no matter where that path takes us. Amen.

Daily Prayers

Morning Prayer
CANTICLE OF ZECHARIAH (THE *BENEDICTUS*)
(based on Luke 1:67–79)
Blessed be the Lord, the God of Israel;
for he has come to his people and set them free.
He has raised up for us a mighty Savior,
born of the House of his servant David.
Through his prophets he promised of old
    that he would save us from our enemies,
    from the hands of all who hate us.
He promised to show mercy to our fathers
and to remember his holy covenant.
This was the oath he swore to our father Abraham:
to set us free from the hand of our enemies,
free to worship him without fear,
holy and righteous in his sight
    all the days of our life.

You, my child, shall be called the prophet of the
Most High,
for you will go before the Lord to prepare his way,
to give his people knowledge of salvation
by the forgiveness of their sins.
In the tender compassion of our God
the dawn from on high shall break upon us,
to shine on those who dwell in darkness and the
shadow of death,
and to guide our feet into the way of peace.
Amen.

MORNING OFFERING

O Jesus, through the Immaculate Heart of Mary,
I offer you my prayers, works, joys and sufferings
of this day
for all the intentions of your Sacred Heart,
in union with the Holy Sacrifice of the Mass
throughout the world,
for the salvation of souls, the reparation for sins,
the reunion of all Christians,
and in particular for the intentions of the Holy
Father this month. Amen.

Evening Prayer
CANTICLE OF MARY (THE *MAGNIFICAT*)

My soul proclaims the greatness of the Lord;
my spirit rejoices in God my savior
for he has looked with favor on his lowly servant.
From this day all generations will call me blessed:
the Almighty has done great things for me
and holy is his name.
He has mercy on those who fear him
in every generation.
He has shown the strength of his arm,
and has scattered the proud in their conceit.
He has cast down the mighty from their thrones,
and has lifted up the lowly.
He has filled the hungry with good things,
and the rich he has sent away empty.
He has come to the help of his servant Israel
for he has remembered his promise of mercy,
the promise he made to our fathers,
to Abraham and his children forever. Amen.

GRACE BEFORE MEALS

Bless us, O Lord, and these your gifts,
which we are about to receive from your bounty,
through Christ our Lord. Amen.

GRACE AFTER MEALS

We give you thanks for all your benefits, almighty
God, who lives and reigns forever.
And may the souls of the faithful departed,
through the mercy of God, rest in peace.
Amen.

PRAYER OF ST. FRANCIS (PEACE PRAYER)

Lord, make me an instrument of your peace:
where there is hatred, let me sow love;
where there is injury, pardon;
where there is doubt, faith;
where there is despair, hope;
where there is darkness, light;
where there is sadness, joy.

O divine Master, grant that I may not so much seek
to be consoled as to console,
to be understood, as to understand,
to be loved as to love.

For it is in giving that we receive,
it is in pardoning that we are pardoned,
it is in dying that we are born to eternal life.
Amen.

Contrition and Sorrow
CONFITEOR

I confess to almighty God
and to you, my brothers and sisters,
that I have greatly sinned,
in my thoughts and in my words,
in what I have done and in what I have failed to
do,
through my fault, through my fault,
through my most grievous fault;
therefore I ask blessed Mary ever-Virgin,
all the Angels and Saints,
and you, my brothers and sisters,
to pray for me to the Lord our God. Amen.

ACT OF CONTRITION

O my God, I am heartily sorry for having offended
you, and I detest all my sins because of your
just punishments, but most of all because
they offend you, my God, who are all good and
deserving of all my love. I firmly resolve with the
help of your grace to sin no more and to avoid
the near occasion of sin. Amen.

Prayers before the Holy Eucharist

THE DIVINE PRAISES

Blessed be God.
Blessed be his holy name.
Blessed be Jesus Christ, true God and true man.
Blessed be the name of Jesus.
Blessed be his most Sacred Heart.
Blessed be his most precious Blood.
Blessed be Jesus in the most holy Sacrament of the altar.
Blessed be the Holy Spirit, the Paraclete.
Blessed be the great Mother of God, Mary most holy.
Blessed be her holy and Immaculate Conception.
Blessed be her glorious Assumption.
Blessed be the name of Mary, Virgin and Mother.
Blessed be St. Joseph, her most chaste spouse.
Blessed be God in his angels and in his saints.

ANIMA CHRISTI (SOUL OF CHRIST)

Soul of Christ, sanctify me.
Body of Christ, save me.
Blood of Christ, inebriate me.
Water from the side of Christ, wash me.
Passion of Christ, strengthen me.
O good Jesus, hear me.
Within your wounds hide me.
Permit me not to be separated from you.
From the malicious enemy defend me.
In the hour of my death call me.
And bid me come to you,
that with your saints I may praise you
forever and ever. Amen.

AN ACT OF SPIRITUAL COMMUNION

My Jesus, I believe that you are present in the Most Blessed Sacrament.
I love you above all things, and I desire to receive you into my soul.
Since I cannot at this moment receive you sacramentally, come at least spiritually into my heart.
I embrace you as if you were already there and unite myself wholly to you.
Never permit me to be separated from you. Amen.

Prayers to Mary, Mother of God

ANGELUS

Verse: The Angel of the Lord declared unto Mary.
Response: And she conceived of the Holy Spirit.
            Hail Mary, full of grace,
            the Lord is with thee.
            Blessed art thou among women
            and blessed is the fruit of thy womb, Jesus.
            Holy Mary, Mother of God,
            pray for us sinners,
            now and at the hour of our death. Amen.
Verse: Behold the handmaid of the Lord.
Response: Be it done unto me according to your Word.
            Hail Mary. . . .
Verse: And the Word was made flesh,
Response: And dwelt among us.
            Hail Mary. . . .
Verse: Pray for us, O holy Mother of God,
Response: That we may be made worthy of the promises of Christ.

Let us pray. Pour forth, we beseech you, O Lord, your grace into our hearts: that we, to whom the Incarnation of Christ your Son was made known by the message of an Angel, may by his Passion and Cross be brought to the glory of his Resurrection. Through the same Christ our Lord. Amen.

MEMORARE

Remember, O most gracious Virgin Mary, that never was it known that anyone who fled to your protection, implored your help, or sought your intercession, was left unaided. Inspired by this confidence, I fly unto you, O Virgin of virgins, my mother; to you do I come, before you I stand, sinful and sorrowful. O Mother of the Word Incarnate, despise not my petitions, but in your mercy hear and answer me. Amen.

REGINA CAELI (QUEEN OF HEAVEN)

Queen of Heaven, rejoice, alleluia:
for the Son you were privileged to bear, alleluia,
is risen as he said, alleluia.
Pray for us to God, alleluia.

Verse: Rejoice and be glad, O Virgin Mary, Alleluia!

Response: For the Lord is truly risen, Alleluia.

Let us pray. O God, who gave joy to the world through the resurrection of your Son, our Lord Jesus Christ, grant, we beseech you, that through the intercession of the Virgin Mary, his Mother, we may obtain the joys of everlasting life. Through the same Christ our Lord. Amen.

SALVE, REGINA (HAIL, HOLY QUEEN)

Hail, holy Queen, Mother of mercy: Hail, our life, our sweetness and our hope. To you do we cry, poor banished children of Eve. To you do we send up our sighs, mourning and weeping in this valley of tears. Turn then, most gracious advocate, your eyes of mercy toward us; and after this our exile show unto us the blessed fruit of your womb, Jesus. O clement, O loving, O sweet Virgin Mary. Amen.

PRAYER TO OUR LADY OF GUADALUPE

God of power and mercy,
you blessed the Americas at Tepeyac
with the presence of the Virgin Mary of
    Guadalupe.
May her prayers help all men and women
to accept each other as brothers and sisters.
Through your justice present in our hearts
may your peace reign in the world. Amen.

THE ROSARY

THE JOYFUL MYSTERIES: Traditionally prayed on Mondays and Saturdays and on Sundays of the Christmas Season.

1. The Annunciation
2. The Visitation
3. The Nativity
4. The Presentation in the Temple
5. The Finding of Jesus after Three Days in the Temple

THE LUMINOUS MYSTERIES: Traditionally prayed on Thursdays.

1. The Baptism at the Jordan
2. The Miracle at Cana
3. The Proclamation of the Kingdom and the Call to Conversion
4. The Transfiguration
5. The Institution of the Eucharist

THE SORROWFUL MYSTERIES: Traditionally prayed on Tuesdays and Fridays and on the Sundays of Lent.

1. The Agony in the Garden
2. The Scourging at the Pillar
3. The Crowning with Thorns
4. The Carrying of the Cross
5. The Crucifixion and Death

THE GLORIOUS MYSTERIES: Traditionally prayed on Wednesdays and Sundays, except on the Sundays of Christmas and Lent.

1. The Resurrection
2. The Ascension
3. The Descent of the Holy Spirit at Pentecost
4. The Assumption of Mary
5. The Crowning of the Blessed Virgin as Queen of Heaven and Earth

How to pray the Rosary

1. Pray the *Sign of the Cross* and pray the *Apostles' Creed* while holding the Crucifix.
2. Touch the first bead after the Crucifix and pray the *Our Father*, pray the *Hail Mary* on each of the next three beads, and pray the *Glory Prayer* on the next bead.
3. Go to the main part of your rosary. Say the name of the Mystery and quietly reflect on the meaning of the events of that Mystery. Pray the *Our Father*, and then, fingering each of the ten beads, pray ten *Hail Marys*. Then touch the next bead and pray the *Glory Prayer*. (Repeat the process for the next four decades.)
4. Pray the *Salve Regina (Hail, Holy Queen)* and conclude by praying:

Verse: Pray for us, O holy Mother of God.

Response: That we may be made worthy of the promises of Christ.

Let us pray. O God, whose only-begotten Son, by his life, death and Resurrection, has purchased for us the rewards of eternal life, grant, we beseech you, that meditating on these mysteries of the most holy rosary of the Blessed Virgin Mary, we may imitate what they contain and obtain what they promise, through the same Christ our Lord. Amen.

5. Conclude by praying the *Sign of the Cross*.

STATIONS, OR WAY, OF THE CROSS

The tradition of praying the Stations, or Way, of the Cross dates from the fourteenth century. The tradition, which is attributed to the Franciscans, came about to satisfy the desire of Christians who were unable to make a pilgrimage to Jerusalem. The traditional Stations of the Cross are:

FIRST STATION: Jesus is condemned to death
SECOND STATION: Jesus is made to carry his Cross
THIRD STATION: Jesus falls the first time
FOURTH STATION: Jesus meets his mother
FIFTH STATION: Simon helps Jesus to carry his Cross
SIXTH STATION: Veronica wipes the face of Jesus
SEVENTH STATION: Jesus falls the second time
EIGHTH STATION: Jesus meets the women of Jerusalem
NINTH STATION: Jesus falls the third time
TENTH STATION: Jesus is stripped of his garments
ELEVENTH STATION: Jesus is nailed to the Cross
TWELFTH STATION: Jesus dies on the Cross
THIRTEENTH STATION: Jesus is taken down from the Cross
FOURTEENTH STATION: Jesus is laid in the tomb.

In 1991 Blessed Pope John Paul gave the Church a scriptural version of the Stations. The individual names given to these stations are:

FIRST STATION: Jesus in the Garden of Gethsemane—Matthew 25:36–41
SECOND STATION: Jesus, Betrayed by Judas, Is Arrested—Mark 14:43–46
THIRD STATION: Jesus Is Condemned by the Sanhedrin—Luke 22:66–71
FOURTH STATION: Jesus Is Denied by Peter—Matthew 26:69–75
FIFTH STATION: Jesus Is Judged by Pilate—Mark 15:1–5, 15
SIXTH STATION: Jesus Is Scourged and Crowned with Thorns—John 19:1–3
SEVENTH STATION: Jesus Bears the Cross—John 19:6, 15–17

EIGHTH STATION: Jesus Is Helped by Simon the Cyrenian to Carry the Cross—Mark 15:21
NINTH STATION: Jesus Meets the Women of Jerusalem—Luke 23:27–31
TENTH STATION: Jesus Is Crucified—Luke 23:33–34
ELEVENTH STATION: Jesus Promises His Kingdom to the Good Thief—Luke 23:39–43
TWELFTH STATION: Jesus Speaks to His Mother and the Disciple—John 19:25–27
THIRTEENTH STATION: Jesus Dies on the Cross—Luke 23:44–46
FOURTEENTH STATION: Jesus Is Placed in the Tomb—Matthew 27:57–60

Some parishes conclude with a prayerful meditation on the Resurrection.

The Way of Jesus: Catholic Practices

THE SEVEN SACRAMENTS

Sacraments of Christian Initiation

BAPTISM: The Sacrament by which we are freed from all sin and are endowed with the gift of divine life, are made members of the Church, and are called to holiness and mission.

CONFIRMATION: The Sacrament that completes the grace of Baptism by a special outpouring of the Gifts of the Holy Spirit, which seals and confirms the baptized in union with Christ and calls them to a greater participation in the worship and apostolic life of the Church.

EUCHARIST: The ritual, sacramental action of thanksgiving to God which constitutes the principal Christian liturgical celebration of and communion in the Paschal Mystery of Christ. This liturgical action is also traditionally known as the Holy Sacrifice of the Mass.

Sacraments of Healing

PENANCE AND RECONCILIATION: The Sacrament in which sins committed after Baptism are forgiven, which results in reconciliation with God and the Church. This Sacrament is also called the Sacrament of Confession.

ANOINTING OF THE SICK: This Sacrament is given to a person who is seriously ill or in danger of death or old age which strengthens the person with the special graces of healing and comfort and courage.

Sacraments at the Service of Communion

MARRIAGE (MATRIMONY): The Sacrament in which a baptized man and a baptized woman enter the covenant partnership of the whole of life that by its nature is ordered toward the good of the spouses and the procreation and education of offspring.

HOLY ORDERS: The Sacrament in which a bishop ordains a baptized man to be conformed to Jesus Christ by grace, to service and leadership in the Church as a bishop, priest, or deacon.

GIFTS OF THE HOLY SPIRIT

The Seven Gifts of the Holy Spirit are permanent dispositions which move us to respond to the guidance of the Spirit. The traditional list of these Gifts is derived from Isaiah 11:1–3.

WISDOM: A spiritual gift which enables one to know the purpose and plan of God.

UNDERSTANDING: This Gift stimulates us to work on knowing ourselves as part of our growth in knowing God.

COUNSEL (RIGHT JUDGMENT): This Gift guides us to follow the teaching the Holy Spirit gives us about our moral life and the training of our conscience.

FORTITUDE (COURAGE): This Gift strengthens us to choose courageously and firmly the good, despite difficulty, and also to persevere in doing what is right, despite temptation, fear or persecution.

KNOWLEDGE: This Gift directs us to a contemplation, or thoughtful reflection, on the mystery of God and the mysteries of the Catholic faith.

PIETY (REVERENCE): This Gift strengthens us to grow in respect for the Holy Trinity, for the Father who created us, for Jesus who saved us, and for the Holy Spirit who is sanctifying us.

FEAR OF THE LORD (WONDER AND AWE): This Gift infuses honesty in our relationship with God.

FRUITS OF THE HOLY SPIRIT

The Fruits of the Holy Spirit are the perfections that the Holy Spirit forms in us as the 'first fruits' of eternal glory. The Tradition of the Church lists twelve Fruits of the Holy Spirit. They are: love, joy, peace, patience, kindness, goodness, generosity, gentleness, faithfulness, modesty, self-control and chastity.

VIRTUES

The Theological Virtues

Gifts from God that enable us to choose to and to live in right relationship with the Holy Trinity.

FAITH: The virtue by which the believer gives personal adherence to God (who invites his or her response) and freely assents to the whole truth that God revealed.

HOPE: The virtue through which a person both desires and expects the fulfillment of God's promises of things to come.

CHARITY (LOVE): The virtue by which we give love to God for his own sake and love to our neighbor on account of God.

The Cardinal Moral Virtues

The four moral virtues on which all other human virtues hinge.

FORTITUDE: The virtue by which one courageously and firmly chooses the good despite difficulty and also perseveres in doing what is right despite temptation.

JUSTICE: The virtue by which one is able to give God and neighbor what is due to them.

PRUDENCE: The virtue by which one knows the true good in every circumstance and chooses the right means to reach that end.

TEMPERANCE: The virtue by which one moderates the desire for the attainment of and pleasure in earthly goods.

THE NEW LAW

The Great, or Greatest, Commandment

'You shall love the Lord your God with all your heart, and with all your soul, and with all your mind. . . . You shall love your neighbor as yourself.'

Matthew 22:37, 39, based on Deuteronomy 6:5 and Leviticus 19:18

THE NEW COMMANDMENT OF JESUS

'Love one another. Just as I have loved you, you also should love one another.' John 13:34

THE BEATITUDES

Blessed are the poor in spirit, for theirs is the kingdom of heaven.

Blessed are those who mourn, for they will be comforted.

Blessed are the meek, for they will inherit the earth.

Blessed are those who hunger and thirst for righteousness, for they will be filled.

Blessed are the merciful, for they will receive mercy.

Blessed are the pure in heart, for they will see God.

Blessed are the peacemakers, for they shall be called children of God.

Blessed are those who are persecuted for righteousness' sake, for theirs is the kingdom of heaven.

Blessed are you when people revile you and persecute you and utter all kinds of evil against you falsely on my account. Rejoice and be glad, for your reward is great in heaven, for in the same way they persecuted the prophets who were before you.

– Matthew 5:3–11

SPIRITUAL WORKS OF MERCY

Admonish and help those who sin.

Teach those who are ignorant.

Advise those who have doubts.

Comfort those who suffer.

Be patient with all people.

Forgive those who trespass against you.

Pray for the living and the dead.

CORPORAL WORKS OF MERCY

Feed the hungry.

Give drink to the thirsty.

Shelter the homeless.

Clothe the naked.

Visit the sick and those in prison.

Bury the dead.

Give alms to the poor.

THE TEN COMMANDMENTS, OR THE DECALOGUE

Traditional Catechetical Formula

FIRST: I am the LORD your God: you shall not have strange gods before me.

SECOND: You shall not take the name of the LORD your God in vain.

THIRD: Remember to keep holy the LORD'S Day.

FOURTH: Honor your father and mother.

FIFTH: You shall not kill.

SIXTH: You shall not commit adultery.

SEVENTH: You shall not steal.

EIGHTH: You shall not bear false witness against your neighbor.

NINTH: You shall not covet your neighbor's wife.

TENTH: You shall not covet your neighbor's goods.

Scriptural Formula

FIRST: I am the LORD your God, who brought you out of the land of Egypt, out of the house of slavery; you shall have no other gods before me.

SECOND: You shall not make wrongful use of the name of the LORD your God, for the LORD will not acquit anyone who misuses his name.

THIRD: Observe the sabbath day to keep it holy. . . .

FOURTH: Honor your father and your mother. . . .

FIFTH: You shall not murder.

SIXTH: Neither shall you commit adultery.

SEVENTH: Neither shall you steal.

EIGHTH: Neither shall you bear false witness against your neighbour.

NINTH: Neither shall you covet your neighbor's wife.

TENTH: Neither shall you desire . . . anything that belongs to your neighbor.

– From Deuteronomy 5:6–21

PRECEPTS OF THE CHURCH

The Precepts are positive laws made by the Church that name the minimum in prayer and moral effort for the growth of the faithful in their love of God and neighbor.

FIRST PRECEPT: Participate in Mass on Sundays and on holy days of obligation and rest from work that impedes keeping these days holy.

SECOND PRECEPT: Confess sins at least once a year.

THIRD PRECEPT: Receive the Sacrament of the Eucharist at least during the Easter Season.

FOURTH PRECEPT: Fast and abstain on the days established by the Church.

FIFTH PRECEPT: Provide for the materials of the Church according to one's ability.

SOCIAL DOCTRINE OF THE CHURCH

These seven key principles are at the foundation of the Social Doctrine, or Social Teachings, of the Catholic Church:

1. *Life and dignity of the human person.* Human life is sacred and the dignity of the human person is the foundation of the moral life of individuals and of society.

2. *Call to family, community and participation.* The human person is social by nature and has the right to participate in family life and in the life of society.

3. *Rights and responsibilities.* The human person has the fundamental right to life and to the basic necessities that support life and human decency.

4. *Option for the poor and the vulnerable.* The Gospel commands us 'to put the needs of the poor and the vulnerable first'.

5. *Dignity of work and workers.* Work is a form of participating in God's work of Creation. 'The economy must serve people and not the other way around.'

6. *Solidarity.* God is the Creator of all people. 'We are one human family whatever our national, racial, ethnic, economic and ideological differences.'

7. *Care for God's creation.* Care of the environment is a divine command and a requirement of our faith.

FAITH GLOSSARY

Abbreviations: CCC = *Catechism of the Catholic Church*; USCCA = *United States Catholic Catechism for Adults*

A

Abba: An Aramaic term of endearment that Jesus used during his agony in the garden (see Mark 14:36) to address God the Father. The term 'Abba' expresses the great intimacy between Jesus, the Son of God, and God the Father. St. Paul teaches that God invites us to address him as 'Abba', as Jesus did.

actual graces: God's interventions in our lives, whether at the beginning of [our] conversion or in the course of the work of [our] sanctification. (USCCA, 514)

adoration: The virtue and gift of the Holy Spirit by which we acknowledge that God alone is God, 'the Creator and Savior, the Lord and Master of everything that exists, as infinite and merciful Love' (CCC, no. 2096). *See also* **Blessing and Adoration, Prayer of**.

Advocate: *See* **Paraclete**.

agape: In 1 John 4:8, 16 we read: 'God is love.' The Greek word used here for 'love' was *agapē*. The word 'agape' describes God's total 'self-gift' of unconditional and infinite love, both among the Persons of the Blessed Trinity and for each and every one of us.

agnostic: Someone who claims that he or she does not know whether God exists and whose life is shaped by that lack of belief.

analogy: Analogy is a literary device or genre that is used to express truths; analogy is used to express truths about God that cannot be fully expressed in human language.

analogy of faith: The coherence of the truths of faith among themselves and within the whole plan of Revelation. (CCC, no. 114)

angel: A spiritual, personal, and immortal creature, with intelligence and free will, who glorifies God without ceasing and who serves God as a messenger of his saving plan. (CCC, Glossary)

Annunciation: The visit of the angel Gabriel to the Virgin Mary to inform her that she was to be the mother of the Savior. After giving her consent to God's Word, Mary became the mother of Jesus by the power of the Holy Spirit. (CCC, Glossary)

apocrypha: Writings about Jesus and God's Revelation that the Church has judged not to be inspired by the Holy Spirit. There were numerous apocryphal gospels being written and circulating during the first four centuries which were not included in the canon of Scripture. The judgment of the Church was that these erred in passing on the Apostolic Tradition and the teaching of the early Church. *See also* **canon of Scripture**.

Apostle(s): 'The title traditionally given to those specially chosen by Jesus to preach the Gospel and to whom he entrusted responsibility for guiding the early Church' (USCCA, 504). The names of the first Apostles, also called the Twelve, are Peter, Andrew, James, John, Thomas, James, Philip, Bartholomew (also known as Nathaniel), Matthew, Judas, Simon, and Jude (also known as Thaddeus). After the Ascension of Jesus, Matthias, who replaced Judas Isacariot, and Paul were also called to be Apostles.

Apostolic Tradition: Jesus entrusted his revelation and teachings to his Apostles. They passed it on by their preaching and witness. Along with others, they began writing the message down in what became the New Testament. (USCCA, 504)

Ascension: 'The entry of Jesus' humanity into divine glory to be at the right hand of the Father; traditionally, this occurred forty days after Jesus' Resurrection' (USCCA, 504). 'Christ's Ascension marks the definitive entrance of Jesus' humanity into God's heavenly domain, whence he will come again [see Acts of the Apostles 1:11]; this humanity in the meantime hides him from the eyes of men [see Colossians 3:3]' (CCC, no. 665).

Assumption: The dogma that when the Blessed Virgin Mary's earthly life was finished, because she was sinless, she was kept from corruption and taken soul and body into heavenly glory. (USCCA, 505)

atheist: A person who denies the existence of God and whose life is shaped by that disbelief.

B–C

Baptism, Sacrament of: The first Sacrament of Initiation by which we are freed from all sin and are endowed with the gift of divine life, are made members of the Church, and are called to holiness and mission. (USCCA, 505)

Baptism of Desire: It may be supposed that persons who seek 'the truth and [do] the will of God in accordance with [their] understanding of it would have *desired Baptism explicitly* if they had known its necessity' (CCC, no. 1260).

baptism of Jesus: In presenting himself for baptism, Jesus was affirming John the Baptist's call to the people to repentance. Obviously Jesus did not need to be baptized in order to have his sins forgiven, but, as the *Catechism of the Catholic Church* states, 'he allows himself to be numbered among sinners' (CCC, no. 536).

Beatific Vision: The seeing of God face to face; being and living in the presence of God in heavenly glory. The Beatific Vision is the foundation of the happiness (or beatitude) of Heaven.

beatitude: Happiness or blessedness, especially the eternal happiness of heaven, which is described as the vision of God, or entering into God's rest by those whom he makes 'partakers of the divine nature'. (CCC, Glossary)

Beatitudes: The eight Beatitudes form part of the teaching given by Jesus during the Sermon on the Mount, which set forth fundamental attitudes and virtues for living as a faithful disciple. (USCCA, 505)

Bible: The books that contain the truth of God's Revelation and that were composed by human authors inspired by the Holy Spirit. The Bible contains both the forty-six books of the Old Testament and the twenty-seven books of the New Testament. (CCC, Glossary) *See also* **canon of Scripture; Old Testament; New Testament; Sacred Scripture**.

Blessing and Adoration, Prayer of: A prayer that exalts the greatness of God, in which we acknowledge that God alone is God; he alone is the source of every blessing; he is our Creator and Father and we are his children.

blessings: One of the sacramentals of the Church. 'All blessings praise God for his gifts. Most blessings invoke the Holy Trinity along with the Sign of the Cross, sometimes with the sprinkling of holy water' (USCCA, 505). *See also* **sacramentals**.

Body of Christ: A name for the Holy Eucharist. It is also a title for the Church, with Christ as her head, sometimes referred to as the Mystical Body of Christ. The Holy Spirit provides the members with the gifts needed to live as Christ's Body. (USCCA, 505)

canon of Scripture: The canon of Scripture refers to the list of Old Testament and New Testament books that are accepted by the Catholic Church as the inspired Word of God. The Catholic canon lists seventy-three books—forty-six in the Old Testament and twenty-seven in the New Testament. The Catholic canon of Scripture differs from the Protestant canon, which also includes writings that the Catholic Church has judged to be apocryphal. *See also* **apocrypha**.

catechumen: An unbaptized candidate for the Sacraments of [Christian] Initiation [Baptism, Confirmation and Eucharist]. (USCCA, 506)

charism(s): Special graces of the Holy Spirit given to the Church and the baptized for the building up of the Church.

charity (love): One of the three Theological Virtues by which we give our love to God for his own sake and our love to our neighbor on account of our love of God. (Based on USCCA, 506)

Christ: The title given to Jesus, meaning 'The Anointed One'; it comes from the Latin word *Christus*, which in its Greek root is the word for *Messiah*. (USCCA, 507)

Church: This term refers to the whole Catholic community of believers throughout the world. The term can also be used in the sense of a diocese or a particular parish. (USCCA, 507) *See also* **Body of Christ**.

clergy: Those who receive the Sacrament of Holy Orders to serve the whole communion of the Church.

Communion of Saints: This refers to the members of the Church through all time—those now in the Church and those members who have already gone before us and are either in Purgatory or heaven. (USCCA, 507)

compassion: In the Bible, the English word 'compassion' is a translation of a Greek word meaning 'womb' and of a Hebrew word that is also translated as 'mercy'. Compassion is the quality of a person who so closely identifies with the suffering and condition of another person that the suffering of the other becomes their own, or 'enters their womb'. The Latin roots of the English word 'compassion' are *cum* and *passio*, which mean 'suffering with'.

conscience: 'Moral conscience, present at the heart of the person, enjoins [the person] at the appropriate moment to do good and to avoid evil. It also judges particular choices, approving those that are good and denouncing those that are evil.' When we listen to our conscience, we 'can hear God speaking'. (See CCC, no. 1777)

consecrated life: A permanent state of life recognized by the Church, entered freely in response to the call of Christ to perfection, and characterized by the profession of the evangelical counsels of poverty, chastity, and obedience. (CCC, Glossary)

consubstantial: A term meaning 'of the same substance' or 'same nature'. The Catholic Church uses this term to teach that Jesus is of the same substance or nature as the Father. She does this to assert her faith that Jesus is truly God, truly divine.

conversion: Conversion means turning around one's life toward God and trying 'to live holier lives according to the Gospel' (Vatican II, *Decree on Ecumenism*, quoted in CCC, no. 821).

covenant: A covenant is a solemn agreement made between human beings or between God and a human being involving mutual commitments or guarantees. The Bible speaks of covenants that God made with Noah and, through him, 'with every living creature' (Genesis 9:10). Then God made the special Covenant with Abraham and renewed it with Moses. The prophets constantly pointed to the New Covenant that God would establish with all humankind through the promised Messiah—Jesus Christ.

Creation: The act by which the eternal God gave a beginning to all that exists outside of himself. Creation also refers to the created universe or totality of what exists, as often expressed by the formula 'the heavens and the earth'. (CCC, Glossary)

Creator: God alone is the 'Creator'. God—Father, Son and Holy Spirit—out of love for us created the world out of nothing, wanting to share divine life and love with us.

D–E

death: Death is the separation of a person's soul from his or her body and the cessation of one's bodily life on earth and the beginning of new life.

Deposit of Faith: The heritage of faith contained in Sacred Scripture and Tradition, handed on in the Church from the time of the Apostles, from which the Magisterium draws all that it proposes for belief as divinely revealed. (USCCA, 509)

discernment, spiritual: The practice of looking out for the presence and the workings of the Spirit in our life. It includes trying to understand the promptings of the Spirit and deciding to act in cooperation with the grace of the Holy Spirit.

Divine Inspiration: 'Divine Inspiration' is the term the Catholic Church uses to describe the gift of the Holy Spirit given to the human writers of the Bible, so that, using their talents and abilities, they wrote the truth that God wanted people to know for their salvation.

Divine Providence: God's loving care and concern for all he has made; he continues to watch over creation, sustaining its existence and presiding over its development and destiny. (USCCA, 510)

Divine Revelation: God's communication of himself and his loving plan to save us. This is a gift of self-communication, which is realized by deeds and words over time and most fully by his sending us his own divine Son, Jesus Christ. (USCCA, 526)

Doctor of the Church: A person from any era in Church history whose sanctity and writings have had a profound influence on theological and spiritual thought. A person is declared a Doctor of the Church by the Pope. (USCCA, 510)

doctrine/dogma: The name given to divinely revealed truths proclaimed or taught by the Church's Magisterium; the faithful are obliged to believe these truths. (USCCA, 510)

dogma: *See* **doctrine/dogma**.

domestic church: Term meaning 'church of the home'. 'The Christian home is the place where children receive the first proclamation of the faith. For this reason the family is rightly called "the domestic church", a community of grace and prayer, a school of human virtues and of Christian charity' (CCC, no 1666).

doxology: A prayer of adoration giving glory to the Triune God, in which the three divine Persons are invoked.

Ecumenical Council: From the Greek word *oikoumenē*, meaning 'the whole world', an Ecumenical Council of the Church is a gathering of all the bishops of the world in the exercise of their authority over the universal Church. An Ecumenical Council is usually called by the Pope, or at least confirmed and accepted by him. It can be called for a variety of specific reasons, among which is to clarify the Church's teachings and mission.

Eleven (the): The name given to the Apostles after Judas Iscariot betrayed Jesus and died and before Matthias was elected.

eternal life: Eternal life is living for ever with God in the happiness of Heaven, entered after death by the souls of those who die in the grace and friendship of God.

Evangelist(s): The word 'evangelist' means 'one who announces good news'; the title 'Evangelist' is given to the writers of the four accounts of the Gospel (the Good News of Jesus Christ) in the New Testament. The four Evangelists are St. Matthew the Apostle, St. Mark, St. Luke and St. John the Apostle. 'The term "evangelist" is also used for one who works actively to spread and promote the Christian faith' (CCC, Glossary).

evangelization: 'This is the ministry and mission of proclaiming and witnessing Christ and his Gospel with the intention of deepening the faith of believers and inviting others to be baptized and initiated into the Church' (USCCA, 512). Evangelization is the primary work of the Church.

evil: The opposite or absence of good. One form of evil, physical evil, is a result of the 'state of journeying' toward its ultimate perfection in which God created the world, involving the existence of the less perfect alongside the more perfect, the constructive and the destructive forces of nature, the appearance and disappearance of certain beings. Moral evil, however, results from the free choice to sin which angels and men have; it is permitted by God, who knows how to derive good from it, in order to respect the freedom of his creatures. The entire revelation of God's goodness in Christ is a response to the existence of evil. The devil is called the Evil One. (CCC, Glossary)

Exile (The): A word meaning 'removal from one's own country. In the context of the Old Testament, the Exile refers to the period between 586 and 539 BC when the upper classes of Judah were exiles in Babylon. A previous exile, from the northern kingdom of Israel, had been enforced in 722–721. (The Catholic Study Bible, Second Edition, *New American Bible*, Glossary)

Expiation: The act of redemption and atonement for sin which Christ won for us by the pouring out of his Blood on the cross, by his obedient love 'even to the end' (John 13:1). The expiation of sins continues in the mystical body of Christ and the communion of saints by joining our human acts of atonement to the redemptive action of Christ, both in this life and in Purgatory. (CCC, Glossary)

F–G–H

faith: Faith is one of the three Theological Virtues. Faith 'is both a gift of God and a human act by which the believer gives personal adherence to God (who invites his or her response) and freely assents to the whole truth that God has revealed' (USCCA, 512).

Fall (the): (1) Biblical revelation about the reality of sin in human history. The Biblical story begins with the original sin freely committed by the first human beings. This primeval event is narrated in figurative language in the Book of Genesis, which describes this sin as a 'fall' from God's friendship and grace, which they had received from God not only for themselves but for the whole human race. (2) In the 'fall' of angels, Scripture and Church Tradition see the emergence of Satan and the 'devil'; the 'fall' of these angelic spirits was due to their freely chosen rejection of God and His reign. (CCC, Glossary)

Fourth Gospel: Another name for the Gospel according to John.

free will/freedom: Our God-given power and ability to choose what we have come to know and understand to be good and true, and to love God, others and ourselves because of our love for God. Our free will and our intellect are the bases of our responsibility and accountability for our moral choices. *See also* **intellect/reason**.

Fruits of the Holy Spirit: The Tradition of the Church lists twelve fruits of the Holy Spirit: love, joy, peace, patience, kindness, goodness, generosity, gentleness, faithfulness, modesty, self-control and chastity. (USCCA, 513)

Gentile: A non-Jew.

Gifts of the Holy Spirit: These gifts are permanent dispositions that move us to respond to the guidance of the Spirit. The traditional list of these gifts is derived from Isaiah 11:1–3: wisdom, understanding, knowledge, counsel [right judgment], fortitude [courage], reverence (piety), and wonder and awe in God's presence (fear of the Lord). (USCCA, 513)

Gnostics/Gnosticism: Gnosticism refers to a variety of Christian 'sects' that arose in the first century AD. Gnostics traced their origins back to Simon Magus (see Acts of the Apostles 8:4–25) and existed into the fifth century AD. Gnostics, who considered themselves 'elitist', falsely claimed to have a special and secret spiritual knowledge; for example, secret teachings that the risen Jesus gave to one or the other of the Apostles. In their teaching, Gnostics also often used a mythology to teach erroneously that the physical world is evil, 'the product of the fall, and is thus to be rejected or left behind' (CCC, no. 285).

Gospel/Gospels: The term 'gospel' comes from an Old English word *godspel*, meaning 'good news'. *Godspel* was originally used to translate the Greek word *euangelion* (Latin *evangelion*), a term the early Church used for the Good News of Jesus. The Church uses the word 'Gospel' to refer to the four New Testament books that proclaim the life, teaching, Death and Resurrection of Jesus. More generally, however, the word 'Gospel' refers to the proclamation of the entire message of faith revealed in and through Jesus Christ, the Incarnate Son of God, the Second Person of the Blessed Trinity.

grace: The word 'grace' comes from the Latin word *gratia*, which means 'free'. Grace is the 'free and undeserved gift that God gives us to respond to our vocation to become his adopted children. As sanctifying grace, God shares his divine life and friendship with us in a habitual gift, a stable and supernatural disposition that enables the soul to live with God, to act by his love. As actual grace, God gives us the help to conform our lives to his will. Sacramental grace and special graces (charisms, the grace of one's state of life) are gifts of the Holy Spirit to help us live out our Christian vocation'. (CCC, Glossary) *See also* **actual graces, charisms, sanctifying grace**.

Great Commandment: The commandment to love God with our whole heart, soul and mind and to love others as ourselves because of our love for God. In this commandment Jesus combined the Old Testament revelation of the Law of Love in Deuteronomy 6:5 and Leviticus 19:18 that is at the heart of God's will and plan for Creation and of the Covenant.

Heaven: Heaven is the fullness of communion with God; it is neither an abstraction nor a physical place in the clouds, but a living, personal relationship with the Holy Trinity. (Pope John Paul II, 1920–2005)

Hebrews: Another name for the ancient Israelites and the Jews.

Hell: Hell is the definitive rejection of God, a state for those who freely and definitively separate themselves from God, the source of all life and joy. (Pope John Paul II, 1920–2005)

heresy: A religious teaching that denies or contradicts truths revealed by God. (USCCA, 514)

hermit: A person who devotes themselves to a life of prayer and solitude.

holiness: Holiness is a state of goodness in which a person lives in communion with God, who is Father, Son and Holy Spirit, and, with the help of God's grace, the action of the Holy Spirit and a life of prayer, is freed from sin and evil. (Based on USCCA, 514)

Holy Days of Obligation: 'Principal feast days on which, in addition to Sundays, Catholics are obliged by Church law to participate in the Eucharist; a precept of the Church' (CCC, Glossary). In the United States of America there are six Holy Days of Obligation for Latin (Roman) Catholics. They are (1) Mary, the Holy Mother of God [January 1]; (2) The Ascension of the Lord [forty days after Easter or the following Sunday]; (3) The Assumption of the Blessed Virgin Mary [August 15]; (4) All Saints Day [November 1]; (5) The Immaculate Conception of the Blessed Virgin Mary [December 8]; and (6) The Nativity of the Lord—Christmas [December 25].

Holy Spirit: The proper name for the Third Divine Person of the Holy Trinity; the Lord and giver of life, who proceeds from the Father and the Son, and who with the Father and the Son is adored and glorified.

Holy Trinity (Triune God): The one true God, eternal, infinite, unchangeable, incomprehensible and almighty, in three divine Persons: the Father, the Son and the Holy Spirit. (CCC, no. 202)

hope: One of the three Theological Virtues 'through which a person both desires and expects the fulfillment of God's promises of things to come' (USCCA, 515). Hope is the desire and expectation of the salvation God promised. It is based on God's unwavering fidelity to keeping and fulfilling his promises.

human person: The human individual, made in the image of God; not some thing but some one, a unity of spirit and matter, soul and body, capable of knowledge, self-possession, and freedom, who can enter into communion with other persons—and with God. The human person needs to live in society, which is a group of persons bound together organically by a principle of unity that goes beyond each one of them. (CCC, Glossary)

hypostatic union: The union of the divine and human natures in the one divine Person (Greek: *hypostasis*) of the Son of God, Jesus Christ. (CCC, Glossary).

I–J–K

'I AM' statements: A key and unique writing technique in John's Gospel is his use of seven 'I AM' sayings or statements to teach that Jesus is divine, truly God. These two words, 'I AM', have their roots in the Book of Exodus, when God reveals his identity, his name, to Moses. When Moses asks the voice in the burning bush, 'If I come to the Israelites and say to them, "The God of your ancestors has sent me to you", and they ask me, "What is his name?", what shall I say to them?', God says to Moses, 'I am who I am. . . . Thus you shall say to the Israelites, "I AM has sent me to you"' (Exodus 3:13–14).

icon: An icon (from the Greek *eikōn*, meaning 'image') is a religious work of art, most commonly a painting. An icon is not a regular painting in the way we think of paintings today. Icon painters use a combination of figures, colors, and symbols, and unite the Church's traditions of asceticism and art to create prayer-portals into the realm of God.

idolatry: Act contrary to the First Commandment; 'Idolatry consists in divinizing what is not God. Man commits idolatry whenever he honors and reveres a creature in place of God' (CCC, no. 2113).

imago Dei: This term means 'image of God'. We are all made in the image and likeness of God.

Immaculate Conception: A dogma of the Church that teaches that Mary was conceived without Original Sin due to the anticipated redemptive graces of her Son, Jesus. (USCCA, 515)

immortality: The quality of the spiritual human soul whereby it survives the death of the body and remains in existence without end, to be reunited with the body at the final resurrection. (CCC, Glossary)

Incarnation: By the Incarnation, the Second Person of the Holy Trinity assumed our human nature, taking flesh in the womb of the Virgin Mary. There is one Person in Jesus and that is the divine Person of the Son of God. Jesus has two natures, a human one and a divine one. (USCCA, 515)

inerrancy of the Bible: Because the authors of Sacred Scripture were inspired by God, the saving meaning or truth found in the Scriptures cannot be wrong. (USCCA, 516)

infallibility: This is the gift, or charism, of the Holy Spirit 'whereby the pastors of the Church—the pope, and bishops in communion with him—can definitively proclaim a doctrine of faith and morals, which is divinely revealed for the belief of the faithful. This gift flows from the grace of the whole body of the faithful not to err in matters of faith and morals. The pope teaches infallibly when he declares that his teaching is *ex cathedra* (literally, "from the chair"); that is, he teaches as supreme pastor of the Church' (USCCA, 516).

Inspiration: *See* **Divine Inspiration**.

intellect/reason: Our God-given power and ability to know what is good and true. Our intellect enables us to come to know God through creation and to know and understand the order that God wills among things. Our intellect and free will are the bases of our responsibility and accountability for our moral choices. *See also* **free will/freedom**.

Jesus (name): Hebrew name that means 'God saves'.

Jesus Christ: The Incarnate Son of God who became one of us in all ways except sin without giving up his divinity. Jesus is true God and true man. He is fully divine and fully human. In the one divine Person, Jesus, the divine nature and a human nature are united. *See also* **Christ**.

Jesus Prayer: 'Lord Jesus Christ, Son of the living God, have mercy on us sinners', which is based on Luke 18:10–14, dates back to the fifth

century and comes to us from the Church in the East.

Kingdom of God: The actualization of God's will for human beings proclaimed by Jesus Christ as a community of justice, peace, mercy, and love, the seed of which is the Church on earth, and the fulfillment of which is in eternity. (USCCA, 517)

L–M–N

Last Judgment: The moment at the end of time when everyone will appear before Christ and receive an eternal recompense in accord with their earthly life. (USCCA, 517)

Last Supper: The last meal, a Passover supper, which Jesus ate with his disciples the night before he died. Jesus' passing over to his Father by his death and Resurrection, the new Passover, is anticipated in the Last Supper and celebrated in the Eucharist, which fulfills the Jewish Passover and anticipates the final Passover of the Church in the glory of the kingdom. Hence the Eucharist is called 'the Lord's Supper'. (CCC, Glossary)

Law of Love: The heart of God's Law revealed in Leviticus 19:18 and Deuteronomy 6:4–5 was fulfilled in Jesus Christ and expressed in his teaching his disciples on the New Commandment in John 13:34–35.

lectio divina: A manner of praying with Scripture; the person praying either reflectively reads a passage from Scripture or listens attentively to its being read, and then meditates on words or phrases that resonate. (USCCA, 518)

liturgical year: The calendar that guides the liturgies and prayers of the Church. (USCCA, 518)

Liturgy: 'Liturgy refers especially to the public worship of the Church, including the Mass and the Liturgy of the Hours' (USCCA, 518). 'The word "liturgy" originally meant a "public work" or a "service in the name of/ on behalf of the people". In Christian tradition it means the participation of the People of God in "the work of God"' (CCC, no. 1069). 'In the liturgy of the Church, God the Father is blessed and adored as the source of all the blessings of creation and salvation with which he has blessed us in his Son, in order to give us the Spirit of filial adoption' (CCC, no. 1110)

Liturgy of the Hours: The public daily prayer of the Church which extends the praise given to God in the Eucharistic celebration. (USCCA, 518)

Liturgy of the Word: The first main part of the Mass during which the Scriptures are proclaimed, their meaning is explained, and the people respond in faith. The Liturgy of the Word is an integral part of all sacramental celebrations. 'The meaning of the celebration is expressed by the Word of God which is proclaimed and by the response of faith to it' (CCC, no. 1190).

Lord: The name used in Scripture for the divine name revealed to Moses. The title 'Lord' indicated divine sovereignty. To confess or invoke Jesus as Lord is to profess that he is truly and fully God.

Lord's Prayer (The): Another name for the prayer more commonly known as the Our Father. This prayer is sometimes called the Lord's Prayer because it is a prayer taught by Jesus to his Apostles and disciples. (USCCA, 518)

love, or charity: One of the three Theological Virtues by which we give our love to God for his own sake and our love to our neighbor on account of our love of God. (Based on USCCA, 506)

Magisterium: The living teaching office, or teaching authority, of the Catholic Church, made up of the Pope and bishops, guided by the Holy Spirit, whose responsibility and task is to give authentic interpretation to the Word of God contained in both Sacred Scripture and Sacred Tradition. 'The Magisterium ensures the Church's fidelity to the teaching of the Apostles in matters of faith and morals' (CCC, Glossary).

Magnificat: The canticle of Mary in Luke 1:46–55 in which the Blessed Virgin Mary professes her faith in God and praises God for his faithfulness to his people.

Marks of the Church: The four essential characteristics of the Church founded by Jesus Christ; they are 'one', 'holy', 'catholic' and 'apostolic'.

martyr: From the Greek word *martyr*, which means 'witness'. In a Christian context, a martyr is 'one who witnesses to Christ and the truth of faith, even to the point of suffering' (USCCA, 519).

Mass: The Eucharist or principal sacramental celebration of the Church, established by Jesus at the Last Supper, in which the mystery of our salvation through participation in the sacrificial death and glorious resurrection of Christ is renewed and accomplished. The Mass renews the paschal sacrifice of Christ as the sacrifice offered by the Church. It is called 'Mass' (from the Latin *missa*) because of the 'mission' or 'sending' with which the liturgical celebration concludes [Latin: '*Ite, Missa est.*']. (CCC, Glossary)

Mediator: The word 'mediator' means 'one who links or reconciles separate or opposing parties'. 'Jesus Christ is the "one *mediator* between God and the human race" [1 Timothy 2:5]. Through his sacrificial offering he has become high priest and unique mediator who has gained for us access to God's saving grace for humanity' (CCC, Glossary).

Mediatrix: The title *Mediatrix* was given to Mary to express her unique relationship to Christ and to the Church. Mary is sometimes called *Mediatrix* in virtue of her cooperation in the saving mission of Christ, who alone is the unique Mediator between God and humanity. (CCC, Glossary)

Messiah: A Hebrew word meaning 'anointed'. The Messiah is the one whom God would send to inaugurate his Kingdom definitively. 'The word "Christ" comes from the Greek translation of the Hebrew *Messiah*, which means 'anointed'. [Christ] became the proper name to Jesus only because he accomplished perfectly the divine mission that "Christ" signifies. . . It was necessary that the Messiah be anointed by the Spirit of the Lord at once as king and priest, and also as prophet. Jesus fulfilled the messianic hope of Israel in his threefold office of priest, prophet, and king' (CCC, no. 436).

miracle(s): Miracles are signs of the presence of God at work among us. 'The miracles and other deeds of Jesus are acts of compassion and signs of the Kingdom and salvation' (USCCA, 80).

moral life: Doing what is good and true, and avoiding what is evil.

moral passions: *See* **passions, moral**.

morality/moral law: Morality refers to the goodness or evil of human acts. For a Catholic, morality 'refers to the manner of life and action formed according to the teaching laid down by Christ Jesus and authoritatively interpreted by the Church' (USCCA, 520).

Mystery (of God): The term has several complementary meanings. First, it reminds us that we can never exhaust God's divine and infinite meaning. Second, mystery tells us that God is 'wholly other' (not us) and yet so near that in him we live and move and have our being. Third, the union of the divine and human in Christ is so unique that we revere it as holy mystery. Fourth, mystery also applies to the celebration of the Sacraments in which God, Father, Son, and Spirit, are present and active for our salvation. (USCCA, 520).

mystic: A person who has an intense personal experience of God, or religious ecstacy. This experience may include a private revelation of God.

natural law: Our ability to know through our use of reason the created moral order, what is good or evil, which is rooted in the fact that we have been created in the image of God. The natural law is an expression of the dignity of the human person and is the basis of our fundamental human rights.

natural reason: *See* **intellect/reason**.

New Covenant: The new 'dispensation', order or Covenant, established by God in Jesus Christ, to succeed and perfect the Old Covenant. The New Law or Law of the Gospel is the perfection here on earth of the divine law, natural and revealed; this law of the New Covenant is called a law of love, grace, and freedom. (CCC, Glossary) *See also* **Covenant (The)**.

New Eve: The disobedience of Adam and Eve brought death and suffering into the world. By her obedience and her 'Yes' to God , Mary became the Mother of Jesus, the Son of God; 'she became the new Eve, mother of the living' (CCC, no. 511).

New Testament: 'The designation for the second part of the Bible, which contains the four accounts of the Gospel, the Acts of the Apostles, Letters or Epistles, and the Book of Revelation' (USCCA, 521). 'The twenty-seven books of the Bible written by the sacred authors in apostolic times, which have Jesus Christ, the Incarnate Son of God—his life, teachings, Passion and glorification, and the beginnings of his Church—as their central theme. The promises and mighty deeds of God in the old alliance or covenant, reported in the Old Testament, prefigure and are fulfilled in the New Covenant established by Jesus Christ, reported in the sacred writings of the New Testament' (CCC, Glossary). *See also* **Bible; canon of Scripture; Sacred Scripture**.

O–P–Q–R

Old Testament: The first part of Sacred Scripture that contains the Pentateuch (the first five books), the Historical Books, the Wisdom Literature and the Prophetic Books. These come to us from the people of ancient Israel before the coming of Christ. The Books of the Old Testament were inspired by God. *See also* **Bible; canon of Scripture; Sacred Scripture**.

original holiness: The state of living in communion with God and sharing in the gift of divine life enjoyed by our first parents from the moment of their creation until the Fall, when they freely chose to disobey God's command (Original Sin).

original justice: The state of living in harmony or right relationship with God and all creation enjoyed until the Fall, or Original Sin.

Original Sin: The personal sin of disobedience committed by the first human beings, resulting in the deprivation of original holiness and justice and the experience of suffering and death. (USCCA, 522)

paganism: 'Paganism' was a term used in the early Church to designate a religion other than Christianity or Judaism whose values were contrary to the teachings of Sacred Scripture. Pagan religions practiced polytheism, or the belief in many gods.

Panagia: A title for Mary, meaning 'all-holy'; Mary was free from all sin from the moment of her conception.

parable: A characteristic feature of the teaching of Jesus. Parables are simple images or comparisons which confront the hearer or reader with a radical choice about his invitation to enter the Kingdom of God. (CCC, Glossary)

Paraclete: A name for the Holy Spirit. The term was used by Jesus in the New Testament (see John 14:16) to indicate the promised gift of the Spirit as another consoler and advocate, who would continue his own mission among the disciples. (CCC, Glossary)

Parousia: *See* **Second Coming (of Christ)**.

Particular Judgment: The judgment of one's life that occurs at the moment of one's death.

Paschal Mystery: In speaking of the Paschal Mystery we present Christ's Death and Resurrection as one, inseparable event. It is *paschal* because it is Christ's passing into death and passing over it into new life. It is a *mystery* because it is a visible sign of an invisible act of God. (USCCA, 522–523)

Passion (of Jesus): The suffering and death of Jesus. Passion or Palm Sunday begins Holy Week, during which the annual liturgical celebration of the Paschal Mystery of Christ takes place. (CCC, Glossary)

Passions, moral: The emotions or dispositions which incline us to good or evil actions, such as love and hate, hope and fear, joy and sadness, and anger. (CCC, Glossary)

Passover: The name of the Jewish feast that celebrates the deliverance of Israel from Egypt and from the Angel of Death who passed over their doors marked by the blood of sacrificed lamb. Jesus Christ inaugurated the new Passover by delivering all people from death and sin through his blood shed on the Cross. The celebration of the Eucharist is the Passover feast of the New Covenant. (USCCA, 523)

Pentecost: The 'fiftieth day' at the end of the seven weeks following Passover (Easter in the Christian dispensation). At the first Pentecost after the Resurrection and Ascension of Jesus, the Holy Spirit was manifested, given and communicated as a divine Person to the Church, fulfilling the paschal mystery of Christ according to his promise. (CCC, Glossary)

People of God: The biblical name given to those called by God to announce and bring about the divine plan of Salvation; first given to the people of ancient Israel and then to the Church. The Church is the new

People of God whom God calls into existence 'as his people centered in Christ and sustained by the Holy Spirit'. The visible structures of the Church are the means intended by God 'to help guarantee the life of grace' for the whole People of God. (Quoted material from USCCA, 523)

perpetual virginity of Mary: Mary was a virgin in conceiving Jesus, in giving birth to him, and in remaining always a virgin ever after. (USCCA, 523)

perseverance: Perseverance is the moral virtue, or good habit, of staying with what is good in times when we are distracted or tempted not to do what we know is the will of God.

person: *See* **human person**.

Petrine ministry (office): The supreme jurisdiction and ministry of the Pope as shepherd of the whole Church. As successor of St. Peter, and therefore Bishop of Rome and Vicar of Christ, the Pope is the perpetual and visible principle of unity in faith and communion in the Church. (CCC, Glossary)

polytheism: The belief in many 'gods'.

prayer: 'The raising of one's mind and heart to God in thanksgiving and in praise of his glory. It can also include the requesting of good things from God. It is an act by which one enters into an awareness of a loving communion with God' (USCCA, 523–524). 'Prayer is the response of faith to the free promise of salvation and also a response of love to the thirst of the only Son of God' (CCC, no. 2561).

preferential option for the poor: The principle of the 'Preferential Option for the Poor and Vulnerable'

which instructs us to put the needs of the poor and vulnerable first. (See USCCA, 423.) The central interest of the Church's social teaching is justice for all, but especially for the helpless and the poor. It involves the removal of the symptoms and causes of poverty and injustice. (USCCA, 427)

Protoevangelium: The term *Protoevangelium* literally means 'first gospel' and refers to the very first Revelation we have in the Bible that God would send a Savior. In Genesis 3:15 God promises to send an 'offspring of the woman', who will crush the head of the serpent—the symbol of temptation and sin. (See CCC, nos. 410–411.)

proverb: A proverb is a succinct statement that is used to make a point or state a well-accepted truth. Their power lies in the use of various figures of sound and sense. The Book of Proverbs is one of the writings in the Wisdom Literature of the Old Testament. Wisdom is not just knowledge reserved for a few highly intelligent people; wisdom can be sought by all. It is found through the difficult process of making well-informed choices in life. The Old Testament Book of Proverbs sought to guide the People of God in making 'wise' choices to live the Covenant. (*The New Jerome Biblical Commentary*, 28:8B and 11A)

public ministry of Jesus: The public life and ministry of Jesus began at his baptism and concluded with his entry into Jerusalem as the King-Messiah. It includes the 'mysteries' of his life that reveal him to be the 'Servant' wholly consecrated to the redemptive work that he would accomplish by his Passion.

Purgatory: Purgatory is not a place but a condition of existence where Christ removes the remnants of imperfection. (Pope John Paul II, 1920–2005)

reason: *See* **intellect/reason**.

redemption: Redemption is the salvation won for us by Jesus by his paying the price of his own sacrificial death on the Cross to ransom us, to set us free from the slavery of sin.

religion: A set of beliefs and practices followed by those committed to the service and worship of God.

religion (virtue of): A virtue rooted in the First Commandment; it is the habit and disposition of giving adoration to God, praying to him, and offering him the worship that alone belongs to him. The virtue of religion strengthens Christians to fulfill the promises of their Baptism. (CCC, no. 2135)

Resurrection (of Christ): 'The triumph of Jesus over death on the third day after his crucifixion. Christ's [risen] body is real, but glorified, not restrained by space or time' (USCCA, 525). The Resurrection confirms the 'saving', 'redeeming' and 'liberating' power of Jesus and the truth of his divinity.

Revelation: *See* **Divine Revelation**.

revelation (private): Private revelations 'add nothing to what was publicly revealed up and through Christ but can help inspire a more profound commitment to what has been revealed through public Revelation' (USCCA, 15). Private revelation is 'intended only for the good of the person who receives it and does not need to be believed by others' (USCCA, 526).

S

Sacrament(s): The seven 'efficacious sign(s) of grace, instituted by Christ and entrusted to the Church, by which divine life is dispensed to us by the work of the Holy Spirit' (USCCA, 526). The Seven Sacraments are the three Sacraments of Christian Initiation (Baptism, Confirmation, and Eucharist), the two Sacraments of Healing (Penance and Reconciliation, and Anointing of the Sick), and the two Sacraments at the Service of Communion (Marriage and Holy Orders).

sacrament of salvation: Name for the Church; the Church is the sign and instrument of salvation in the world. She is both the means and the goal of God's plan for humanity.

sacramentals: These are sacred signs instituted by the Church. They prepare people to receive the fruit of the Sacraments and sanctify different circumstances of life. Among the sacramentals, blessings occupy an important place. (See CCC, nos. 1667–1678.) There are blessings for persons, meals, objects, places, and ceremonial occasions such as graduations, testimonial honors, welcomes, and farewells. All blessings praise God for his gifts. Most blessings invoke the Holy Trinity with the sign of the Cross, sometimes with the sprinkling of holy water. (USCCA, 505)

Sacred Scripture (Bible): The inspired written Word of God. 'The books that contain the truth of God's revelation and that were composed by human authors, inspired by the Holy Spirit, and recognized by the Church' (USCCA, 527). *See also* **Bible**.

Sacred Tradition: The Tradition of the Catholic Church refers to the body of teaching of the Church, expressed in her beliefs, doctrines, rituals and Scripture, that has been handed down from the Apostles to their successors, the Pope and the bishops, through the ages, in an unbroken line of succession.

sacrifice: Sacrifice is a free offering, a gift, made by a person for the welfare of others. The word comes from two Latin words meaning 'to make sacred'. Such a gift is deemed to be sacred—a special and a sincere sign of love and life. The greatest sacrifice of all is to give one's life for another. In a religious context a sacrifice is 'a ritual offering made to God by a priest on behalf of the people as a sign of adoration, gratitude, supplication, penance, and/or communion' (USCCA, 527).

Sacrifice of the Cross: The perfect sacrifice was Christ's death on the cross; by this sacrifice, Christ accomplished our redemption as high priest of the new and eternal covenant. The sacrifice of Christ on the cross is commemorated and mysteriously made present in the Eucharistic sacrifice of the Church. (CCC, Glossary)

salvation: Salvation is the forgiveness of sins and restoration of friendship with God, which can be done by God alone. (CCC, Glossary)

salvation history: The story of God's reaching out to humanity to fulfill the divine plan of Salvation, and also of humanity's response to God.

sanctification: The term comes from Latin words meaning 'to make holy'. Sanctification is the work of the Holy Trinity attributed to the Holy Spirit. It is the 'healing of our human nature wounded by sin by giving us a share in the divine life of the Trinity; . . . the work of making us 'perfect', holy, and Christlike. (CCC, Glossary)

sanctifying grace: The word 'sanctifying' means 'that which makes holy'. Sanctifying grace is 'a habitual gift of God's own life, a stable and supernatural disposition that enables us to live with God and to act by his love' (USCCA, 514). *See also* **grace**.

Savior: Title for Jesus Christ. The Hebrew name 'Jesus' means 'God saves'. The Son of God became man to achieve our salvation; he is the unique Savior of humanity. (CCC, Glossary)

Second Coming (of Christ): The glorious return and appearance of our Lord and Savior Jesus Christ at the end of time to judge the living and the dead, when history and all creation will achieve their fulfillment.

senses of Scripture: Tradition notes that there are two senses or aspects of Scripture—the literal and the spiritual. The literal meaning is that meaning conveyed by the words of Scripture and discovered by exegesis following rules of sound interpretation. The spiritual meaning points to realities beyond the words themselves. (USCCA, 527–528)

Sermon on the Mount: The summary of Jesus' teaching on discipleship found in Matthew 5:1—7:29; it is a blueprint on how to live as his Church, the new People of God.

sin: 'Sin is an offense against God as well as against reason, truth, and right conscience' (USCCA, 528), in which a person freely and knowingly chooses evil over good. Sin involves a serious lack of effort in meeting duties and responsibilities to God, to others and to oneself. Sins are mortal or venial. **Mortal sin** is 'when we consciously and freely choose to do something grave against the divine law and contrary to our final destiny' (USCCA, 520). **Venial sin** is a less serious offense. *See also* **social sin**.

social sin: Sins that produce unjust social laws and oppressive institutions. They are social situations and institutions contrary to divine goodness. Sometimes called 'structures of sin', they are the expression and effect of personal sins. (USCCA, 528)

Social Teachings (Doctrine) of the Church: The official social doctrine developed by the Catholic Church in response to the industrial and technological revolutions. This social doctrine is built on the Church's reaching out and responding to orphans, widows, aliens and others from the days of the early Church. (Based on USCCA, 528)

solidarity: 'The principle of solidarity, also articulated in terms of "friendship" or "social charity", is a direct demand of human and Christian brotherhood' (CCC, no. 1939). This involves love for all peoples that transcends national, racial, ethnic, economic, and ideological differences. It respects the needs of others and the common good in an interdependent world. (USCCA, 529)

Son of God: The Second Divine Person of the Holy Trinity. 'The title "Son of God" signifies the unique and eternal relationship of Jesus Christ to God his Father; he is the only Son of the Father; he is God himself. To be a Christian, one must believe that Jesus Christ is the Son of God' (CCC, no. 454).

Son of Man: The title used by our Lord of himself in the Gospel. This title connotes a relationship with the eschatological figure of the 'Son of man appearing in clouds and glory' (Mark 13:26) in the prophecy of Daniel (Daniel 7:13). (CCC, Glossary)

soul: 'The soul is the subject of human consciousness and freedom; soul and body together form one unique human nature. Each human soul is individual and immortal, immediately created by God' (CCC, Glossary). 'The immortal spiritual part of a person; the soul does not die with the body at death, and it is reunited with the body in the final resurrection' (USCCA, 529).

Stations of the Cross/Way of the Cross: A devotional exercise which follows the 'way of the cross' in the Savior's steps, observing stops or 'stations' to meditate on the path Jesus took from the Praetorium in Jerusalem to Golgotha and the tomb. (CCC, Glossary)

steward/stewardship: A steward is someone who has the responsibility of caring for what belongs to another person or group of people. In the biblical accounts of Creation, God designates humanity the responsibility to have dominion over, or serve as the stewards of, creation. The root word for 'dominion' is *domus*, which means household. God has entrusted creation, his household, to humanity.

T–U

temptation: Temptation is 'an attraction either from outside or inside oneself' to choose to sin, or to act in ways that are contrary to the will of God.

theologian (of the Church): A person who reflectively studies 'Revelation as found in Scripture, in Apostolic Tradition, and in Church teaching' (USCCA, 530).

theology: Theology is 'faith seeking understanding'. It is the study of God in which we use reason assisted by the grace of the Holy Spirit to deepen our understanding of Revelation and the faith of the Catholic Church.

Theological Virtues: Gifts 'infused by God into the souls of the faithful to make them capable of acting as his children and of meriting eternal life' (CCC, no. 1813). The Theological Virtues are faith, hope, and charity (love).

Theotokos: Word meaning 'God-bearer'; a title for Mary professing that she is truly the Mother of God.

Tradition: *See* **Sacred Tradition.**

traditions of the Church: The diverse ways the people of the Church authentically celebrate and give witness to her Tradition and faith in various times and places throughout the world.

transcendence: Transcendence refers to the idea that God is so 'beyond' the universe, and so different from anything else that exists, that God cannot be directly experienced by human beings. A shorthand way of saying that God is transcendent is: 'God is the absolute Other.'

Transfiguration: The mysterious event in which Jesus, seen speaking with Moses and Elijah on the mountain, was transformed in appearance—in the sight of Peter, James, and John—as a moment of disclosure of his divine glory. (CCC, Glossary)

transubstantiation: A term used to describe the unique change of bread and wine into the Body and Blood of Christ. By the consecration, the substance of bread and wine is changed into the substance of Christ's Body and Blood. (USCCA, 530)

Trinity: *See* **Holy Trinity (Triune God).**

Twelve (the): The Apostles chosen by Jesus before his Death, Resurrection and Ascension. From among the Twelve, Jesus appointed St. Peter to be the leader of the Apostles (see John 21:15–19).

V–W–X–Y–Z

virtue of religion: *See* **religion (virtue of).**

Visitation: The visit of Mary to Elizabeth after the Annunciation; Elizabeth was an elderly relative who was six months pregnant with her unborn son, St. John the Baptist. The account of the Visitation is found in Luke 1:39–56.

vocation: The term given to the call to each person from God; everyone has been called to holiness and eternal life, especially in Baptism. Each person can also be called more specifically to the priesthood or to religious life, to married life, and to single life, as well as to a particular profession or service. (USCCA, 531)

Way of the Cross: *See* **Stations of the Cross.**

Word of God: The entire content of Revelation as contained in the Holy Bible and proclaimed in the Church. In John's Gospel, God's 'Word' means his only-begotten Son, who is the fullness of God's Revelation and who took flesh (the Word incarnate) and became man for the sake of our salvation. (CCC, Glossary)

Works of Mercy: Charitable actions by which we come to the aid of our neighbors in their bodily and spiritual needs. The *spiritual works of mercy* include instructing, advising, consoling, comforting, forgiving, and patiently forbearing. *Corporal works of mercy* include feeding the hungry, clothing the naked, visiting the sick and imprisoned, sheltering the homeless, and burying the dead. (CCC, Glossary)

worship: Adoration and honor given to God, which is the first act of the virtue of religion. Public worship is given to God in the Church by the celebration of the Paschal Mystery of Christ in the liturgy. (CCC, Glossary)

YHWH: The divine name God revealed to Moses in Exodus 3:13–15; the Hebrew letters YHWH are the first letters of the words meaning 'I Am who I Am', or 'I Am He Who Is', or 'I Am Who Am'. The divine name is so sacred that the people of ancient Israel did not speak it, nor do Jews today. In its place they use the Hebrew word Adonai, or Lord.

Acknowledgments

Scripture quotations taken from or adapted from the New Revised Standard Version Bible: Catholic Edition, copyright © 1989, 1993, Division of Christian Education of the National Council of Churches of Christ in the USA; used by permission; all rights reserved. Excerpts from the English translation of the *Catechism of the Catholic Church* for use in the United States, second edition, copyright © 1997, United States Catholic Conference, Inc., Libreria Editrice Vaticana; all rights reserved. Excerpts from documents of Vatican II from A. Flannery (ed.), *Vatican Council II: Constitutions, Decrees, Declarations* (New York/Dublin: Costello Publishing/Dominican Publications, 1996). Excerpts from the *United States Catholic Catechism for Adults*, copyright © 2006, United States Conference of Catholic Bishops, Washington D.C.; all rights reserved. Prayers from *Catholic Household Blessings & Prayers*, Revised Edition, copyright © 2007, Bishops Committee on the Liturgy, United States Conference of Catholic Bishops, Washington, D.C. Excerpts from the English translation of *Rite of Baptism for Children* © 1969, International Commission on English in the Liturgy Corporation (ICEL); excerpts from the English translation of *The Roman Missal* © 2010; all rights reserved; used with permission. Story of Christian faith in action, p. 40, taken from Thomas H. Groome, *What Makes Us Catholic: Eight Gifts For Life* (New York: HarperOne, 2002), reprinted by permission of HarperCollins Publishers, copyright © Thomas H. Groome, 2002. Excerpt from 'The wider role of bodily sense in thought and language', p. 57, by E.T. Gendlin, in M. Sheets-Johnstone (ed.), *Giving the Body Its Due* (Albany: State University of New York Press, 1992), copyright © E.T. Gendlin, 1992. 'Sharon's Christmas Prayer', p. 72, by John Shea, from *The Hour of the Unexpected* (Allen, Texas: Argus Communications, 1977), copyright © John Shea, 1977. Cesar Chávez's 'Farm Workers' Prayer', pp. 79–80, used with permission of the Cesar Chávez Foundation, copyright © 2012 the Cesar Chávez Foundation, *www. chavezfoundation.org*. Prayer, p. 111, by Henri Nouwen, from *With Open Hands* (1995); used with permission of the publisher, Ave Maria Press, Inc., PO Box 428, Notre Dame, Indiana 46556, *www.avemariapress.com*, copyright © Joyce Rupp, 1995. Excerpts, p. 104, from General Audience of Pope Benedict XVI, August 26, 2009, and from Pope Benedict XVI's Message for the Celebration of the World Day of Peace, January 1, 2010, copyright © 2009, 2010 Libreria Editrice Vaticana; used with permission. Excerpt, p. 104, from homily of Pope Francis at inaugural Mass, March 19, 2013, copyright © 2013 Libreria Editrice Vaticana; used with permission. Information about CCHD, pp. 119–20, adapted from the Caritas Internationalis website: *www.caritas.org*, copyright © Caritas Internationalis, 2011. Excerpt, p. 122, from General Audience of Pope Benedict XVI, December 1, 2010, copyright © 2010 Libreria Editrice Vaticana. Excerpt, p. 130, from *In Search of the Beyond* by Carlo Carretto, published in 1976 by Orbis Books, Maryknoll, New York 10545; reprinted by permission of Orbis Books. 'Anger is a Poison', p. 139, from *The Five People You Meet in Heaven* by Mitch Albom (London: Little Brown, 2003), copyright © Mitch Albom. Excerpt, p. 148, from *Down These Mean Streets* by Piri Thomas (New York: Vintage, 1997), copyright © Piri Thomas, 1997. 'Hymn to the Holy Spirit', p. 150, by James Quinn, S.J., text copyright © James Quinn, S.J., Selah Publishing Co. Inc., North American Agent; *www.selahpub.com*. Quotation in relation to Nelson Mandela inspiring people, p. 158, from *Divine Energy: God Beyond Us, Within Us, and Among Us* by Donal Dorr (Liguori, Missouri: Liguori Publications, 1996), copyright © Donal Dorr, 1996. Jean Vanier's description of how L'Arche began, pp. 163–4, adapted from *www. larcheusa.org/*, copyright © L'Arche International. Quotation, p. 169, from Blessed Pope John Paul II, General Audience, October 22, 1997, from *L'Osservatore Romano*, 29 October 1999, copyright © Libreria Editrice Vaticana; used with permission. Quotation, p. 181, from *Redemptoris Mater*, copyright © 1987 Libreria Editrice Vaticana; used with permission. Story of Dorothy Day, pp. 226–7, adapted from 'Illuminating Lives', a series of biographical essays by Beth Randall, *www.cs.drexel. edu/~gbrandal/Illum_html/Day.html*, copyright © Beth Randall, 1996. Quotations, pp. 254–5, republished with permission of Crossroads Publishing Company, from *Against an Infinite Horizon: The Finger of God in Our Everyday Lives*, Ronald Rolheiser, 2002; permission conveyed through Copyright Clearance Center, Inc. Quotation, p. 266, from Pope Paul VI, *Indulgentiarum Doctrina*, copyright © Libreria Editrice Vaticana; used with permission. Quotation, p. 268, from Ronald Rolheiser, 'The Communion of Saints' (November 5, 2006), *www.ronrolheiser.com/columnarchive/?id=23*, copyright © Ronald Rolheiser, 2006. 'Something in me is stirring...', p. 273, from *May I Have This Dance?*; used with permission of the publisher, Ave Maria Press, Inc. PO Box 428, Notre Dame, Indiana 46556, www.avemariapress.com, copyright © Joyce Rupp, 1995. 'Prayer for Vocations', p. 277, from the National Coalition for Church Vocations, copyright © NCCV, www.nccv-vocations.org. 'Canticle of Zechariah (The Benedictus)', p. 277 and 'Canticle of Mary (The Magnificat)', p. 278, International Consultation on English Texts (ICET).

Image credits

Cover: *Main image:* Detail from *Man of Sorrows*, 1994 (acrylic on canvas) by Laura James (Private Collection/The Bridgeman Art Library). *Left center:* World Youth Day © Pascal Deloche/Godong/Corbis. P. 7: Photo: Rama. P. 12: Photo: Ralph Hammann. P. 14: Photo: Varga Csongor. P. 20: Photo by Chris McGrath/Getty Images. P. 22: Photo: Hank Walker/Time & Life Pictures/Getty Images. P. 23: Photo: Marie-Lan Nguyen. P. 36: Photo: Gunnar Bach Pedersen. P. 37: Photo: Laurom. P. 50: Photo: Reinhard Hauke. P. 55: Photo: GREG WOOD/AFP/Getty Images. P. 56: Photo: Wolfgang Moroder. P. 60: Photo: Godong/Getty Images. P. 61: Photo: David Monniaux. P. 68: Photo: Jastrow. P. 71: *The Holy Family*, copyright © 2007 Janet McKenzie (*www.janetmckenzie.com*); Collection of Loyola School, New York, NY. P. 76: Photo: ROBIN UTRECHT/AFP/Getty Images. P. 78: Photo of Cesar Chávez, used with permission of the Cesar Chávez Foundation, copyright © 2012 the Cesar Chávez Foundation, *www.chavezfoundation.org*. P. 86: Photo: Paterm. P. 89: Photo: Kostisl. P. 90: Photo: Piotrus. P. 93: Photo: GFreihalter. P. 112: Photo: Clio20. P. 114–15: Photos: Nick Michael. P. 116: Photo: Yair Haklai. P. 118: Photo: FILIPPO MONTEFORTE/AFP/Getty Images. P. 122: Lady Julian of Norwich, illustration by Stephen Reid. (Private Collection/The Stapleton Collection/The Bridgeman Art Library). P. 128: Christ Crowned with Thorns (wood), West African, 20th century (Private Collection/The Bridgeman Art Library). P. 129: Photo: Jozef Sedmak. P. 130: Photo: Manfred Heyde. P. 136: Photo: Otourly. P. 140: Photo: FA2010. P. 144: Photo: Transromanica Association. P. 149: Dove of the Holy Spirit coin (Classical Numismatic Group, Inc. *www.cngcoins.com*). P. 153: Photo: Daderot. P. 154: Photo: Neithan90. P. 155: Photo: Giovanni Dall'Orto. P. 156: Photo: Schiwago. P. 158: Photo: Media24/Gallo Images/Getty Images. P. 160: Photo: Wessel de Jonge. P. 163: Photo © Philippe Caron/Sygma/Corbis. P. 164: Photo: Sailko. P. 173: The Mother of God of the Sign icon, late 17th century Russian School (Private Collection/© Richard and Kailas Icons, London, UK/The Bridgeman Art Library). P. 174: Photo: Frank Vincentz. P. 175: Photo: Béria Lima. P. 180: Photo: Brandmeister. P. 191: Photo: Marsyas. P. 202: Photo: Ralph Hammann P. 203: Photo: Schuppi. P. 205: St. Maria Goretti © Fr. William Hart McNichols. P. 211: Photo: Vassil. P. 213: Photo: Copyright © Mary Evans Picture Library. P. 214: Photo: Fingalo. P. 215: Photo: Andreas Praefcke. P. 221: Photo: Gunnar Bach Pedersen. P. 224: Photo: Wolfgang Sauber. P. 226: Photo: Bettmann/CORBIS. P. 233: Photo: Vassil. P. 235: Photo: Andreas Praefcke. P. 236: Photo: Neithan90. P. 243: Photo: Yoav Dothan. P. 247: Photo: GFreihalter. P. 249: Photograph of Thomas Merton by John Lyons, used with permission of the Merton Legacy Trust and the Thomas Merton Center, Bellarmine University. P. 254: Photo: Raja Patnaik. P. 259: Photo: Vassil. P. 269: © Danny Lehman/CORBIS. P. 270: Elizabeth Ann Seton, © Mary Evans Picture Library.

Index